ILLUSTRATED INDIA
ITS
PRINCES AND PEOPLE

INDIA.

ILLUSTRATED INDIA
ITS
PRINCES AND PEOPLE

UPPER, CENTRAL AND FARTHER INDIA, UP THE GANGES AND DOWN THE INDUS.

TO WHICH IS ADDED

AN AUTHENTIC ACCOUNT OF THE VISIT TO INDIA OF HIS ROYAL HIGHNESS THE PRINCE OF WALES

CONTAINING 123 FULL-PAGE ENGRAVINGS AND MAPS

JULIA A STONE

GYAN

Published by

GYAN

Gyan Publishing House
5, Ansari Road
Daryaganj, New Delhi-110002
Phone: 011-47034999, 9811692060
E-mail: books@gyanbooks.com

Distribution Network
gyanbooks.com
India, USA, Canada, UK, Australia, France

ISBN : 978-81-212-4527-2 (HB)
First Published, 1877

2nd Impression 2020

Printed at: Gyan Press, Delhi.

ILLUSTRATED INDIA:

ITS

PRINCES AND PEOPLE.

UPPER, CENTRAL, AND FARTHER INDIA,

UP THE GANGES AND DOWN THE INDUS.

TO WHICH IS ADDED

AN AUTHENTIC ACCOUNT OF THE VISIT TO INDIA OF

HIS ROYAL HIGHNESS,

THE PRINCE OF WALES.

BY MRS. JULIA A. STONE.

CONTAINING 123 FULL-PAGE ENGRAVINGS AND MAPS.

HARTFORD, CONN..

AMERICAN PUBLISHING COMPANY.

1877.

A STATE PROCESSION, INDIA.

PREFACE.

THIS volume makes no pretensions as a History of India; that wide field must be occupied by an abler pen. To impress the mind of the reader, by a portrayal of sights and incidents that passed under her observation during the years of her life spent in India, (the wife of an U. S. Consul there,) as deeply as her own mind was impressed by them, has been the earnest aim of

THE AUTHOR.

Contents

CHAPTER I.

SINGAPORE AND VICINITY.

CHAPTER II.

LIFE IN THE TROPICS.

CHAPTER III.

THE ISLANDS OF THE ARCHIPELAGO.

CHAPTER IV.

GOING UP THE COAST OF THE PENINSULA—MALACCA—PENANG—BURMAH.

CHAPTER V.

LIFE IN BURMAH.

CHAPTER VI.

CALCUTTA.

CHAPTER VII.

THE HOME OF NOOR-MAHAL.

CHAPTER VIII.

BENARES; THE ETERNAL CITY.

CHAPTER IX.

CHUNAR, MIRZAPORE AND ALLAHABAD.

CHAPTER X.

CAWNPORE AND LUCKNOW.

CHAPTER XI.

AGRA.

CHAPTER XII.

THE TAJ.

CHAPTER XIII.

FUTTEHPORE-SIKRI—BHURTPORE—DIGH.

CHAPTER XIV.

DELHI—THE FORTIFIED PALACE OR CITADEL.

CHAPTER XV.

DEWAN KHAS, OR THRONE-ROOM AT DELHI.

CHAPTER XVI.

RAMBLES ABOUT NEW AND OLD DELHI.

CHAPTER XVII.

THE ROAD TO OLD DELHI.

CHAPTER XVIII.

THROUGH THE PUNJAB COUNTRY.

CHAPTER XIX.

DOWN THE INDUS.

CHAPTER XX.

BOMBAY.

PART SECOND.

List of Illustrations

MAPS.

STREET LEADING TO THE BAY OF SINGAPORE.

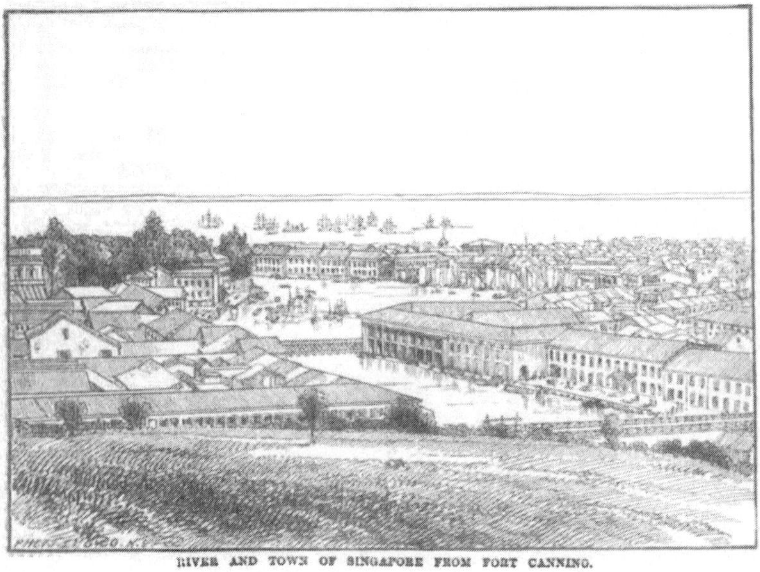

RIVER AND TOWN OF SINGAPORE FROM FORT CANNING.

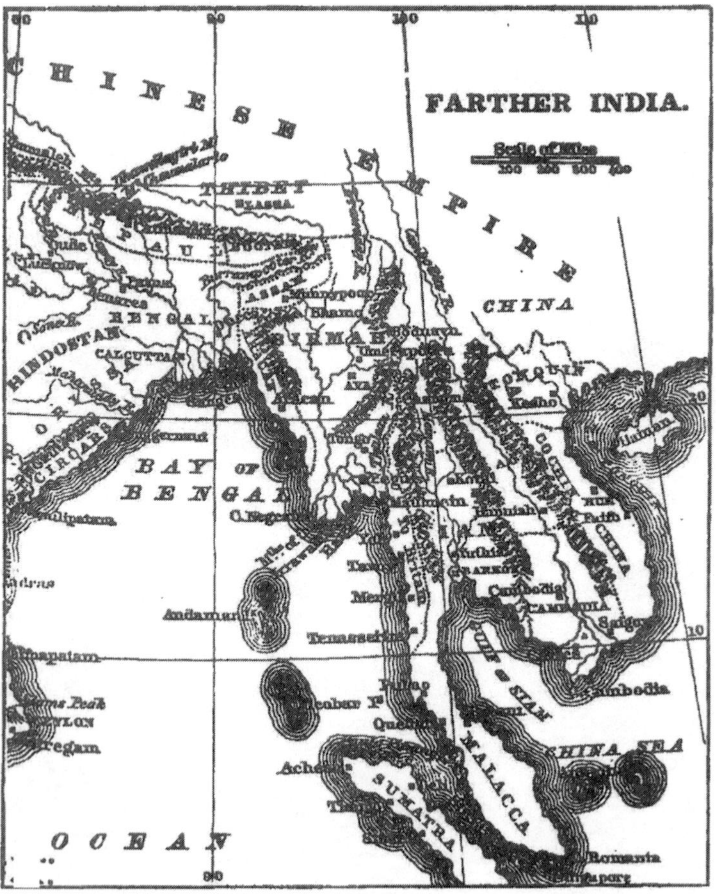

MAP OF FARTHER INDIA.

FOR GENERAL MAP OF INDIA, SEE PAGE 558.

CHAPTER I.

SINGAPORE AND VICINITY.

"PLEASE Tuan," said Coachee, making a very profound salaam, one morning, during our residence at Singapore, "will Tuan lend me four dollars on next months wages?"

"We will see about that Coachee, when we know what you want to do with it."

He hesitated and the question was pressed, "What do you want to do with it?"

"I want to get married."

"Oh that is it, I thought you wanted to bury your grandmother,"—the usual excuse that these servants make, when they want to raise money for a gay time; and it sometimes happens after several burials, and the money or food stops coming to her, the enraged old woman will walk in with a salaam to the Tuan, and expose her own hopeful's villainy.

"*Tega ringet* (three dollars) build me *atap* (house), half a dollar buys me white cotton *baju* (coat), half a dollar I pays the priest."

"But man, you have in your hand your past month's wages—six dollars."

"*Sia tah*, I know; but I must make a present to the girl's father and mother, and I must make a big supper of rice and curry, for all the friends on both sides."

One could not afford to lose an opportunity of conferring so

2

much happiness by denying a good servant so small a favor. So it came to pass in the course of another two weeks, that another small thatched house presented its gable among the row on a back street, and a modest good-looking Malay girl came into it as a bride. A very happy light brown face often peeped out from it shyly, when Coachee sat on his box, and we were taking our evening drive.

This establishment was comfortable the whole year, in that genial climate; and the wedding feast met their simple, frugal tastes, and only cost ten dollars more than Adam and Eve's wedding. Notwithstanding this primitive state of things, Europeans often find themselves rather straightened—with their tastes and habits—to meet the wants of themselves and families in this place, on salaries varying from two hundred to eight hundred per month, while the servants on wages of six dollars have a surplus over.

Perhaps there is no people on earth more grossly misrepresented than the greater part of the Malay people. The stereotyped idea that stared at us from our school books thirty years ago, yet retains its place, without any palliating explanation. It suggests that the usual occurrence among men of this race is, to get intoxicated with opium and then arm themselves with a sword in each hand, and rush into the streets and kill every one they meet. A horrible pastime truly if this were so. There are two very great mistakes in these two lines from our school geographies. The first is this—the Malays are not in the habit of using opium in any form; it is a custom particularly Chinese. The second is,—in the few "Amocks" that are known to Europeans, to have been run, no one has been killed except the man who ran it. The truth is, this people never commit suicide, they have not the nerve to kill themselves; but nevertheless there are times when some despondent one wishes to die, and death will not come unsought, so he rushes out into the streets with a grand flourish of two short swords amidst the shouts of "Amock! Amock!" kill! kill! turning neither to the right or left, striking this way and that, without aim, and soon meets the death that he is endeavoring to provoke.

The Malay has very little of that cringing dissimulation that characterizes the people of Hindustan. He loves passionately, and jealousy or despondency prompts him as naturally to this act, as it does a Parisian to seek a pan of charcoal and quietly suffocate himself. It is only a different way of doing the same thing. Of late years, the natives give timely notice to the town police, of any suspected despondent persons among them, and have them locked up, until their mental horizon brightens.

Nurtured kindly by nature in a climate so sweetly tempered with heat and moisture that there is not a month in all the year that does not ripen fruits, a small amount of labor producing sufficient for his daily wants, the native becomes a total stranger to that form of avarice that prompts one to labor and hoard up a store of anything; and yet a Malay beggar is never seen in the streets. If no friend offers rice when he is needy he can always find fish in the streams or the sea, and a never failing supply of wild fruit in the jungle; the cold he has never known. His hospitality extends to dividing the last morsel of rice with an acquaintance, or saying to one of his friends:

"If you are tired of working now I will give you food to eat two or three months, if you want to be idle, and then you may work and give me food, and I will rest."

Sir Stamford Raffles while governor of Java during the period that the English held possession of that island, found many interior villages where our common crimes: murders, thefts and drunkenness were so little known that they had to be enlightened on the use of prisons and executions in christian countries. The Patriarchs of these simple communities were horrified, saying, "England very bad country, your people must learn of Malay," and protested that they had no use for anything of the kind, for in their government, the customs of their fathers were followed, and the rules of hospitality and kindness so seldom violated, that they rarely ever were obliged to resort to the very unusual severity of a reprimand of any person before the assembled fathers of the village.

Sir Stamford wisely gave up trying to enlighten the people; probably those virtuous heathens would have sent missionaries to England and America, if he had unfolded our state of society much more.

During the years 1863 and '64 the sympathies of the Mahomedans, more especially of the better class of Arabs residing at Singapore and Batavia, were greatly exercised by the drunken and demoralized condition of European sailors in those ports. The Rev. Mr. Jeffreys of the Scotch Presbyterian Church of the former place informed me, that it had been ascertained, that about forty converts to the Moslem faith had been made, and they had publicly joined the mosques and put on the long robe and turbans, and after being instructed in the doctrines of the Koran, they were finally sent on a pilgrimage to Mecca at the expense of benevolent Mahomedans, to confirm their faith.

The same statement was further confirmed by Mr. D— Chief of Police at Singapore, who related an interview that had taken place in his office. An Arab resident of the city came in with several European sailors and one American, from Marblehead, Mass. When the Arab had called the attention of the Chief of Police to the nationalities of the men, he bade them ask Mr. D—'s permission to unite with them in the Mosque. The English sailors and the Yankee said they would not do it, for they had a right to "jine the Mahomets or any religion they pleased." Among them were Danes and Swedes, and three were Irish, whom Mr. D— bade go to the Catholic priest: the Rev. Father Beuril. The Arab then asked if it was true, that an English subject could join any religion that he pleased; and on being informed it was so, the parties withdrew.

The city of Singapore is situated in Lat 1° 17′ N. on the south side of an island of the same name, which is only separated from the southern extremity of the Malay peninsula by a narrow strait. Its greatest extent east and west is twenty five miles, and it is about fourteen north and south. It was purchased in the year 1819 by Sir Stamford Raffles for the

East India Co., of the Sultan of Johore. The Tumongong or Prince of Johore and his heirs receive a perpetual annuity from the sale. Where the city now stands there was at that time only a small fishing hamlet; but the sagacity of this gentleman at once grasped its importance, from its direct situation on the great ocean highway to China.

The Honorable East India Co., had held possession of Bencoolen on the coast of Sumatra for more than a century; but its location was ill chosen for trade, it was too far from the track of vessels, to become a great mart of commerce, while Singapore, the new site, stood just in the gate, where all must pass through.

The former inhabitants of the island were Malays who had come from Sumatra and drove the aboriginal tribes over to the mainland of the peninsula; they, in turn, were invaded by the Javanese about the year 1200 and driven up the coast, where in time they founded a kingdom whose capital was Malacca which was captured by Albuquerque in the year 1511.

Finding they were unable to expel the Portuguese, they centered their power in the lower part of the peninsula and founded the kingdom of Johore, from whose Sultan the purchase of the island was made. At that time, all the islands in the straits were the rendezvous of hordes of pirates. From every sheltered nook and inlet, when a merchant vessel was passing, would swarm out fleets of native war boats, which were propelled by numerous oars, and often contained from two hundred to three hundred men.

Every trading vessel, then, was obliged to carry one or two small cannon and plenty of muskets and sabers; if they were not on the alert with their guns well shotted with grapnel and in a position to shatter and sweep whole boat loads from the face of the water, they could scarcely escape capture from the hosts that would very soon surround the ship. There never failed to carry out that old tradition of pirates, "dead men tell no tales." When every article of available plunder was removed from it, the ship was sunk or burned.

The hostility of the different Christian colonies,—the

English, Dutch, French and Portuguese—was a perfect training school of piracy for the native seafaring population of this region, as the history of the two hundred years of strife clearly shows; and out of this grew the gigantic "Honorable East India Company," as its members usually style themselves.

This state of peril to voyagers continued, though in a less degree, for eight or ten years after the purchase of Singapore, and until the Hon. Co.'s "apostles of civilization:" war steamers, could reach with their broadsides all the hiding places of these miscreants. It is very doubtful if sailing vessels ever could have cleared these seas, so that the commerce of Singapore and Penang could sufficiently develop to attract the population and trade that they now have, and offer remunerative honest labor to native people. There have been some instances since, where a tendency to lapse back into the old state of things has been manifested; for Sumatra an island of eight hundred miles in length, has a vast uncounted population, that has never been brought under any civilized rule. A few years since, a small steamer was fitted out from an adjacent port to carry pilgrims to Mecca. As these devotees never go empty handed to the shrine of the Holy Prophet, it came to be known that there was considerable treasure on board. Some quondam pirates were among them, who found the temptation to add one more foul crime to their lengthy list too strong for their feeble piety.

The third night out at sea, they got possession of the steamer; the captain, officers, and all of the pilgrims who were not in league with them, were speedily assisted to "shuffle off their mortal coil." An engineer, a helmsman and a waiter boy were reserved from the general slaughter till they could be conveniently spared by the pirates. It was in the plan however, to give these three a sea burial before they should reach land. It was not a cheerful prospect, but the waiter-boy was the first to see a breaking rift in the gloom. When the pirates' labor was done, and they wished to rest they ordered him to prepare the *hubble-bubble*, a pipe in which tobacco smoke is drawn through water. This he did once or twice much to their satisfaction, in the ordinary way to throw them off their guard; then he skilfully mixed a well-known drug in the ingredients of the pipes, and in half an hour after they began to smoke they all lost their senses in a hasheesh dream, and while wandering through its mazes, every one of them irrecoverably *lost* his *head* before the second half hour. A few days after, that same little steamer put into a port with considerable treasure that had piously been intended for the Prophet's tomb at Mecca, but with only *three* living souls on board, an engineer, helmsman, and waiter; there were also a great number of useless bodies and bones which no mourning friends dared to claim.

Sir James Brook, cotemporary of Sir Stamford Raffles, was the first efficient teacher of civilization to the pirates and Dyaks of the broad populous island of Borneo, whose murderous crafts swarmed over all the adjacent seas. Though he went to them in a fleet of gunboats, he was nevertheless a man of peace, a wise, resolute, determined character, who clearly saw what was necessary to be done and had the nerve to do it.

The pirates—who were incorrigible after they had made a vigorous attempt to capture his steam-pinnace, in which they nearly succeeded—he very effectually admonished through the mouth of his cannon.

With the wily old Sultan, Muda Hassen, he made a treaty by which he compelled that ruler to prohibit all piracy on his coast; and watched, with guns well shotted, to keep him from swerving from the very letter of the compact. The Dyaks were the agriculturists of the interior whom the Malays of the coast constantly harassed by their plundering expeditions into their country, and the Dyaks as persistently retaliated by rushing down to the coast to cut off human heads with which to decorate their temples. A young Dyak was not considered an eligible match for one of their blushing maidens, who could not point to one or two human heads, hanging like pictures on the wall, that he had cut off and preserved and placed there. With this wild tribe, Sir James entered into treaty to protect them from the depredations of the Malays, conditioned that they would cut off no more heads from the coast people, and would bring their camphor and gutta-percha there to sell.

"Only nine or ten heads," counting on his fingers, "only just a few, a very few, for the grand festival and dance in the temple," implored their chief.

"Not a head," said Sir James, unless you first take mine." So peace settled down on the beautiful waters of the summer seas that encircle Borneo, and piracy was said to be suppressed.

The city of Singapore stands on the margin of a most lovely bay, studded with charmingly green islets, with a spacious sweep of shore rounding away in the distance, lined with great plantations of palms and other glossy-leaved trees which fringe even the water's edge, outrivaling far, in natural beauty, the famous bay of Naples. Behind the city rises a background of conical hills, whose summits are crowned with the fair residences of the European population, embowered in tropical shade and fragrance. The city has now completed its first half century of existence, and has attracted from nearly every nation of the earth more than 100,000 people, three-fourths of which are Chinese. About five or six hundred are of the different nationalities of Europe with a few Americans. The remaining portion of the inhabitants, are gathered from every clime and country. The faces and the costumes that are daily met in the streets, are as varied and striking as those seen at a masquerade or a world's fair, indeed some one has called this city a world's fair with the fair (sex) left out, because there are so few white ladies visible.

Each one of this multitude is engaged in sharp pursuit of the dollar, and is contented under English government, because it is strong and rigorous enough to protect him in his legitimate gains. The Chinese are generally centred about the busiest part of the town, on the west side of the river. They form the great body of reliable laborers, servants and artisans. Their chief object in coming here, seems to be to accumulate

ILLINOAN PIRATE AND SAGHAI DYAK.

a few hundred dollars and then return to China, where their families are, and where their mode of living is so very cheap, that with such a sum they can make themselves very comfortable in their native village. Though they largely outnumber all the other nationalities put together, the government seems to manage them quite as easily as the smaller proportion of foreign population in the cities of America are managed. Java and Malacca have had a large Chinese population for a century and a half, but they are as separate and distinct from other people, to all appearance, as when they first came. A Coolie may be anything, or nothing, while he is poor; but when he has acquired property, he aims to be intensely Chinese, which only means respectability, with his people.

A Chinese gentleman's son after completing his education in the University of Edinburgh, returned home in European dress. The father said to him:

"My son, you may be a very good Chinaman with your education and wealth, and influence our people greatly for their good; but you will, at best, make a very poor sort of a European and as such have no influence with any one." This shrewd advice was not lost on the young man; he went for a few months' travel in the "Pagoda land," and on his return, all indications of his western world proclivities had disappeared, except that he brought a wife home with him that had *natural* sized feet.

From observations in these parts, any American would soon dismiss from his brain the idea of absorbing the Chinese element into our newer civilization. If we should give them suffrage and education they will accept them, and are shrewd enough to profit by them where they can; but they will still govern each other by Chinese customs and usages, through the agency of secret societies or combinations. It is believed that every individual going from China to Singapore, is included in either one or the other of the two Chinese secret societies, which as far as possible carry out their own laws upon their members, even to the execution of the death penalty. These societies are fully imbued with all the rancor and hatred engendered by rival districts of country and clans of people in their own land.

In 1854 these animosities grew so fierce that the rival societies fought regular battles in the streets of Singapore. The combatants would instantly disperse on the arrival of any force sent to quell them, but would meet and fight it out in some other place. Penang was similarly disturbed in 1866, by the barricades and battles of the Chinese Hoey (secret societies) in the streets of that city. "These Hoey," it is stated in *Our Tropical Possessions in Malayan India* "interfere with the administration of justice in the courts."

A few years ago one Chinaman was killed by another, when a comrade was eye-witness of the murder. When brought before the magistrate, he testified to what took place. His testimony happened to be against a brother member.

Before the final trial came on, this witness was smuggled out of the reach of the court; but the rival society was interested to have the offender punished, so they brought forward a man that very closely resembled the missing witness, who had been taught the story that the first had related and testified to it in court. He had nearly finished his evidence when the police magistrate came in and detected the deception and gave notice to the judge. The whole machinery of these societies is framed to compel the members to perpetuate their laws and customs wherever they may be, and thus keep them distinct from the people that they live among.

The other divisions of the city of Singapore, both European and native will be best shown, in a sort of panoramic survey, by a drive through the different streets and quarters. The evening drive and the morning walk, whatever they may be in other parts of India, are no obsolete traditions here. The charming roads are much enlivened by the number of European ladies and their children, who "*jalan machan anging*," (walk to eat the air)—as the Malays say—before seven o'clock in the morning; when, if there is any spot of earth where a literal realization of the ideal clime, born of poet's dreams, is to be found, you will be likely to meet it here. Fruits and flowers here never know of the "sere and yellow leaf;" a single ripe leaf falls and another immediately takes its place, so a stem of ripe fruit is plucked, and flowers soon come out near it, and another cluster ripens. Thus flowering and fruitage are the daily unvaried routine of the vegetable kingdom, through the whole twelve months of the year. This constant growth makes some sorts of wood so dense that they sink in water as readily as iron.

We are now driving through the European quarter over splendid roads, all green-bordered and fringed with growing hedges of ratans, clipped and shaven into smooth green walls, throwing out long graceful sprays of feathery foliage, fifteen or twenty feet high, flanked here and there with towering palms, like plumed sentinels guarding the beautiful inclosed lawns and large, substantial, white stuccoed dwellings, standing among glossy leaved trees, trailing with orchidaceous plants.

Phaetons whirl past, with coachmen and footmen in tall white turbans and long white coats, which bespeak their nationality and caste. Inside there are daintily-dressed European ladies and children enjoying the evening air so sweetly mild, that it is a luxury to move in it and breathe it. Old *hack gharries*, (Indian carriages), creak along, drawn by sorry, dejected, diminutive Indian ponies, that look as if doing penance for the sins of a past existence, by drawing overloads of native men, while the drivers in pity for their beasts have dismounted and draw with them at the shafts. We turn now into the extensive Botanical Garden and thread our way along its charming drives, over its graded and shaven hills, and round its miniature lakelet, where gigantic lilies—the Victoria Regia—bloom as freely as if in their own broad Amazon. Here roses blossom perpetually and one would think from the great abundance, that the spirits of flowers that had been pinched and frost-bitten in colder lands were sent here to enjoy their Elysium.

We will now turn our horses city-ward. Our road is a broad smooth avenue; on either side of it huge trees stand contiguous like giant neighbors with clasped hands far above our heads shutting out the glare from the track below, while we pass in the cool soft light, orchards of nutmeg trees, mangosteens, and cocoanut plantations. The dust and seeds of parasitic plants lodge in the rough bark of some old sago-palms, or on the surface of some old stone gate-post, and forthwith the moist air fosters it with such loving tenderness that the rough unsightly support is soon draped with ferns and wild orchidaceous plants, trailing their long pendant sprays.

We now wind around the base of the hill where the signal-flag staff stands within the fort on its summit, to give us the first news of a steamer's arrival, or that of any other vessel that may chance to be coming into port. Just here, a little stream that has been flowing between banks so thickly set with ratans bending their lithe tips down to its waters, as to hide it from view, *débouchés* into the sunshine, and here *Doughbys* or washmen stand all days of the week in the cool waters, and thwack clothes against the rocks to wash them, with a vertical sun pouring its powerful rays on their heads and bare shoulders and backs. Their ancestors washed in just that manner on the banks of the sacred Ganges and Kristnah two thousand years ago, and gave their clothes the same snowy whiteness that they do. There is a legend that a philanthropic American brought them out a washing-machine and set it up, and put forth commendable exertion to enlighten their benighted minds on the economy of muscle, and use of soap and hot water; and went through a sprightly little pantomine of rubbing clothes by hand. The *Doughbys* could do the rubbing to perfection when dry clothes were in their hands, but the machine was a profound mystery to the wisest men of their profession, an ugly nightmare to all the old croaking *Doughbys* who saw it.

The first washing done by it looked decidedly grey, and the philanthropist very blue; but as the next was about the average whiteness he took courage and praised the *Doughby* who had performed the operation. But unfortunately the truth oozed out after this fashion:

NATIVE WASHERMEN.

A NATIVE BARBER AND CUSTOMER.

NATIVE CARPENTER.

SWEEP WITH RATTAN BROOM.

"Me steal 'em away down to the river, thwack 'em six hours, bleach 'em all dis day, and they all very good now. Big machine that!" The importation of washing-machines did not flourish.

From country roads we turn into city streets, and soon come out on the Esplanade, a narrow plain on the beach, with a circular drive, a faint suggestion of the Englishman's Hyde Park, for all the *élite* of the town drive here to enjoy the sunset, sea, and music, when the band from the fort plays. Day and night are always evenly balanced here, and promptly at six the sun closes his day's march by hanging up piles on piles of his most glittering, gorgeous tent-curtains in the western sky. The tall spire of the church, and every leaf and drooping branch in that row of grand old senna-trees, has borrowed some of the glitter.

At the east end of this plain stands the Raffles' Institute: a school for natives, founded by Sir Stamford Raffles; and the Gothic Church. On the west is the Town-Hall and Library, Court-House and Post-Office, all fine substantial buildings, each surrounded with its cool shady lawns. Beyond them is the river bank lined on either side with rows of great commercial warehouses; whose ships laden with pepper and gambier are floating on all the navigable waters of the globe. This stream is always covered with a nondescript fleet of small boats, the carriers between the ships in the bay and the shore; among many queer kinds of craft there are the curious little Chinese *sampans*—boats with large eyes painted on the bow—which skim over the water propelled by one oar, and the irrepressible Chinaman standing bolt upright in the stern; his baggy coat and trowsers flapping in the wind—the first moving thing seen here in the morning and the last at night.

The band from the fort have taken their stand in the centre of the circular plain and have commenced a very creditable musical performance. They are all *Sepoys*, or native soldiers, and have been long under the drill of a skilful European master. But as we want to sketch hastily men and things as we see them in the crowd, we will pass them, for the plain is now full. Gay horsemen, gentlemen in American buggies—by the bye, one never sees a lady here in one of those high-geared carriages—and nice family *gharries*, filled with pretty European children in charge of their native nurses, or *Ayahs*—those in the Madras and Bengalee costumes are very picturesque—and wealthy Chinese gentlemen with shaven heads, enjoying the soft air of evening, in fine English turnouts. *Parsees* or *Ghebers* are there also, mounted on fine Persian horses, wearing hats modeled after the fashion of a basket with the bottom stove in, so as to resemble some burnt-out crater in their old home by the Caspian Sea. Pony phaetons with jolly bachelors smoking, the footman in tall white turban, carrying the lighted joss-stick, in case their pipes should go out, merchants, bankers, barristers, and judges in fine carriages with the ladies of their families, are there too, with a sprinkling of *hack gharries* and Malay drivers airing their gaudy-sky-blue, pink and magenta-colored coats, and handkerchief *toupees.* The ring completely surrounds the plain, and all are moving in a circle, like children in the merry-go-round cars in a French Garden, only with a gravity that borders on the ludicrous. Yonder falls into line a fine English turnout, the mingled yellow plush, gold lace and scarlet on the coats and peculiar turbans of the coachman and two footmen, show that the establishment belongs to the Government House. It is Sir St. George Ord and Lady Ord, the present Governor of the Straits Settlements.

"Why has the garden wall of that fine house on the beach been built up recently so high that one can scarcely see more of the building than the attic and roof?" asks one.

"An Arab merchant has bought it," is the answer, "and his wives do not like to be looked at by us infidels and barbarians."

It would not repay, if one could see their vacant faces, but be assured that they see all that passes from behind their *parda* or screen, which is so contrived that they can see without being seen. Hence it becomes in their own opinion, an act of great levity to show themselves. Like an overgrown infant the Arab lady is bathed, dressed, and combed, and sits among her cushions on the *dais* or raised part of the floor, her genius is only allowed by her position and caste to vent *itself in cooking*, and that is among them a much-coveted accomplishment.

That equipage on the right is the *Tumongong's*, or as he was styled when in England, "His Royal Highness the Prince of Johore." He did not spring from royal blood, but is a prince without the so-called Divine right.

Strange that six months in no colder climate than that of England should have taken away all that coarse burden of fat flesh, and dull uncomfortable look, which once distinguished him; but such is the fact. Fatness really is often more troublesome than disease here, for the latter can be treated with medicines; but nothing so effectually burns out this redundant "mortal coil" as cold weather.

The prince is now of medium size and compact form; with skin of a clear light-brown color, and dark, intelligent, pleasant eyes; very courteous and cordial in manners. His costume is neither Arab nor Malay. He wears a neat head-gear, made of velvet and gold lace, a sort of compromise between a turban and an English hunting-cap. This he adopted after grave official consultations; for it was not considered at all admissible for him to make his appearance in Europe in the handkerchief *topee*, his national head covering.

He never uncovers in any society, whether at the table or in the drawing-room or street; he is thoroughly moslem in that particular. Instead of the Malay *baju*, he wears a short sacque coat, which much resembles its predecessor the aforesaid *baju* in shape. It is heavily trimmed with gold lace and wrought gold. He is certainly a most desirable person to hold by the button, as each one of those ordinary coat appendages consists of a large diamond of the purest water. If the ladies are accused of envying him his diamonds, I would not undertake to estimate the number of gentlemen who covet his knighthood, conferred by the Queen—the Order of the Garter and Commander of the Bath—which are represented by the decorations on the left breast. It was said that after he had been presented to the Queen, and had been sumptuously entertained by dukes, lords, and lesser aristocrats, in short, had been lionized to his heart's content, he exclaimed:

"I have seen all your riches and grandeur and how you nobles live, I want now to see the condition of the poor, that I may compare them with *my* poor people."

They took him in winter to Whitechapel, London, and there he saw more lean, haggard, squalid want and poverty, about the same amount of heathenism, and certainly more evidence of vice and crime, than in his own country. He remarked:

"My people do not suffer as yours do."

He came back well satisfied with everything, except his own roads; so he secured an engineer to construct roads for his territory.

But let us return to the drive. There passes a group of four Arabs of the higher class sauntering along on the greensward. Counting-rooms are all closed, and business operations too for the day, before five o'clock P. M. Chatting sociably, strolling up and down the beach, they contrive to pass the remainder of the daylight. One of them has been to Mecca, hence he wears the color sacred to St. Patrick and Mahomet—a bright grass-green robe of silk reaching to his ankle. All good Arabs will pay him great respect and make their most profound salaams, for he is a *Hadji*, a pilgrim to the Prophet's tomb, but they will not trust him a cent more for this sign of his piety, as they invariably recall the Turkish adage, "If thy neighbor has been to Mecca, remove to the next town;" which does not require great profundity or learning to translate, thus—"This person has all his piety in his show window."

Another has on a red dress, and evinces a fashionable feminine taste as to its particular shade of color, for it is a magenta-red. Huge white turbans form the head-gear of each.

Yonder come sauntering, two young men: young Arabia probably. They are of a different caste, just a notch or two lower. One wears for a head-piece, a *tarboosh*—in plain Anglo-American, a red woolen skull-cap with a black tassel. Please don't think that the *tarboosh* is quite empty, for there is something of a head in it, but it is just as void of anything except conceit and contempt, as a London cockney's or a New York exquisite's. The owner looks upon the crowd as if his Arabic might shape itself into the words, "Atrocious Europeans, driving in the same carriages with your wives and daughters."

Ah! the features unbend! the frown vanishes! *Seyd Abdullam* is taking a saunter down the esplanade. Will he notice these young men? Oh no! he has seen the *Hadji*; and bringing his hand to his head he makes a profound "*salaam*," approaches and kisses his hand. I shall not undertake to translate the Arabic words of greeting.

The *Seyd's* outer garment is a long frock reaching nearly to the ankles, made of white muslin, perhaps just a shade or two more transparent than the kind we call nainsook.

Now let your imagination put on over this man's vest, a back and front, both of dark cloth; no sleeves but those of the gown, braided over in patterns with gold braid or some gay-colored silk, and then you have just an outline of aristocratic Arabia; but it is not complete, for I have forgotten those nondescripts called Oriental slippers.

These are heavier than any of Paddy's brogans, and were made per order down at the heels; so the wearer walks with a delightful skuff on the pavement or bare floor.

Seyd or *Said*, for it is spelled both ways, means Prince *Emir*, *Sheik* or some one of those indefinite titles, but definite so far as it signifies aristocracy among Arabs. The Seyd I speak of is known as a merchant here, and as a moslem of royal blood is not allowed to cross the sea. He is one of the solid men on change, and a solid Arab is no light distinction I can assure you, in this mart, where *Kling* traders outjew the Jews. His rich cargoes and ships

3

float on the Indian seas where the dreaded *typhoon* engulfs whole fleets, but no policy of insurance will he spread over them, for if *Allah* wills it, they go down and he will not contravene His purposes. If his losses are heavy he will simply say "God is great,"and as a poor man will quietly begin to climb the ladder of life anew.

Yonder comes a *Sheik* with a name as long as his skirts, for the *Sheik* wears skirts, but mind you no crinoline.

Skirts—perhaps I should say petticoats—were the normal garments of men in the cradle of civilization, and are still of those who have not strayed far from the old crib.

The lords of creation of my own land, will be I fear, exceedingly shocked at such an assertion and hint that it is not true, or if it is, that it had better be suppressed; but I assure those presuming upstarts of a nation of yesterday, that I have the whole Chinese history as authority for asserting that when garments were first shared out to men and women, the ladies took the trowsers, and as Chinese history goes back to four thousand years before the world was *created*, and tells of changes of the moon, and all about the dynasties of Cheng this, and Chang that, and of god like elephants that they reverenced, and that Cheng was first cousin to the moon, but in all that time does not record a single change of fashions, it is evident they have worn them ever since.

Just look at that China-woman's trowsers over there, do not the loose ample folds become her tiny figure? Tradition enters more into the details, but corroborates history in the main; it runs thus:—

"When Mr. and Mrs. Noah and family had nearly finished their perilous voyage from the sunny land of Shinar, they found their stock of fig-leaf aprons quite exhausted; and even had there been an abundant supply, they would have had to shiver sadly in the winds that blew down from the cold heights of Mount Taurus. In this emergency a conjugal council was held, in which they concluded to make garments of the skins of the beasts they had slain to supply their table. Mr. Noah, willing to lighten the women's work, (an example worthy of imitation) concluded that he could make his own garments; but having been a ship-builder for a hundred and twenty years, his hands were stiff and clumsy, and the best he could do—between bothering with the log-book and the ark's coming to port—was to put one seam into his garment; thus producing a *petticoat*. Mrs. Noah being twice as nimble with the needle and having a taste for such work, put in two seams and made *bona-fide* trowsers, which the mothers of mankind have kept ever since.

The change of garments between the sexes is thus accounted for.

"Western Europe was peopled by the tribes from the regions of Mount Taurus and of the Black and Caspian seas. They got along very well in their westward travels, having no mistakes nor mishaps until they came into the regions of the vine. Here the men freely imbibed until their brains were so muddled, that rising in the dim morning light with a splitting headache, they could not tell one seam from two, and got into the wrong garments; the women, poor feeble things, were left no resource but to put on the others and say it was all right. But let one of the men venture back into the regions around the Black sea, without going back to first principles in fashion, and he will be taught a lesson that he will not forget in regard to skirts.

The *Sheik*. He is not very dark skinned, has gray eyes and gray beard. His flaunting skirts are of most immaculate whiteness; his face turned upward as if waiting for the appearance of the Prophet or that tall chicken that the *Koran* tells us about, whose height, reaches from the third to the seventh heaven. Mounted on a splendid light-gray Arabian horse, he is always punctual to time, on the beach, at the hour when European ladies are driving there, and his gray eyes are occasionally seen leering through their corners, at the carriages passing. It is hinted he is sighing to transplant some European beauty to his *harem*, which, may all good angels forefend.

But evening is upon us and we must end our drive.

CHAPTER II.

LIFE IN THE TROPICS.

THE moon pours down such floods of soft luxurious rays, that our senses are entranced with the voluptuous light and the soft delicious atmosphere we breathe. Deep masses of shade are gathered under the broad-leaved plantains and palms. Here and there, a leaf reaches out beyond the others and catches on its surface a light that silvers it over with beauty. Even the old cluster of bamboos, whose slender stems seventy feet in height, writhe in the most fearful contortions when the wind goes howling through them, now bends as gracefully as a bunch of silver-tipped plumes over the low roof of the cook's domains, decorating with its lofty coronet the humble home of the dusky ones that feed the fountains of life by kitchen toil.

Yonder the notes of a piano steal out through a lattice of green and silver leaves and waken suggestions of feet tripping to the giddy waltz. Across the valley the light and mist give a weird-like appearance to the scene. Here and there is a rift in the veil, where the water gleams through like molten silver poured over the lowland by the tide marching up the river. In a white bungalow on its bank a party of bachelors seem to be revelling in champagne and cigars, perchance booking bets for the coming races.

The distant baying of dogs comes to us through the ambient air, whose voluptuous softness mellows and tones away all its harshness. Pariahs though they may be, moonlight like this brings out all the poetry and feeling of the faithful creature.

Thug! thug! goes the carpenter bird; it is driving imaginary nails. In this soft silvery light, there is a something that will not let it cover its head with its wing, and go quietly to sleep as it would in darkness. Thug! thug! it must work on till daylight, with its imitation nail driving.

Frogs and crickets keep up an incessant chorus in the distance, and an uneasy crow, in a gorgeous Ponciona Regia tree in the garden, flaps his lazy wings and wakens a dozen of his sleeping comrades, who, thinking dawn has come, set up a cawing; then making one or two circles or short flights, return to their perch again.

On the silvery, sleeping waters of the bay, ride the crafts of all nations, their slender masts throwing long slanting shadows on the waters. Creeping in through the opening amid the verdant islands, comes a steamer. Her trailing column of smoke looks almost white in this moonlight while a shadow creeps up on one side of the full-orbed moon. Instantly all of the Chinese tom-toms of Singapore start into full drum beat. Fire-crackers without number snap and sparkle. Bamboo fiddles shriek their shrillest squeaks, and tin kettles rattle their loudest din. Every available noise has been brought into requisition that could be possibly thought of by the Chinese gentry or the long cued servants, who have suddenly slipped away from their post of duty and are now raising bedlam in the streets.

We rush out to see what is going on; when we find long processions of Chinese passing through the streets marching up and down, carrying lights, and making all the din and noise their energy can put forth.

Their great temple is in a full blaze of illumination; so we sagely conclude that it is some sacred time with them, and we return, thinking that we will get Apa Geon's account of it in the morning.

"Apa, what was all that noise about last night?" I did not say music, though these boys are excessively fond of their bamboo fiddles, and doubtless it was his private opinion, that omission was owing to a want of correct taste and judgment.

His first look was one of blank astonishment at such profound ignorance, setting down in his own mind, no doubt, that it was all owing to being born one of those unenlightened "Mellicans," as they call the Americans, that are not even fortieth or fiftieth cousin to either the sun or moon. Suddenly his face brightened with the thought that he might enlighten my darkness.

"*Ulat machanlah bulan,*" that is, a dragon was eating the moon, and then he added, "we make great noise, and he give it back."

Here his steps assumed the firmness of a person who knows that he has conferred a benefit upon the world. Talk of benefactions; by what name shall we call saving the natural light of the world, and conserving the beauty of moonlight to the race of man? This simple servant-boy felt that he had done a good act, had performed a time-honored duty, and wore the dignity of merit. No amount of refinement or knowledge will make a Chinaman forego this ancient ceremony of driving away the dragon that is swallowing the moon during an eclipse. When every other argument fails him, he will say: "It has always been our country's custom, and this is sufficient for them.

A Chinaman is shrewd in his worship, rather than otherwise, and jolly rather than gloomy. His *Joss*-house may be a costly temple, or a tiny thing like a little girl's doll-house.

I was walking in a wealthy Chinaman's garden, and saw what I thought was a child's doll-house. I went to it, thinking to discover how the Orientals "did" the toy business; when I found that this house, three feet in height, and about the same in width, contained only the square bit of red paper said to have written on it in Chinese characters the name of their god *Joss*, a box of matches, some bits of the sacred yellow paper twisted up like cigar-lighters, and a little bronze cup, about the size of a small tea cup, in which the garden servants burn the sacred paper at sundown—this burning constituting their evening worship.

The evening of the twenty-eighth of August had been fixed upon by the Chinese residents of Singapore for their great annual sacrifice or feast for the dead. The evening proved dark and rainy; but knowing that the ghosts of the dead mind neither mud nor rain, we wisely concluded that there would be no postponement on account of weather, and the coachman was directed to drive to that part of the city called *Tuleo Ayer*, to the residence of a rich Chinaman, the "Spirit Farmer of Singapore." This word sacrifice is horribly suggestive to the ears of the western world. However, do not picture to yourselves altars flowing with the blood of slain beasts. Though the Chinese revere the Queen of Heaven, and claim cousin-ship for their Emperors with the Sun and Moon, yet rumor hath never said that they, like the ancient Mexicans, had altars streaming with human gore.

On nearing the place, we came in sight of a table between seven and eight hundred feet long, brilliantly lighted with gas and Chinese lanterns. The food was arranged in tall pyramids, from ten to twelve feet in height, round a form which the food perfectly concealed. Among them were flowers and green leaves, unintentionally forming a mimic Nile valley. Pyramids of cakes alternated with others of yellow oranges; some of sweatmeats with those of green mandarin oranges, sugar-coated preserved fruits, ducoos, mangosteens, pine-apples, rambatans and rambas; indeed the pointed style prevailed, except for meats. Pork, or pig meat, as they call it, and ducks and chickens were in great abundance.

Riding slowly past, making our way with great difficulty through the dense crowd, which would only open at the sight of a policeman's club, we reached the house, in front of which, in the street, stood this immense table. Our host, a prosperous business man of the city, who spoke English very well and was sufficiently conversant with European customs, to receive visitors in that fashion, met us at the door and conducted us in. There were a few persons present in a spacious reception room on the second floor.

Some cake, confections, and preserved fruits, were presented to us—some of the most perishable, as mangosteen, and ducoo, were crystallized in such a perfect state that only a patient, pains taking Chinese lady could have accomplished. Choice cookery with them is a fine art, with which they do not permit servants to meddle or make. Within the limits of a certain charmed circle, lies their peculiar privilege; and rumor says they are content within that sphere.

Tea like nectar, was served in cups about half the size of an egg-shell. Query.—Did Jupiter ever send for a second cup? We did. From the front windows, we looked down upon the table with its burden of eatables, and the dense crowd of shaven heads waiting there in the rain. The food that the rain could injure, had been protected by propping up immense umbrellas of a peculiar mushroom pattern over it.

Eleven o'clock came, the crowd grew denser; those near the table held their places firmly and patiently. Half past eleven; still the rain pattered unremittingly, but it did not harm whole fruits, and all the rest were safe. The gas still gave a good light, but the lanterns had caught more of the rain—some of them had gone out.

The clock struck twelve. The crowd of shaven heads was as still and reverent as possible. No doubt, many a weary one was striving with unutterable longing to pierce with human sight the veil that hid a lost one's face. Not a word was heard; the haunted hour had come, all were serenely satisfied. The air round the table was supposed to be filled with the spirits of the dead.

Half-past twelve came, half an hour was supposed to be sufficiently long to wait for their ghostships; then the food was distributed among the crowd, by persons round the table.

Numbers carried their portions to the graves of departed comrades—such kindly tributes may often be seen on Chinese graves. The Chinaman remembers one that was his companion in wandering from the pagoda-land: his paradise of all the earth, and he places his gift on the rude piece of wood or stone, as a special tribute to his ghostly friend, who he thinks will come and partake of this food in some mysterious way, not very comprehensible to the living, but very satisfactory to the dead. After that, the coolie eats the food and creeps back to his sleeping-place—home he has not; his usual bed is the pavement under some verandah—as satisfied with the performance of his duty, as many a millionaire, who has reared a costly monument to his friend.

"It is not to be supposed," said the host, "that the more intelligent classes of Chinese believe that we actually feed the dead; it is a sacrifice *in honor* of the dead. In order to be accounted worthy to offer this sacrifice, we must first go through many services in the temple; prayers and sacrifices must be offered during a night of vigils. We know the poor are fed by it, and that is well. This sacrifice is connected with our religion, and has through many centuries, been the custom of our country."

Truly it does not seem to be a bad ceremony, for the "heathen Chinese." Such a yearly feeding of the poor might be copied in our own Christian country, without reducing us to heathen.

I will mention a pretty conceit in regard to Chinese burials. When a corpse is carried to the grave, as the friends start for home they begin to drop bits of gilt pasteboard about three inches square, which, it is supposed, the ghost will see and thus be able to find its way back to the old homestead. It is only a token to trace the way, and is never omitted. The material may be of gold foil, or silver, or tin, according to the wealth and position of the dead. These are the shining steps that lead the spirit, at ghostly hours, back to living friends.

Tigers, snakes and other wild beasts, and reptiles are

found upon the Island, and life here is not wanting in incident and adventure.

Some coolies who were working on a distant pepper and gambier plantation, which bordered on a wet piece of jungle, caught sight of a boa-constrictor. Coolie Geon was at once on the alert for speculation.

Rumor had told him, that the government paid a bounty of fifty dollars for every tiger that was caught in the island. He reasoned from that fact, that a serpent, a great dragon in his estimation, would bring him almost a fortune. So the coolies followed the serpent's trail and saw him at his huge gambols when he was throwing himself in coils from a tree to which he had fastened by one or two folds of his tail. They watched him at meals, taking good care that he did not serve one of their own number up, at one of his unostentatious rural repasts.

One day when his snakeship had been rather intemperate in the use of swine's flesh, having quietly sucked down an unfortunate pig and then laid down for a digestion nap of three days, the coolies whisked a strong noose over his neck and made it fast to a tree, then another over his tail; one or two wooden hooks judiciously driven down, pinned him to the earth.

It was a hot Sunday afternoon, when half a dozen coolies made a sensation among all classes, by bringing into town, on a long pole, a limp, lifeless boa-constrictor about thirty feet long, and two feet round the body. His skin was gorgeously laced with green and gold color, on a black ground.

Coolie Geon did not realize very heavily, in commercial phrase, on the "*Ulat busar*,"—great dragon,—for there was no market, no government bounty. So he concluded to turn showman, and admit white gentlemen at one dollar, and the natives for whatever they would give, to see the boa.

He would have prospered in this business had it not been for the disagreeable odor, which was certainly not very attractive. His show was popular only an hour or two the next morning; after which it was thrown into the sea to bait the sharks. Coolie Geon considered this a downright waste of meat. A few merchants made up a purse of about twenty dollars for them, and the coolies went back to picking pepper. As no more great dragons were brought to town, if there were any caught, it is safe to conclude that anaconda-steaks took the place of rat-fricassee, in the coolie restaurants.

An American gentleman obtained a young boa-constrictor which he intended to bring up as a household pet. He kept it in a large glass jar, and tenderly fed it with raw eggs until it became strong enough to throw off the cover and indulge in quiet strolls about his bedroom, or adjoining rooms when doors chanced to be left open, where it would amuse itself by hiding in unlooked-for places, as a bed, or a wardrobe. The fates seemed to frown on this infant snake's rambles, and one day its thread of life was clipped—he was found dead. Some suspicion was cast on a tame mongooz whose principal pastime was killing reptiles.

To the credit of the anaconda and boa family, it should be said that they have never manifested such an unseemly liking for Chinamen flesh as the tiger family possesses; having in this island, confined themselves literally to animal diet.

One unusually, rainy week, when we only caught fitful glimpses of the sun and had to kill the time by counting the showers, or listening to the cronish, gossipping chatter of a hundred or two sparrows in a tree close by, a real sensation made its appearance in the yard, in the shape of a huge, black creature of the lizard family, six or seven feet long. Instantly all the dogs in the neighborhood seemed to be on the spot, barking in the highest key. The servant-boys ran here and there and caught up anything that would deal a heavy blow, as poles, sticks, shovels and tongs. One was fortunate enough to find a piece of board, four or five feet long, with which to meet the lizard, on his march across the yard.

The reptile fought them well, lashing them with his long slender tail. Every stroke told as though it had been a thong of leather on the bare legs and arms and thinly clad bodies of the native servants, who thwacked away with their bamboo poles, which did not seem to be heavy enough to do much execution. This lizard did not appear to belong to the crocodilė species, as the head and jaws were short, and he did not make much fight with them; he evidently knew where the strength of his artillery lay. One after another the dogs were sent yelping away, and only skirmished at a safe distance afterwards. A poor little black-and-tan terrier, getting a blow, retired to the house and delivered his barks from the open window.

Old Jacko, the monkey, joined his fiercest yells to the barking of the dogs, and went with them towards the intruder the full length of his chain. At length, when the din was at the highest pitch and the creature had nearly fought its way across the yard against eight or ten servants and as many dogs, the man with the board got a chance to deal it a stunning blow; they then threw a noose over its head and made it fast to a tree, where they continued to beat it until its valiant tail lay still and lifeless.

"What will they do with it?" was asked of the stable boys who went fiercely into the fight.

"*Bekin banya busas machan*," replied one or two. "Make great eating, plenty Malay men give one dollar, little piece,—" measuring it off on his hand. "It make one man very strong, he live very long time," said another boy who had acquired a little broken English that he was very fond of airing on every occasion. From this I concluded that lizard was not a regular article of diet among them, but was taken as our own people take rowing and gymnastic exercise, to improve their strength and add a few years more of life to that which is usually allotted to man.

The jungles of Singapore will not admit of grand tiger-hunting. In this they are unlike the plains of Burmah or Bengal, where the kingly elephant comes in as the powerful ally of man,—a sort of monster setter that snuffs the approach of game, and gives the signal to the hunters when to open their battery of fire-arms, by elevating his proboscis out of harm's way.

A CATTLE-LIFTER.

Word comes into town that a tiger's track has been seen in a certain vicinity. Instantly every gentleman who is, or fancies he is, a good shot, is on the alert; guns and ammunition are eagerly sought after, and all betake themselves to the supposed haunt of the tiger, to bait the animal.

The body of a goat, pig, or bullock is fastened to the ground so that it cannot be too quickly snatched away, and the sportsmen conceal themselves in some tall tree that overlooks the spot, where they remain watching through the night—the early dawn being the time when the tiger is most likely to seek for food. Great care must be observed so that he may not smell the hunter, for he is a wary creature and quickly suspects something wrong.

Some acquaintances told me that they watched by turns a bait like that, for one whole week, without getting a shot. Usually, one night of watching in such an elevated and constrained position, so cools a gentleman's love of the sport, that he returns to town, and the watching is continued by native convicts, who are detailed for that purpose, until the animal is shot, or is known to have changed his quarters.

One day, word came to our quiet town that a huge tiger had been trapped eight or ten miles out, and his Malay captors were bringing him in alive. Native men and boys rushed out to see him and followed in his train. By the time they reached town, he had a retinue that might fitly represent one of the old decaying princes of Bengal. His royal highness did not seem to relish the attention that was paid him. He was rather savage over it, and pitched, and plunged, and howled in a terrific manner. These antics only added spice to the entertainment. His captors turned show men, for this was the next thing to a real wild-beast combat, and made the exhibition prosper for two or three days.

When the excitement had subsided a little, we drove down to the Malay part of the town to see the tiger. We found him in a rude cage made of iron and strong bars of wood, within a walled enclosure, with a man at the gate to take the "backsheesh."

The animal was a monster of his kind. He was lying on his back with his feet up; his paws were badly swollen; the claws, or nails, had all been extracted, and the flesh left raw and bleeding. This was done ostensibly to protect the keeper, but the claws always find their way to some native jeweler's hands, and are made into brooches and bracelets, for which the Straits of Malacca are famous. The peon on duty there, said the head measured twelve inches between the ears.

The full-grown tiger soon pines away in confinement; to tame one it must be caught when quite young.

The Malays have a method peculiarly their own, of capturing this animal. They dig a pit fifteen or twenty feet deep, in the path the creature is supposed to travel, and cover it over with ratans, ferns, and grass, laying them on with great skill and naturalness, to make them look as if they really grew where they were placed; for they believe that a tiger would notice anything displaced as quickly as a hunter would; and lastly a bait is placed over the centre of the pit. As the tiger always pounces upon his prey, he goes to the bottom, and is quite unable, with his utmost efforts, to jump out.

When his rage and strength are somewhat exhausted, and he has been without food for some time, a strong cage is let down, baited with fresh meat, but so arranged, that, when the bait is disturbed, the door closes and shuts the animal in; then the cage is drawn out of the pit. The natives contrive to pull the paws through the cage, and with pincers, extract all their claws.

It sometimes happens that a cub falls into one of these pits; such an incident occurred during the first year of our sojourn on the island. Mr. Cameron relates this affair in *Our Tropical Possessions:* of which I give the substance.

Several natives were known to have been carried off within a short period, from a certain district, and considerable excitement was felt by all classes of the inhabitants. People driving at night along roads bordered by jungle, felt very nervous, and it was even rumored that tracks had been seen in the Botanical Garden, only four miles from town. The local paper, the

Straits Times, revived the tradition that had almost lapsed into oblivion, that native men enough were killed to average one for every day in the year. The editor, Mr. Cameron, in a very fair and candid way went on to show, that although not half of that number were reported by the police, he was convinced that it was very near the truth, for the pepper and gambier planters were interested in concealing all such deaths, for fear their plantations should get the name of being in a dangerous locality. These are all in the interior, and at such a distance through the jungles that it would be exposing another man to a like fate, if he were sent to report a death. Consequently they announce no deaths, while those reported are nearly all Malay wood-cutters working on their own responsibility; though the former laborers are equally exposed, and outnumber the latter in the proportion of ten to one.

Squads of convicts were sent to the infested districts, attended by police-peons, and several pits were dug; the watch and guard went on nightly in the old way, when one morning a half-grown cub was found in one of the pits. They knew the mother could not be far off, and as the object was to kill her as well as to secure the young cub, it was allowed to remain in the pit, unmolested, while they sent the news to town.

On the following morning, about ten native peons armed with muskets arrived at the spot, under the charge of the Deputy-Commissioner and two European Inspectors of Police.

They took their way cautiously to the mouth of the pit, and were looking down at the cub, when suddenly, with a fierce growl, the mother-tiger bounded from the jungle into their midst, tearing the sides of the pit and scattering those around it, but directly attacking no one. All were petrified for a moment, for the animal was actually brushing against them.

When the first surprise had a little passed off, an ill-directed random fire was commenced by the native peons; the effect of which was certainly fatal, but in the wrong quarter. The tiger retreated reluctantly to the jungle, apparently scathless;

but it was discovered that one of the peons had received a shot through the body, and he died from the effects of it, that evening. The Deputy-Commissioner also received a shot through the sleeve of his coat, in the encounter. No near approach was made to the pit again that day, but the watch was kept up. Though the tigress showed herself several times, she escaped the few scattered shots that were fired at her.

On the third day, a person of some experience took the direction of affairs. He threw down a large piece of wood, causing the cub to howl out loudly. On hearing the cry of her young, the tigress bounded fiercely to the mouth of the pit, and received in her breast the charge of a well-directed rifle. The young tiger was then taken out, and brought to the city with great rejoicing, by the peons at least, for they were able to claim two bounties and the price of the skin, besides having a tigerling to train up, to take a place in some menagerie when he developed into fair tigerhood.

CHAPTER III.

THE ISLANDS OF THE ARCHIPELAGO.

TO the west of Singapore, for eight hundred miles, the great Island of Sumatra stretches its varied coast-line towards the south-east; A fertile land; a vast country where kind nature feeds her primitive children, and toil is scarcely known.

But in Singapore we know it only as the great barrier against those fearful storms, that come with such awful force from the southern ocean, sweeping the seas, and breaking in fury on the coast. Western-world civilization has never reached its pleasant hills and mountains, which we see from the steamer's deck, rising away in the far interior. God never made so fair a land to remain forever the home of barbarians. The world must certainly have a large part of its allotted time yet to run, for there are so many rich fields in it, which have not yet fulfilled their apparent mission.

Under its shadow, basking in an unruffled sea, which it shuts in, lie almost innumerable smaller islands; while further to the south and east, Java adds five hundred miles more of barrier, with only the interruption of the narrow Strait of Sunda.

Then come other narrow channels, and Madura, Bali, Lamboc, and Sumbawa, with their lofty volcanoes.

The islands, Flores, Adenahra, Lombatta, Timor, Sarawatha and the Great and Little Keys, stretching away through the ocean, 85° on the Equator, appear like stepping-stones, ready for the giant race which is to come and people a land more favored by nature than any other that the sun has ever looked upon.

On the north of these lies Borneo, almost a continent, where salubrious summer ever fosters fruits and flowers.

Sarawak is the capital of what is called the settlement of Sir James Brook in the island of Borneo. It is a small territory entirely under his control; that is, it is independent of England and not under the jurisdiction of the Sultan of the island. There are regular sailing vessels, but no steamers, plying between Singapore and this port, which is about six days' sail from the former.

The broad estuary of a river forms a very good harbor. Its waters are gathored on the western slope of a mountain-range, far interior, that nearly equally divides the island into the eastern and western parts, watering, on the way to the sea, forests of huge camphor, teak, gutta-percha, sandal-wood trees, and jungles of bamboos and ratans, that have supplied the commercial world for centuries with those articles.

The Malay Sultan of this island, as before mentioned, ceded to Sir James this portion of the western coast. It was a fair bargain and grant, peacefully made, for certain sums of money, goods, and services rendered, and neither Sultan nor Rajah Brook or heirs have broken treaty. The white residents of this little Rajahdom scarcely number twenty-five of both sexes; a little handful truly, but, dwelling peacefully and dealing fairly, they constitute a strong commercial bond, standing as they really do, at once the mediators and defenders between the almost innumerable semi-civilized Malays of the coast-country, and the wild, untamable Dyak tribes of the interior. The bankers and merchants drive a very thrifty trade in the various natural products of this wonderful island. The Mateo diamond was taken from the mines of Borneo which lie on the western slope of the mountains.

A lady-friend who, with her husband, had resided two years in one of the Malay towns of the island, where they enjoyed the unenviable distinction of being the only white residents in the place, described the climate as very charming indeed. She said:

"Coming from a northern latitude and bracing winter air, we suffered from no fevers, or any other sickness worthy of notice, during our stay. The only depredation committed on our premises, was by the very numerous wild pigs from the forests and jungles; who had a remarkable taste for the sweet-potatoes in the garden. The common people are happy and quiet, neither addicted to strong drink, nor overwork, nor worry. The women spin and weave the native cotton into cloth, and sometimes print it in elaborate patterns, with indelible colors extracted from the juice of plants. The men cultivate the gardens and fields of rice. Wood-cutters fell and chip up the huge camphor-trees into small bits, and place them in caldrons and boil out the gum, which is allowed to settle and crystallize upon a net-work of twigs. A species of palm, when grown about half the height that it would naturally attain, is also felled and split in halves; at that period of growth it is found to contain a large amount of starchy pith; this is scooped out and cooked for food; it is also washed and granulated, and then it is the sago of commerce."

To the east of Borneo and separated from it by the streets of Macassar lies Celebes with its vast unknown forests, its broad bays, gulfs, and rivers; it is said to be very sparsely inhabited. The cultivated fields, the populous cities that are to be, and the commerce that is to whiten its fair waters, seem now to lie very far in the future; but they will come. Civilization will some day come to these new-old lands, as it has come to New Zealand and Australia.

Three days' steaming to the south-east, from Singapore lies the Island of Java. A regular line of steamers plies between this city and the ports on that island, connecting with the English mail-steamers. There are numerous islands lying along this route; one of them is Banco, known for centuries for its mines of tin.

The principal ports of Java, are the well-known towns, Batavia on the north-western, and Sourabaya on the eastern coast of the island.

Batavia is built on a large bay, thickly studded with islands: very charming they appear with their numerous cocoanut and areca palm-trees. Some are fortified, others converted into docks for repairing ships; but none are of sufficient length to act as breakwaters to protect the harbor in a severe storm from the north-east. A canal leads from the harbor to the town, and one has to leave the steamer and take a sail-boat to reach the city.

No stranger is allowed to enter the country without a passport, stating his profession, and the length of time which he expects to remain on the island; but the Dutch Government-officers are said to be very obliging when these requirements have been attended to.

The great counting-houses are near the river. Each one has its own plot of ground, planted with trees. These houses are built of red brick, and ornamented in stucco, in the old Dutch style, above and at the sides of the windows.

The European part of the town has fine spacious shops, occupied by tailors, milliners, chemists, and those who follow the various mechanical arts. It has some very elegant dwellings the most noticeable of which is the Government Palace, which is occupied by the Governor-General during a part of the year; the remaining part is spent at Buitenzorg, his country seat. There are one or two fine club-houses.

Further on is an extensive green park; which is intersected with roads and driveways planted with trees. It is really a charming half-Enropean and half-tropical place. Here the *élite* and fashion of the Dutch metropolis in the East are seen driving at five o'clock, in splendid phaetons brought out from Europe.

There is plenty of smoking here. Batavia is a sort of paradise to which the souls of smokers go when released from existence elsewhere; gentlemen are always puffing like locomotives; they smoke, driving or walking, as well as sitting at

HOUSE AND WOMEN OF BORNEO.

business; even in the presence of ladies the cigar is not always laid aside. It cannot be that they have acquired such strong habits in one short state of existence.

The ladies drive at this hour in full evening dress, as if going to a party or ball. The hair is ornamented, and costly jewelry worn, just as they will appear in the drawing-room during the evening. Bonnets are only worn at church, and hats are worn in the morning ramble.

All the European citizens take a morning walk, either just before or just after sunrise. Costume at that hour, *négligé*. Fashionable ladies are in print wrappers, and gentlemen in loose flannel jackets and pajamas.

Returning from the walk, the next thing on the day's programme is a bath in the usual Indian style—buckets of water thrown over the head and person. All then dress for the morning meal. A collation of bread, cold meat, eggs and coffee is served, after which the gentlemen drive to their places of business, and the ladies superintend their household arrangements. Eastern servants require much more supervision than European domestics or American "help."

The wealthy citizen comes home to breakfast, as it is called, at twelve o'clock, and does not return to the counting-house that day. When the meal is over, he stretches himself on a lounge, and takes a nice little nap of a couple of hours. He awakens about four o'clock, bathes, and smokes again — if the cigar has been out of his mouth at all except while eating. There is some ground for a suspicion that he does not smoke while sleeping, because he always calls for fire and cheroots, the first thing after waking in the morning. He then dresses for the evening drive, as I have mentioned, and is accompanied by his wife and daughters; or perhaps he may prefer a promenade about the beautiful streets, all bordered with trees and choice shrubs; while the ladies drive in their phaeton, attended by coachman and footman in jaunty costumes.

People manage to pass much of their time in society very pleasantly here. Each lady selects her evening for an "At

Home;" and that is understood, or announced among her friends. When the evening comes, she illuminates her front balcony or verandah brilliantly, and all her acquaintances whom she has been in the habit of meeting at other "At Homes," consider themselves invited to spend the evening at her house.

Where the balcony is broad and spacious, as it usually is here, it is hung with ratan curtains, so as to protect it from the sun, and is furnished like a parlor. Here the host and hostess receive their guests; the great drawing-room, back of it, is reserved for the dancing-hall. Refreshments are served at about eleven o'clock, and guests then usually return to their homes, to spend the next evening at another friend's house in the same manner. Though, on some occasions when the music and the dance are more than usually fascinating, the "wee sma'" hours are struck before the host and hostess find themselves alone.

Samarang, another seaport town of Java, is two days steaming from Batavia, down the north side of the island. It stands in a region that is teeming with rice and coffee; in the background rise the Chundy mountains, and near by also rises a lofty mountain called Gunong Sampi.

Perhaps no country in the world abounds in such magnificent and ever-varying scenery as the island of Java, or has a lovelier climate. Sourabaya, at the eastern end of the island, is reached by Dutch mail-steamers every two weeks. The city is almost surrounded by the river Kederia; which rises in a lake of the same name: it divides into two branches, the Kali Mus, gold river, and the Kali Permeang.

The Yenger Mountains are in the vicinity of Sourabaya, the point of departure for visitors to the volcanoes. A carriage takes the tourist over a good road to Passerpan, at the foot of the hills. There the carriage is left, and ponies are required for the ascent to the Government Bungalow at Tassari; which is fifteen thousand feet above the level of the sea.

The Bromo, a volcanic mountain, is three miles from the Government Bungalow, and it occupies about an hour for a pony to climb up the mountain road.

After leaving Passerpan, the hills are wooded for some distance. Tree-ferns grow to such a height that they look like palm-trees; flowering shrubs fringe the way, and beautiful orchidaceous flowers and plants cling to the bark of the trees. Wild hogs, fat and burly fellows, are as common as the monkeys, which appear to be very numerous, chattering at one from every tree. We saw an old one sitting on a rock, tending her young with very amusing maternal gravity, hunting the fleas and wood-ticks out of its fur.

Birds of gaudy plumage flit through and among the tall bamboos and broad-leaved chantizy; but at a certain altitude the trees dwindle in height, and are seen at rarer intervals; they are a different species from those lower down. The slopes are covered with a tall coarse grass, and a shrub called the kut-i-sang, that reminds one of the rhododendron. The following is from the pen of Mr. J. D'Almeida:

"Having arrived at the edge, there is a descent of more than eight hundred feet to the floor of the Dassar-sand sea. The path down the side of this old crater is very precipitous; but the mountain ponies are admirably adapted for the descent, if held with a tight rein. Leaving the rim, on descending, the burnt stones, charcoal, and cinders, are almost within sweep of the hand, as one trudges over the calcined rocks. What imagination can paint a scene, such as this ancient crater once presented—a heaving mass of lava and fire, fifteen miles in circumference! It is now a sea of fine sand, with two or three peaks in its centre, only one of which is an active crater, and that is called Bromo—a corruption probably of Brahma, the Hindoo deity; and this supposition respecting the name is further strengthened by the fact that the natives pay particular reverence to this volcano, though now professing to believe in the Koran."

The partition between the Mohammedanism of these Malays and image-worship, is very thin; they are probably about half way between the two religions; though their nominal conversion took place more than four hundred years ago. They would not worship an image, and yet they believe that a deity resides in a volcano. They also still venerate the peepul-tree, as the natives of Hindustan do. The kosambie and cotton trees, they believe, are inhabited by evil spirits who delight in killing children: which is only a relic of their former belief in the hideous goddess Kahle. Sowing the rice crop, too, is still attended with peculiar rites and ceremonies.

The Javanese keep a sacred festival on this mountain top, at which sacrifices are thrown into the burning crater, to propitiate the spirit of Bromo and secure success to themselves and all their undertakings for a year: the more hazardous the scheme, the greater the necessity for sacrifice.

The pilgrims gather from the adjacent islands and all parts of Java, with an offering to cast into the flames. Though leagues on leagues of sea or land be traversed, they must be at the burning crater's brim at sunrise, each one offering, it may be, a chicken, a rice-pot, some coin, a rosary of flowers, a new sarong,—anything, in short, that is of value to these simple people. Bromo is not particular; his fiery tongue laps it all down; but whatever it is, it must be sprinkled with water, and blessed by the priest, and offered at sunrise. None are so poor as to come without a gift for the great fiery mouth of Bromo.

The priests do nearly all the praying and interceding, kneeling in rows on mats, at a certain distance from the crater; while clouds of perfumed smoke curl up from clumsy wooden censers. They go through all the forms of prayer; that is, so far as their knowledge of the Koran goes, for "much learning" will never cause madness in these priests. Nearly all this time the people surrounding them have been driving bargains, chatting, and joking, in the easy, good-humored way peculiar to the Malays. It did not take them as long to say all the prayers they had learned, or else they were more expeditious than the priests, and gained time to make a few more bargains. Now comes the sprinkling of the offerings, and another prayer in which the crowd join—the last bargain will get its share of Bromo's blessing.

The oldest priest (clad as they all are, in long white muslin

JAVANESE PRINCE IN HOME DRESS.

gowns, with gay yellow scarfs on their shoulders, and turbans) rises and gives a signal.

The crowd rushes forward pell-mell. Each one is for himself; the one great desire of the pilgrimage is urging him on. This last stage is to be the test of all his schemes. If he can only be the first to reach the brim of the crater and throw in his offering, success is bound to come to him.

Just when he has nearly out-distanced all the others, some limping old priest will call a halt, and order more prayers; Bromo is not yet quite ready to be gracious. No one can afford to neglect prayers when Bromo is to be propitiated for a whole year and will make one the winner in every enterprise, or crown with success some darling project; so the devotee stops and prays.

As the priests arrange themselves in front, nearest the crater-god who is to be worshipped, they have the start of the others in the last short race, but do not always run as well as the village athletes.

The fortunate one stands on the crater's edge; and away down, down, two hundred feet, among the heaving, seething sulphurous fire and smoky vapor, he hurls his offering. It is the first; but there are many more to follow it. The first to sacrifice is a happy fellow, and is looked upon as a rising man in his village; he may come to be tax-gatherer, perhaps, as people have little use for post-masters there.

It was interesting to watch the offerings as they were flung into the crater. Large cocoa-nuts gave only a faint boom, when carelessly thrown; hit the sides of the crater and stopped short. Huge jack-fruit went bowling down the shelving slope. If it split on a rock and did not reach the fire, the object of the pilgrimage was lost, and deep disappointment wrote itself on the face of the one who threw it. Live chickens, among other things, were thrown into the awful mouth of the volcano. A few of the stronger birds changed their fate into flight, and alighted on the rock, safe from fire and vapor, and the steady trade-wind carried them safely away from the pilgrims.

If one were to ask this crowd what they wish for most, the answer would probably be very much the same as would be given by a promiscuous assemblage in any other country.

That keen, weazened-faced fellow would say, that he has sent a venture in a boat, but it has been gone a long time and he has heard nothing of it; so he came to Bromo.

There is a cleaver-faced Shylock, who has loaned out money, and is fearful he shall lose it; so *he* came to Bromo.

There are young girls among the crowd; but it would never do to ask them what *they* came for: they would not tell you.

Doubtless there also are many representatives of praying Hannah; for these Asiatic women, if they had a legion of sons, would ask for one more.

On descending from the crater many games are played, by which those who have taken part in the festival try to lift the veil from the time to come, and get a peep behind it, to see what there is in store for them. These games give the laggards in the race to the crater another chance to try their fortune.

A favorite form of divination consists in walking three times round a high mound and then hurling a stone over it. If the first stone that one hurls goes over without hitting, success will take kindly to him during the ensuing year.

The volcanoes in this part of the island are Bromo, Lamongan and Smeroe. Lamongan is six thousand feet in height, and is near lake Klaka. From the Government Bungalow, among the mountains of Arjuno, these three burning mountains can all be seen lighting up, at the same time, the cloudless evening sky. The sight on a clear starlighted evening is indescribably grand; the lurid glare of the fiery volcanoes falling on the nearer peaks, making them stand out from a sea of gloom and misty vapor, which hovers over all the valleys and lowlands away to the seaward.

First Bromo; for he must in those old days have had the preference, a sort of higher rank than the others, when he uplifted to the face of night a lake of fire, fifteen miles in circumference. He belches out a full blast of flame, as if

Vulcan himself were at the forge below, blowing the bellows with a giant arm. Then Lamongan sends up his tongue of flame, as though the forces which had just been so active under Bromo, were transferred to Lamongan; while the former falls into a state of half semi-repose, taking a fresh breath.

Lamongan having finished his fiery blast, then Smeroe or Bromo suddenly flash up afresh, as if the force were transferred again from one to the other, by some subterranean channel common to all three. This circumstance has given rise to a belief among the common people of the island, that these volcanoes are connected with each other. Though they are all visible from this elevated point in the Arjuno-mountains, yet their distance from each other is over thirty miles.

There are many very extensive ruins of palaces and temples in the middle and eastern part of this island, which show plainly a former high degree of civilization, before the conquering Arabians came to propagate the religion of the Koran. The great temple of Borobodo is still majestic in its ruins. It is in the vicinity of the Prahu (boat) Mountains (named from their resemblance to the outline of a boat); not very far distant from one of the volcanoes. It was built round a conical hill, in a series of ten terraces. Four of these are square, having a grand arched entrance on each side; and six are circular. The lower terrace is about four hundred and thirty feet on each side, and is built of blocks of stone so perfectly dressed that there does not seem to be any cement required to join them. On the perpêndicular walls is sculptured the legend of the god Rama, and the history of Buddha.

The summit of the hill is paved, forming a wide court, in the centre of which is a pagoda with a mutilated, gigantic image of Gandama. This centre temple is surrounded by seventy-two smaller ones, similar in shape and arranged in three rows at exact distances round it.

Four days' journey north from Singapore, by steamer, is the city of Bangkok, the capital of Siam. It is located some little distance from the sea on the broad river Meinam, the Mother of Waters, which, like the Grand Canal of Venice, is also its great highway and place for pageants and other great displays.

In place of roads and streets, it has canals. One has only to keep a boat and boatmen instead of a carriage and horses, and then the comforts and conveniences are about equal.

The river Meinam drains a valley of inexhaustible fertility, about six hundred miles in length, which is bounded on either side by a range of mountains, separating it on the east from the valley of Cambodia, and on the west from the narrow coast-possessions of the English and Burmese.

The surface of this river is as populous as the "black streets"—as the native quarters of an Oriental city are usually called. Thousands have their birthplace and dwell all their lives on it. The houses of the poor are built on stout corner-posts extending down some distance into the water, and framed into immense rafts which are fastened by chains to piles. Between these posts is confined a quantity of bamboo poles, which, containing a large amount of air in their cavities, and the bark being impervious to water, will by their buoyancy float rows of small houses for several years, and then have only to be replaced by new ones. Even the location itself can be readily changed in calm weather.

The Buddhist temples are generally solid structures, with niches for the reception of the image of Buddha: they are surrounded by paved courts where the people congregate. On the pyramidal-shaped shrines is lavished untold wealth, in gold, and jewels, and curious and beautiful decorations of fretted and carved work. Some of the smaller images are said to be composed wholly of precious stones, one of emerald and another of amethyst, etc. Intelligent Buddhists repel the idea that they worship the image before which they bow. They assert positively that Buddha is a spirit; the image is only a reminder of him. All classes of the people are remarkably generous to their religious institutions, the temples and monasteries; giving their goods to feed the poor. Persons are often met with who have given their whole fortunes, and afterwards led a life of toil and privation.

THE LATE FIRST KING OF SIAM.

The white elephant is revered, because he is supposed to contain the spirit of some very exalted person, a great king, a warrior, or some saint; for it is believed that pure spirits enter into creatures that have white forms. Such a spirit dwel ing among them, even in such an unwieldy shape, confers great blessings on those that entertain him, and the country also. Hence the great respect entertained for him is manifested in about the same manner as homage is paid to their king: by entertaining him with music and shows, and prostrating themselves before him as if he were more than mortal.

The climate is mild and healthful like that of the Straits of Malacca, particularly on the higher ground away from the river; here also reigns perpetual summer. Europeans suffer much less from heat than in Hindustan. There are many health-resorts in the mountains easily accessible from the city.

The late king is generally conceded to have been the wisest, most learned, most tolerant, and best native ruler in all Asia. He came to the throne about the year 1851. His father died in 1825; and he being the son of the crowned queen should have succeeded then, but for the usurpation of an elder brother, a son of one of the lesser lights of the harem, while he, the rightful heir of the throne, retired to a monastery and led the life of a Buddhist priest for twenty-five years. He was, during this long probation, a most diligent student of all the Oriental languages, especially the Sanscrit and Pali, so closely interwoven with that of the Siamese in all their sacred books on religion and law. He also made himself familiar with history and the natural sciences, geology, chemistry, astronomy, and the English language. In the last, he was the pupil and familiar friend of the American missionaries, and from them gleaned the ideas of European strength and civilization, that were so manifest in his reign. Unlike the rulers of China and Japan, the sovereigns of this small kingdom, almost in their shadow, have for two centuries shown an enlightened wish to cultivate trade and friendly relations with Europe.

The Kralahome, or prime minister, the son of the half-brother who usurped the power for twenty-five years, is a man whose talents and executive ability compel respect, both from foreign residents and the native people.

It is not my intention to go into any minute description of this country, or Borneo, or Java, but only to show that they are all interesting and comparatively untrodden fields, not yet so much worn by the footprints of travellers as to lose their novelty. They do not lie too far off the grand highway round the world; they are all easily reached from the city of Singapore. The ruins of Upper Egypt have long been considered to be the greatest architectural works near the Equator; but here, many hundred miles nearer to it, within the torrid zone, in Siam and Cambodia, are curious and beautiful remains of long-forgotten cities, and immense temples built of ponderous blocks of stone, with fortified inclosures equalling in size the cities of Delhi or Agra, and rivalling Thebes, Karnac and Luxor, in details and grandeur of proportions. They were not built for the disciples of Buddha, as the sculptures on the walls plainly show; hence they were reared before Gandama's disciples came here to convert all this peninsula to the then new religion of Eastern Asia; which time of coming could not be far from the birth of our Saviour. They were cotemporary with Rome, Athens and Palmyra, and have been preserved best of all. Near the ancient capital of Cambodia, a high graded road stretches away over mountains and rivers, which are spanned by solidly-built stone bridges; all perfect enough for use, should the ancient owners come back to them to-day. With a liberal prince on the throne of Siam, and the French at Saigon, controlling Cambodia to a certain extent, students and tourists will there find abundant materials for study and inspection.

CHAPTER IV.

GOING UP THE COAST OF THE PENINSULA.

WE BADE adieu to bright, summery Singapore, its fadeless verdure, and perpetual succession of flowers, and went on board the steamer *Mahratta*, about three o'clock in the afternoon. Our old friend Mr.——, was already standing on deck. He seemed to be a sort of genial link between the past and present, for he had completed his seventy-third year, with the serene temper, spirit, and health of a man of thirty or forty. He had not been in the temperate zone since 1816.

Among the passengers here, I noticed two Sisters of Charity, and two brides-elect. The Sisters of Charity, were probably from some sickly coast-station, and had been to our salubrious little island to recruit their health.

The brides-elect were from Scotland. They came round the Cape of Good Hope by the Steamer *Ajax*, and were brought on to Singapore. The screw of the steamer having broken, they were unable to put in to Penang, where they were to meet their intended husbands. It was hinted that their laggard lovers were not at hand.

The Malay boys that dive here for "backsheesh" must, I think, belong to the original tribe of tadpoles that the savans pretend were our progenitors.

You may have seen a string of winking, blinking frogs sitting listless and disconsolate on a log; when something would attract them, and then there would be a twinkle of legs, a plash in the water, and a green streak going down through the depths. The boys were just like these frogs. Patter, patter into the clear water, went a handful of small coin from a passenger, over the side of the steamer. Instantly there was a rush from a crowd of log dug-outs, a swift twinkle of brown legs, and a brown streak in the direction of the money sinking down into the water; then, a moment after, a blowing and snorting from brown upturned laughing faces; and then they took from their mouths the doits that they had caught before they reached the bottom, where they would have been buried and lost in the sediment.

"*Cashi wang pootch!*" (give white money). This produced as greatly accelerated a twinkling of legs as electricity from a battery would. The silver was brought up before it had travelled far towards the bottom of the harbor; and while looking at these boys one came very near believing in the tadpole theory.

Ah! there come the good-humored faces of two friends, Mr. —— and Mr. ——. Riding three or four miles to New Harbor, just to bid outgoing friends good-bye, does not seem to be regarded by the gentlemen of Singapore as a task.

Steaming out among the beautiful islands, toward the golden sunset, the western sky is all piled with crimson and gold-burnished clouds. It is one of those gorgeous sunsets that are so frequent here, when nature seems to get up a splendid pageant, in the midst of which the sun may retire after his day's march. Whatever may be the fame of the Bay of Naples, I am sure that it must have many drawbacks in comparison with the Bay of Singapore and the lovely scenery of the Straits of Malacca. There, at Naples, would be the fading and falling of the foliage, the dry, parched, midsummer look; while here is an unvarying temperature, daily showers, an unfading green. This island, and the innumerable islets in the vicinity, always appear as they do this December day—clothed with the bright emerald hue of Spring. Passing out from the island of Pulo Brani, the neighboring hills are crowned with white bungalows, making them doubly beautiful, half hid as they are among the graceful senna-trees, (the elms

SINGAPORE FROM THE HILLS WESTWARD.

of the Orient) the betel-nut, the gorgeous ponciana regia trees, and a great profusion of broad, glossy-leaved trees and shrubs.

On the verandas, ever and anon could be seen the flutter of a white dress, and, passing about the grounds, we saw the white-and-red turbaned servants.

I watched the golden track which the sun had painted on the smooth, still waters, and which our boat seemed to follow, and my heart accepted the omen which the bright way indicated.

There was the jingle of a bell. I looked round, and beheld the dinner-table spread on deck. Could anything be in more perfect harmony,—the golden sunset streaming in long slant rays across the deck, through the gaps of the awning:

> "Tapering away in a line so sweet,
> Where the golden sun and waters meet,
> Paving a path fit for angels' feet."

As the day ended, a cool breeze sprung up from the land, and good soft woollen blankets would not have come amiss on any berth that night.

When the dawn crept over the waters, we dropped anchor before the old Malay, Portuguese, or Dutch town of Malacca.

Albuquerque made an unsuccessful assault on this town in 1508, and had to withdraw. Renewing the attack in 1511, the town and country adjoining fell into the hands of the victorious Portuguese, whose many descendants form a large portion of the present population; retaining the habits of their ancestors, through both Dutch and English rule. During the one hundred and thirty-one years of their rule the town was strongly fortified, and became one of the great commercial marts of the East Indian trade. In 1642, the Dutch took possession, and enlarged and strengthened the place. They have left their impress on everything, for all the ruins seem to bear the Dutch stamp.

As the regular steamer between Singapore and Malacca cast anchor at the same time, only a few boats honored the

Mahratta with a visit. Not being in readiness to go in these, we were in danger of losing the opportunity altogether, when we caught sight, out of our cabin window, of one of the steamer's officers, just shoving off for shore, who kindly offered us a passage with him, which we gladly accepted.

There was a strong breeze blowing off the land, and we were three miles out in the roadstead, so there was hard pulling for the rowers. Very beautiful was this December morning, so unlike any December anywhere else than in the Straits. There was a touch—just a dash—of northern September in the air, without the gorgeous foliage on the land.

A few purple and golden clouds were scattered and piled about the rising sun, who appeared looking as though he had thrown off his shining garments overnight, and no one had tidied up his bed-chamber. Be that as it may, we could, and did, stare at him while on the horizon, as we would not have dared to do, hours after, when he had put on his burning fierceness. The buoyant waves, and the fresh breeze, sent a thrill of vigor through our veins, as our boat went skimming over the sparkling water, pulled by four native rowers.

The view of the hills, the walls of the old ruined fort and church, and the rows of graceful senna-trees, with here and there a betel-nut or a cocoa-nut tree to give an Oriental touch to the landscape, is very picturesque. The old Portuguese and Dutch fort was dismantled and levelled early under the English rule. The old church, built three hundred years ago, has long been without a roof, and the grass has woven a fine soft green carpet over the aisles where the good, old Dutch housewives and frauleins prayed. In one corner a propiya tree stands, flourishing, and bearing fruit; growing out of the brink of a grave, like Roger Williams' pear-tree. I could not relish that fruit; I should almost accuse myself of cannibalism if I ate of it.

It seems that all the notable ones of that early day had an ambition to be buried in the church aisles. We noticed one tomb, as old as 1563, recording in a Latin inscription the virtues of the deceased. Another tablet had been erected to the memory of an English officer, within the last decade of years. With the exception of three monuments, the slabs were all level with the aisles, which had doubtless echoed with the tread of irreverent, as well as reverent feet, for this old building has stood through many changes. St. Francis Xavier officiated at the altar of this old ruin; and one may also add that he, on one occasion, commanded the most efficient battery of the fort when the Sultan of Acheen made a fierce attack on the place. The Sultan's fleet of boats was entirely destroyed.

The English have taken advantage of this old church on the hill, to build a lighthouse against its western wall.

We took a drive down the beach, along a most charming street, which had a few nice houses and very many bungalows, nestling under the shade of cocoa-nut and betel-nut trees. Indeed, here as well as at Penang, cocoa-nut trees are everywhere planted among the shade-trees, which produces a very beautiful effect on the scenery as a whole. Buckah Chine is quite a steep hill, with very many curious Chinese graves (Buckah is the Malay name for hill).

Finding it nearly time for the steamer to leave, we drove down to the river bank to find a boat. Here we encountered the Klingmen, a class of people who will to the end of time outjew the Jews. Seeing that we were strangers, they only asked one dollar and fifty cents to take us on board; but a half-caste man interfered, and told us the regular price was forty-five cents; which was then readily taken by the boatmen, who when they found that they could get no more, said they would wait in readiness till we wanted to go. The half-caste said that he was a Christian, and did not think such ways were right; which spoke well for this man, for the Klings probably remembered him to his cost.

Casting my eyes once more towards the church on the hill, with its rows of beautiful trees in full clear outline against a sky that could vie with that of Italy, I found that we were just in front of what I suspected must be the old Dutch Stadthaus. It was so brightened up with stucco and paint that I was at first uncertain; but a moment's reflection told me that there was nothing either English, or very modern beneath the paint; and so it proved.

There was something that strongly reminded me of the old Dutch buildings that once gave such a quaint look to the lower part of New York, particularly the Old Dutch Church in William street. The bricks used here were probably brought from Holland, and were of the same style as those used in that country; and the windows were of the same diminutive pattern, but presented a stronger contrast to the present style, here in the East Indies where nothing but a venetian blind and a door-frame make a window.

What a burning shame to a city like New York, to allow every old Dutch landmark to be removed!

Here are quaint and curious old rooms, that were thought to be so stately, two centuries ago; but no Vandal hand has been allowed to touch them. Here pompous, stiff, old Dutch governors gave audiences and receptions, and quaint, dignified dames glided about in the old Dutch dances, at about the time and in the style they did when William the Testy and Wouter Van Twiller were governors of what is now New York; the date of Anthony Van Corlear, that horn-blowing ambassador to the pioneer settlers of Connecticut.

I was devoutly wishing that some quaint old dame of an ancient governor, in her stiff brocade, might step in through the doorway; when at that moment, the church bells rang, and I remembered for the first time that day, that it was the Sabbath.

The sound of the bells, quivering and pulsating through the bright, breezy morning air, disturbed my reverie and dispelled any clairvoyance that might have entranced me, for no door opened, no ancient dame in stiff brocade rustled near me. Had I been near the dwelling of Dame Van Twiller I should have desired above all things to see her in her morning costume. I have such a boundless admiration for her capacious pockets, the profound depths of which no one dared to fathom while she lived, but from which, when she departed, were brought to light sundry silver spoons and wooden ladles, with whose disappearance the servants had long before been wrongfully accused.

On this spot the first wedge of civilization and Christian government entered a continent of paganism. All thanks to those old pioneers, whatever may have been their aims, who encountered so many dangers, and endured such complete isolation from the rest of the world.

Fifteen minutes brought us back to the vessel, though it had occupied two hours hard rowing to take us to land.

Along the coast were tall forests, reminding one of those seen in passing over the railroad in Michigan; the grand old trees looked like natives of our own wild woods dropped down here on the sea shore. Then came stretches of cocoa-nut plantation. I never yet saw one of these trees growing entirely wild: some human habitation was always near. Far interior was a chain of mountains, the watershed of the peninsula; between them and the coast is a low range of wooded hills which rumor says is the home of wild elephants, who live in herds, free from the trammels and restraints which man imposes on them when they are trapped into servitude.

There also live the Jacoons, the original inhabitants, who peopled these shores before the Malays came from their islands. Only a remnant of them is left; they number now about nine hundred. They build a platform on the huge branches of old trees, and on that, erect huts for their families and themselves; ascending by means of strong bamboo ladders, which they take up with them at night. They live on fish and fruit, and do not trouble themselves much about clothing, fashion, or caste. Father Borie a worthy Roman Catholic priest, has for years, been teaching them Christanity, and how to build their huts and cultivate the soil.

I sketched the outlines of the hills and the upper lighthouse, and then we stood off from the shore.

While at breakfast on deck, we sighted the hills of Penang.

The captain said they were fifty miles away, which we thought was a long distance, but the air was free from cloud and vapor. We anchored off Penang about three o'clock, and waited for a pilot to take the boat into harbor.

Having received an invitation from a friend, to spend our time at his house, we lost no time in going on shore.

In our hasty departure from the ship, we just missed our friend, who went out in a boat to meet us on board, but he arrived at the landing about the same time that we did, conducted us to a carriage, and drove with us to his house, which was situated on the margin of a beautiful bay. The streets away from the business portion of the town are delightfully shaded; indeed, in many cases, the front part of the grounds attached to the house is so thickly studded with trees that the dwelling is completely hidden from view.

The wide, smooth roads charmed us. Graceful areca-palms, cocoa-nut and senna-trees—the last reminding us of the elms of our own climate—all interlacing each other, and trailing with fringes of vines and parasitic plants, made the highway, except at noon, one long shady aisle.

At five in the afternoon, we drove out to the baths, and then walked across the fields, to see the waterfall at the foot of the hill. There was scarcely water enough to arouse enthusiasm or make it worthy of its name.

The island of Penang presents a bold hilly outline from the south. The summit of the highest peak gives an average difference of nine degrees cooler temperature, than the town on the narrow plain on the southern shore of the island. This is called Government, or Flagstaff Hill, because vessels are signalled from that place; it is about six miles from the town, and easily reached. Government has here erected bungalows at convenient points, which are furnished ready for occupation, and rented at a merely nominal price, for sanitary resorts.

The mean temperature of the town is 80°, and the season like that of Singapore, is one long unvarying summer. The mercury having only a range of ten degrees.

The yearly rain-fall in town, is sixty-five inches; on the

ENGLISH LIFE IN FARTHER INDIA.

hills it is one hundred inches. It is so equally distributed throughout the year, as to make this warm climate one of the loveliest conceivable.

There is no shaping of the seasons to bring a harvest at one time of the year, more than at another. Growth and fruitage is a constant, daily recurrence; vegetation knows no rest, except what the nightly withdrawal of the sun may give. Oranges and bananas bloom and ripen at the same time, throughout the year.

Probably no spot of earth will ever be found better adapted than the islands of the Eastern Archipelago, to the wants of primitive man. No scorching drouths with their storms of hot sand, like those of Hindustan, Persia and Arabia, ever blast the daily supply of luscious pineapples, and other fruits, which grow almost without culture, far outrivalling those of other parts of the world in sweetness and delicacy of flavor.

Unlike other tropical regions, these two islands are singularly exempt from fevers; and the cholera, that sweeping scourge of other lands, when it comes, seems almost wholly to confine itself to the native population, whose habits of life make them easy victims. They always build their habitations over low, marshy ground; and this, with their long Mohammedan fasts, succeeded by nightly feasting, and gorging themselves on crude fruit, renders them peculiarly fit subjects for the disease.

Next morning we arose early, intending to walk down to the margin of the lovely bay, overlooked by our bedroom and veranda; but the dew lay heavy on the grass and leaves, so we spent the time in sketching the shore of Province Wellesley opposite, and noting the waiting-boys decorating the breakfast-table with fresh-gathered roses and superb sprays of Fran Japanese flowers, while the softest air of summer came in through the ever-open windows, this New-Year morning.

A Venetian blind is considered ample night protection in this lovely climate.

From the profusion of roses here, and at Singapore, I

judged the "Last Rose of Summer" was an unknown and un seen flower. I question if Eve in the primæval garden was ever able to welcome the New Year with such a profusion of flowers as had here grown and been gathered, and would be grown and gathered daily, until the New Year should wane into the Old Year; and so on, to the end of time.

Breakfast over, we bade adieu to our kind host, and went on board the steamer again. The day was one of those bright, breezy, delightful days, known only in colder climates, in May or early June. The mercury at 79° Fah. The sky was without a cloud, and the summer sea without a ripple, for we had chosen our time at a season of the year when the trade winds fly on easy wings, and the furious cyclone sleeps far away in the ocean caves.

We felt no inclination for games, and very little for conversation, while there was so much beauty of earth, air, and sea to enjoy. We wished to imprint the scene upon our memories forever. The delicious air was a luxury of which other and more beloved lands only gave faint yearly reminders. It was gliding past us, and we wished our whole souls to revel in it while it lasted. We knew that northern skies would seem more stern, and northern, blasts more piercing, after such a sweet Elysium; so we eagerly inhaled the breeze, or, "ate air," as the Malays express it. January the 2d was bright, balmy and cool. The mercury was at 80° at 2 P. M., having risen only one degree, since sunrise. During the past night, the wind had freshened and the steamer now rolled so much that one had difficulty in dressing, and felt some dizziness, much as if shaken in a box. We left our cabin and went on deck about eight o'clock. Our good steamer was walking the water with a very elastic tread and continued to roll as screw steamers with wind amidships are wont to do. The breakfast-table was spread on deck, as it had been every morning since we had left Singapore. Though the viands looked inviting, I forbore to eat, adhering to my rule to take no food at the beginning of rough weather; thus avoiding much seasickness.

The coast of Province Wellesley and that of Tennasserim lay not far to the right. The shore was heavily wooded down to the water's edge, and had quite a new-world look about it. Back a little distance was a large mountain ridge. One mountain in this chain, is called Mount Ophir; it is situated lower down the peninsula. Who can certainly say that this mount had not an ancient fame, since it is conceded, from certain ruins in Java, that a colony of primitive Egyptians must have been planted in that island; attracted there probably by its mild climate. Behind the mountain, at no very great distance, roll the the waters of the Gulf of Siam.

The Malayan peninsula is really very narrow and stretches down a thousand miles, separating the great waters of the Bay of Bengal, from those of the Gulf of Siam and the China Sea. So narrow is it in one place, that there is only a a portage of twelve miles. A canal across the upper part of this peninsula would save the commerce of nations trading to China, a voyage of more than two thousand miles,—no small item in the season of the cyclones, when whole fleets of merchantmen are swallowed up when crossing the China Sea. We passed some desert islands belonging to the Mergu group. They were covered with low shrubs, and stinted brown grass. The third day after leaving Penang the sea began to look turbid, indicating our approach to the Gulf of Martaban. At five o'clock that evening we came in sight of the light-house, at the mouth of the Salwen, and anchored until morning, as it is a difficult river to enter at night.

In the morning we passed Amherst Point, where Dr. Judson and his co-laborers in this missionary field lie buried. We went on deck, and found ourselves steaming up a broad, beautiful river. The Salwen is two miles wide near the sea. The banks are low, and thickly-wooded with gigantic trees. Many kinds of timber are produced here, by this ever-verdant climate, which are so very dense in fibre, that they sink in water like iron.

Steam saw-mills are seen at little clearings here and there, for sawing the famous teak-wood which is much used in

Europe for ship-building. The fame of the elephants that work about these mills has travelled further and faster than the fame of the mills. All the passengers on board the *Mahratta* were on the lookout for elephants, and were not very particular whether they were tame or wild, single or in herds. Our friend and fellow-passenger, Col.——, who had been for years in Burmah and was there during the English war, told us very many amusing things of the elephants which roam over the wild inland districts, very much as wild buffaloes do on our American prairies. He stated, that there is a sort of moral law among these herds; that when one of their number becomes viciously wicked, the patriarchs of the community hold a council, and pass sentence of banishment upon him; which sentence is rigorously carrried out.

The Colonel was not certain, he said, whether or not the offending one is tried by a jury of his peers; but there can be no doubt that, after the mysterious conference, he is turned over to the tender mercies of the warriors of the herd; who fall into rank, and commence belaboring the "rogue" elephant, as he is called, with tusk and trunk, until he is glad to betake himself to distant parts, and never more trouble his former companions. The "rogue" quadruped does not always improve by severe discipline and a lonely life, for driven from his haunts, he is obliged to hover round the settlements of man, where his wanton acts frequently bring him to an untimely end.

As we steamed up the river we observed numerous pagodas rising from a distant bluff which ran parallel with the right bank. These Asiatics have a conveniently short road leading to their "neibban" or heaven. If at any time a man has led the life of a robber and has amassed great wealth, he has only to build a pagoda, and heaven's gates will be opened wide to him.

We had been for some time in sight of the golden-pagoda of Moulmein when, upon turning a bend of the river, that city came in full view. As we neared the landing-place, the passengers generally showed evident symptoms of a deter-

SURF BOAT AND BOATMEN, INDIA.

mination to see the lions—and elephants too—of this place; for they were all on deck, with covered heads, the only necessary preparation under a rainless sky. Our fellow-voyagers, the brides-elect, were watching very intently the curious, long, black boats, dug out from huge trees, and covered with awnings. A gentleman remarked to them "Look carefully, you may see a friend come out of one of those floating logs." Just then, a Scotch gentleman was discovered in one of the boats that was making its way to the landing-steps of the steamer. One of the brides-elect saw him too. There was a quick breath, a little blush on her face, and a flutter of a handkerchief in her hand; then the lady went below to receive her future husband in the cabin.

We secured a boat to take us to land, for steamers in this part of the world seem never to come alongside of a wharf. Indeed I think that wharves are not counted among possibilities here. Our boat would have been a great acquisition for Barnum. It was thirty feet long, and four feet wide at midship; dug out, or burnt out, from some huge tree; and tapering trimly each way to a very sharp bow and stern. A sort of round basket-awning was just above and almost touched the heads of the seated passengers, helping to give the boat the appearance of a long black log as it was rowed swiftly through the water by four diminutive brown men. The fare demanded was only one-half rupee—twenty-two and a half cents.

Safely landed, our first want was a gharry, or carriage; for, though it was January, the midday sun was so powerful that we could not have walked a hundred paces with comfort. We did not wait long, for several Jehus, who were lurking near by in shady ambush, charged down upon us, and noisily offered to drive us untold distances for half a rupee. Selecting one that looked the freshest, and freest from dust, we took our seats; coachee mounted his perch in front; and we drove off. Our carriage was not very stylish, but closely resembled a flat-roofed, square house on wheels. And as for our steed, how shall I describe his points, how can justice be done to his portrait? One might have fancied that he was originally a mouse, nibbling in one of the great rice-granaries, until some wandering fairy had passed her wand over him, and he became a pony about three or four feet high. We almost felt a vague misgiving that he might possibly become a mouse again if we tarried long or travelled far.

We drove down the lower main road, past rows of queer little native shops about as large as a pepper-box, and smelling almost as pungent. They were stocked with water-cups and queer little earthen and brass pots, which are here used by the natives as cooking-utensils; while here and there diminutive piles of rice, and strings of cayenne pepper, were exposed for sale. Two dollars would be a liberal capital to set up one of these native shops, and would place the proprietor far beyond the reach of financial panics. The wants of the native customers are few and simple, and I could not help envying a people so fully emancipated from the tyranny of artificial requirements.

We passed by rows of tumble-down native houses, tenantless and roofless; and we noticed that the bazaars, had a sluggish look, as if what little commercial life there was in the place was fast dying out. Beyond the skirts of the town, we came out upon cultivated fields of rice. And there I made a discovery. I had always associated rice-growing with low, marshy ground; but this land appeared as though good wheat could be raised upon it, if the climate were cool enough for it to thrive. The tilled ground is all divided into little patches, thirty or forty feet square, surrounded by a low turf wall, ten or twelve inches high, which holds the water that falls upon it during the rainy season. Towards the close of the rainy season, which lasts only three months, the rice is sowed in the water, and oxen are driven about in it, dragging a bush or a clog to cover the grain, which soon springs up, and is thinned by transplanting to other fields.

Dust! dust! everything seemed turning to dust. It came through the venetian blinds like a cataract. We closed them; but there were other crevices, especially a wide space just under the top of the carriage, which could not be closed; so we resigned ourselves to our fate. There had been no rain for six months past, and nothing but the reversal of the laws that govern the trade-winds could bring any for three months to come. It was a marvel that there was a single green thing left alive. The leaves of the trees out of the way of the dust kept their glossy look; but the grass was as brown as if it had been dried in a kiln.

Our journey began to seem long; we were getting too much for our half rupee. We had passed several steam saw-mills without stopping, and we were half afraid that there was something wrong; but as we spoke no Burmese, and the driver no English, there was little chance of finding out anything by calling a parley. There was no alternative but to exercise faith, particularly in Burmese humanity in the person of our coachee.

And here I cannot resist the temptation: I must give you coachee's portrait.

Imagine a brown man,—do not think I mean sun-brown,—but a genuine, fully-developed brown; a butternut-brown if you will. His face is oval, his features very angular, and his head is shaved close to the scalp. His limbs are slender, and his body light as a half-grown girl, and not a large pattern of a girl either. An old strip of thin blue cloth, resembling bunting in thinness and color, wound round his head, so as to form a very shabby low-caste turban, with the long end of the strip hanging down his back nearly to his waist. It was decidedly amusing to see it flapping with every jolt and every movement of the breeze. This cloth served a double purpose; it formed a protection from the sun, dust, and mosquitoes, and was also a sort of imitation jacket to cover coachee's back. His chest and arms were clothed only with their own brown color; which under this warm sky never seems quite as naked as white. His lower garment was a red-and-white plaid cotton cloth, fastened in that indescribable Madras-fashion, already mentioned, about his hips, by a sort of Oriental upholstery much in vogue here, and supposed to be favorable to physical development.

Presently our house-on-wheels rolled into a shady lane, and then turned into a mill-garden. Coachee got down and opened the door for us; then pointed out the way that we should take. When we got out of the carriage we had more respect for the little dot of horse-flesh that had carried us safely over four miles of dusty road, than when we entered it.

The superintendent of the mill was a Portuguese, but he spoke English well. We handed him the note from his employers, and he very kindly set about showing us the elephants, which were now taking a bath in the river.

Picture those enormous animals rollicking, sporting, spouting, and flapping in the water. It was a comical sight, such ponderous creatures bobbing up and down like Jack-in-a-box, doing the fantastic. One in particular attracted our attention. Sometimes the head and trunk only were above the surface of the water; the poor driver appearing like a frog on the animal's neck, close behind its ears; while a perfect deluge of water was blown from the elevated trunk over the neck and shoulders of the elephant and the whole person of the man. As a large quantity of the sediment of the river was mingled with the water, it can well be imagined that the driver presented an interesting appearance. But the next moment both animal and driver were beneath the surface; the long trunk alone rising above and sending forth mimic waterspouts. At other times the huge creature would sit on its haunches, like a dog, with his head and back exposed; and then he would turn about in a sort of elephantine gambol—the great leviathan at play in a very small sea!

The driver all this time kept tapping with his goad, and scolding the elephant in the most approved Burmese fashion. He even accused the creature of unfairness in attempting to roll over in the water, with his driver on his back. No good elephant does that. These mahouts, or drivers, firmly believe that the elephant understands all that his keeper says to him and so they go on reproving gently, as a father would his son. The superintendent called for one of the drivers to

EASTERN MACHINERY.

bring his charge out of the stream, in order to commence work. The creature had not had enough of the water, and the pigmy driver of this mountain of flesh, tapped and goaded at all assailable points, adding a vast amount of urgent reasons and fretful expletives, before the elephant would obey its master's commands and go on shore. As soon as they reached firm ground the driver dismounted, for the animal always shakes himself, like a dog, whenever he comes out of the water.

A kind of saddle was then placed on the animal's neck, upon which the driver perched himself. After that, a sort of harness was put on; very strong double ropes were passed round the body, and a similar rope across the breast. Into this rude rope-gear was hooked at both ends a very long, heavy chain, and another chain was hooked into that, the other end of which was fastened to a piece of teak-timber, about thirty feet long and one foot square, the estimated weight of which was about three tons. A stick of this teak-wood unsupported, sinks in the water like a piece of iron.

The elephant walked off with his burden, without any apparent effort, to a high pile of timber of the same description, upon which they wished to place this piece also. Having arrived at the right point, the elephant turned round and dexterously unfastened the chain from the timber, with his trunk, then walked to the end nearest the pile, and settled back, without sitting down, until he could thrust his huge tusks far under the timber; he then brought his proboscis over it to hold it on, and slowly rising and bringing himself to the right position, he raised it above his head and placed one end of the timber on the end of the pile. It did not, however, rest firmly at first; so the driver sputtered away at the elephant in a fretful tone, tapping vigorously with his little goad.

Finally, Mr. Elephant looked very seriously at the timber, and seemed to comprehend that he had not done his best, and must make another effort. So, taking hold in the same manner as before, he lifted the wood down, and then placed one end on another part of the pile where it would rest more firmly. Then walking to the other end, that still rested on the ground, he coiled up his trunk, and placed it against the stick, and shoved it on to the top of the pile, with as much apparent ease as a man would lift a piece of ratan of the same length.

After that the superintendent ordered the elephant to carry a piece of the same timber, of similar dimensions to the first, lifting it by the middle, clear off the ground, across the yard, to form a new pile. The timber was drawn from the place where it left the saw, in the same manner as the first; and after unfastening the chain from it, the elephant went to the middle, directed by the driver on his neck, and settling back as before, placed it on his tusks, and held it on with his trunk; then slowly raising himself up erect, he walked off with ease, carrying it quite clear from the ground and very evenly balanced, a distance of some twenty rods across the yard, and there deposited it, as the beginning of the new pile.

Several other pieces were carried in a similar way by this elephant. Some of them were less in size than that already mentioned; but there was one nearly double the thickness, and about half the length, also weighing not less than three tons, which he carried, we thought, easier than the others; for though the size made it more difficult to place on the tusks, the length was not so troublesome.

The goad consists of a short round stick, about twenty-four inches in length; at the end there are some triangular pieces of tin or iron, which serve to make a slight impression on the animal's thick hide. The tapping is gentle, as are also the tones of the driver's voice, if the elephant's conduct is good and his work satisfactory. These huge animals are ruled more by the kindness of their keepers than by the goad. When they are very vicious they are chained by the feet to the ground, as at such times they are dangerous and would destroy everything that came in their way.

A friend told us a good story about an elephant working

NATIVE BURMESE CARRIAGE.

at one of these mills, piling lumber, which showed the extraordinary sagacity of these animals. His work, one afternoon, had not been as good as usual, and the driver's tone had been very complaining and fretful. At their supper Mahout was not as social as usual, and Elephant was grieved. The chief food of the elephant is cut grass, and he finishes his meal with large cakes made of ground pease; the driver also eats the same kind of cakes, and as his sleeping-place is never very far from the elephant's they lead a rather social life. The driver of this particular elephant, waking up in the moonlight part of the night, was surprised to find that his charge had left his stall. On going round the mill-yard, he found him re-arranging the timber that had been piled so very unsatisfactorily during the day. The driver patted the great sleepless head, and freely forgave its sagacious owner for all his shortcomings. Some twinges of self-respect must have disturbed his sleep, or perchance his keeper's reproaches had been more stinging than his goad, and he resolved to earn his approbation.

The elephant, and the long-horned blue buffalo are the beasts of burden of Burmah. The Burmese ox, carrying his head proudly and stately, is preferred by the natives for their carriages—carts, perhaps, we should call them. They will trot nearly as fast as a pony, and endure heat and labor much better; and attached to the fantastic Burmese carts, they do not seem out of place.

The elephant whose labors I witnessed was still considered youthful, as he was only fifty years old, for here, in their native land, they are known to live and work three times that number of years.

We bade the kind superintendent good-bye, with many thanks for his attentions to us, and much pleased with having added to our vocabulary two Burmese words—"*Naow*," stop, and "*Daw*" go; for now we fondly dreamed that we could drive anywhere: perhaps we might, but not to any place in particular.

Passing back to town by the upper road, we came in front

of a fine gateway, on either side of the entrance to which stood a huge surpliced image of a tiger, which like many other shams was very fierce and imposing, though only formed of brick and stucco. We drawled out "*Naow*," and the driver reined up at the gate.

We strolled into the inclosure in careless sight-seeing fashion, and wandered about the ground, which were laid out in cool shady walks. In the midst stood a large building, the gables of which were very peculiarly carved and decorated. From photographs that we had seen, we at once recognized it as a phoongee or priest-house, with a school attached to it, as a matter of course. Every Buddhist priest in Burmah is bound by the nature of his office, to instruct the male youths of his country. In this place the teacher and his pupils occupied during the hours of tuition a broad roomy verandah with a fine outlook, having a spice of open-air life about the whole concern. The minds of the boys seemed to have nearly as much aptness for wandering away from their studies when they saw us, as those in our own American schools would if an elephant were passing. To the little Burmese our visit presented an equally rare sight. It was quite a novelty for them to know that just out there,—an Ingles "Meim Sahib" (English madam) was walking about in the garden, in those curious western garments. Could they not go down and see her? Permission was accorded, the teacher probably being quite as curious as the taught; and the scholars came pouring down, and did a good amount of staring. But we had no right to complain of this, as we ourselves were also on a staring tour. Indeed they were very gentlemanly little heathen, and did not rudely crowd around us, as some saucy little heathen would that are growing up in American cities.

Two or three boys came forward with a gesture that we took to be a sort of salaam, and seemed to vie with each other in showing what they deemed the rarities of the place. One supposed that some very beautiful flowers that he pointed out would interest us; another pointed, and seemed ready to

BUDDHIST PRIEST'S HOUSE AND SCHOOL.

lead the way into the cool shade of a fine group of trees, surmising that rest in the shade was what we might desire, and a look of disappointment came over him when he saw that we did not seat ourselves. They did not seem to think that the building could be a novelty to us.

Seeing the spire of a small pagoda or dgodis, a little further on we endeavored in dumb show to ask the question, may we go in? The boys readily understood, and at once led the way. It proved to be one of those solid bell-shaped monuments, about thirty feet high, crowned with a high cap of tinkling bells, suspended over the rod which forms the extreme pinnacle of the structure. Every breeze rocks it, and rings a multitude of little sweet-toned bells, whose music is only faintly heard below. The pagoda was coated over with lichens, and grey moss, and discolored with dust. It was without niches for images; but near it, was an old dilapidated building, filled with gigantic images of Gaudama, and the attendant spirits, or 'Nats' as they are called in the Buddhist mythology. These images, like the tigers at the gate, were built of brick and stucco, rounded and smoothed into human likeness, and arranged against the walls of the room. They were superannuated gods, which had retired from the fatigue of being adored. Begrimed with the smoke of incense and sitting in about as much dust and dirt, as his godship—Buddha—did twenty-five centuries ago when a student near the holy Hindoo city of Benares.

One of the little boys seeing me look in at the dirty door, eagerly pressed by me into the temple, and pointed out the divinities therein, one by one, chattering in a very edifying manner; but it was all labor lost, except the kind intention, and that we still remember with a kindly feeling. When we turned towards a new building standing to the left of the one just mentioned, invitingly near and bright in the fresh glory of six new gabled roofs, and innumerable steel-colored wood-carvings, which bristled up from every possible place, he shook his head signifying that we could not go into that temple. I half suspect that it was some priest's sanctum, the vestibule of which no womankind could ever be permitted to pass.

We thanked these little native gentlemen, who were not enlightened enough to be rude to strangers, and they bowed very politely to us as we entered our carriage and drove away. We at first supposed that we were posting off to the large pagoda, the gilded spire of which gleamed and flashed in the sunlight; the same pagoda that we had seen far down the river, but which now loomed up very far above the tall trees that lined the roadside, crowning the brow of the hill beyond the city, on which it stands. We soon found, however, that we were passing every road that led in the direction of the hill, but were unable to ask any questions, or give any new directions. Just as we were turning down toward the river where the steamer lay, we met a procession of shaven-headed priests with saffron-colored robes, if such scanty clothing could be called a robe, following a Burmese cart and oxen, wherein were tom-toms and gongs, beating out a dolorous music. The oxen were garlanded and decorated, and a small image on a stick was placed in the yoke. Curious to know what they were about, we motioned our driver to follow, for we saw that they were going to the Great Pagoda. The driver could not pretend that he did not understand where we wanted to go, but we strongly suspected that he intended to ignore our wishes. As, however, we had no alternative, we waited very patiently for him to make up his mind. We turned back into a road thickly shaded with the dark-green, dust-laden foliage of trees, among which peered out sometimes in groups, and sometimes singly, the tapering spires of pagodas, grey with lichens and age. There were no inscriptions, and each so closely resembled almost all the rest of these solid structures that but for the marks of age, it might be supposed that one hand built them all. Some few had niches constructed in the side-walls in each of which a solitary image of Gaudama was seated, absorbed in a profound meditation, a veritable brown study on the "Great Good," the way to Neibban, the Buddhist paradise.

Incense-smoke had blackened the plaster and gilt around

these images and had not given the great Buddha a very pure look. Near the foot of the hill were several priests' houses, noticeable for their graceful and elaborately ornamented gables. Near them, were two large cars or wagons, with curious platform-frames mounted on them, to which the upright coffins of the priests are fixed when they are carried to the funeral-pile to be burned. The funeral-pile is gorgeously decorated, and the bodies of the Talapoins—a higher grade of priests—are quite overlaid with gold-leaf, while during the burning, tom-toms, or small drums, beat as joyously as if it were rather a good thing for a priest to die and give the people a gala day.

We are on holy ground now, for small pagoda-spires shoot up from almost every rod of practicable ground, as thick as stalagmites from the bottom of a cave. Our driver halts before two surpliced colossal tiger-dogs, in brick and plaster, guarding the grand entrance to the two hundred steps leading to the Great Pagoda, up which the worshipper must climb to offer a prayer at this famous shrine. As we felt a little out of place following a procession of heathen to their temple, we allowed them to pass on, before we began to climb the steps, which were broad and solidly made, following the surface of the hill, with one or two wide landings or resting-places. At one of these places we stepped through the opening in the low parapet-wall, which protects each side of these steps, to examine two small but extremely beautiful pagodas. They were covered with very minute tiles, or rather, small pieces of sheet-iron, covered with a glaze or enamel of a very brilliant green, rivalling emerald in hue. The rays of the sun in the west were flashed back in a flood of dazzling light from every square inch of their surface. In the niches in the side-walls are found the Buddha Gandama, blackened with incense-smoke, showing that many a pious heathen had turned aside to pray there.

At the top of the steps, we found ourselves in a broad paved court surrounding the pagoda. Near the steps and at other points about the court were old wooden one-story sheds, enclosed on three sides and open on the fourth, which seemed to be used as storehouses for old dilapidated gods and their attendants, who looked very much as if they needed to recuperate in a health-retreat, or wished to be excused from attendance in the pagoda, so that they could go at once to Neibban.

We passed a woman sitting on a mat, who among other things had prayers to sell—ready-made prayers fastened to a staff like a child's flag. Some were written on paper and others on copper or tin-foil, and then inserted in the split end of a little stick. They were sold at the rate of four prayers for one cent. While we were looking at the articles which composed this woman's little store, a Burmese man came up and bought a prayer, for which he put down a quarter of a cent. He took also a candle about the size of a pipe-stem, and only just long enough to burn while his godship read that short prayer. Things are very exactly adjusted; if the candle is long the prayer will be long also.

We were curious to see how that kind of praying was done, and followed the man. We entered a one-story square apartment, built so that the back of the room should abut against the large central pagoda; and in a low niche, which seemed to belong more to the huge structure, than to the room we were in, was an image of Buddha, but so much blackened by smoke that we did not perceive it until the man with the prayer thrust his little taper almost at the nose of the god, and lighted up its features. The man then kneeled on one knee and held his light close to the image, while he waved with his right hand the little stick that contained the prayer, close to Gandama's eyes, very much as if he thought the god was asleep. When the light burned low enough to scorch his fingers, the prayer was finished, and he walked away as if he had done his duty.

Just then throngs of women and girls, came tripping up the steps, and at once bought their prayers and offered them with great promptness. The Burmese women are a shade or two lighter in color than the Malays, but their average

GAUTAMA IN THE SMALL PAGODA, RANGOON.

height is only about four and a half feet. They are more slender in form than the Malay women, and we thought, had a similar cast of features, though their cheek-bones were not so prominent. They disfigure their ears by inserting in the lobe, an ornament resembling an ordinary spool of cotton, made of gold or glass, according to the means of the wearer. The size and weight of this trinket thrust through the soft part of the ear, combine to stretch it down and render it very unseemly. These women enter into all sorts of traffic and trade with a zest that would make an advocate for woman's suffrage think that the millennium was not far off. Not the slightest objection is raised here, to their working on railroad embankments, or in any other way, and certainly as far as our limited observation went, they could carry a hod as well as a Burmese man. The "hod" of which I speak is a strong stone jar filled with brick or mortar and balanced on the head, leaving the hands free to hold on to the slender bamboo-ladders that are used there.

We strolled along among the different apartments that joined the central pagoda, till we came to a new one hardly yet completed. The masons were still at their work making some new colossal 'gods' of brick and stucco. These 'gods' could not have been less than twenty feet in height; and being in a room and standing on the same level with ourselves, they appeared to us much larger than they really were. It would be interesting to know what were the ideas of the masons about their labor and the way in which the common brick and stucco were, through their instrumentality, converted into a consecrated body. Perhaps, after all, it might not be more difficult to explain than changing the bread and wine into the corporeal presence of Christ.

Having satisfied our curiosity in the praying-places of the pagoda, we retired a little distance to the shade of some sacred peepul trees, where we could take in the whole view of the unique structure before us. It looked like an immense inverted bell, three hundred and fifty feet in height, with a diameter of the same dimensions. It has not lost much of its beauty, but in the palmy days of the Burmese empire all the central and upper parts of the structure were overlaid with gold-leaf; from which circumstance its name—the Golden Pagoda—was derived. The circular or upper part rests on a hexagonal platform or foundation. On the outer edge of this platform are erected many small pagodas, twenty-five or thirty feet in height, surrounding the grand central structure. Some are grey with age and covered with lichens, others look as if recently finished, and we thought it probable that some penitent rogue, instead of purchasing heaven by building a new pagoda, had attempted to secure the same prize by putting a new exterior on one of these old ones.

The view from the steps is very beautiful. The town of Moulmein lies at your feet with the river Salwen flowing through its midst towards the sea, deepening and widening into a broad placid stream two miles in width near its mouth. It filled its bank the day we saw it from the pagoda, the same as if the drouth which was then of six months duration had not lasted six days. The jungle and the tall forest-trees along its banks are of the same dark-green, glossy color in January as in June; they have worn the same unchanging hue since the morning when they first uplifted their heads to the light of day. Steam is rapidly sweeping these from the bottom-lands of this river, and from the myriad islands which guard its mouth and that of the great river Irrawaddy.

Lofty bluffs extend in continuous line far into the distance, above which are glimpses of fertile table-lands stretching far away into the unknown interior of Burmah. How my wishful eyes peered into that dim distance up the river, to which an exploring party, then fitting out, was about to proceed from these coast-cities, in search of the old forgotten portages or roads, by which eight centuries ago the merchandise of interior China found its way from the banks of the river Yang-tse-kiang to boats that bore it down the waters of the Salwen. In those far bygone centuries, according to Burmese history, an embassy was sent down these waters from the emperor of China to the king of Burmah, to establish friendly relations, and to compare notes on the respective magnificence of each ruler. There were knotty and tangled

TEMPLE AND COLOSSAL TIGERS NEAR MANDELAY, BURMAH.

questions of etiquette connected with royal receptions, in those days, which were oftener cut with the sword than solved in any other way. The Chinese uncover the head in the presence of superiors, in token of respect, but never uncover the feet. The Burmese, like all the people of India, uncover the feet; uncovering the head has no significance at all with them. The Chinese ambassador refused to appear at court with bare feet, and in attempting to approach the king with feet covered, the palace guards slaughtered him and all his retinue. As a matter of course war was declared between the two nations, and the Chinese government gave the Burmese a lesson in politeness that they remember to this day. The Salwen has remained closed until the present time, and the old passes in the mountains have long been forgotten; but English capital and commerce will no doubt ere long seek out, and divert from a long and dangerous sea carriage of four or five thousand miles, a trade which these rivers long ago floated directly from China to the cities of Burmah.

We descended the huge stairway of the pagoda, and made our way to the steamer. From its deck we saw the glittering spire shining resplendently in the declining rays of a beautiful sunset. We listened for the sweet sound of the tiny silver bells, but they whispered no music to our ears as we watched from afar the grand old structure fading into the night.

The anchor was weighed at sunrise, and we were off for Rangoon, one hundred and thirty miles distant. This city stands at the junction of the Rangoon and Pegu rivers which are the outlets of the Irrawaddy. As we rounded the point and entered the mouth of the Rangoon river, a remarkable scene met our view. Our boat and the wooded banks of the stream were faithfully photographed on the cloudless sky. The water was smooth as a mirror, and this strange picture was high enough above the bank to leave a narrow belt of hazy vapor-like cloud between the real and the unreal banks. We gazed on this spectacle for several minutes, and then it either faded away, or the boat carried us out of a favorable position for seeing it, for it slowly vanished from our sight.

CHAPTER V.

NATIVE LIFE IN BURMAH.

THE population of the city of Rangoon is about one hundred thousand. Since the English have held a sort of protectorate over Burmah the population of the cities bordering on the coast has steadily increased, for the natives find a better opportunity for trade in them than in the interior, and also more security for life and property. Mandelay the capital, is situated on the Rangoon river, far up in the interior, it has greatly decreased in population in the last fifty years.

Just before we came to anchor, we passed a very substantial-looking house on the left bank, decorated with a large amount of bunting, wrought into every sort of flag, streamer, and signal that a seaport population would be likely to recognize. A gaily decorated boat shot out from the jetty and came alongside to welcome its owner—the husband of one of our bonnie Scotch brides. The poetry of their first days of wedded life was ended; they now settled down to its realities, in their home beside the river.

As soon as the anchor was dropped, long, black, sharp-pointed dug-out boats, the model of which might have hung over the taffrail of Noah's ark, surrounded the steamer. As we stood peering over the bulwarks into the boats, we recognized the good-humored, kindly faces of two gentlemen whom we had known in Singapore. Surely no one need be told how pleasant such a meeting was, when one only expected to meet with strange faces.

One of the two gentlemen, Mr. ——, had come on board

to meet his bride-elect. He had not seen her for five long years. Her gentle face and quiet manners had won our hearts, as we saw her, morning after morning, in some quiet place on deck reading the Bible to her father who was just a little hard of hearing; and we thought that such devoted love when transferred to our friend, would make his life in the East one long happy day. They met, as was most becoming, away from the eyes of curious strangers: alone, in the cabin; but when her betrothed handed her down the steps into the boat, I saw that happiness hung over her features like a veil, making her look, as I thought, radiantly beautiful. Love had spread his sacrament for those two, and from all our hearts blessings went forth towards the youthful pair.

The banks of the Ragoon river like those of the Salwen, are low from the sea up to the city—a distance of about thirty miles. We landed, took a carriage, and drove directly to the Great Pagoda of Ragoon. This shrine is very ancient, and is supposed to be one of the first points where the Buddhist missionaries, about twenty three centuries ago, began to teach the then new religion of Gaudama. As his life and teachings were so much purer, and the rites of his religion so much more simple, it is no marvel that Burmah, Siam, Cambodia, and southern China should at once discard their innumerable, sensual, and disgusting deities, and the worship of the Sun and Water for faith in one God alone, whom they now recognize under the name of Buddha. They believe that all who lead good, pure and benevolent lives, will hereafter be absorbed into his being; in other words, return and become a part of God and exist in him in some mysterious manner. This constitutes their Neibban, or state of heavenly blessedness.

Their former religion, Brahminism, taught them, if a man led a good, pure and holy life through several existences, he might at last become a sacred cow, the favorite animal of Vishnu. To become a sacred cow, or to become a part of deity himself, are the dissimilar inducements held out by the two religions, and these poor people made their choice before our Immanuel walked among the Judean hills, and taught a purer religion still, than that which was taught by the lips of Buddhist priests. There is a tradition that the king and court of Burmah held out longer against the new religion than the people, and that on this spot some Buddhist saints of those distant days, performed such miracles and wrought such notable works that even these royal doubters were at last converted, and then, as with Christianity in Constantine's time, the new religion became the religion of the kingdom. Ever since that time, the spot where those miracles were said to have been wrought has been considered sacred ground. The priests affirm that the pagoda erected upon it is of very great antiquity, but they are unsupported by any historical testimony, and it is probable that the present structure dates no further back than the beginning of the fourteenth century. This solid monument, as far as any signs of age or the wear of the elements are concerned, might be as old as the priests claim, or it may be comparatively recent, for nothing less than an earthquake, or a mine of powder exploded under its base would ever harm it. All ordinary defects are easily covered with stucco and gilding. Like the one at Moulmein, this pagoda stands on a high hill, a part of which appears to be the work of man. It was defended by a wall as recently as the year 1852, when the English captured it.

Near the base of the hill we ascended a terrace, and entered a gateway leading through the wall. We passed through a lofty entrance hall, the carved and gilded ceiling of which was supported by columns made by merely smoothing and rounding to an even surface huge trunks of trees. They could not boast of either pedestal or capital, but they had once been overlaid with beaten gold, which is yet bright and good, as it is above the reach of the greasy hands and oily bodies of the natives. I should think from the wrinkles which appear in the gold that it was laid on when the art of gilding was in its infancy.

We emerged from the hall, ascended more steps, and at once found ourselves in the spacious courtyard of the temple. A poor blind Burmese girl was singing very sweetly and

GATE IN THE PAGODA-WALL, RANGOON.

plaintively some songs in Burmese, and the passers-by tossed her some small copper coins. This was a strong reminder of our own Western customs and the one solitary instance that I can call to mind of an unfortunate being in the Oriental world, attempting to arouse sympathy and obtain money by singing.

Surrounding this temple were old sheds containing dilapidated gods that had been set aside for newer ones, exactly like those which we had seen at the golden pagoda at Moulmein, and about the same number of new ones ready to receive adoration. I have an idea that space is the only limit to the number of the gods of these people.

This pagoda is about four hundred feet in height, and the diameter of the base is very nearly the same as the altitude. The small pagodas within the enclosure, are much more numerous than those at Moulmein. Not far from the great hall, we saw a gigantic image of Gaudama, in brass, in a recumbent position, his features wearing the same expression of abstraction and deep meditation. This statue was about fifteen feet in length, and the corresponding proportions of body and limbs suggested a great weight of metal, and this, with the finish, made me suspect that it might have been cast in Birmingham. It has often been hinted that one of the most liberal subscribers to the missionary fund was a Birmingham founder, who cheerfully paid in his money for the conversion of the heathen, while his workmen were casting idols for them to worship. This statement I am half inclined to believe is true, as I have elsewhere met with idols which appeared to be of English manufacture.

On one side of the pagoda court is an enormous bell, said to be either larger in size, or to contain more metal, than the great bell at Moscow. It has a rude unfinished look compared with bells cast either in Europe or America. A large amount of both silver and gold is said to enter into its composition; for the native people, when a bell is being cast for any particular temple, consider it a very favorable opportunity to propitiate their god by throwing into the molten metal, their gold and silver ornaments.

This bell is said to measure thirteen feet in height and about eight feet across from edge to edge. It was cast in Rangoon. The thickness of the edge of the bell was such, that it just fitted in or would cover the space between the elbow of a tall man and the tips of his fingers. That certainly is not a standard measure, but it will give some idea of the thickness of this huge casting. It is not rung in the ordinary way, but a native man strikes it with a sledge hammer. In the English and Burmese war, in 1854, this pagoda and its defences were considered one of the most difficult places to capture, on account of its commanding position on the summit of the hill. Our friend and fellow-passenger, Colonel ——, of the English army was then a young man and engaged in active service during the war. He was present at the capture of the pagoda, and pointed out the place where the troops passed the outer wall and ditch and scaled the hill, and also the spot where the hand-to-hand fight occurred at the wall of the temple enclosure.

After the capture and occupation of this strong place by the English, they wished to carry away the great bell as a trophy, when they left the country. So they took it down from its huge wooden supports and after long and toilsome efforts—for they had no proper machinery—they brought it to the side of the vessel which was to convey it to England, but by some accident, when it was being hoisted aboard ship, it fell into the water. They thought it was safe enough there, and that they could return at some future time with the proper mechanical contrivances, raise it out of the river bed, and carry it off. Their ships however, had scarcely left the river's mouth, before the priests set about recovering the lost bell. They assembled the whole population for the work, dragged the bell from the water, built a cylinder about it, and then actually rolled it up the hill, and on the fourth day put it in its old place again.

Throughout India there are places which are considered to be environed by a peculiar sacredness because they possess real or supposed relics of Buddha Gandama. Beneath the

NEAR VIEW OF THE GREAT PAGODA AT RANGOON, BURMAH.

pagoda at Rangoon some of the god's hair is said to be buried. Gaudama's tomb, it is asserted in the sacred writings of his followers, was opened two hundred and fifty years after his death and the relics found in it divided among different kingdoms that had embraced his religion. A noted temple in Ceylon claims great sanctity among Buddhists, because it possesses a *bona-fide* tooth of Buddha carefully preserved in naptha, in a jar of gold, handed down through all the twenty-five long centuries which have elapsed since his apotheosis. The author of "Our Possessions in Malayan India" relates the following story which illustrates the veneration felt for Buddha's relics:

In 1845, the king of Siam sent a mission of priests to this famous temple at Kanday, in Ceylon, with presents valued at £5,000 ($25,000,) to obtain a sight of the sacred tooth, and permission to rub a little lock of cotton upon it. This cotton was then to be taken back to consecrate a golden jar of otto of roses for his majesty's use.

The Kanday priests received the presents; but utterly refused the request to show the tooth, or consecrate the king's golden jar. They declared it was a favor altogether too great to be purchased by a foreign prince, for the small sum of twenty-five thousand dollars; and then dismissed the disconsolate mission.

As the disappointed priests were leaving the city of Kanday, they fell in with the son of the grand vizier of the ex-king of the Kandians, named Tickory Bandah. I may here mention that when the island of Ceylon fell into the hands of the English, the new government took Tickory and his two brothers and educated them in the English language, and Tickory in particular, became, as he says, quite a favorite. When Tickory heard the story of the failure of the mission, he, presuming upon his influence with the Governor, immediately offered his services to obtain for the disappointed priests the desired view of the holy tooth if they would wait three days; he, on his part, giving into their hands a cheque for two thousand rupees, or about one thousand dollars, as a guarantee that he would fulfill his promise. He then went immediately to the Governor and represented very forcibly the imposition that must have been practised upon the king of Siam's holy mission. The Governor sympathized with Tickory and the Siamese, and said that the relic might be shown to them with as little delay as possible, for as both Kandians and Siamese were Buddhists there could be no harm in doing so. It happened however that the keys of this holy shrine were kept at the house of the resident councillor, who was away from home for a few days, elephant-hunting. Tickory, therefore, requested permission to present the Governor's compliments to the resident councillor's wife, and ask that a search be made for the keys, as it was not at all probable that her husband would include them in his shooting outfit. The Kandian priests were then notified that the great relic was to be exhibited, and their assistance in the capacity of guardians would be necessary on that occasion.

Accordingly, on the third day the shrine was opened. The Kandian priests and worshippers were on one side, and Tickory Bandah and the Siamese mission on the other; the judge of the Queen's bench and the governor being in the centre. The Siamese after making all due offering to their great deity, stated their request—their high-priest acting as mouthpiece—and the Kandian priests stated their objections. The holy tooth was then brought out; when the Governor, apparently not quite understanding the whole matter, required an explanation. Tickory saw his chance, and knew that then or never was the time for his *coup-de-main;* but he was perfectly self-possessed and equal to the emergency. Suddenly taking from the hands of the Siamese priest a small piece of cotton, together with the golden jar of otto of roses, he turned to the Governor, saying: "this is what they want, your Excellency. They wish to take this small piece of cotton—so; and dip it in this otto—so (suiting the action to the words); they wish to rub it on this sacred tooth —so (again suiting the action to the words); and, having done this, return the cotton to the golden jar of otto of roses—so; thereby, your excellency, consecrating the whole contents."

All this was only the work of a moment. Though the Governor understood perfectly well that such unceremonious proceedings were against all precedent, he probably did not comprehend the difficulty quick enough to interfere. The Siamese of course received the consecrated jar with demonstrations of fervent gratitude, but the Kandians were highly indignant, while the Governor patting Tickory on the back said "Tickory, my boy, you have settled the question for us; a pity it is that you were not born within the precincts of St. James's; for you would have made a splendid diplomatist."

Next morning Tickory received a *douceur* of $5000 and his own guarantee of two thousand rupees that he had left with Siamese priests. He has ever since been held in the highest esteem by the king of Siam and the Buddhist priests of that country, who look upon him as a holy man; though now for some misadventure he serves in the chain gang in the convict lines, at Malacca. From the late king of Siam he received substantial as well as honorary tokens of royal favor. He has *carte blanche* for drawing on the treasury for any amount; but he has as yet contented himself with the moderate sum of $700. This custom of presenting offerings to holy shrines and holy men, has been going on in Oriental lands ever since the Syrian monarch sent Naaman with his camels and gifts to Elijah, and was doubtless in existence long before. The priests here pile up untold secreted wealth in their pagodas, while every morning's sun looks down on them, begging their bread in the streets, in compliance with the vows of their priesthood. Gandama himself gave up the throne of his native country, now known as Oudh—to beg in the streets as a priest.

We now descended and made our way to the garden which Pagoda Hill overlooks. It is a charming spot, one of those combinations of park and garden, with artificial lakelets, graded hillsides and shaven lawns, that in the tropics make the loveliest imaginable pictures.

Yonder is a serpentine sheet of water, spanned by a gaily painted bridge, which opens a way into a region of flowers, lying in shadowy coolness, beckoning our weary souls into the dim shady recesses. But our feet were tired and refused to obey the call. So we seated ourselves in a little nook under a tree, the tough, leathery leaves of which seemed to have been made of parchment, painted green and overlaid with one or two coats of varnish. Such is the provision which nature makes to protect vegetation and fit it to her children in the spot in which she has placed them. The sun can never scorch and burn up a leaf thus protected, as it would the leaves of our trees in the temperate zone. All this dark-green, glossy foliage was hymning out a rustling, murmuring music, as if the glad rains had only yesterday fallen on it, instead of the cloudless sky and the burning sun that has hung over the earth for the past six months. Up among the branches peered out wierd parasitic plants feeding on the life of the tree, and tasselling its giant branches with purple and golden blossoms. I pulled off some of them and put them in the pocket of my dress. Two weeks afterwards I chanced to come across them and they were not withered in the least. I think they would have grown again if they could have been placed in their favorite position.

A native woman kept an eating-house on a square yard of matting not far from the entrance to the pagoda, and as thirst began to wither us, with no chance of allaying it at hand, visions of her oranges, pine-apples, and bananas rose before us. So we sent for her to bring her stores. She came, and our intolerable thirst left us, but her entire stock-in-trade was sold out!

Strolling through one of the walks we came upon a vine clambering over a little tree, making all its top such a dense mass of orange-red bloom that the green leaves were entirely concealed. Long sprays hung swinging down, fringed so thickly with slender tubular flowers, as to be not very unlike a string of Chinese fire-crackers. Flowers are

THE GREAT PAGODA AND SMALL TEMPLES, RANGOON,
SHOWING THE TWO HUNDRED STONE STEPS LEADING TO THE SUMMIT.

less plentiful here in Burmah, than at Penang or Singapore.

That evening we dined with an old friend from Singapore, a pleasant chatty gentleman, with enough cheery good-humor about him to make any occasion, however ordinary, extremely pleasant. The party was small and our conversation turned on our proposed route of travel through the valley of the Ganges and the quaint old cities and ruins scattered through it. Delhi with its wondrous old ruins, and Agra with its magnificent Taj; and the cities on the head-waters of the Indus.

As we were desirous of carrying home an image of Buddha from Burmah, our friend very kindly offered us a beautiful one which he possessed; we, on our part, volunteering to send him a large photograph of the Taj; which was afterwards forwarded to him from Bombay.

Leaving Rangoon we passed down the river by daylight; the banks were low and monotonous, yet the giant trees with their dark, glossy foliage, were a rare and gladsome sight to our eyes, they are so very unlike those seen on the river banks of the old world. All night the *Mahratta* pitched and rolled in a strong northeast monsoon, which came over the mountainous coast and sweeping down the bay carried the steamer out of her course. Many of the passengers were greatly discomforted by the motion. About one o'clock P. M., the engine stopped, something had given away and must be repaired, here, in mid sea. For awhile the *Mahratta's* great throbbing heart stood still. Away down in her lowest depths anvils were ringing, and we could hear the strokes of the huge hammers busily at work. The sound came up through the place where the great iron shaft now stood motionless. I began to be very much alarmed. With noiseless steps and many foolish fears in my heart, I crept out of my cabin and peered down into the region whence the sounds proceeded, and which might almost have been taken for the abode of Vulcan. For a moment I half envied those whose seasickness had divested them of all anxiety as to whether they went on their course or off it or even to the bottom.

However, after drifting about for three hours we started again, whether on our way or not it was difficult to determine, for the chronometer was not reliable enough to point out our exact position; but, with a clear sky and plenty of sea-room, we were told by the captain that matters would all mend. We were now in the track of the many memorable typhoons which have surged their gigantic waves up this bay, then up the Hooghly and other outlets of the Ganges, destroying boats and shipping in its way, sweeping all the villages and plantations along the banks, and threatening Calcutta, notwithstanding its distance from the sea.

THE TYPHOON OF 1864.

Some little waves, one mild October day, away down in the Indian Ocean, began a gentle, dreamy, whirling sort of waltzing motion. Bright, sparkling, joyous things, gladsome were their first gyrations! Others were now disturbed; move they must for nature never rests; she hates a standstill, for mobility is an attribute of her reign.

The changing monsoon rode on the wings of the storm-cloud, and piped for the dance of the waters.

Wave joined hands with wave, each whirling aloft snowy wreaths of foam. Their trailing sea-green robes, all fringed with gems, sweep through crimson and golden sea-weed bowers, where ocean shells have slumbered undisturbed for ages. On through the deep-sea caverns, where mariners' bones have bleached through silent centuries; on, the troubled waters sweep; over the green, slimy, mouldering hulks of the old Portuguese navigators; over snowy coral pinnacles of ocean reefs; over unfathomed caves and grottoes; deep calling hoarsely unto deep, and answered in the same terrible tones.

On whirl the circling waters, gayer, giddier, madder! Wider and wider grow their fearful gyrations. With the violence of the tornado they sweep the whole surface of the great Bengal Bay, enclosing in their fatal mazes every barque upon the bosom of the ocean. The wind howls with terrific force, lifting the foam and spray till sea and sky are one bewildering gloomy mist.

The shivering vessel shrieks in every timber. The cordage rattles in deafening tones; sails are rent away and spars wrenched from their places and washed overboard; wave-washed, rudderless, and trembling, they stagger pitifully. The frenzied waves come on, seething, surging, then retiring; wreathing in and wreathing out; rushing, swelling, lifting subsiding. The doomed ship staggers, driving wildly, fearfully, then plunges—and is gone! A moment more, and the mad waves are dancing over the limp, lifeless seamen, tossing their pallid faces up amid snowy sheets of foam.

On, toward the northeast, sweeps the mad carnival of all the Storm Spirits. The air is thick and blinding with the spray. Helpless hulks are hurled against each other, and then vanish into the depths. Steamers are broken like cockle-shells, and anchor-chains are snapped off like spiders' threads. No friendly island breaks the violence of the waves. They pass the great Sand Head and roll madly up the river, tossing their foamy crests over whole villages and plantations, uprooting trees, and spurning banks and bounds, mingling in one inextricable floating mass, human beings and their huts, boatmen with the wreck of boats, tigers, pythons, hyenas, trees, jungle, weeds, and grass.

Such was the terrible cyclone of 1864.

The wave that swept up the Hooghly to the city of Calcutta was so great that it lifted ships up into the streets. One ship of a thousand tons burden was carried up into the Botanical Garden, opposite the city, crushing down everything in its way. The underwriters excavated a canal to float it back into the river. The loss of life among the poor natives was immense. Of the famous avenue of gigantic elms, three miles in extent, leading from this city to Barrackpore, only three or four remained standing. The city looked very much as if it had been sacked or ruined by an earthquake.

When our steamer arrived at Sand Head, the mouth of

the river, we dropped anchor, and waited for a pilot, till daylight. The pilot was a native man—a Mussulman, I judge from his dress—probably one of those natives who are brought up on this river, and become pilots by virtue of knowing it inch by inch, and foot by foot, and rod by rod, from Calcutta to the sea; it has become their inheritance. His fee for piloting a steamer up or down, says Capt. S——, is between $3000 and $4000, a nice little income for him! The Hooghly is a deep swift river, with low monotonous banks, bordered with rice-fields and cocoanut plantations, which have a sicklier look the farther they are from the sea, and at last they disappear altogether. For miles below the city we passed almost continuous brickyards. One would think that they might supply half the globe with brick; but work is never driven here as in other countries. With the first glimpse of the city the anchor drops into the river. The law compels all vessels to stop here and wait for the down tide to turn the steamer round, which if done too swiftly would result in damage among vessels in the roadstead; so the stern of our vessel will get to the city first.

Formerly it was not very uncommon when raising anchor, to find human bodies entangled with it. The soil of this delta probably once breathed and lived. The English Government have done much of late years towards preventing and discouraging the Hindoos from burying their dead, or committing suicide in the Ganges, but it is quite impossible to completely guard a sacred stream that is one thousand five hundred miles long, every rod of which a Hindoo fully believes would float his dead body safely to heaven. Eating fish from that river is only one remove from cannibalism.

The villages along the Hooghly are generally built in the shade of the clustering cocoanut trees near the river—so that their owners may not have very far to go to pray—or at least near some tank, as the water reservoirs for irrigation are called. The banks of these reservoirs are planted with different species of palm, as the cocoanut, betel-nut or areca, with some bananas. The native houses on this part of the

ROADSTEAD IN THE HOOGLY.

river are built of a wicker-work of ratans, or any reed from the jungle, plastered over with a very compact light-blue clay. The roof is thatched and projects far enough to protect the walls during the rains. The ridge-pole rounds up in the centre so there is a descent in every direction from that point. The floor forms the foundation. It is constructed by pounding down layers of blue clay, one above the other, until a compact, hard, smooth surface is obtained, which can be kept much cleaner than one would at first imagine. Compared with the cellars and garrets and tenement-houses inhabited by the poor of the great cities of Christendom, such dwellings are found much better adapted to the wants of the natives of this climate, than the first are to those of the poor in more northern countries. The wants of the people are fewer and there is less of discontent in their appearance. Some years ago Garden-Reach was one of the pleasantest localities about the city of Calcutta. Since that time the charming villa on this beautiful stretch of river bank has been the residence of the ex-king of Oudh and his court. It is said that the nightly orgies now held there, make the vicinity an undesirable residence for Europeans.

CHAPTER VI.

CALCUTTA.

THE BOATS in common use on the Hooghly are peculiarly constructed, with a very high bow and stern. They glide along this exceedingly rapid river, like ducks, and float, even when caught in the great waves called the *bore*, caused by high tides acting with the swift current.

The sun was just setting when we came to anchor, and the short twilight faded into night amidst the hurrying of porters bringing the baggage on deck, and waiters who were particularly officious just now in expectation of a *douceur*. The boatmen gesticulated and flourished their boathooks, shouting very forcibly in the most convenient Bengalee language that they could manage, each determined to be first at the boat-stairs and hold firmly there to prevent being carried away by the strong current, or crowded aside by some larger boat's party before they had received any passengers for themselves. For angry gesticulation, commend me to one of this class.

At last we found ourselves on shore and safely stowed in a hack gharry. The word was given to coachee to drive to Wilson's Hotel, and in a few moments he drew up before a large house, intimating that we had arrived at our destination. On looking out we saw 'Great Eastern' in very large black letters, across the whole front. Pointing it out to coachee, he said, "All same, all same!" We hesitated and consulted together. Finally our Jehu settled the matter for us by bringing out a clerk or waiter of some sort, who told us that Wilson's Hotel was the former name, but that it had

A STREET IN CALCUTTA.

been changed to Great Eastern. Next day returning from a visit in the town and driving up on the other side of the hotel, in the next street, we found 'Aukland House,' painted in equally large black letters. To our look of surprise, coachee again said, "All same, all same!" This time we did not dispute him, but thought how convenient it must be to have several names to a house, if they were all good to draw custom. On a third occasion we found that they had hoisted the 'Wilson' flag again, but that time, used to the chameleon-like nomenclature of the house, we did not put coachee to the trouble of saying "All same, all same!"

It was January, and the winter months constitute the gay season in Calcutta, if it can be called winter when the mercury does not fall below 65° Fah. On enquiring for a good suite of rooms we were told there were none to be had at present, at least for three days to come. The difficulty was how to get over those three days. We were not birds—we could not tuck our heads under our wings and fold our feathers about us and go to sleep standing! Something must be done. So one of our party ran over to Spencer's Hotel, but found that it was also full. After much consultation, word came to us that the Wilson-Aukland-Great-Eastern Hotel could give a room to "the party with the lady," but the others, being gentlemen, must camp down where they could.

It was about ten o'clock at night when we found ourselves in a cheerless room, the dimensions of which were twenty-six by sixty feet. We were shivering with cold, though the mercury stood at 65°; but that was fifteen to eighteen degrees lower than we had experienced for four years, and clothing did not seem to supply the place of the heat of the sun. So shiver we must, for there were no places for fire.

There were sixteen gas-burners in the room and three were lighted, but for some cause connected with the gas department, that night, they did not burn; so we called for a candle and began to explore the mysteries of the apartment. I went peering down one side of it and up the other, and finally found four sash-doors but no windows. A fair supply of doors surely! The knobs were all gone except one, which could hardly be called a liberal number, but as there were the usual number of bolts for fastening securely, we became somewhat reconciled.

Our furniture was equally scanty. There was a lank sofa with two or three gouty springs in the last stage of collapse; and also an enormous punkah, or fan, forty feet long. This punkah hung in the middle of the room. It was rigged with ropes, one of which passed through the wall so that the boy who pulled it could stand outside. The punkah-wallah was not on duty that night, and the machine hung motionless. This was another inconvenience, for though wrapped in our shawl-blankets and shivering with cold, we had a strong desire to raise a breeze with this great fan, just to blow the mosquitoes out of the room.

The "Bearer," as the chamber-man is called, improvised a double-bed, out of two small iron bedsteads, by placing them side by side in order to economize one great friendly Scotch blanket which would cover two very cosily. Indeed I strongly suspect our having any bed at all that night, was mainly owing to the suggestive width of that blanket, for that was our only covering. Oriental luxuries, indeed!

Morning came to us cold and cheerless. As soon as breakfast was over we took a carriage in order to get out into the sunshine, and drove to the Chittypore road to see life among the lowly. This street is a great native bazaar filled with the queerest little shops, each one a *fac-simile* of a baker's oven—soot and all—except the oven door: small ovens, too, for these places are only ten feet square and five or six in height. Here were exposed for sale the queerest looking trinkets imaginable, for native wear; cheap bracelets for the arms and heavier rings for the ancles. Here, too, tailors were sitting cross-legged on the narrow verandah, almost brushed, by every passenger, but giving no heed to anyone or anything except the snowy muslins which they were making up. Besides these there were other diminutive

OLD COURT HOUSE STREET, DALHOUSIE SQUARE, CALCUTTA.

shops, all gay and glittering with tinsel-embroidered caps, a sort of *tarboosh* worn by genteel native men, and heelless slippers that were the glittering counterparts of the head-covering.

One man sat in a little cupboard, only just wide enough to hold him, twisting silk with bobbins. The silk had evidently been reeled from the cocoons. The thread seemed to pass through a ring over his head and was twisted by some wooden bobbins worked in his hands; the toes on the right foot held the thread that passed through the ring, very firmly, while those of the left foot were employed in guiding the thread and keeping it straight until reeled. This mode of spinning is probably the oldest on record; and is the honored ancestor of the silk manufactures of France and England. In this bazaar there were also provision stores, dingy and dark, with queer little piles of seeds used in the curry-powder, and dingy strings of dried cayenne pepper, and piles of grain, and a sort of dried pease, food for man and beast. The only familiar things among them all, were the piles of hulled and unhulled rice. In a doorway, brushed by all the bustling crowd, sat a native man as serenely and collectedly painting delicate patterns on beautiful enamelled boxes, as if in the most secluded place imaginable. Indeed, it was some time before we could call off his attention and make him understand that we wanted to buy some specimens of his workmanship.

Along one side of the street ran a neatly cemented open conduit through which poured water from the Ganges. It was nine o'clock in the morning as we passed, but the native barbers and customers still sat *a' le Turc* on the pavement beside the conduit waiting to be shaved, and seemed as contented and happy in the morning air as those who frequent the gay dressing-saloons of Paris or London. No rent-day troubles the native Calcutta barber, for he shaves his customer wherever he finds him. When he is able to get up more style he may be called to the sleeping-room of some European gentleman, and become a thriving man; for his charge is determined by the complexion of his customer.

Here we found open sheds with mangers where hack gharry-ponies were dozing, while their owners were sleeping beside them on little bedsteads three feet by four in dimensions. Tape, or listing, in the place of cords, is the only bed or bedding needed; but they sleep as softly and sweetly as ever did the grand Inca of Peru in his embroidered hammock.

Further on, we came to coppersmiths at work in curious little places—so very small that one could stand in the centre and touch either wall. These smiths fashion and shape all sizes of brass pots, on a long piece of iron which resembles the horn of an ordinary blacksmiths anvil, the identical patent got out by Tubal Cain, the recorded father of those who first wrought in brass or iron.

Chouringhee road and the Maidan, or driving park, are in fact the Hyde Park of Calcutta. From five to six in the evening, they are the scene of the greatest gaiety the city presents to a stranger's eyes. All the pomp and state that each individual or family can possibly muster, is trotted over these drives at that hour of the day. It is the only escape from the weary monotony that haunts one in a climate that permits of no active exercise. All classes of persons avail themselves of it. The Governor-General's grand turnout with outriders and retinue is occasionally seen; but the throng of splendid carriages, containing the beauty and fashion of this Indian metropolis, is there every evening.

Two native servants in gay livery stand instead of sit at the back of every carriage, for slender East Indians could never hope to attain to the dignified pomposity of an English footman, sitting with his strong arms folded across his ample chest, as if he bore on his own shoulders the honor of all his master's family. Native footmen could never do that; dignified presence is not a strong point with them. But standing there in their favorite colored costume—scarlet and black, or scarlet and white—skilfully flourishing their fly-drivers, which are made of glossy white hair from the tail of the yak, they give about the same effect and tone

GOVERNOR GENERAL'S PALACE, CALCUTTA,

that a brace of peacocks would if hanging on their perch in a picture of a landscape.

The army is well represented on the drive by gay horsemen and officers in rich uniforms, mounted on fine chargers that prance and curvet among the throngs of carriages. The native princes and noblemen who visit or reside in or near the city, have abandoned the palanquin, or palkee, as it is now called, as well as elephant-riding, for the English phæton. I confess to a little regret at this. An elephant richly caparisoned bearing some up-province Nawab, attended by lancers and spearmen, as in the olden time, would have proved, I doubt not, a very attractive feature in this crowd of pleasure seekers. In the palmy old times of the Moguls, a royal palkee was as elegant as a jewel-box. There is one exhibited in Windsor Castle, that was presented by the Emperor of Delhi to one of the kings of England, about two centuries ago. The frame is of sandal wood, richly inlaid with turquoise and other precious stones, in a running pattern, and all round the edges of the frame is an inlaid border of seed-pearls. It is curtained with heavy scarlet silk embroidered with shreds of pure gold.

Near the Maidan, the Hindoostani name for esplanade, or parade-ground, is Fort William the strongest fortress in the country at the present time. The cathedral grounds join the Maidan on the south, and the gardens and grounds surrounding the Government House are only separated from them by an open square. The palace of the Governor-General is by far the largest and finest edifice in the city. It consists of two semicircular buildings placed back to back, uniting by a great hall in the centre, making both sides alike. There is a dome over the grand central hall which is sufficiently lofty to be quite imposing. Rows of columns decorate the porticos, and the size and proportions of the edifice as a whole, give it somewhat of a majestic air. It is built of brick and stucco. As might be supposed the vicinity of the Government House is the fashionable quarter, like the west-end of London. Fronting on these grounds are the finest private residences where the members of the Governor-General's council and other high officials live in a luxurious and princely style.

Calcutta has been proudly styled the "City of Palaces." We found, however, that there was a dark side to this gorgeous picture. Once, when driving through one of the great thronged avenues, we thought to return to our hotel by a nearer way and without knowing definitely whither we were going, passed down the first street that we came to. In an instant, as if by magic, the scene was changed. All traces of civilization seemed to be left behind. The houses were mean, low, and small. Wattled cane and bamboo, plastered with clay, took the place of the substantial brick and fine white stucco of the avenue. The roadway was narrow and filthy, open sewers sent up their reeking stench, and children with scarcely a shred of clothing played in the dirt, while old toothless, haggard crones basked in the warmth of the sun. This is called the "Black Town of Calcutta.

The city of Calcutta is a modern place, there are no remains of antiquity near it. In 1686 on its site stood a small mud-village called Halee-Ghât, Halee, the name of the Hindoo goddess of death, and Ghât, a bathing-place, or steps leading down to the water. The present name is only a corruption of the two words. It is supposed to contain about 600,000 inhabitants, but a stranger would not estimate the number as high as that, until he knew how densely the native quarters are packed.

There are no regular theatres in the city, but private theatrical entertainments and private concerts, got up by amateur players and singers, with frequent balls and dinner-parties, make the cool season at Calcutta seem almost a paradise of delight, compared with the unvarying monotony of an up-country station. Both army-officers and civilians, look upon being sent to small distant stations, very much as they would upon exile. It is impossible to estimate the utter loneliness of young men from good families and pleasant homes in England, who are sent to frontier stations far from

GATEWAY TO GOVERNOR GENERAL'S PALACE, CALCUTTA.

the great routes of travel, where there is no European society at all, aside from the officers of the army-corps, with which they are connected, and perchance a magistrate. Those who are thus situated and can contrive to escape to Calcutta for a few weeks at this season of the year, are considered by their friends remarkably fortunate, and, as can be readily believed, they make the most of their time. Hence the crowded state of the hotels while we remained in the city. The afternoon of the second day after our arrival, some guests at the hotel—very fortunately for us—took their leave and we were enabled to get a good suite of rooms fronting on the street. The sun shone into them cheerfully and we were very grateful for its warmth, and when we sat down to our dinner, spread for us in our cheery sitting-room with a good Bengalee boy to wait upon us, our ruffled spirits became more tranquil.

We found it necessary to hire a waiter, all to ourselves, for one can hardly get helped to food at table unless he specially engages a servant. Even the private rooms are quite without attention. If one is at all urgent, the waiters enquire, "Do you want a boy?" We were not a little surprised, after the cloth had been removed and everything attended to for the night, when the waiter in attendance informed us that if we did not hire him for a month he should charge four annas (twelve cents) *per diem* for his services; which he seemed to think was such high wages that we would prefer to pay three dollars and engage him for a whole month. "All right!" we said, and he went away in a state of perfect happiness to take his rice with his family and tell his friends what high wages he was to receive if we failed to keep him a month, and probably dreamed all night of a new coat that would cost one entire rupee. An American lady, whose family consisted of her husband, herself and one child, said she had repeatedly tried to get along with less than thirty servants, but could not.

"Caste" has been religiously handed down through the long centuries, and has brought with it numberless divisions and sub-divisions of labor. People of one caste cannot associate with people of another. They are not even allowed to travel beyond certain prescribed limits, and thus, where the individual himself is disposed to be tolerably useful, his religion and the customs of his country effectually prevent him. But in some instances they lose caste. Much of the religion of the natives consists in eating according to caste rules, bathing in the Ganges, and other ceremonies, and those whose caste has not been kept quite pure, or whose ancestors have married into the rank next lower and therefore cannot themselves be permitted to officiate as priests, consider it quite an honorable position to cook the food and wait upon one whose genealogy goes back to the demi-gods. Of late years low-caste Brahmins, even, have been willing to engage as waiters in the service of Europeans, but such men would not sweep a room if you were to give them a fortune, neither would they wash an article of clothing — men here perform such offices — or a dish, or draw a drop of water, for they would then lose caste; but they would find some one to do the work for them, and would see that it was done properly. Their caste, however, will permit them to become accountants, and very many Brahmins of the inferior order are thus employed. The caste next lower to the Brahmins affect a great nicety, not as to the manner of doing your work, but as to what part they will condescend to do at all.

Complicated housework brings with it, or rather requires for its satisfactory management, a host of servants of different castes, who swell the cost of living enormously, without a proportionate amount of comfort. There is a vast amount of hair-splitting in this division of labor — the priest and cook are the highest dignitaries.

The English Government of late has been taking hold, in a fair, impartial, business-like way, of the education of all classes of native children, and will probably do a great deal for them and for India. The government stands pledged to pay to any man of good moral character who will so teach a school, that it will satisfactorily pass the requisite examination, a certain amount of money. This offer is open to dissenters, as well as Church of England teachers, and many of our missionaries have availed themselves of it.

The traveller from the New World will find that the Indian Museum will well repay the trouble of a visit. It contains a large collection of antique curiosities gathered from all parts of this old, old world. The departments of mineralogy, conchology and zoölogy are very good; but there appears to be a great deal of slovenliness about the management; things are stowed in odd corners, and everything is covered with as liberal a supply of dust, as if the desert sands had settled upon them. At least so we found it. Possibly this may not be the usual condition of things, but may have been occasioned by alterations which were in progress at the time of our visit.

The bathing ghâts at sunrise, present a novel sight. How remarkably have these two prominent Oriental systems of religion — the Hindoo and the Mohammedan — blended personal cleanliness with religious rites. The author of the "Institutes," as the holy Hindoo books are called, must be credited with a great deal of shrewdness and a firm reliance on his followers' love of water. Before Aaron made that golden calf in the wilderness, it is asserted, that this Brahminical religious code compelled untutored Hindoo races to stand in the water and raise the pure element in their hands while saying their prayers, with their eyes looking upon the rising sun. The personal cleanliness that has ensued from this daily immersion — for I believe, once at least during the prayer, the head must be put under the water — must have operated through all those long centuries as a powerful civilizer. This hydropathic ritual must be rather agreeable to the devotees during four-fifths of the year. The force of habit and the idea of peril to their souls if they neglect these ablutions, secures their observance of these ceremonies, even during the cooler season of the year.

We arrived at the bathing ghâts in the chill, grey dawn

of a January morning, the mercury registered 60° when we left the hotel, and we shivered in our woollen wraps, as we looked down on the crowd of heads in the water. The faces were of all shades of color from yellowish-brown to negro blackness. How the fine, clear-cut Caucasian features and decided oval *contour* of face, ever came to be covered with a sooty black skin, is quite beyond my power to conjecture. Young and old of both sexes are clothed in white muslins, a shade or two thinner than our ordinary white cloth. The women wear a large square piece, or an over-garment, called in some parts of India a 'chudder.' The priests keep their brown shoulders covered by a few yellow threads, passed over one arm and then under the other. When the disc of the sun was fairly above the horizon, this great crowd rushed into the water with apparent glee; each one carrying with him a large or small brass pot, which is called a 'lota,' and is used for dipping up and pouring out the water while looking toward the sun, which they do as if devoutly addressing their prayers to that luminary rather than to the river. Some carried rice with them to cast into the water; others carried a sort of rosary made by stringing together very small natural flowers, like the petals of the white lilac, or others made of yellow flowers, which seemed to be counted over during the prayer and then left floating on the stream.

The thought was suggested at once — may not this Hindoism or Brahminism be only a species of that sun-worship which prevails in mountainous regions of India, where scores of their finest youth, even now, bleed annually on altars dedicated to that luminary.

Substituting the Ganges-water in the washing away of sins, for the heart's blood of a human being, was doubtless a great progressive step, away in the far off ages,—ages so long gone that only the progress of the stars can fix their date. It is to be regretted that so little progress has been since made.

When those in the river had concluded their devotions,

TANK IN GOV. GENERAL'S GARDEN, CALCUTTA.

they began washing their outer garments. That being done, they filled their lota-pots in the water where hundreds had bathed and washed, and took home the holy liquid to drink and cook their rice in, but if the shadow of an unbeliever were to fall upon it, they would call it unclean and throw it away. They seem to carry these praying-pots with them everywhere, so that they may be always prepared for worship. I saw one man running at full speed,—for he was late—without stopping he caught up a handful of fine dust, polished his brass pot as he ran, and dashed into the water with the crowd.

They came out of the water and up the steps, shivering like aspen leaves, in their wet clothing, and hastened away to their homes, holding out their outer garments so as to catch the wind, in order to dry them as they walked.

Among the preparations for a trip to the northwest provinces from this point, it is important to obtain letters of credit on the bankers of the various money-districts, and thereby avoid the inconvenience of carrying a weight of coin.

Leaving Calcutta, we crossed the Hooghly to the village of Howrah on the opposite bank. Everywhere along the river in Hindoo countries the ghâts, with their massive stone steps leading down to the water, invariably attract the attention of strangers from the Western World; their substantial construction forming a striking contrast to the flimsy habitations of nine tenths of the people. They are built of immense blocks of dressed brown stone laid upon very deep, solid foundations and fastened together with strong iron clamps; for these banks are subject to great periodical inundations and nothing but the most substantial masonry can resist their violence. Adjoining is the quay and depôt-buildings of the Great Indian Railway. The old-fashioned coach-cars, such as are common in Europe, are provided for first-class passengers, but the only evidence of luxury which we could discover about them, was a good, fair ratan seat and back, which at night could be transformed into a berth for one to lie down upon. The third-class carriages, judging from what we could see from the station-house windows, appeared to be a sort of travelling pen. The car is only the ordinary height, but divided into three stories or compartments, one above the other, giving the native people, who never use seats or chairs in their homes, just sufficient room to sit on their folded legs and feet. It must certainly be admitted that the sides of these cars are so made as to give a free circulation of air, for they are only enclosed just sufficiently to prevent the slender bodies of the natives from passing either in or out through the bars or slats. These carriages are built in lofts or stories, one above another—the inmates sitting on the floor and their heads almost, if not quite, touching the ceiling or division which separates them from the floor above. The passengers mount a ladder, in single file, to the second and third lofts, and then seat themselves as best they can in true Oriental fashion; in this way a great saving of car furniture is effected. By this economical arrangement, the fare is brought down within the reach of the poorer natives, who throng these cars and even perform their pilgrimages by railway, instead of wearily measuring their way on foot, as undoubtedly the founders of their religion expected them to do. The fare charged is about one half-cent per mile.

Thirteen miles north of Calcutta, is Serampore, formerly a Danish trading-settlement. It was founded in 1598, when the clumsy looms of India produced the finest fabrics in the world, when the soft, silky, gossamer muslins of Dacca were the coveted robes of princesses, and the famous shawls of Cashmere, only at rare intervals, graced royal shoulders in western Europe. After one hundred and forty-seven years of growth and decay, the settlement was purchased in 1845 for twelve lakhs of rupees (about $300,000) by its rival colony the English, at Calcutta. There was an avenue of grand old trees which in such a warm climate as that must have formed a very attractive feature; but they were all destroyed by the cyclone of 1864.

But scant signs have been left of the old traders: of how they amassed princely riches or became beggarly poor, we know

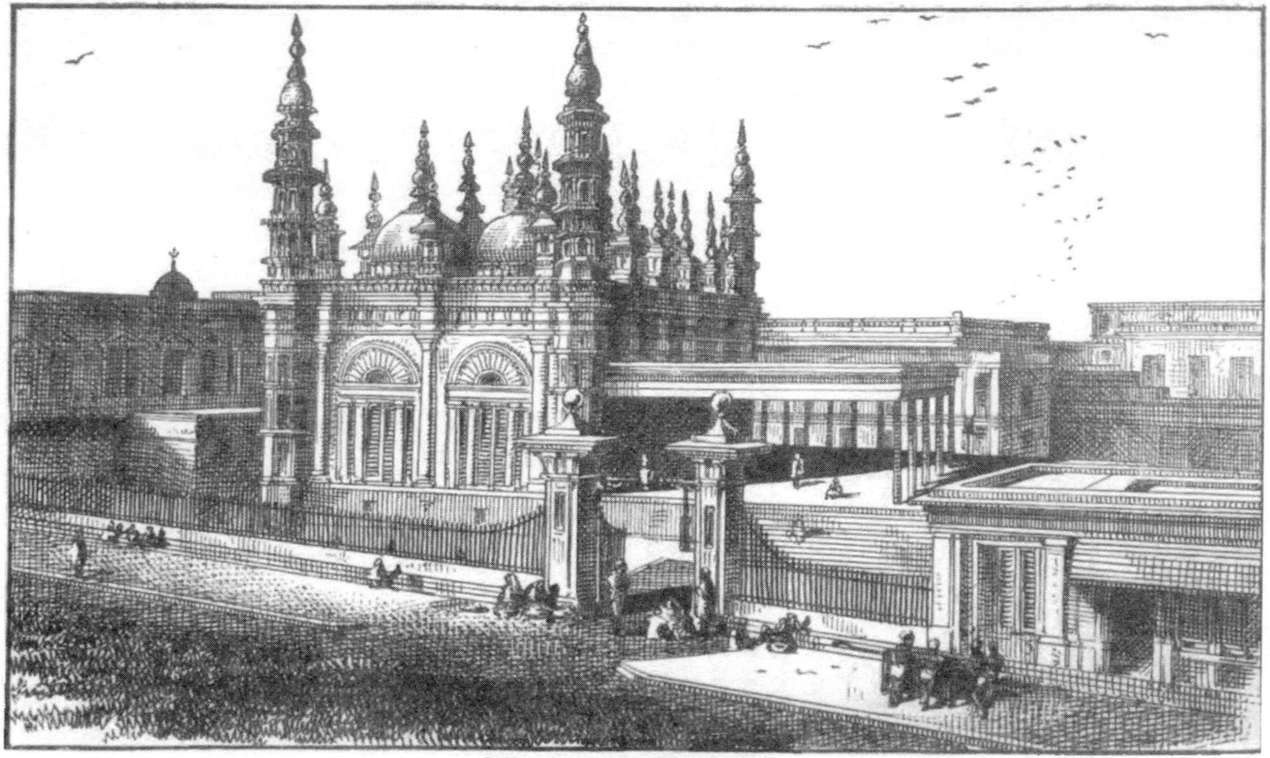

DHUMUNTOL MOSQUK, CALCUTTA.

little now; except the old dilapidated warehouses on the river banks and a few local traditions, but few traces of them remain. But the names of the pioneer missionaries, Drs. Cary, Ward and Marshman, who sleep in the little burial-ground, are yet fragrant in the memory of all Christian people. The Serampore College, which was erected from their own private funds, is their own monument and memorial. It is a substantial building on the banks of the Hooghly river, and has a well-arranged library, containing some rare works on India. Between the college and the river, once stood the house of the sainted Cary; but the water has played so treacherously with the banks, that its site is now some sixty feet or more out in the river. Dr. Cary established the Botanical Garden, which at the beginning of the present century contained three thousand species of plants. His garden, contained six acres; it has now been sold for business purposes. There is also a Roman Catholic chapel and convent here.

On the opposite bank of the river, is Barrackpore, the great military station for lower Bengal, and in a beautiful park within view, stands one of the vice-regal residences. Here the Governor-General and his family retire for rest during the cooler months of the year when wearied with the routine of the Goverment House. During the hot months they betake themselves to Simla, nestling among the foot-hills of the Himalaya, which has a climate like the temperate zone.

Twenty-four miles from Calcutta, is Hooghly, the first foothold of Europeans in India. It was purchased by the Dutch, and a trading colony founded, in 1625, sixty-one years before Job Charnock founded Calcutta, and seventy-three years before the Danes began their settlement at Serampore. This town has had many masters, one after another, Dutch, Portuguese, French, and finally the English, who now possess it by right of purchase. In Akbar's days when the Mogul empire had reached the zenith of its glory, the Dutch colony of Hooghly excluded the English from the trade of the Ganges and then began hostilities, which only ended when the English finally had purchased or captured the forts and trading-posts of their competitors in India. Hooghly was then considered the granary of Bengal, and the river floated down to it the products of a vast and fertile region. When a Portuguese settlement held possession of the town, the Roman Catholic religion was of course openly professed, and the worship of the Virgin and the saints is said to have been so obnoxious to the beautiful Moomtaj-ie-mahal, wife of Shah Jehan, after the conversion of her daughter Jehanira, that she importuned the Emperor to destroy the "image-worshippers," until at length he issued the infamous order to exterminate the whole colony. Their little fort sustained a seige of three months by the whole Moslem army which lay encamped about it. When the fort became untenable, its brave band of defenders retired to their ships, but even there misfortune overtook them, and one of the largest ships, on board of which were two thousand people, was blown up by its captain, who considered such a death preferable to falling into the hands of the infuriated Moslems. Of sixty-four vessels anchored in the river, only three escaped.

The Emambarra is an interesting place and the mosque is a handsome structure. There is a lofty, massive clock-tower with a remarkably fine chime of bells at the entrance to the Serai, one of those Oriental institutions for the accommodation of native travellers, that have passed down to the present time, from the days of Joseph and Mary.

Two miles away is the Roman Catholic College built by a French gentleman, Monsieur Perron, a general who went into the Mahratta service and acquired an enormous fortune. This institution has been endowed by a Moslem gentleman, with an annual income of fifty thousand rupees (about $25,000.) It has two departments of instruction, English and Oriental, and usually has about six hundred native pupils.

Satgan, a few miles above, on the Hooghly, now a miserable village near the great railroad-bridge which spans the river of the same name, was once a noble city, which flourished in commercial glory from the days of Pliny down to the time when the Portuguese acquired possession of Hooghly and drew the trade from Satgan to that place. The Romans are said to have traded here, and if so their caravans must have wended their way up through the Ganges valley, across the wide valley of the Indus, up the famous Kyber pass, through the grand old Hindoo Koosh Mountains, teeming with warlike inhabitants, across the desert to Persia, across the plains to the city of Zenobia, thence across the plains to Damascus; thence across northern Palestine to the Mediterranean, where they would take shipping to Rome, if they did not turn off and go by the way of the Persian Gulf and Red Sea, or embark from some place on the Malabar coast. It is difficult to conceive how such a long and perilous journey could have been accomplished, but that the Romans did trade with India, there can be no question, for silk from Hindoo looms, and other treasures from the distant Orient, adorned the palaces of the Eternal City in her palmy days.

Satgan, in the very heart of the ancient Hindoo kingdom of Gour, had its citadel and royal residence, and through fifteen centuries its riches drew traders from far-distant countries. There was a golden halo about it in those old days, but its glory is departed now.

Pundoak also, was one of the loyal cities centuries ago, though now it is sunk to such a lowly condition. It is only fourteen miles from Hooghly. It was fortified with a wall and deep trench, five miles in circuit, and for that time and the mode of warfare in those days it must have been a strong city. The long line of kings, who reigned within those old walls the outline of which even can now scarcely be traced, counted up to the sixty-first monarch — a list of monarchs numbering nine more than all the Afghan and Mogul emperors who reigned in Delhi since their invasion in A. D. 1103.

The final subjugation of the country and fall of this city, took place in 1340, when Mohammed Yogluck sent his nephew Shah Sufi to the capital of Gour to avenge an insult offered to his interpreter residing at that court. It is said, that that functionary had butchered a cow, to celebrate a feast on the birth of his child — a horrible crime in the eyes of a people who consider those animals sacred. The interpreter carefully buried the bones of the animal in his own enclosure, so as to avoid offence to the cow-worshipping Hindoos; but in the night the jackals, as is their wont in that region, dug up the bones for a second picking, and left them exposed to the sight of the too suspicious Hindoos, who immediately rose *en masse*, and demanded that the offender should expiate with his own life the death of so sacred an animal. The mob surrounded his house, seized the child who had been the innocent cause of all this trouble, and killed it on the spot, to propitiate the wrath of their god. The father appealed to the king for protection, but got no redress of his wrongs; so he took up the body of the murdered child, and carried it to Delhi and laid his complaints before the emperor in person, who only needed the shadow of an excuse to send his army to conquer the country and annex it to his own dominions.

The army came, commanded by Shah Sufi, and laid seige to the town. The Hindoos fought bravely, believing that all who were killed, if immersed in their sacred tank, or well, would be restored to life, and be able again to join the line of battle, but it is needless to say they were disappointed. The wily Moslem commander then contrived a plan by which some cow's flesh was thrown into this sacred reservoir, and then no Hindoo, however great his sufferings, would use the water. Thousands of them might have been mown down by Moslem guns and sabres, and still men would have come to fill their places; but this bit of beef in the water with which they performed their acts of worship, and which they must drink, and in which they cook their food, was a far greater calamity; it was a disaster which they could not repair. It would entail upon their own souls and their children's souls through an indefinite number of lives and transmigrations, the severest penalties which the angry gods could possibly mete out to them. The fear of committing such a crime subdued them, and thus though plenty of water was

RAJAH GHOSAL'S RESIDENCE, CALCUTTA.

within reach, no Hindoo would drink it, nor could any amount of purifying ever make that great reservoir clean, to a son or daughter of Sieva.

Only Mussulmen live in Pundoah now. The tank so unfortunately connected with the fate of the old city is the one pointed out to the traveler, about six hundred feet from the modern railroad-station. There are also other tanks; one on the left-hand side of the village is called the Pir-pookur; it is surrounded by monuments to saints; some say Moslem saints, and the tame alligators that live in it and the keeper who feeds them — for a fakir acts as their keeper — seem to be more Mohammedan than Hindoo. The alligators are fed with live fowls, but I do not suppose they would refuse a dog, or a pig, on account or koran or caste, unless their training has made them particularly fastidious. Perhaps in that far-distant day, benevolent mothers offered them a baby for breakfast. This tank was probably dug before the city fell into the hands of the Moslems, or else immediately after, and was only enlarged and cleansed for the new occupants—the conquerors, who settled in Gour. That event took place five hundred and thirty-four years ago. This large tank, (reservoirs are called tanks here) cannot be of much later date than that, for since then the population has been decreasing, and the demand for water also. On the other hand, it may be twice that age, if it was constructed by the Hindoos.

The trees on the bank, and the ruined tombs, are memorials of the Moslems who fell during the seige and they give to the locality a very picturesque appearance. There is also a fine mosque two hundred feet in length. It has sixty domes, which reverberate sound like a whispering-gallery. It was built by the conqueror Shah Sufi; the raised platform in the centre was the place where he spread his praying-mat, and performed his devotions. Near this is another tank, called Shimbasan, where devout women go to pray for what Hannah besought; only there is this difference — these women instead of laying their gifts before the altar, place them carefully on the water, on anything that will float, and if by any chance a breath of air, or movement of the water sends it towards them, they consider the answer favorable, and the fulfillment of their wishes certain, and they go home in as strong faith as did the pious Jewess of old.

During the reign of the Toglucks, a passion for crowding a great number of domes on the roofs of the mosques seems to have prevailed. There is one within the city walls that has fifteen, and another near old Delhi, built about the same time, that has no less than *eighty-nine*! A tower one hundred and twenty-feet high, was erected near the mosque at Gour to commemorate the victory of which I just spoke; probably both mosque and tower were erected to memorialize that event; the tower serving the double purpose—of a monument of victory, and a minar from which the muzzin might call the faithful to their prayers. In those days the mosque sprang up where the sword of the Moslem prevailed.

There is a peculiarity about the tower at Gour which is worthy of notice,—an iron rod like a lightning-conductor, runs up the wall and projects from the top. Did these Mogul chiefs five hundred years ago know how to guard against lightning? or was this iron rod merely a freak or fancy of the architect who constructed the tower?

It is said that the emperor at Delhi offered the government of Bengal to the successful commander, Shah Sufi, but that the latter declined, preferring to lead a life of piety in the place where he had so signally defeated the Hindoo image worshippers. A little distance from the tower, his tomb was pointed out to us. Perhaps after all there was not so very much self-denial on his part, when he declined the honors of the Bengal governorship. The Emperor Mohammed Togluck came to the Mogul throne, by slaying his father, and when seated on it could not feel secure, until thirty-two of his blood-relations had fallen victims to his sword; all through his life he displayed an insane desire to shed blood. Obscurity in such a reign is more to be desired than prominence.

Thus far we have travelled through a rice-growing region;

on every side as we came along we observed the little plats for rice-culture, fifteen or twenty feet square, surrounded by low mud-walls only eight or ten inches high, to hold the water that falls during the rainy season. These plats begin on the slope of the hill and extend as far as the land can be rendered level, and the water — if there is any to be utilized — is allowed to flow off on to a lower level. Sometimes the rice-fields are watered directly from the great tanks or pools, which are such a prominent feature in this part of the country. Previously to this I had supposed rice could never be raised on land that is naturally dry—but this land was certainly as dry as any wheat-growing land in Ohio. All this region in fact, would be a desert during three-fourths of the year, but for constant irrigation; hence the pools of water are as precious to the inhabitants as a mine of gold, for with out them famine would soon depopulate the country. A large amount of labor and capital, however, must be expended in excavating and keeping them in repair, and this circumstance alone, will always prevent the land from being cut up into small farms. In the course of events the government will probably own the land, and dig and control the pools.

Sometimes circular wells, similar in appearance to those in western countries, but very much broader, are sunk down to a great depth. Then an inclined plane is built up on one side of the well with the perpendicular at the brink. A purse-like bucket, of a novel pattern, is made by taking an immense round of leather, as large as will fit the surface of the well, through which holes are made in the outer edge, a long rope is passed through each, and the bucket spreads itself out on reaching the water, and contracts like a purse when it is being drawn up out of the well, which is done by a rope passing over a windlass to which a yoke of oxen is attached. By the time the oxen have reached the foot of the inclined plane, this great bucket has reached the level surface of the ground; a man is stationed there who seizes it, and pours its contents into the mouth of open conduits or furrows which run through the field about ten or twelve feet apart.

CHAPTER VII.

THE HOME OF NOOR-MAHAL.

IN Hindoo history Burdwan is called Koosumpore, the Flowery City. The rajahdom of Burdwan, is one of the richest in India.

The Rajah's estates extend seventy-three miles in length, by forty-five miles in breadth. He pays a yearly revenue to the English government, of £40,000 sterling—nearly two millions of American dollars—and strange to say the Rajah enjoys paying it. He probably finds himself more prosperous under the protection of a powerful government than if he were one of a host of weak, petty rulers; each one liable at any moment to be invaded by his neighbor, or be entirely blotted out by a combination of all the neighboring petty states. The Rajah of Burdwan is a member of the Governor-General's council; a sort of parliament in a small way, modelled after the great one, the head of the Island Empire.

To this city, the beautiful Moomtaz-ee-Mahal, who lies buried in that marvellous shrine, glittering with gold and precious gems, at Agra, came with her husband, Shah Jehan, when his attempted revolt against his father, the Emperor Gehangire, in the latter part of his reign, had been crushed, his fortunes were at the lowest ebb, his army almost annihilated, and he himself was retiring before his father's victorious generals. Burdwan was considered a strong place, two hundred years ago, and one can readily imagine the refreshing feeling of safety which the fair Moomtaz-ee-Mahal must

PAGODA, EDEN GARDEN, CALCUTTA.

have felt who, together with her infant daughter, had followed the fugitive Shah in all his campaigns, sharing with him the changing vicissitudes of fortune, at a time when both court and army were so full of plots, and counter-plots, that Jehan one day occupied the position of favorite son, and the next day was fleeing for his life. Only a few months before, Shah Jehan had almost felt himself upon the throne of the empire; the emperor, his father, was a close prisoner in the hands of one of his most powerful nobles, who had suddenly surprised and captured him in his own camp on the river Jhelum; while Noor-Mahal, the beloved Noor-Mahal, his wife, had been vanquished while leading on the army in the vain but almost heroic endeavor to liberate her husband.

In this part of Bengal, if not at this point, lay the jagir to which Akbar, the wise and good, sent that dangerous young beauty and her loving lord, Shah Afgan, to live at a safe distance from the court of Delhi and Prince Selim. Hither also, in a little time, when they had learned to know and love each other well, came the sad news that the wise emperor was dead, and Prince Selim—Gehangire—who coveted the young wife, reigned in his stead. There was a brief council held to determine what course they should pursue, for they were true to each other, and the husband's haughty Persian blood fired at the thought of giving up his wife, the mother of his infant daughter, to his rival, although a king. No; rather than that, he would give up his commission in the army, surrender the territory and command which the Emperor Akbar had assigned him; forsake everything indeed, and, with his young wife, seize the first opportune moment, and take their way back to Persia, the fatherland of both.

These hasty plans had scarcely been suggested, when across their fertile fields came a viceregal hunting-party; resplendent in the gorgeous dress of the Afghans of the hills—hunters, lords and nobles, men-at-arms, stalwart followers in gaudy trappings of scarlet and gold, and members of the new governor's court. Here and there were gay and gallant bands of horsemen, mounted on fleet Arabians, the body-guard of the great Nawab of Bengal.

There was a tramp of horses' feet, and Shah Afgan, the Persian, turned to see a messenger, who made a low obeisance and then delivered his message, commanding his attendance on the new emperor's foster-brother, now Governor of Bengal, at a banquet that evening. Brief were the words signifying his compliance, for he knew that it was a message of doom to him. Shah Afgan went to pay the visit, with a dagger concealed in the bosom of his Persian robe; he was not put off his guard by the marked courtesy with which he was received by the new favorite of the emperor. As the evening hours flew by, amidst the noisy revelry of the hunting-feast, the proposal came for Shah Afgan to give up his wife, and as a reward for his complaisance receive high promotion in the army. No words can adequately express the burning indignation of the insulted husband. Prudence for a moment restrained his tongue, but when the disgraceful proposal was followed by threats of punishment in case of refusal, his fury knew no bounds. Utterly regardless of consequences he rushed upon the Viceroy and thrust his dagger into his heart; the next instant he himself fell fatally wounded beneath the weapons of the favorite's body-guard.

Noor Jehan watched with a foreboding heart all through the hours of the night for the footsteps of her husband, and at early dawn was seized by the officers and guard and immediately conveyed to Delhi as a prisoner, on a charge of conspiring with her husband to kill the Viceroy. Upon her arrival in Delhi, instead of being tried, according to Moslem custom, by the laws of the Koran, the Emperor met her with a proposal of marriage, which she refused with such firmness and disdain, as to cool his love, and he handed her over to his mother, the Grand Sultana—who, regardless of her birth and former position, installed her as her waiting-maid—and for a long time appeared to have forgotten her, and refrained from pressing his suit. Time and the reflection that she was now wholly in his power—for she was to all intents a prisoner, and could not leave the palace without the Emperor's consent—induced her to think more favorably of his proposals, which he renewed in about a year after the assassination of her husband; and finally she accepted him. The marriage was celebrated at Agra with great pomp and display, and the beautiful Noor-Mahal was raised to honors such as had never been enjoyed by any consort of an emperor of India, although of royal blood. It was after this cruel fashion that the "Light of the Harem" was wooed and won; and these are the stern facts upon which the poet built his glorious fiction.

My heart cried out, for the Noor-Mahal and Selim, the hero and heroine of Moore's poem, and refused to be consoled with these hard facts, and give up the sweet picture of the two lovers. Selim, in the poem, always appeared to me a charming prince, a splendid fellow about seventeen, with large black eyes and thin, fondly-cherished whiskers, and very large, brilliant diamonds, which he did not cherish at all, but just scattered among his friends, for fun; a prince who always had a large number of nice young men to take supper with him, while jugglers and dancing Nautch-girls, were performing to dream-like music. Noor-Mahal flitted through the picture, just sweet fifteen; she never had loved and never would love anybody but Selim, never would let anybody smile at her again, if he would only forgive her and love her just as he did before. Then she steps out to find a witch who will teach her how to win Selim's love again, and the witch tells her to run out in the dew and pluck some flowers that the moon was shining on, and be sure to bring in some of the pale rays of the moonshine, and that would fetch Selim at once. There was some difficulty about getting the moonshine; that broke the spell, and Selim did not appear according to prediction. Then Noor-Mahal, as a last resort in her misery, gave one of her diamond rings, or some other precious jewel to the head Nautch-girl, to exchange dresses with her, and allow her to put on her trappings, and go in and dance before the prince and his friends. Well, she was dressed at last, and tricked out with bells and tambourine, and went in and danced, her heart trembling all the time like a frightened little dove. But it was all thrown away upon the recreant prince. Selim continued sulky and looked down on the ground; then she thought she would try singing, and if that failed she would go away to some lonely place and languish, and die. But when she began to sing, Selim knew her voice, and clasped her in his arms, and she was forgiven and loved once more.

Well, that is the picture which the poem suggested to me, but I cannot put it on paper in the glowing words of Moore. It is very hard to demolish such a sweet romance and look at the real unmitigated Prince Selim — the tyrant and murderer of poor Noor-Mahal's husband.

The prince was the eldest son of the Emperor Akbar, who was cotemporary with Queen Elizabeth of England. The Tamerlane rulers of Hindoostan, in this reign, reached the zenith of their power and magnificence; it was the son of Prince Selim that built those wonderful structures, adorned with jewel-mosaics—the Taj, the baths and the magnificent throne-room at Delhi. Selim was no mere youth when he ascended the throne, with the title of Gehangire, his heart already fired by mad love for the Persian beauty who had grown up from infancy in the capital. He was forty-seven years of age, and had, long before he saw his Noor-Mahal, married two wives, daughters of powerful Rajpoot princes, and at the time he made love to her, had two grown-up sons whose development gave promise of a better manhood than Selim's had been. The eldest son was Prince Koshroo, who lies buried in the Koshroo garden at Allahabad, and Shah Jehan, the second son, the successor of his father, now lies in the Taj, at Agra, by the side of his wife, the beautiful Moomtaj-ee, who was niece to the real Noor-Mahal. It is cruel to give such dry details, when they are so damaging to romance, but the truth must be told. I jot down the facts because I wasted some sympathy over the queen's tomb in the Taj, between counting the jewels in her sarcophagus and reading a muddled sort of a statement by a

THE ONLY UNMARRIED LADY IN TOWN.

traveller, that led me to think that I was at the tomb of the real Noor-Mahal, who is buried hundreds of miles away on the banks of the Ravel in her own tomb, built during her widowhood, near Gehangire's, just across the river from Lahore.

Akbar during the later part of life had thought of bestowing the throne on his grandson, Koshroo, because Prince Selim had disgusted all the respectable Mussulmans of the court by cruelty to his prisoners of war, some of whom the wretch skinned alive, and to fill the measure of his cruelty, had put out the eyes of his own son Koshroo. He was an insatiable lover of brandy, which is forbidden by the Koran, but carried on all his orgies between sundown and morning, not offending decorum in the daytime, in the least, or neglecting to attend to business, but daily presided on the judgment-seat, as was the custom of all the great Mogul emperors of his family. This was the sort of hero, whose portrait was drawn by the English ambassador, Roe, who was sent by James the First, of England, to the court of Delhi. His Noor-Mahal's influence over him was so great that to a certain extent she mitigated his cruelty and even introduced many reforms into the palace, which she greatly embellished by her superior Persian taste.

Noor-Mahal's father was a Persian nobleman whose fortune had sunk so very low, that it is said, he emigrated to Hindoostan, from Teheran, bringing his family and all his earthly effects in one bullock cart. During the journey through the mountain-passes, Noor-Mahal was born. The father from utter poverty decided to abandon his child and placed it by the wayside, hoping that some wealthy merchants in the caravan, would see it, as they passed along, and take compassion on it; and bring it up as a slave-girl. The plan succeeded, for the child was beautiful, but the good Turk who found her was a little embarrassed on the subject of food, which the little one must have or die. Searching for a nurse, he found the child's mother and learned the straightened circumstances of the family, whom he kindly

9

assisted on their way to the court of Akbar. The father and his sons entered the emperor's service, and rose rapidly to good positions. The mother had free access to the royal harem, where she recited very acceptably the traditional poems and songs of her own country, which were eagerly listened to by the grand sultanas and their daughters. The little Noor-Mahal all unconscious of her future fate, accompanied her mother on tambourine or ziraleet, in the recitations and songs at the palace.

It was on one of these occasions, that the Persian mother's heart was pained by the rude attention which Prince Selim paid to her daughter, who was already betrothed, and she stated her complaint to one of the princesses, who in turn brought the matter before Akbar, who advised that the young girl should be married at once, and immediately bestowed a jargir, or military command in Bengal on Shah Afgan, the new-made husband. It was supposed that the matter was finally settled and would soon be forgotten, but Selim never forgot the young girl whose charms had captivated him, and the result was as I have related. Noor-Mahal was a power in herself, but, I must add, *not behind* the throne, but on it and around it; and her infatuated husband relied implicitly upon her judgment in every emergency.

Once, when the imperial household was travelling with a large retinue, on its annual visit to the court of Cabool, one of the most powerful of the great nobles of the Mogul empire, Mahowhut Khan, suddenly swooped down on the royal *cortège*, in the grey of the morning, and having captured the guard, entered the tent where Gehangire was sleeping. The Prince suddenly aroused by the unusual tumult, sprang from his bed with drawn sword and on seeing the Khan, demanded the cause of this strange intrusion. The chieftain dropped on his knee in the act of reverence, and said, "Your very humble slave, has for a long time been anxious to pay his homage to his sultan; but there were always some evil-minded traitors that barred my approach, and now when the army, all except your body-guard, has crossed the river Jhelum, I resolved to capture you, and do homage at leisure. You are now my prisoner."

Gehangire saw at once, the position of matters, and without surprise, or change of countenance, signified his readiness to go wherever the Khan desired, as soon as he had made his toilet; and under this pretence tried to escape to the apartments of his queen. The haughty Khan placing his sword across the door said, "Whatever toilet the Sultan wishes to make, must be made here! there will be no chance of slipping out of my presence; you must mount and accompany me!"

The royal toilet was as lengthy as the Sultan could make it, but came at last to an end, and Gehangire was led over his slaughtered guards to mount the Khan's elephant. The Sultan's own elephant-driver pressed up to mount and guide the animal; but a sword-stroke from the Khan cut him down; another pressing up, shared the same fate. None of his own attendants, except his cup-bearer was allowed him.

While this was taking place, Noor Jehan (the Queen's title in later years) disguised herself as an ordinary woman of the country, entered a common dingy palkee and passed through the Khan's army, as a woman belonging to the camp, and reached the imperial troops in safety. The next morning she led out the royal army and marched to rescue the Emperor.

The bridge of boats over the river Jhelum had been destroyed by the Khan's soldiers; and the Empress, and her brother, supported by the principal commanders of the imperial army, were obliged to lead their forces over a narrow ford lower down. She was mounted on a royal war-elephant, with her grandchild in the howdah, as sultans in those days were accustomed to go into battle. With this advance detachment she gained the opposite bank, where a furious conflict soon raged around her. The river ford was deep and dangerous, the detachment was in a state of confusion, and the main body of the army as it advanced to support her, was driven step by step down the bank to the water, where a terrific hand-to-hand encounter ensued. The Empress's elephant-driver and attendants were all killed, and her brother was taken prisoner by the enemy; her elephant received a sword-cut on the proboscis, rushed wildly into the water, and swam down the river, carrying the Empress and her grandchild in the howdah, until the sagacious beast finally effected a safe landing. Noor Jehan now gave up trying to rescue the Emperor by force, and humbly petitioned the Khan, to allow her to share his captivity, to which that chief consented, thinking it was decidedly safer to have her in his own keeping than to risk the desperate efforts which she might make on behalf of her husband. She had, however, formed her own plans. The royal pair got up some very passable quarrels, in the presence of Mahowhut Khan, and the rebel chief was astonished that a woman who seemed to care so little for her husband when with him, should have been so anxious to rescue him. Gehangire grew very confidential with the chief, and told him he was afraid she wanted to get him out of the way, so that she might raise his fourth son, Sheriar, her daughter's husband, to the throne; suggesting that there ought to be a general review of the army in that part of the realm, when her plot would probably be discovered and steps might be taken to frustrate it.

Now, to the Empress Noor Jehan in the days of her power had been assigned the revenue of a large province, which was required to furnish a certain quota of troops for the royal army, but, as might be expected, this expensive requisition had not often been exacted of the favorite wife; it was hardly to be supposed that she would like to spend her pin-money in equipping soldiers. Gehangire of course knew this, and affecting to be suspicious of her loyalty, in the presence of his captor, swore by the beard of the Prophet (to a Mussulman a very blasphemous oath) that his wife should provide the contingent required of every other subject; whatever troops there were in her territory, must be assembled, there should be no concealment or further evasion.

Noor Jehan, in turn arose, and there was a great amount of indignation and quite a scene between the royal husband and his imperious wife; it was a shame, a burning shame, she said, to make such a demand of her—his queen, his Sultana, his Noor-Mahal,—the waste of money thus entailed would ruin all her plans of planting a broad avenue of shade-trees, all the way from Delhi to Lahore, digging wells, and building houses of rest for travellers at every mile and a half of that distance. The mosques, too, which she desired to build at certain distances, for the establishment of prayers, according to the law of the Prophet, could then never be erected. No, she would not be compelled, like any petty rajah or commander in the army to waste her money, on the equipment and payment of troops. She did not profanely mention the beard of the Prophet, but her mental resolve was as firmly formed as if she had taken the most solemn oath; probably in her secret heart she was gloating over the idea of the cudgelling her Afghans of the hills of Roh would give those Rajpoots and this hated Khan, the Punjabees and Marwarees.

It fell out as she expected. The contingent from her territory was mustered, notwithstanding her pretended opposition. They crossed the Indus at the old ford of Attock, where all the conquering hordes, under Semiramis, Alexander, Seleucus, Mohammed Cassim, Mohammed of Ghazni, down to Timorlane and Baber, had come like the besom of destruction—though this appeared to be only a common summer excursion—and they took their way up that grand old Khyber pass.

The Afghans began to sniff the freedom of their native hills and once when the Rajpoots fell out with a small foraging party of Afghans and killed nearly all of them, their leader demanded justice from Mahowhut Khan, who however answered him evasively. The next day the Afghans fell upon detachments of Rajpoots to avenge the Mussulmans that had been slain; the fight spread to the camp, and the rebellious Khan was in mortal fear, and fled to his prisoners for safety.

The day came at last for the great review of Noor Jehan's contingent; the Afghans had gathered from the hills, they had come, as the ants and the locusts come, and the Queen had been allowed to go away to superintend the muster. The Emperor, after the skirmish in the camp, had become very solicitous for the safety of his jailer, the rebellious Khan, and told him, that he would not quite like to take the responsibility of having such a highly-valued friend ride with him along the Afghan lines of troops, in their present state of excitement. A subordinate officer, a deputy-commander of the Rajpoots that guarded the Emperor wherever he went, would be sufficiently respectful and would honor his exalted rank. So the Khan remained at a little distance off, at the head of the Rajpoots, while the Emperor and the deputy rode along the line of Noor Jehan's contingent. As he approached the centre of this line of stern Moslem troopers they opened and the Emperor rode in and was free! The Noor Mahal commanded there; and all his old Mohammedan troops were posted at convenient distances. There was no particular quarrel between Gehangire and the Empress now; the pretended quarrel was over, the royal couple reconciled. It was a bloodless victory; but freedom was just as sweet as if it had been purchased on the battle-field.

The Khan now clearly saw through the deception and knew that he had been out-generaled; he moved his troops away rather quickly to a strong position, where he might venture to open a treaty with his late prisoners and secure forgiveness for his audacity.

The lord-treasurer, the Queen's brother, Asaph Khan, was yet in his power, and through his means reconciliation was brought about, and the rebel obtained his pardon.

The next summer-excursion was made to the valley of Cashmere, and there Gehangire was seized by a deadlier foe —paralysis; he attempted to return to Delhi, but died on the way and was buried at Lahore. Then followed a contest between his two sons for possession of the empire; Shiriar was slain and Shah Jehan came to the throne. Noor Jehan survived the Emperor about twenty years, and spent her great wealth in useful public works.

* * * *

When we visited Burdwan, we stayed at the only hotel in the place, which is of very diminutive proportions, but they gave us a good bed and well-served meals. There is here, also, a Dak, or travellers'-bungalow, an institution peculiar to India. It grew out of the wants of the servants of the government; officers, civil and military, must travel at all seasons of the year to distant stations among people who sincerely believed that even the shadow of a European would defile their dirty huts. So the government erected substantial buildings of brick and stucco, containing several suites of apartments; each suite is designed to accommodate a family or an individual, and consists of a sitting-room, bedroom and bath-room. Those rooms are only equipped with heavy furniture, such as matting on the floor, a bedstead with a bottom of cane or listing, sufficiently soft and cool for that warm climate, a table and chairs, wash-stand and ewer, and the bathroom is fitted with 'chattahs' of water ready for a *douche* bath.

Whether one stops at the hotel or at the travellers'-bungalow, it is indispensable, if he would wish to live there without contracting disease, to carry his own bedding; that is, sheets and a large blanket, or woollen shawl, which, with a rubber pillow that can be readily inflated, are all that one requires. Never by any means should the traveller omit to have a good supply of towelling and napkins, and a change at least of table-linen, drinking-glasses, knives, forks, and spoons. The price of the rooms is regulated by the government-agent at a fixed tariff; one rupee if you stay but an hour to get a meal, and two rupees for twenty-four hours. Each of these bungalows has a few servants, who are kept there by the agent, and also a Khansamah, or housekeeper, who also acts as cook, and will buy anything in the market, that one may choose to order, and will render a proper account, adding a small charge to compensate him for his trouble. This will give a tolerably correct idea of the accommodations to be found in any part of India, outside of the great seaboard cities. One does not meet with sumptuous fare, but at the same time he need not suffer for any rational want. Of course there are in such places, as elsewhere, innumerable petty vexations and disappointments such as are the lot of travelers in every country ; Hindustan is not an exception to the general rule.

Having taken our rooms, when tiffin (mid-day meal) had been served, we sallied out to view the show-places of the Rajah of Burdwan.

We drove first to the new palace, which is furnished and upholstered in the latest European style. Indeed the whole establishment, exterior and interior, looked so very foreign by the side of Oriental architecture and Hindoo temples, that one could almost believe that one of the old Magi, who used to travel about on flying carpets, had picked up a moderate-sized palace on the continent of Europe, and had dropped it in the vicinity of a Hindoo city, while flying over it. It looked like a stranger, so sharply was it contrasted with its surroundings. The houses of the Rajah's servants elbow it very closely.

No members of the Rajah's family ever reside in this palace; it is in the common phrase, a show-place, where he entertains European guests in European style. The floors of the grand drawing-room, picture-gallery and dining-hall, were of grey-and-white marble; the tables, chairs, sofas, and other articles of furniture, were all of Paris or London make, and of course had no novel attractions to us. The dining-hall contained portraits of the Rajah's family. We noticed one of himself, and one of a younger brother, taken when dressed in a long 'chupkin,' or coat, of white merino trimmed with a sort of gold trimming called 'kincob.' The head-gear was a sort of brimless hat, covered with gold embroidery.

LIFE AMONG THE LOWLY IN BENGAL.

The gallery contained, I should judge, three or four hundred pictures, all modern; but they did not interest us as much as the ivory miniatures; among which was one of the Noor-Mahal—Noor Jehan. As it is very like the one in the first king of Oudh's tomb, at Lucknow, it probably was copied from it; there was also one of Rungeet Singh, the last king of Lahore of any ability; also one of Nana Sahib, who planned the butchery at Cawnpore, during the mutiny of 1857.

In the throne-room, or Durbar-hall, the floor, at the time of our visit, was then in process of being laid in a tessellated pattern, similar to the one in the palace of St. Cloud before the Communists fired it. The Rajah's state-chair is a gilt and plaster concern—the gilding was rapidly falling off, making it look about as dilapidated as the old coronation-chair in Westminster Abbey, without having any of the worm-eaten antiquity of that interesting relic. A gallery runs round part of the room, showing that when his Highness did not choose to occupy it, it could be used for theatrical representations and the Nautch-girls' dance; royalty looking on from the gallery.

The Dilkhoose palace is built on the margin of one of the largest of the large pools or tanks of water found in this region, which seemed to be blessed with a greater number of them than any other place along the route. Stone ghâts, or steps, led down to the water, and gave to these miniature lakes a finished substantial look. On the cool margin, among the shrubbery was a herd of two or three hundred tame deer.

In the gardens adjoining, among the trees, were some of the gentler animals of the Rajah's large menagerie, which he maintains at a cost of eight thousand rupees per month.

As we were making the circuit of the garden, we came to a couple of contiguous pits where a gnu, and some other horned animals were having a free fight all to themselves. The door between them had been pushed aside and the gnu's intruding visitor appeared to be getting the worst of it. Possibly it was only a mild sort of rehearsal of parts which they were to perform in the evening at the after-dinner entertainment, before distinguished visitors. A little further on were lions, tigers, bears, wolves, hyenas, etc., a whole list of fierce wild beasts, confined in strong cages. Under the old *régime* it is said an evening entertainment was not considered *comme il faut* without at least one combat between a tiger and a buffalo—the common animals of the country; if anything more fierce was to be had, so much rarer the sport. The Dilkhoose was occupied at the time of our visit and strangers were not admitted.

What a novel treat it would be indeed, to pass freely through the palace of such a wealthy Hindoo prince, and understand all its quaint and curious appointments, just as they stand ready for the occupants to use. The Burdwan family are Hindoos of the Hindoos, and like many other families along their sacred rivers, could boast of great antiquity at the time when the Druids were sacrificing in Stonehenge.

It puzzles one to see how the Buddhist religion ever spread, as it has done, so as to embrace so many millions of people; since its professors never make proselytes or receive converts. How did it begin? There are at this place one hundred and eight temples of the god Siva, the destroyer. It hardly seems possible that men of this family, possessing as they do so much intelligence, can worship such disgusting idols. Over there among the trees arose the spires of a Christian place of worship, showing that the ark had come to Beth-Dagon. The railway close by, with all its faults, is bringing progressive ideas, and slowly, but surely, lifting the curtains and introducing the blessings of western civilization—free-schools and other means of educating the masses of the people; in good time it will be said, there is light in the home of Dagon.

I can almost forgive the natives the worship of the Ganges; for a part of the year it is a broad, majestic, rapid river, and captivates the imagination and arouses whatever reverence there may be in the soul, for the sublime in nature. But the worship of this monster Siva, or Kahlee—I believe she is called by both names—feasting on human flesh; or as she is frequently represented, just staying her appetite a little, by eating an infant — this puzzles me; it is decidedly further down in the mire, than I can understand any phase of human nature, and certainly does come very near the lowest depths of degradation. As might be expected from the number of temples dedicated to Siva, this was once holy ground for the Thugs, her fanatical devotees.

It is said that the tank opposite the Christian church, on the right-hand side of the road, was very frequently used by the Thugs to hide the bodies of travellers, murdered by those monsters in human shape, as they came on their pious pilgrimages along the Grand Trunk road, over which formerly passed nearly the whole travel of India. From Calcutta it stretched up through this valley, a distance of one thousand six hundred miles across the Indus to Peshawur and the historic Khyber Pass. An enterprising Thug, once on this road, was sure to become very devoted to Siva, and very rich and prosperous, until Colonel Sleeman, the English avenger, overtook him. This officer was as thorough as St. Patrick, in banishing these vipers from the face of the earth; there was, however, a remnant of them saved for a time. We saw a high-walled enclosure, like a little city or fortress, in Rajpootana, where four or five thousand Thugs, including all their families, old and young, male and female, who had been convicted of Thugism, were placed and closely guarded. In later years a few have been allowed to come out on ticket-of-leave; but on breaking any law of the realm they could be hung for the old crime without further trial.

The hotel stands near the margin of a very large tank or reservoir, not less than four hundred feet on each side. The usual stone ghâts are on one side; the other three sides appear to be only earth, probably fine clay beaten down, layer after layer, until it is capable of holding water for a long time. Its inviting banks had beckoned me the day before, to walk under the wide-spreading peepul trees, (a sacred tree of the Hindoos) and the Indian elm or senna trees; but the sun was too hot then, and the grey dawn of the next morning was the first suitable opportunity for a visit to its banks. A stately elephant marched out from among the trees on the margin, and went past me, carrying his mahout perched upon his head between his ears. I watched them until they reached the further side; at that distance the driver appeared about the size of an ape. Some few of the hotel servants were standing in the margin of the water, with their praying-cups in their hands while they said their prayers. On the left men were irrigating a garden by the basket method—two men standing a little apart down the bank, holding the end of a rope which was attached to a platted palm-leaf basket; slacking the rope, the basket fell into the water and filled; giving the rope a sudden jerk together, brought it up, sending the water out of it into a little pool higher up the bank, where two more men were stationed, who threw their basket in such a manner as to dash the water into a furrow or trench running through the garden. This mode of irrigation is a modified form of the Egyptian shadoof.

I walked down to the garden and looked over the hedge, and recognized some old friends, garden vegetables of the temperate zone, growing here without rain in the month of January. The sun in summer scorches their leaves to tinder in a few hours. The pease, beets, and carrots seemed to thrive as well on the moisture that the water-baskets brought to their roots as if it had first fallen in showers on the plants themselves.

We left Burdwan and were soon all aboard the train once more, rattling across the plains and rumbling over bridges; but there were no forests here to scream through; we were travelling towards the hill-country. We passed over some stupendous bridges. One just before entering Burdwan, boasted of two hundred and eighty arches, built entirely of brick; we only had a distant glimpse of it after passing.

We crossed the Adjar river on a fine bridge of thirty-six

arches, of fifty feet span each. We left the rice-fields behind us and were soon nearing the highlands; a branch of Vyndhya hills, which stretches up from the southeast, and crosses the Ganges at Rajmahal. These hills are of volcanic origin; one of them sends forth clouds of smoke, so hot that any combustible with which it comes in contact quickly takes fire. A branch-railway strikes off here for Rajmahal. Every mile of ground in the vicinity is haunted by old traditions; it was thickly peopled when Abraham lived under the oak at Mamre, by tribes which still linger among northern mountain fastnesses, and who make pilgrimages to the old ruined sites of ancient cities and temples, in the same way as the Jews go up to Jerusalem to die within its walls and lay their bones in its sacred soil.

It was at Rajmahal that the infamous Surajah Dowlah was captured; he who placed his prisoners, that awful night, in the "Black Hole" at Calcutta. After the battle of Plassey, during which his vizier went over to the English with nearly the whole of Surajah's army, he thought it was time to make a quiet little trip up the Ganges: somewhere out of the way of the English and the vizier, whom they helped into the office of Nawab of Moorshedabad. For this latter piece of good service Meer Jaffier, the new-made king, gave the East India Company an immense sum of money and a large extent of territory round Calcutta, with the privilege of driving out the French from their possessions on the Hooghly river, if they could. When Surajah Dowlah had reached Rajamahal, his few boatmen mutinied; they had some scruples about rowing the fugitive tyrant out of the way of his pursuers, in short they had learned that another king sat on his throne, who would, doubtless, pay more for their delay than they would get for rowing. Surajah Dowlah then attempted to escape by disguising himself in a peasant's garb and hiding in a deserted walled garden, where he was captured by his pursuers, in this once splendid city.

This city was long the residence of the Mogul Viceroy in the palmy days of Shah Jehan and Aurungzebe. Suja, the brother of the latter, built a splendid palace in the vicinity of a beautiful waterfall, called the Mootee Ghurra or Cascade of the Pearl House. It was probably at this palace that the ill-starred marriage between Aurungzebe's eldest son Mohammed, and the daughter of Shuja, was celebrated. They had been betrothed when mere children, at their grand-fathers's palace at Delhi. When the conspiracies of Shah Jehan's four sons culminated in his dethronement, the expulsion and death of the heir-apparent, and the usurpation of the throne by Aurungzebe; the latter could not feel safe, though Morad, his fellow-conspirator, was confined by his orders in the state-prison at Gwalior, for his brother Shuja was still at large, having taken up his abode in the Viceroy's palace in Bengal.

The imperial army under Mohammed and one of the old, trusted commanders, was sent after Shuja. When the army approached the Viceroy's palace, an interview was brought about between Mohammed and his uncle. Mohammed was about twenty years of age, and may be excused if he forgot the warrior and the throne, and when in the vicinity of his fair cousin began to play the part of a lover. The dream of love aroused all the emotions of his early manhood, with resistless force; what were his father's schemes for power and lust of blood? had he not seen his grandsire in his hopeless imprisonment, and his father pass to the throne over the bleeding bodies of three of his near kinsmen?

How painful his thoughts must have been during those few days of anxious deliberation, it is difficult for us, so differently circumstanced, to imagine. One day he forgot the throne, his father's plans and the army, and went over to Shuja's and married his betrothed bride. His dream of happiness was short, however, and he soon found that his father was determined to destroy him as well as his uncle. The wily Aurungzebe contrived to have a letter fall into the hands of Shuja, purporting to be an acceptance of an offer that had emanated from Mohammed to betray Shuja, his father-in-law, into Aurungzebe's hands. This brought on the young man his uncle's distrust and suspicion, and resulted in their final estrangement and separation. Shuja pursued his lonely flight to Assam, where he soon after died. Mohammed now had no resource left him except to endeavor to make his peace with his father. But Aurungzebe was never known to really forgive anyone who at any time had offended him, or who had done him an ill turn, and in the case of his eldest son and heir, he made no exception to his general rule. Mohammed was sent to that counterpart of the Bastile, the fortress of Gwalior, where an uncle and two cousins were already imprisoned, and there he and they lingered out their lives.

Twenty-five miles beyond the opposite bank of the Ganges are the ruins of Maldah, an ancient city extending a distance of eighteen miles in length by six in breadth. Broken arches and fallen towers, which still attest the skill of the former inhabitants lie scattered over the plain. The lofty gateway yet stands in the ruined wall, and a mosque lined with black marble very elaborately carved, shows dimly something of its former splendor. It was another of the old royal cities of Gour, the former name of Bengal, and already had a long history, reaching far away into the dim past, when the Afghan rule was first established in the valley of the Ganges, about the year 1193. Two or three centuries ago the Ganges ran close under its old walls, and its vast population daily bathed and worshipped in the sacred waters. But one day during the rainy season the river ploughed for itself a new channel down by Rajmahal, and all the people followed their water-god to that place, only to have it desert them there in the course of time, and their descendants are now piously waiting for the river to come back to them.

There is always a charm about the ruins of an old deserted city, which one knows has been the theatre in which much past human history has been enacted; the heart will ever vibrate to the same thoughts and feelings that actuated those who have turned to dust long ago.

At Sahibgunge we were all eager to get our first view of the real Ganges, for it must be remembered that the Hooghly is only one of its numerous mouths. The scenery here begins to change, the hills are now in sight, the rocks on the river-banks and hill-sides are honeycombed with cells, where Hindoo, and Buddhist, and Moslem saints have burrowed, one after the other, through a period of twenty-five centuries, from the time when Gaudama wandered through this region, uttering the first protest against the Brahminical religion. Lank, cadaverous-looking old men, bowed and bent with long-continued abstinence, make pilgrimages to these places and weep and pray, over old ruined temples and cells, in a very edifying manner.

Every city in this vicinity yielded to the preaching of Gaudama; caste was banished for the time, and men of wealth, nobles and kings, vied with each other in building monasteries, where men led studious lives and instructed the youth of their own sex. Women, too, heard him and caught his inspirations, and wished to study the "Greatest Good;" and monasteries — prototypes of the convents of later centuries — were erected, that they might enjoy similar facilities for instruction.

Gaudama's religion was never enforced like Mohammed's at the point of the sword; though he died at the age of fifty-five, yet he had lived long enough to see his doctrines spread all through this great valley, and after his death those well-trained missionaries Thauna and Onttara, travelled as far as Burmah in the year 306, B. C. Ceylon and Java received the faith a little later. It must have spread with great rapidity, for before the birth of Mohammed, Buddhist pilgrims came from China to the fatherland of their Buddha; and, with book in hand, made such accurate descriptions and measurements, that from their diaries the sites of long-lost cities have been recently discovered, and *savans* have been able to construct a tolerably accurate geography of this region in ancient times. They were no swiftly-flitting travellers; they came to copy the religious books, and with their patient Chinese habits, they collected and subsequently carried home with them all the knowledge that could be gleaned from the countries and places where the founder of this religion had lived and taught. Fa-Hian came in the second century of our era, and remained three years in India and two in Ceylon, and then visited Java. Two hundred years later came another Chinese pilgrim, Hwen-Tsang, with note-book in hand, on the same pious errand as the former, and spent *sixteen* years in his researches. They both passed through Thibet and Tartary, and crossed that part of the Himalayan range, called the Hindoo Kush; they entered by the way of Cabool and Peshawar, crossed the Indus at Attook; and thence passed over to the Ganges Valley, very minutely examining as they went all the places mentioned in the Buddhist writings; visiting Benares, Paliboothra, and the sacred places in South Behar. Patna, according to the diary of Hwen-Tsang, is on the site of that grand old city Sandracottus, where the old Greek ambassador, Magasthenes, came to arrange the treaty for Seleucus, the general who received the eastern part of Alexander's empire. It has been questioned whether it was the actual site of the city, for the Greek describes a river uniting with the Ganges larger than would answer to that in this vicinity, and some are therefore to fix the locality at Allahabad.

Patna must have fallen little by little, as the long list of centuries passed over her, for she is still a populous city, though nothing is left to attest her ancient grandeur. The pilgrims of old are precise in stating their course from point to point and from river to river; they passed to the western bank of the Gunduck, then turned south, parallel with that stream, and then crossed the Ganges to Paliboothra, or Pataliboothra,—for both names are applied to the same city,—and Patna is supposed to be derived from the latter.

The Buddha Gaudama, was a king's son, whose capital stood on the banks of the Gogra at some distance nearly north of Benares, where he was sent to be educated, and where he renounced the Brahminical religion, whose oppressive absurdities disgusted and pained him. He retired into a forest to study the "Greatest Virtue," or "Greatest Good;" there he developed the purest moral code ever set forth by man unaided by inspiration. He renounced his kingly inheritance, gave all his wealth to the poor, and led a wandering life of humility.

The bridge across the river Soane, is a very solid structure; the cars rolled slowly over twenty-eight arches, each having a span of one hundred and fifty feet. The river here must be more than a mile in width during the rains, judging from the extent of sand on either side of the now shrunken stream. Railroad-bridges in India, on account of the great rise in the rivers, are built with the utmost regard for the strength and solidity of the foundations. Those of the bridge over the Soane are said to go down thirty feet below low water level. The coach-compartment-cars, used on these lines of rail, are certainly pleasant, if a small party of acquaintances can have one to themselves, as we had thus far, for we felt quite at home and were able to read, write, and enter into, conversation, without the intrusion or observation of strangers.

VIEW OF BENARES.

CHAPTER VIII.

BENARES; THE ETERNAL CITY.

IF any city in the world can truly merit the title—the Eternal City—it is this Jerusalem of the Hindoos.

What a motley crowd is now being landed on the platform. Three-fourths of them are pilgrims, who do not make their way here slowly and painfully, as in former times, traversing many weary leagues of distance, to perform some vow at one or more of the thousand temples that the city, on the opposite bank of the river, is said to contain. Now they come with railway speed, regardless of proximity to a lower caste person. The greater number of these pilgrims have a lean, hungry, anxious look; and if appearances are any indication of the inner life, I should judge a good hearty meal would do them vastly more good than a bath in the Ganges, or wasting their food and substance on oblations; one would think it was almost sufficient penance to live on boiled rice without denying themselves even that.

The baggage that had been landed on this platform would create quite a furore if landed on the stage of any comic theatre in the western world. One would think that Falstaff's ragged regiment had turned pilgrims and come to Benares. It looks as though Brahma, Vishnu, and Siva had all passed a very sleepless, busy night, commanding one follower after another, to take up his bed and walk.

There comes a portly Baboo *gentleman*; he has none of that haggard look, which darkens the countenances of his fellow-pilgrims; his conscience appears easy, and the amount of flesh on his bones indicates that he is neither a poor nor a half-fed pilgrim; if indeed he is a pilgrim at all; very possibly he may not be. Over his cashmere dress, this chilly morning he wears a quilted, scarlet bed-spread. He walks with a considerable amount of conscious dignity, followed by two servants; the first carries his bed, consisting of sundry quilts and cushions, and the second bears his *cuisine* and brass pot for praying with in the river.

There, again, is the opposite extreme of native Hindoo life, pouring out of that third-class car; a sort of three-story tenant-packing house. There is not the slightest approach to trunk, box, or travelling-bag, among the crowd; but each one has a queer little bundle of traps, consisting of his lota, or prayer-pot, and if he pretends to any earthly possessions at all, he will have them all stowed away somewhere about him, and the bundle will constitute his bed at night, or if very poor or very fanatical, he may perhaps only carry a rag, or a bit of coarse woollen blanket. Quilted cotton "comfortables" are so numerous, and bare arms and legs, so persistently thrust themselves out from all shades of white cotton cloth, that the whole throng has much the appearance of having been suddenly ordered out of bed.

The Ganges at Benares is bridged with boats, which rise and fall with the water at the different seasons of the year. In the month of January the stream reaches its lowest mark, and consequently we found by far the larger number of the boats embedded in the sand, at unequal depths, giving a delightful corduroy surface to the bridge. We drove to the Victoria Hotel; a house of modest dimensions to be named after a Queen—I should say, the Empress of India. I begin to suspect from seeing so many great names on small houses, that our American fondness for "big" titles is a part of our old-world inheritance; we were, however, very comfortable at her majesty's hotel. As usual in Oriental cities a number of guides were on the alert to meet us; they seemed to 'snuff' a stranger from afar. This one who appropriated our luggage was a graduate of the Victoria

College at Benares, a very intelligent man, but a Hindoo still; he was very ready to leave the stall where he sold books, to act as guide, for five rupees per day.

Very many of the streets of this city are too narrow for a carriage to pass through them; in fact, by extending the arms one may touch the houses on both sides of the way. We were advised to charter an elephant of the commissioner, as the best mode of locomotion, and the one usually employed here, for passing through the streets. However, on applying to the agent, for the government owns all the elephants, there were none to be obtained that day; so a gharry was substituted. I should mention that the European portion of the inhabitants are located at Secrole, a suburb about four miles from the bridge across the Ganges.

There is a wide "Maidan" or parade-ground, which we overlook from the hotel. It has a dreary Sahara-like look, as though all vegetable life had long ago become discouraged and died out, excepting bunches of reed grass called the *silkie*. If trees ever grew on this holy ground, they were long ago translated to the celestial bowers of Vishnu. The cavalry and infantry lines, the civil-offices, the post-office and church are all located so as to overlook the maidan. There is a small river that empties into the Ganges, on this side of the town. The dwelling-houses, with their wide verandahs, stand in a garden of tropical trees, and look cool and breezy contrasted with the dry, glistening sand of the ground without. Good English roads lead in various directions.

We drove into the city to the great bazaar, where some festival appeared to be in progress, for every available foot of space was crowded with human beings. Looking up the street, over the gaily colored crowd, red, yellow, and white predominated to such an extent as to recall the trite comparison of a bed of tulips, only these were very exaggerated tulips, each with a little glittering skull cap on the top. The carriage had proceeded about half way through the street, when coachee came to a stop, whether for us to view the crowd, or for the crowd to view us, was at first rather difficult for us to decide. Finally we came to the sage conclusion that a thousand persons could do a thousand times more gazing than one, so we motioned coachee to drive on, but he did not pay the slightest attention to our polite request. Then we called the guide and asked if that was the best he could do for us, for if so we should have no further use for him; if we spent the day there in the carriage coachee would know the way back to our hotel without him. He listened attentively and was soon seen elbowing the throng about the little pony, and then the gharry began to move.

We had gone but a short distance further in the direction of the Golden Temple, when he came to the door and said the street was too narrow to admit of the carriage passing through, and that we should be obliged to walk. So we alighted and walked down a street, with a dead brick wall on the right, so narrow that one might have thought it was a cellar passage, but for the bright blue sky above. However, we soon discovered that on our right was the wall of the temple court, and we moved in that direction. In order to get a good view of the top of the temple, which is the chief architectural attraction, we were shown up to the second-floor verandah, of the house on the opposite side of the way. As we were going up we noticed a low-caste servant perched on a balustrade, quite out of our way, but on seeing him the guide muttered something between his teeth; and then went over to him, and gave him a push with his foot that sent the poor man down on the stones in the street below. I expressed surprise at such harsh treatment of any human being, but the guide shrugged his shoulders, saying: "He is only a low-caste fellow."

We obtained a good position to look down into the temple enclosure. The temple-proper is a very moderate-sized building, it has neither dome nor spire, strictly speaking. It has three pyramidal towers, but the lines on the sides are not straight, they swell from base to summit, but not enough to dignify them with the name of domes. No command of the decalogue had been broken by the builders, for they are not made "in the likeness of anything in the heavens above or the earth beneath." But when seen, they are readily distinguished as the roof of a mundra or temple. Two of these towers are made of gilded copper, and were constructed in England, — the work shows that for itself, as the natives do not understand the galvanic method of gilding.

We entered the temple enclosure; there is nothing striking about the gateway, it might lead into any ordinary yard; it is dirty and damp, and noticeable only for its musty, mouldy smell. Sacred cows, which are treated with great reverence by the Hindoos, meet one at every turn. A Hindoo would consider his life in this world richly rewarded if, at his death, his spirit might be permitted to enter and inhabit one of these grass-eating bovines. What noble aspirations must actuate the hearts of these devotees! Constant kindness to these animals has made them exceedingly tame and gentle, yet I should feel a decided objection to be mixed in with a crowd of them.

The temple itself stands on a platform, and consists of three rooms, each not more than twelve feet square. There is no ornamental work on the interior of any of them; everything is as plain as a prison wall. In each is a stone cylinder three or four feet high, rounded at the top, and rising from a stone basin sunk in the floor. Offerings of rice or flowers are laid on the cylinder, on which the priest pours some water from the Ganges, which washes the offering down through a channel below the floor, flowing out into the sacred well beneath. The devotee then receives a mark on his forehead, equivalent to an assurance he has that day performed 'poojah' or worship. They showed us an image with an elephant's head, called Gunesh—god of wisdom; he had rather a corpulent body, and the four-post chair that he seemed to be squeezed into, appeared essential to keep him from running over and covering a large extent of territory, or perhaps invading the region of some other god, for the 'gods' are rather near neighbors here. The god of wisdom was not much patronized. We did not see anyone inscribing the mark of this 'beast' on their foreheads, at his shrine; I fancy wisdom is somewhat at a discount here. The stone cylinders are called Mahades. This image is the deification of Lingam, or the creative principle.

The Golden Temple was built by Rungeet Singh, the Sikh king of Lahore. He also built a palace, as did almost every other Hindoo Sikh prince in India; no matter what distant part they rule over, they have an interest here; each has built a temple or palace in this city. It seems indeed, to be a popular investment; a prominent palace or ghâts is estimated by them equal to a lot in paradise, since all who die in this city are admitted to heaven without any questions. In an adjoining enclosure, is a flat stone roof supported on columns; it covers the sacred well, the mouth of which is protected by a strong iron grating to prevent those who are too eager for immortality, from jumping down into the very arms of Vishnu, who, as tradition says, leaped down there when the Emperor Aurungzebe pulled down his temple and built this graceful mosque on its site It must be a long time since any living waters came from that well. It is the most offensive pool imaginable, and it is to be devoutly hoped that his godship has not a delicate sense of smell, for he would suffer untold tortures there.

All the flowers, rice and grain, offered by thousands of people, have been washed down through channels into this well for the last two hundred years at least, and perhaps for ages before Aurungzebe disturbed their temple. Another well here called Mankarnika is equally offensive, though it is said to be so holy that there is no sin so heinous that its waters will not immediately efface. I have not the slightest doubt that a drink of it would poison even one of these priests, accustomed though they are to its odors, but as it is safely grated over, only villainous perfume can come up from below. There are, as it has already been stated, nearly or quite, one thousand temples in Benares; very many are

THE TEMPLE OF APES.

attached to palaces, and are in fact, private property. We passed one of those palaces, a small, white marble structure, on one of the narrow streets leading to the ghâts. It was such a pleasant contrast to the damp, foul-smelling place that we had just left, that I lingered awhile to look at it, in great danger of losing sight of the guide and our party, by some turn in the narrow winding street.

The Doorga Kond, or as it is usually called, the Monkey Temple, stands at the upper end of the city, about half an hour's drive from Secrole. This temple stands on the margin of a very spacious tank or reservoir, with massive stone ghâts, or steps leading down to the water; it stands within a walled enclosure. Its graceful tower, in the form of a pyramid, is carved with representations of all the animals which are held sacred in the Hindoo mythology. Clusters of small turrets relieve the stiffness of the straight lines, and elaborate carving harmonizes and softens the whole into comeliness. Strangers are not likely to pass this place without notice; its throng of apes are always on the watch for travelers, and they often drop alone, or in twos and threes, upon a carriage, chattering and playing their antics in a harmless way; but when one comes to the gate the whole tribe turns out to investigate matters, and see what they can appropriate or gain from the visitors. They know how to chatter and clamor for backsheesh, as well as their Hindoo neighbors.

Our guide said that there were four or five hundred of these monkeys in all. We invested a few coin in koll—a kind of parched pease, and some coarse sugar, and gave the whole troop a good meal. The old patriarch of the tribe, hung menacingly over the gateway, as if determined to have no visitors before he and his friends had breakfasted; he came down and mingled with the others in the most amusing scramble we had ever seen for the largest lumps of sugar. They retreated to gnaw and chatter furiously over their gains, when they saw they were not likely to succeed in snatching any more. Several young slips of monkeyhood were in imminent danger of being trampled to death by the throng; however, their wits did not desert them, as human wit often does in an emergency; for they turned over, and as they could not reach the backs of those treading on them, they reached the under side, putting their arms and legs so firmly round the tall fathers of the tribe, that they could not shake them off. Some clutched at them very peevishly, and one went skipping over the wall and up a tree to get rid of this burden, but it was of no use, for baby monkeys know how to hold on, and it made very little difference to them which one they held on to, if one shook them off, they made no ado, but darted under another, and made themselves safer if possible than before. Some of the older ones were huge, strong fellows of tawny yellow color; others wore the small mouse colored, Malacca variety.

While the monkeys were busy with their breakfast, we seized the opportunity to go inside knowing their religious scruples would only be quiet while the sugar lasted. Why do the Hindoo people revere and care for these brutes? do they in some way consider them atoms, or particles of their great ugly monkey-god that captured Ceylon? Had I faith in the Darwinian theory of man's origin I should say that these priests were taking good care of their grandfathers, to whom they have a strong family resemblance. Revering a noble majestic river, such as the Ganges, which bears on its broad placid bosom such floods of temporal blessing to a land on which, for eight months in the year, no cooling drop of rain ever falls, is almost excusable in a people whose minds as yet are but dimly lighted by truth and knowledge; but worshipping a monkey is really inconceivably absurd. The boasted grandeur of human intellect will meet with a most humiliating show at Benares.

The court of this temple is paved with stone; it is wet and littered with offerings. Round the inside of the wall extends an open colonnade, and in the middle of the court, stands the temple, upon a low platform, from which rise stone pillars, which support the tower, the top of which, as

I said before, rises above the wall. The idol which is here enthroned is a disgustingly hideous thing, and it is very difficult to tell why, or for what he is worshipped; but the people are grossly ignorant and debased, utterly incapable of reasoning for themselves, and they submit blindly to the guidance of a priesthood as ignorant as themselves. Their mythology is full of the most absurd contradictions, which these hereditary priests never take pains to explain, or reconcile, nor do they instruct the youth, as the Buddhist priesthood are accustomed to do. To the civilized mind such a condition appears almost impossible; how such abject submission on the part of the people could be perpetuated, and thirty-six centuries of mental stagnation maintained so perfectly, is really a greater wonder than the building of the pyramids.

Twenty-five centuries ago, there came a little tremor over all this dead dullness, a little rift in the mental night. The son of a chief, or prince, came to this city to be educated as befitted his rank, by the priests belonging to the Brahmins' caste. There probably was then no less sin, ignorance or misery than there is now; perhaps there were more shrines to those beastly sensual gods than there are at present, but the people were just as benighted and debased as now. The young man—he was no ordinary youth—studied the problem of humanity, he brought his heart into sympathy with the suffering and misery of men oppressed under the iron heel of caste, at a time when the penalty was death for a Soodra (the lowest caste) to attempt to read the sacred books, or offer in any way the slightest disrespect to the dominant castes. He spent his time in the lonely solitudes in the quiet recesses of the forest, thinking out the mystery of the "Great Good," and his meditations resulted in a system of religion infinitely higher than the Hindoo worship in which he had been educated. He taught the doctrine of *one* Supreme Being whose law was summed up fully, in the practice of the "Great Good." Alas! he knew of no atonement, no Saviour for past sins; the doctrine that he taught, was a deliverance from future transgressions, if mankind would follow the pure morality which might be attained to, by meditation, and fasting, and prayer. He gave to the poor the treasure which he had inherited from the long line of monarchs from whom he claimed descent, and commenced the life of an itinerant teacher; wandering on foot over a large extent of country, along the Ganges and the Dewah or Gogra rivers, toiling, teaching, doing good, and leaving behind him a memorial of his labors which remains even to this day.

Sarnath, only eight miles from the holy city of Vishnu, where Gautama studied when a boy, became one of the principal seats of learning, where his religion in after years was taught. The Buddhist king, Athoka, who wrote his religious edicts on huge, polished stone pillars forty-two feet in height, one of which now stands in the college gardens of this city, lived two hundred and seventy years before the Christian era, and about the same length of time after the death of Buddha. Gautama, died at Magatha, now Behar, about the time that the prophet Daniel was coming into great repute for wisdom, at Babylon, and forty years before Socrates taught, in Greece, the unity of God and the immortality of the soul.

Taking a boat about sunrise, we drop leisurely down the river, taking in, with one sweep of the eye as we float along, the grand panorama on the banks. Massive stone steps lead from the water to the terrace eighty feet above its level, where lofty palaces present an almost continuous front for two miles, among which, the domes and tall minarets of Aurungzebe's mosque are conspicuous objects. It is the grandest and at the same time the most animated river view in this country. The margin of water is crowded with bathers and devotees, for this is one of the holiest places on this holy river, and sunrise is the hour for worship. The bathers are all dressed in white clothes; with heads uncovered and standing waist-deep in the water, they make with great solemnity their offerings of flowers; some seem

A FESTAL DAY ON THE GANGES.

to use a kind of floral rosary which appears very appropriate. All castes are present, princes, pilgrims and horrible old saints, too disgustingly loathsome to describe. The morning air is chilly, and the first plunge in the cold water sends a shiver through the frame, which is at once repressed by a strong mental effort, but the effects are felt with double force after the devotee leaves the water and walks homeward in his wet clothes. On the terrace above the ghâts stands the sacred ox, not an image, but a *bona-fide* bouvine, sleek and fat, looking down serenely on the crowd, as if aware that he was receiving worship and felt flattered by it. I confess that the sight of his godship made my thoughts wander off to beefsteak and breakfast.

We landed and went up the hundred steps leading to the mosque, which twice a day are thronged by pious worshippers ascending and descending. The ghâts are built of very compact brown stone; they are worn very smooth with the constant patter of bare feet for many centuries, until even the hard stone has worn away. On them are displayed all sort of wares, a thousand and one trinkets, from a bangle for the ankles, or a penny ring for the nose, to a jewel for a prince. Gold filigree jewelry, polished pebbles, attar of roses, paintings on ivory, and household goods, are sold here on the upper part of the ghâts. The vender comes and spreads his mat, and raises a huge umbrella; instead of rent he pays a clerk, for so we will call him, to hold this cloth roof over him. He is now established in business here—for this one hour—the next, he may find a more eligible location; or he may espy some stray tourists whose steps he will haunt until he drives a bargain with them. The musjid, or mosque of Aurungzebe does not present its front to the river. The reason for this doubtless is, that the worshipper *must* face the west at prayer, he *must* look towards Mecca—if not, it is all waste time. This requires the back or dead-wall of the building with the kiblah in it to face the west, while the end fronts the river.

The mosques in this country are unlike those of Egypt or

Constantinople, in form. Here, the mosque always opens on a cloistered court-yard, with the inseparable tank in the centre, for the ablution of the faithful, before prayer. The outside walls of the whole enclosure are without windows or openings of any kind, except the gateways which are usually very grand in their way. This one is not as imposing as many others on account of the limited space allotted to it.

The musjid of Aurungzebe was not built because there was such a place of worship needed by actual believers at that time in Benares, but as a memorial of Aurungzebe's victories, and the triumph of Mahomedan faith and arms over Brahminism. His predecessors had been very tolerant; for three successive reigns the Hindoo temple and the mosque flourished together; at least the mosque did not oppress the temple; for it is said that during that time no Hindoo suffered death for his religion. But when the bigoted fratricide seized the throne, he pursued a very different course, and oppressed those who differed from him in religion. The Hindoos were taxed so much *per capitum*, for the privilege of worshipping in their own way. His army in the Deccan plundered the temples and broke the images. On this site where the musjid now stands, once stood a temple of the Hindoo god Vishnu, which he in the pride of his victory pulled down and in its place erected this religious monument. The dispossessed Brahmins had now to find some plausible reason for removing their temple to another locality; so they said, his Godship, disturbed by the pulling down of his house, after mature deliberation, gave one great leap and jumped down the Gyan-Bapi—the sacred well in the adjoining enclosure—and passed underground to the Golden Temple before mentioned. This Temple is built of the same reddish-brown stone as the ghâts; it comes from Chunar, I believe, and is used very much in this country for building purposes.

The mosque itself is a high-arched colonnade connected by three great arches with the court, the central arch being much larger than the others. The court presented a very lonely appearance; there was not a single worshipper there. The roof is flat, and is surmounted by three domes, which are supported by the arches below. The most prominent features of this building are the graceful minarets that rise from each side to the height of more than one hundred and forty-seven feet from the terraced floor of the musjid, which distance, added to the height of the ghâts, makes a total of two hundred and twenty-seven feet from the water. These minarets spring from a base only eight feet three inches in diameter. Though so very slender, there is a winding stair of one hundred and thirty steps leading to the little kĭŏsk on the top, from which a splendid view of the country is obtained. You look down upon the roofs of the city dwellings, the most of which are flat, and into queer little corners, where native life goes on the even tenor of its way—men sewing, men spinning silk up in very breezy places. There was something refreshing in sitting down in this place, so severely chaste, dedicated to Allah, the same Jehovah whom we worship, where there were no images of beastly, sensual gods staring at one, nor anything to offend the most chaste mind. Certainly any one might pray here.

After our surfeit of Hindoo gods, sacred wells, mahadoes, sacred oxen, and sacred river, I felt like thanking God for such a reformer as Mahomet; and I never before realized what a vast stride forward, all Asia took, the day he first denounced the images in his own city. Gautama's religion was a reform which we can only correctly estimate, by weighing the character of the man and the moral code he taught, by the character of the Hindoo gods and their laws. Mahomet's religion was as much higher than Buddhism, as the worship of God is higher than the adoration of men. Doubtless some rumor of the wonder-working, all-powerful God of the Jews, had reached Mahomet, and he wrought on that imperfect report.

The Observatory of Jei Singh, a nobleman of Hindoo origin, was built in 1680, yet it is said to be the oldest authentic building in this ancient city, which dates back, according to Hindoo books, to its founder king Kasika, who, it is supposed, then ruled over this country, and if Hindoo chronology is of any value, must have been cotemporary with the Pharaohs of Egypt. He was commanded by Vishnu, about sixteen centuries before the Christian era, to build a city on this holy spot, and on this particular side of the river, and was promised that all who were so fortunate as to die within its limits should pass immediately to heaven, without further transmigration of the soul. Vishnu denounced, in equally decided terms, all who should live or build on the opposite bank. It is quite probable that king Kasika did not own any land over there. The railway station buildings are the only ones that rear their contumacious fronts, to-day, on that side of the river. No Hindoo, during all those long centuries, has ever raised his habitation there. The building material of those days must have been of a very destructible kind, as few remains or ruins are visible.

The Observatory is a square stone building, somewhat dilapidated. The chief attraction is on the roof, where, engraved on stone, are several charts of the heavens, and a map of the world which represents the earth as a flat surface resting on an elephant, and the elephant standing on a tortoise. What the tortoise stands upon, has not yet been determined; the poor creature has apparently a poor footing, with a heavy load upon his back. There was no difference of opinion among the people as to the mountain which appears in the centre of this map of the world, for the Ganges flowed from the foot of it, and they all knew where the Ganges was. In short, they considered themselves about as near the axis of the universe, as the Boston people are wont to do. Did they not see the sun go around them every day.

This Rajpoot prince had a passion for astronomy: and besides the observatory above spoken of, he built another at his own capitol, Jeipoor; and he is said to have been the founder of the one at Delhi, built nearly forty years later.

Both of these institutions were endowed by their founder; but their revenues have long since been plundered.

Victoria college in this city is a fine gothic building, surrounded by well laid out grounds and gardens. It contains a museum which, I should judge, was a collection worthy of more care than it seemed to receive. The manual labor required in the care of the college and surroundings is performed by natives, low caste fellows, who have not the slightest conception that dust is a detriment to anything, they have such a strong and deep affection for it themselves. Our visit was on a holiday, and we saw no class exercises. I think there were no pupils residing in the building, they lived at their own homes, and were what are termed day scholars. The instruction is free, and the attendance is quite full, we were told. It is supported by the government. It has a library which contains many rare old oriental manuscripts, which afford great facilities for studying the Pali, Sanscrit, Yamul and Persian tongues. The last mentioned, though never the venacular, was the polite language, while the first three were written languages of the different sections of the country. The Ovrdoo is a sort of commercial compound of all of them put together, and forms a kind of circulating medium that grew out of the wants of the army of the Empire.

In the complicated system by which England rules over so many nations, with so many languages and a multitude of dialects, they long ago adopted a system of competitive examinations. For every petty office in the army or in the civil service of the Indian Government, the young Englishman coming out, before entering on duty, must pass examination in one of these languages; and with every promotion, a new examination is required. One gentleman, who had been in the service twenty years, was telling us of a very desirable position which had been offered to him. On receiving our congratulations, he said: "The rub is, I am compelled to study more Sanscrit, and as I am more than fifty years old, that will not be easy for me now."

Near by we saw the noted Monolith, one of the edict columns of King Athoka, which I have alluded to before. The grandfather of this king was the Sandrocottus mentioned in Greek history, as king of Palibothra; with whom Seleucus Nicator formed a *prudent* treaty, when he met him on the Indus river with an army of 600,000 men; promising to leave him in quiet possession of his own country, for a tribute of five hundred elephants. The inscription containing the religious edict, is written in the ancient Pali, or spoken language of the third century before Christ. The alphabetical characters which are used on these pillars, are of the oldest form that has yet been found in India; yet each letter is clearly and sharply cut; only a very few are lost by the peeling off of the stone. That was a skillful hand that traced these lines so clearly, so long ago, really writing his own epitaph with his king's, for little else is known, even of him. What changing scenes, has this old column looked down upon. Julius Cæsar had not dethroned Queen Boadicea, and the Druids were sacrificing in British groves, when this old stone was hewn into its present shape.

We drove to the Burra bazaar again on our way home, and bought a few trinkets; among which was a "Ganesh" —the elephant god—and a small brass cup called a lota, used to hold the sacred water of the Ganges, or Gunga, as the natives call the river. All the shop keepers and petty traders wear the chupkun, a long coat, fitting very tightly, and short waisted, with a sort of double front—opening on the right breast if the wearer is a Hindoo—and on the opposite side, if a Mussulman. This class of people, whether Mahomedan or Hindoo, wear pajamas, or trowsers; a lower caste of Hindoos than this, wear the hotee, a white cloth about a yard wide and quite long, so that it may be wound and draped in a very queer manner, quite indescribable. One of this class of servants usually wears his own skin for a coat, and is never troubled with tailors' bills. He is an enfranchised man, not any more troubled by caste than he is by clothes; is a water carrier and sweeper by birthright, his ancestors having enjoyed the same privileges, centuries ago; and yet his modesty does not allow him to boast very much of his old family, although they lived in this valley before the Brahmins came.

Shop-keepers, tailors, clerks, waiters and coachmen, all aspire to the dignity of owning a coat; not so much for warmth or protection, as for embellishment. This coat is long, reaching below the knee, and is made of calico or merino of some glaring bright hue—to set off their brown skins; indeed, they seem to bloom naturally into scarlet, magenta, rose pink, or white, with yellow or red border trimming. The Hindoo masculine head-gear of this caste is a dainty little scull-cap, embroidered and spangled.

The women wear trowsers in Asia, from the shores of China to the Mediterranean. It is very discouraging to think not one has ever become a man by it. The experiment is not worth trying in any other country, after such a failure; four to six thousand years is a painfully long time to watch the solution of such a problem; it is worse than wearing skirts. The fact, however, furnishes substantial proof that there has been an usurpation in other portions of the world. Dress was instituted first in this eastern part of the globe, and women wear trowsers here by right of inheritance. Mrs. ——— ought to look into this matter.

The pajamas of the Hindoo women differ from those of the Turkish, by being very tight around the ankles, but quite full about the waist and hips. Over these they wear a piece of cloth, eight or ten yards in length. They begin at one end and wind this once or twice around the waist to form a skirt, then by looping and draping it, they form something like an overskirt; then it is passed under a girdle and across one shoulder and under the other arm, then brought up over the other shoulder and falls across the chest. It may be used for a veil for the head and chest. It is called a sarree. The under garment is a tight fitting jacket of white muslin. The pajamas and jackets of ladies of high rank are made of kincob, a very rich silk on which figures are inwoven with shreds of beaten gold. The sarrees of such ladies are of the finest gossamer muslins for which the east was once so famous, and the end used for the veil, is often bedecked with pearls and diamonds. It is said one old prince reproved his daughter for wearing so much fine Dacca muslin, when the young Miss replied: that she thought forty folds about her was just as little as a person in her position of life ought to think of wearing.

Benares has long been famous for the manufacture of kincob. We went to the manufactory, and were shown into an upper room, where a man sat on a low bench weaving the most gorgeous silk that I ever saw, in a very primitive sort of loom. It was patented doubtless in the reign of Pharaoh. The silk was white, very fine and heavy, with a gloss greatly superior to any that I had seen before of the silks of India. Near him were silk bobbins, and shred gold on bobbins; the weaver was motioned by the master to stop, because he hoped to make some bargains, and the noise of the looms would render talking difficult. Judging from his dress, he was a Mussulman. A sittringee: a stuffed floor cloth was first spread down, but our guide asked for seats for us; then two or three low stools or benches were brought in. After we were seated, betel-nut was handed to each one of us; it was strongly scented with attar of roses; so, instead of eating it, or rather chewing it, we enjoyed the smell of it very much. Another sittringee was spread, on which the master seated himself; while a servant brought him rolls of this gold and silk fabric, which also seemed to be permeated with the perfume of attar of roses. Each web of kincob is only four and a half yards long; and the price per piece, varies from seventy-five to two hundred dollars, according to the amount of pure gold woven in, which is always carefully weighed. No amount of greenbacks woven in would produce such a gorgeous glitter. Having no use for so few yards of material with so much value in them, I bought a kincob scarf and came away.

We spent a half-day in visiting the funeral ghât, where the fires never go out which consume the bodies of the faithful who are fortunate enough to die in the sacred city. The souls of such are believed to go directly from the funeral pile to heaven. Sick people are brought hundreds of miles that they may die here—the very gate of paradise. The smoky atmosphere is repulsive, and a person treads carefully upon the dust beneath his feet, and gazes with deep horror upon the half-naked men who attend the fires—seeming more demon than human.

That night we made arrangements with the landlord to provide us a carriage for the morning, and to waken us about four o'clock for a cup of coffee and a four mile drive to the railway station. We got off in good time, and just in the gray light of the dawn we crossed the Ganges on the old rickety bridge of boats. Going up the steep river bank, our pony became so discouraged that he refused to go any further; thereupon, a host of human spiders, all arms and legs, came out from all sorts of places in the old half buried boats, and swarmed around poor pony's head and legs, and all over the wheels until they began to roll, and pony was forced to go because the carriage was going up hill without him, and he feared some danger if he stood in the way of it. We moved off amid a chorus of "backsheesh."

CHAPTER IX.

CHUNAR AND ALLAHABAD.

THE Benares Railway station is the only building that has dared to raise its audacious front on the south side of the river in defiance of Vishnu's maledictions, so long since uttered, but so well observed.

No train ready. From this platform we took our last survey of the grandest river front in all India. The sky was cloudless, as it always is at this season of the year, but a rosy tint stole over it just as the sun made its appearance on the horizon; this was the lovely background of the picture; against it, stood out in light and shadow, the domes and tall minars of the great mosques, with their airy little kiosks perched on their tops; the meridian wall of the observatory breaking the uniformity of the long line of palaces of nearly all the princes of India, including those from the upper valley of Napaul nestling among the higher Himalayan Mountains, and the Rajah of Oudh, whose broad lands skirt their foot-hills, down to the Ranas, whose greater or lesser dominions extend over the table lands of the Deccan and the sunny hill slopes of the lower part of the peninsula. All of these have secured eligible building lots in this gate of Hindoo paradise, on the banks of the sacred river; and instead of building dingy warehouses, and incumbering the bank quay with boxes and bales innumerable, they have built lofty palaces and massive brown stone ghâts or steps leading down some eighty feet to the water's edge. Those ghâts join and form one colossal broad flight of stairs along the whole city front, three miles in extent. A half-million of people I think could find safe standing room on them to worship. Vast treasure even now, annually finds its way to the holy Hindoo shrines of Benares; and all castes—from the priest in the temple, to the pious Thug strangling his victim by some lonely roadside—hope to be fortunate enough to be permitted to die in some nook, however small, in this ancient city.

Its exports, though far reaching, require no lumbering wagon trains, no fleets of heavy freighted river boats; they consist of its ancient inexhaustible superstitions, which come and go in the hearts and heads of the host of pilgrims, like those seen at the station, who require only brass pots to use in prayers and to hold water for drink, and mats to sleep on.

At last the whistle sounds. There are a few puffs and snorts of the locomotive, and then we are whirling past rich fields, that do not suggest by any worn look that they began feeding a vast population before Rome was built or its founders born, and have known little idleness through all the long ages since; their one great task has been to grow grain.

Once more at Mogul Serai, and once more seated in the compartment cars of the main line of the great Indian Railway, we make ourselves ready to devour something or some place, provided it has a history that reaches with one hand far into the arena of the dim past, where all the multitude of active human passions swelled and surged through the manifold phases of life, and with the other hand, holds a firm grip on tangible, active, present existence—like the famous old fortress of Chunar, a few stations west. No one has ever ventured to tell which one of the kings of Behar first thought of guarding this western frontier, from brave old Sandracottus marching to meet Alexander at the fords of the Indus, down through the long line of kings that ruled Behar and Bengal. Four centuries and a half have elapsed since Timorlane drew up his vast hords of Mangolian Tartars around this fortress, and planted his battering rams against its walls. It is recorded that the garrison held out so stoutly and caused the great Tartar so much delay and trouble, that although he had agreed to permit it to be ransomed, he gave the order, after its surrender, that every person be put to the sword. So great was the amount of treasure taken—by Timorlane's own account of it—that the private soldiers would take nothing but gold or jewels; silver was too burdensome to carry.

The mode of warfare has changed, and the old fortress has changed its masters many times only to make its defences stronger with every new ruler. Before the Tartar Moguls came, it had passed from the Hindoo to the Afghan Mohammedan rulers of Delhi. A little more than a century after that conquest, Baber, king of Cabool and Khandahar, a descendant of Timorlane, came down through the famous old mountain passes of the Hindoo Koosh, and passed the fords of the Indus, and swept his victorious legions down the valley of the Ganges to the plain of Paniput, where he met and defeated the Afghan Emperor of Delhi, Ibrahim Lodi. The following story by the ancient chronicler shows how this fort Chunar passed into the hands of Sher Shah, who had recently made himself king of the great province of Behar, and with this accession of power soon conquered Bengal and Delhi. and made himself Emperor of Hindoostan.

THE LADY MALIKA'S DIAMOND WEDDING.

When Sultan Ibrahim Lodi heard of the advance of the king of Cabool and Khandahar upon his dominions, he very prudently sent a large amount of treasure to the fortress of Chunar in view of present and possible emergencies, and appointed for its commander or governor, one of his great maliks or generals named Taj Khan-sarang-khani, that is, Taj Khan, the great lord of the robes.

The Lady Malika, as her title was given, was his favorite and it would seem his most entirely beloved wife, though neither a beauty nor the fortunate mother of sons, which are the usual passports to power. Neither was she a newly-made wife, enjoying extra freedom and petting during honeymoon; she had long been the loved wife and trusted councilor of her husband, while younger and fairer women had been

ADVANCE OF BABER.

married by him only to hold subordinate positions in the household. She, as well as her husband, was born of Afghan parents, of that famous old tribe of Roh, that came to Delhi with its chief when the father of Ibrahim Lodi was very closely pressed, during a rebellion of his Hindoo subjects.

When the insurrection was put down and peace and order restored in the city and realm, the tribe began to long for its native hills again. The old chief bowed at the foot of the throne, saying, "The cause of God and the Prophet has triumphed and the Sultan is at peace within the walls, now let your humble slaves depart to their own hills again." The Sultan consented and offered him costly presents of gold and jewels. But the hill chief rose up grandly and said, "I came not to Delhi to sell my wounds; your Majesty is a kinsman of our tribe, and when the Afghans of Roh heard that the honor of Moslem women was in danger, they flocked to your help like the ants and the locust." Those of the tribe that chose to remain in the Sultan's service, were given appointments in his army and became high nobles of the realm.

The Lady Malika had perfectly won the heart of Taj Khan, by her lovely spirit and wit on all occasions and her keen preceptions of the true condition of things that came under her observation, also of that which was best to do in sudden emergencies. The empire was already on the brink of falling into other ruler's hands, and every Khan was ready to seize on the possessions of his neighbor, and thrust himself forward into some desirable position at another's expense.

So, shut up as Taj Khan was, his one only trusted confident was this favorite wife, the Lady Malika. She also won the heart of the whole garrison by her sweet winning way of scattering plentiful backsheesh among the officers and men, thus cementing their loyalty to the Khan, without even dreaming of the test of it to herself, that lay in store for her. Next to her in the Khan's confidence, were three own brothers, slaves from Turkistan, whom he had long since purchased, and bound to himself by generous trust and acts of kindness; finding they had rare abilities, he made them his lieutenants in command. Their names were Mir Ahmed, (blessed) Mir Ishak, and Mir Dand (David.)

Now, while the Lady Malika so sweetly charmed all others, it must be confessed that she completely failed to charm the other wives of the Khan. They compared dresses, and jewels, and rations, and held consultations and endless confabulations, and came to the conclusion that they did not and could not love the Lady Malika; because all the handsome dresses and richest jewels and best sweetmeats found their way to the Malika's apartments. The sons warmly espoused the cause of their mothers, whose rights and dignities they supposed were invaded, curtailed and suppressed by the favorite wife, who had no son to take her part in these cabals, or to apprize her of the small volcano extending under her feet.

One day, soon after, the mother of the eldest son found the rations not quite to her taste, and the Lady Malika had been seen in more than her brilliant attire. She broke out in bitter complaints to her son, a fiery youth just emerging into manhood. He drew his sword and vowed he would right his mother's wrongs, and rushed sword in hand into the Lady Malika's apartment, who received a sword cut on her arm and then ran to the apartment of the Khan for protection. The husband was enraged beyond measure at the undutiful son who had dared to wound his father's wife. He vowed by the beard of the Prophet he would slay him at once. There was a hasty meeting between father and son, each with sword in hand; the youth parried the heavy strokes skillfully, and lunged with such extraordinary success, that there was occasion for a great funeral in Chunar. Three days after, the Khan lay in his grave, and hired Persian mourners wailed the usual requiem. The Lady Malika took up a portion of the duties of her late husband, with a sad heart and gloomy forbodings for the future. The news of the fall of the empire, and of the death of the Sultan at the battle of Paniput, and that the Tartar conqueror had seated himself on the throne at Delhi, came to her about this time. How soon he might be at Chunar was a problem she could not solve.

The son who had caused the death of his father the Khan, now came forward when the troops were on parade, and raised his standard to show he was going to assume his father's command and his titles. His heralds proclaimed him Khan-sar-ang-khani; but no one did him obeisance and honor. He then issued his commands to the troops, but they moved not; he raged and stormed; but the soldiers rent the air with their shouts: "The Lady Malika!! the Lady Malika!! we will obey no one except her and the late Khan's lieutenant Ahmed." The youth was compelled to retire to his own apartments, for not an officer or soldier would obey him.

In this condition things remained in Chunar; till one day a holy dervish besought admittance at the gate, and being allowed to enter sauntered about. till he caught sight of Ahmed, and then signified to him that he had a private communication for him.

The Lady Malika sat in her balcony turning over in her mind the many dangers that threatened the fortress, well knowing her widowed condition and that, however loyal the troops might be to her, the position, wealth, and strength of her fortress, only invited conquest and total spoilation, from Baber the new Tartar Emperor. Then she reflected that she had a dangerous neighbor in the Afghan Sher Shah who had risen from tutor, to be the Grand Vizier of the young ruler of Behar, and had finally displaced the Sultan and was ruling in his stead, while his liege was a fugitive at the court of a neighboring prince. There was another who was honestly and anxiously endeavoring to solve the problem that this strange and unlooked for situation of things had brought about, and that person was upright, trusty Mir Ahmed; for a secret messenger (the holy dervish) had come to him from Sher Shah, to propound just this confidential question: "Has Mir Ahmed anything to communicate to Sher Shah? If so, send only Mir Dand to me." The dervish departed as quietly as he had come, nothing could induce him to divulge more.

That evening saw the elder brother in close council with

the two younger, over their *nargileh*; he puffed volumes of smoke, laboring to mature mentally some plan; while the younger men, from long habits of love and respect, sat silently waiting; at length Ahmed spoke. "He shall marry her, and I will arrange the dower. My master, on whom rest the Prophet's blessed peace, trusted me, and trusted you, and I will not betray his trust, or the Lady Malika. It is a sin to charge Heaven with the mistake that she was not born a man; but our master often said she had all the attributes of a great commander; but I put it to you, what could she do; what could even our late master do, if here to day, with this great Mogul warrior Sultan on one side, and that sly tiger lord, Sher Shah, who has driven out his king, on the other? This day he has sent to ask me if I have anything to communicate to him. Does he think I will betray my master's family? No! I will stipulate! he shall marry her and protect my master's family from dishonor; and it shall be well for them and us."

The younger brothers responded: "It is well!" Then Ahmed and his brothers sought the audience hall where sat the Lady Malika, making profound salaams. Her first, calm, penetrating look at Ahmed told her at once something of importance was on his mind. She said speak out without fear, you are in the place of a father to me, desolate as I am. Making another salaam, Ahmed stood up and said, "Be not angry with your servant, for I have a plan to unfold of great importance, it is to marry you to Sher Shah, whom the late malik regarded as a great commander, and to give the fort and the royal treasure as a dower; if the plan suits you. He shall bind himself to protect the honor of my master's family. This day he has sent a message tempting me. Sooner or later—now our beloved Sultan Ibraham has fallen—this immense treasure and fortress will be overwhelmed and wrenched from your control; let us choose our master while we may. Sher Shah is of the same race as yourself,—may God and the Prophet enable him to keep the place against the Mogul. As for us we will obey your commands whatever you decide."

The Lady Malika saw the danger of waiting for either to come unasked, and said: "Send Mir Dand at once to Sher Shah; if he must come, let it be with only a small retinue." Sher Shah had already two wives, and many sons; but the Lady Malika trusted to her own inherent power and good fortune, to rise to a good position among them. Mir Dand, or David, travelled to Behar, as secretly as the dervish had come to Chunar, and with the skill of a consummate diplomat, stipulated warily for *this* honor and *that* advantage for his dead master's family and his beloved mistress, all the while feigning he feared the Lady Malika could never bring herself to accept such a position as the harem of a man of such humble origin, and binding the Shah by an oath, that he would himself protect him, in that event, against his mistress' displeasure.

Sher Shah was anxious for the treasure, and the fortress; liked weddings better than battles; and was entirely ready to agree to any proposal; in fact, would marry a whole regiment of rich women, for a fortress; a few wives, more or less, did not matter. So the treaty was speedily arranged; the obscure ambassador little dreaming that he had made a marriage contract for his mistress, with one of the most noted Emperors that ever reigned over Hindoostan; and that the beloved Lady Malika would be Queen at Delhi.

Sher Shah with only a few attendants and Mir Dand, travelled to Chunar, leaving his great army of gorgeously equipped Afghans a day's march behind them. He was quietly admitted by Mir Ahmed before the garrison suspected what guest the Lady Malika had the honor of entertaining. The lady charmed him, and the wealth awaiting him as owner, dazzled him; while the strength and position of the fortress now set his brain on fire to conquer the empire, drive out the Mogul, and ascend the throne himself. The Lady Malika's presents to her new husband on this occasion, says the old historian, were 150 of the most *exceedingly valuable* jewels, about 560 pounds weight of pearls, and 12,000 pounds of pure gold.

This famous fortress occupies the rocky crown of a low range of hills, that rise abruptly from the south bank of the Ganges, to the height of one hundred and forty six feet. Its north frontage on the river, is not far from one thousand feet; while its extent in the other direction, is more than twice that measurement. It is surrounded with a rampart varying from ten to twenty feet in height, as the surface of the hill requires, with towers at intervals built of the fine brown stone, which is quarried here. On the highest point within the enclosure stands the ancient Hindoo palace. It is a gloomy, massive, vaulted building, with nothing about it that can ever decay, and nothing attractive connected with it except its great antiquity, which probably saves it from demolition, and gives it respectability. Beneath it is a great well or cistern, sunk very deep in the solid rock—the water reserve for seiges. It dates further back than either Afghan or Mogul rule; it is greatly venerated by the Hindoos because there is a tradition that Brahma sits upon a marble block in the court yard adjoining, nine hours of the day, in the shadow of a noble peepal tree. The remaining fraction of time is given to Benares, and the world in general goes on without him. One may get a faint idea of the insufferable pride and exclusiveness of a sect of priests who believe that they hold a sort of monopoly of the deity to such an extent.

The fort also contains an elegant English built residence for the Governor, and pretty bungalows for other officers, and hospitals and a prison.

Sher Shah managed to keep the fortress during the four years reign of Babes, by tribute and feigned submission; but the Emperor said he liked not the looks of the man, for he had the sign of rǒyalty too plainly written on his face to be trusted long. Accordingly, when the brave young Humayun his son ascended the throne soon after, he marched his army to Chunar, and its commander pacified him, as he did the father, and he withdrew. But Humayun was not long satisfied, nor would he keep treaty, but marched his army down there the second time. By this time Sher Shah felt himself firmly in command of the province of Behar, as king, and marched out of his stronghold, and challenged open fair battle with his Emperor in the plains, and their forces met near Kananj. Humayun was defeated, and barely escaped capture by making his elephant swim the Ganges. The bank was too steep for the elephant to land, and the pursuit very sharp; a soldier who had gained the top, seeing the Emperor's danger, unwound his turban cloth and let it down, and hauled him up safely.

His queen, Humayun was compelled to leave in his camp on the battle field. When Sher Shah rode in, she came out of her tent; the Shah dismounted from his elephant in token of his respect, and bid her make any request and it should be granted; she only asked that her ladies and herself should be protected. The Shah replied, that every lady and every woman, high or low, should be sacredly cared for. This is mentioned as a very magnanimous departure from the rule in those days, for all females were usually sold into slavery. Four hundred of these slept in freedom and security around the queen's tent that night; and this low-born and kingliest ruler sent them home under safe escort.

For sixteen years from that day, Humayun was a fugitive, and when he came back he brought a new wife to reign in his harem. In the mean time, the Shah took possession of the capitol, ascended the throne of the empire, and built the old ruined city called Delhi Sher Shah.

Warren Hastings once went to Benares with a small retinue; he shut the Rajah up in his palace and placed his own guard around it, while he tortured the prince to compel him to give him more treasure, which the Rajah was rather slow to part with. When the people of the city came to know what was passing in the palace, they rose *en masse*, and Hastings found the most prudent thing for him to do, was to withdraw in the darkness of night and take shelter in Chunar. This important fortress came into the possession of the English by treaty in the year 1768, and was to them the key that opened Delhi, and all the North West provinces.

About a mile and a half from the station we crossed a magnificent bridge of seven immense arches of great length, built of fine grained brown stone. The banks are high; as we looked from the windows, we saw a very slender stream, a mere succession of pools of water, at this season of the year—with a very wide extent of water washed sand on either side of it. I should like a view from one of these fine bridges at the close of the rainy season when the rivers are pouring their great angry floods through them with their utmost violence; it would awe one I think by the impression of its power, like the rapids above Niagara.

All along our route that day, were fine fields of wheat—if they can be called fields, where the only divisions were low mud walls, scarce a foot in height—on which, in the gray light of the morning, we saw troops of women and children plodding along to their work—weeding the fields—clad only in their dingy white cotton trowsers and an equally dingy cloth or saree about the shoulders, their long hair streaming in rather a wild improvement on our own late fashion.

The wheat fields were interspersed with yellow blossoming mustard, and small patches of castor beans; in one field, the plants could not be less than fifteen feet in height. Occasionally we passed large orchards of mango trees, very much resembling old apple orchards. Excepting these orchards, trees are seen only at rare intervals, that is, fruit bearing trees; the exceptions are very fine leaved miamosa. It is a wonder that the country has not been turned into a desert by this almost universal destruction of trees.

Mirzapore, or the city of Mirza—Pore, being the Hindoo word for city, contains a population of 80,000 inhabitants. The chowk, or chok and gardens are said to be worth seeing, as well as the numerous mosques and Hindoo temples; but we did not stop. This region was formerly the great resort of Thugs; there being a temple in this vicinity dedicated to their favorite divinity. Col. Sleeman hunted Thugs over almost every mile of the region to the south of this, and freed the country of one of the most dangerous secret bands that the world has ever known.

CLERK IN NATIVE STORE.

A RICE FED COOLIE.

THE OLD KHANSAMAH.

CLERKS IN ENGLISH STORE.

Two miles before reaching the city of Allahabad, we cross the Jumna, a river about the same width and volume as the Ganges; these two sacred streams unite at the city, which makes that spot very holy ground, in the estimation of the Hindoos. The bridge at this point is considered here, one of the most stupendous works of its kind. Its entire length is about 3,224 feet, which is nearly a thousand feet shorter than the one across the Soane, a stream of much less volume and rapidity two hundred miles farther down the Ganges. There are fifteen arches said to be about two hundred feet each span, their substructions extending down fifty feet into the bed of the river. The annual rise of water below the junction, in the rainy season, is forty-five feet.

The city of Allahabad is built on the point of land formed by the junction of these holy rivers. A city has doubtless stood on this site ever since these rivers have been worshipped. When Aaron was moulding that golden calf for the Israelites to worship, more than thirty-three centuries ago, the Hindoos were here venerating living cows and oxen. Killing or eating beef, has been considered through all these years, one of the greatest sins man could possibly commit, and out of all the dark list of crimes here, the one least committed. This feature of their religion would seem to point to their having emigrated very early in the history of the world, from the valley of the Euphrates. Possibly they came to redeem the lost prestige of the Queen of Babylon's army, and her improvised elephants. This is also one of the supposed sites of the ancient city of Palibothra that has been troubling the antiquarians so long to settle; and which like the ghost of Banco, will not down at their bidding, for it still wanders from Patna here. The position at the confluence of two great rivers and the old stone monolith with its ancient Pali inscription, seem to make it probable, at least, that this was the place where the vakeel, ambassador of Seluecus, Alexander's general, came to conclude a treaty with Sandracottus, as the Greeks called him; or Tsandragutta as the Hindoos name him. Whatever that old city or its old king may be to us, Tsandra-gutta, or Sandracottus, was very evidently no myth to the Greeks, for this king was able to march to meet them on the banks of the Indus, at the head of 600,000 fighting men, three centuries before the christian era. King Athoka was the first known Buddhist ruler of this region; he was the grandson of Tsandra-gutta and lived about 273 years before Christ. He wrote his religious edicts on immense stone columns and caused them to be erected in different parts of the kingdom. He is often referred to in their history. It appears also, that his illustrious grandfather was a foundling, brought up by a cowherd who found an infant concealed in a jar in his cow pen. He liked the looks of the child and gave him to his wife Tsandra; her name was joined to his, as was often done to label the children where there was more than one wife in a family.

A Brahmin who was conspiring to dethrone his king, heard of the acuteness and brilliancy of this boy, and bought him of his foster parents for a thousand pieces of silver, intending to make use of him in future. He had already one adopted son, and he determined the two should fare and share alike; they were dressed in the same manner, and each wore a splendid necklace of gold. One day the father ordered the elder boy to take a sword and go to Tsandra-gutta, who was asleep, and take off his necklace without cutting the string or untying it. He went as directed to his adopted brother and studied over the matter awhile and then returned to his father the priest, and said he could not find a way to do it. The father neither expressed pleasure nor displeasure, or changed countenance at this report. A few days afterwards when the older brother took his siesta, Tsandra-gutta was ordered to take a sword and go to his brother while sleeping and take of his necklace, without cutting the string or untying it. The boy went to his foster brother as directed, and considered the problem a few moments; he saw that there was but one way to do it, so he drew his sword, and with one stroke severed his brother's head from his body. He carried the necklace entire, according to orders, and laid it at his father's feet, who neither expressed displeasure nor approbation, but remained silent.

The father soon after, however, gave him all his riches, and told him that he was destined to take the throne of the reigning king, the father's personal enemy; and then withdrew to another country. The young headsman Tsandragutta with the treasure thus left him, levied men and went on from one success to another until he got possession of Paliboothra, and killed its king Damanda. (Life of Gaudama, page 374.)

Bindusura was his son and successor; he was the father of one hundred and one sons; among them Athoka and a brother Tseise who were born of the same mother. On the death of his father, Athoka took the throne and slew all of his brothers except Tseise. He was brought up in the Hindoo religion, but became a Buddhist after he ascended the throne. The old stone monoliths and their well cut inscriptions show the progress and civilization of that olden time.

Previous to the rebuilding of this city by Akbar, it bore the name of Deeg. He re-named it Allahabad, the city of God. It was the custom of eastern kings when they rebuilt a citadel or palace, or greatly enlarged and improved an old one, to change its name.

When the Chinese pilgrim, Hwen Tsang, before alluded to, travelled through this valley—in the year A. D., 629—in his notes he described a city on this spot, half in ruins, with an old column—precious in his eyes—lying on the ground near the water, where the rivers met. That ruinous old Buddhist city was called Prayag Junction. The tide of Brahminical persecution had already swept up through the valley leveling temples, colleges, monasteries and this old stone pillar, which even then had a respectable antiquity—being nine hundred years old—and which he doubtless thought was passing away. He studied and mastered the ancient Pali language and patiently transcribed all the words engraved upon the stone, never dreaming that those old characters would fade out of the memory of the race living near it for more than twelve centuries, and the pillar be claimed by hated Brahmins as a walking staff for their monster gods, until the day when his little diary should travel back to this valley and in the hands of a Briton—at that time a rude, unlettered western people, whom the Romans had rather benevolently spent some centuries in endeavoring to elevate—become the master key to unlock the hidden lore, and authenticate its object and origin.

This monolith, which is a solid cylindrical shaft of light grey granite, forty-two feet seven inches in height, now stands in the middle of the fortress, and is a sister column of the one at Benares. It contains three inscriptions; the first is that of King Athoka, 270 years B. C., ordering his religious edicts for the propagation of Buddhism to be written on stone pillars, that they might endure forever; the second inscription is that of King Samudra Gupta who reigned in the second century of our era, describing his extensive dominions when Buddhism is supposed to have been in full power. After that period, there came ruin; and fanatical fury swept the column down. When Jehan-Gir, the son of the great Emperor Akbar ascended the throne of the Moguls, A. D. 1605, he raised up the fallen pillar and placed a third inscription upon it, mentioning his accession. When the English took possession of this city and undermined the citadel in 1838, the old pillar was again reset in its present position. There is said to be a similar fallen, broken monolith at the village of Kosam, about thirty miles from Allahabad, lying amid huge piles of ruins, but it contains no inscriptions earlier than the second century of our era; this was also described by Hwen Tsang, the pilgrim.

The citadel—the fortified palace of the old rulers—stands on the point of land, and the two rivers add much to the strength of the defense. With its lofty towers and ramparts, and the charming kiosks that adorned its walls two centuries ago, it must, though bearing the scars of war, have looked very imposing and grand, as late as when Bishop Heber saw it. The principal gate, surmounted by a dome with a wide hall beneath it, was surrounded by arcades and galleries, which he pronounced the noblest of entrance to a place of arms. Modern ideas have marred its beauty sadly.

There is a Hindoo temple beneath the fort, its roof being supported by pillars. It is entered by a sloping passage and is a dark and gloomy place, with monstrous, hideous images of Gunesh, the elephant god, and Mahadoes. There were always very many Hindoos in the army of the empire, some of whom, as Rajah-Man-Sing, were its trusted and ablest commanders, whose daughters and sisters married into the royal family, and were wielding such powerful influence as mothers of the Sultans always do. Every one else may plot to the son's ruin; the mother, never! So this temple probably came to be spared through some such consideration, even by such a fierce image breaker as Aurungzebe.

Jehan-Gir built the palace at Allahabad—at least, the Hall of Audience called the forty pillared pavilion is ascribed to him. He resided here while Viceroy of Oudh, during the great Akbars' lifetime. It was here, doubtless, where that fatal estrangement began between him and his eldest son Koshroo, which a late writer attributes to the intrigues of his last wife, Noor Jehan. Had this writer made himself familiar with historical facts, he would have found that Jehan-Gir's marriage with Noor Jehan took place in the second year of his accession to the throne and after his hatred and cruelty had already culminated in blinding Koshroo and impaling 700 of his retainers, who had raised the standard of insurrection during the first four months of his reign. While these poor victims were writhing in the last agonies of the cruelest of all deaths, and while Koshroo's fate was yet held in suspense, this ferocious father ordered the prince to be conducted on an elephant along the line of victims that he might witness their death. Jehan-Gir's cruelty in the early part of his life, contrasted strangely with his father's tenderness and perfect abhorrence of unnecessary pain. His deep, passionate love for Noor Mabel, was the only redeeming trait in his character, and through her influence many of his former barbarous usages were suppressed; and if that leopard's spots could not be changed altogether, it was a great and good thing to modify them.

There can be no doubt that the true cause of his hatred of this son was in the fact, that Koshroo, although young and unfitted for the position, was nevertheless the powerful rival of his father for the crown of the great emperor. He had been brought up at Akbar's court, ostensibly for the greater advantages that he could enjoy there; but in reality, a hostage at first, for the good behavior of his father. The Emperor entertained serious thoughts of passing by his son, and giving the throne by will to his grandson. This so aroused Jehan-Gir, that Akbar was convinced that to save the life of one or the other, he must forego his purpose. Accordingly in Akbar's last illness, he summoned both aspirants to his bedside; and in the presence of all his nobles, and with his own hands, buckled the imperial sword on Jehan-Gir and gave him the royal canopy and regalia which constitutes oriental investiture of power; and died believing that he had saved a resort to arms. The young man was enraged and disappointed, retired at once from court and went to Lahore, where he raised the standard of insurrection, and where he and his partisans were defeated and captured.

The historian says the mother of Koshroo, who was buried here at Allahabad, was so shocked, and her feelings were so humiliated on account of her son's behavior, that she drank poison and died; and this further exasperated the father against the son. It is perhaps well that the statement comes ready-made, for there is room for suspicion that the treatment her son received had much to do with her suicide.

After Koshroo's eyes had been put out by his father's command, Shah Jehan the second son begged the favor of being allowed the care of his *poor brother*; and was granted his request. Koshroo died very mysteriously about the time of Shah Jehan's last insurrection against his father, while with his brother in his camp in the Deccan.

THE SERAI AND GARDENS OF "SULTAN KOSHROO."

The Serai was built by the great Emperor Akbar, for the accommodation of travellers, as was the custom of the Emperors of Hindoostan. Some of the wiser and better of these rulers seemed to have had great building proclivities, and showed what would be called to-day, very commendable benevolence. One of these, Firoz Shah, who began to reign in the year 1353 and continued on the throne thirty-five years, must have been a wise, active and provident king. Elphinstone thus enumerates his public works:—one hundred caravansaries; forty mosques; thirty colleges; five canals for irrigation; thirty tanks, or great reservoirs for irrigation; one hundred public baths, or bathing places for the people; one hundred and fifty bridges; and one hundred hospitals.

It is doubted whether any monarch in Europe in that age built as many hospitals, and otherwise expended as much money, for the benefit of the middle and lower classes of his subject, as this record of public buildings shows.

All of these were wisely made free by being endowed by grants of land for their maintenance and repairs. This Emperor was afraid that all cases of oppression of the poor did not reach him, so he raised a great bell in his palace yard, that any might come in unobserved and ring it, and he would hear his case. He also built a tomb for his cruel predecessor, who had hunted and slain his subjects as if they were wild beasts. He sought out the survivors of such families as had been injured by his predecessor, and made such restitution as lay in his power, until they fully and freely signed a written pardon of the old tyrant; which voucher he placed in a strong box in the tomb of the dead man. Very sensational document, at this day that old manuscript would be.

This Serai is built on the same general plan as they are found all over the country, namely: a quadrangular enclosure with a high wall, aronnd the inside of which runs a row of cloisters; where people can spread their sleeping mats under good shelter for the night; where they can take their own few and scant cooking utensils, bake their own chew-patties (unleavened cakes) made of coarse wheat flour, and eat in the separate apartments according to caste rules. The centre of the court is reserved for laden camel's and elephant's, carts or drays with their loads of grain or merchandise, which can be drawn up where the owners can watch them from their little cloisters, until they are ready to go on their way again. The strong gate and the high wall, under the present rule are quite sufficient protection against petty thieves; but when those fearful robber bands were scouring the country, sentinels were placed on the walls to give speedy warning of all comers. This Serai is square and about 500 feet on each side.

One American traveller, speaking of this Serai and garden, says: "These may have been founded by that monarch, who died about seven hundred years ago," but he entertains a doubt about the present building being quite as old as that, and well he may; for by going back seven hundred years, we shall find that not even Shaha-oo-deen, the first Sultan, and his viceroy, had as yet reigned in India.

One of those magnificient gateways of graceful Saracenic architecture leads from the Serai to the garden. It is about sixty feet high, and fifty feet on the sides, with a high arched passage through the centre, and apartments on either sides. The garden is spacious. At the further end of it are three tombs which stand on stone terraces raised fifteen feet from the ground. The tombs are all nearly of the same size, about forty feet square, and are built of stone, surmounted by a white marble dome. The sarcophagus of the bégum, or queen, has the form of the moslem slate, the same simple manner in which is denoted any Mahomedan woman's grave.

The usual pen roll marks the sex of the sleepers in her sons' graves. After leaving Allahabad the railway takes its course through a very level, monotonous country; through whose soil we see, here and there, channels, now dry, ploughed by the fickle rivers in their raging floods. The landscape is barred with yellow mustard blossoms on green, and framed in by dusty land, from which the crops have long since been gathered. Countless multitudes have eaten bread that was reaped on these river banks during the forty centuries that they are supposed to have been cultivated, and a countless host will yet eat bread from them. If there is any spot of earth where one is in danger of eating their remote ancestors with their loaf, it would be the denizens of this valley. Indeed one morning I so far forgot the locality I was in, that I took a little fried fish at the hotel in Campore; it had such a strong Hindoo flavor, that I immediately marked it among forbidden articles of diet, at least to me. Whenever I recall it, I fancy I can almost see the Ganges, and the fish feeding on the human bodies that are thrown into it for burial.

CHAPTER X.

CAWNPORE AND LUCKNOW.

THE elevation of this place (Cawnpore) above the level of the sea is 580 feet. Lat. 26° 28′. Long. 80° 2′.

We arrived weary, and very late in the evening, at the station after a duller day's travel than usual. The train had been detained two hours, by the engine running off the track. We drove to the hotel and retired directly, and slept soundly under a stuffed quilt, until a late hour in the morning, intending to leave by the mid-day train for Lucknow. The old khansamah, or head waiter, knocked at last, at our door and inquired if we had any orders to give about our breakfast. The directions were given, and we made our toilet while the meal was preparing.

As there were two or three hours before train time, we concluded to spend them in the Memorial Garden. The top of its gothic screen was visible from the window of our room. It is the only really interesting object in Cawnpore; unless we except one, the Ganges canal which, to the residents, is almost a stream of life blood, because it has changed such a large extent of arid soil, into fruit producing fields.

The landlord of a hotel in the East is generally invisible. I do not intend to say that he is of such etherial, or spiritual substance, as to be without flesh and bones like other men, but the eyes of travellers rarely catch so much as a glimpse of him. The house is operated by native servants, with rare opportunities for rascality. The proprietor however, makes

BIRD'S-EYE VIEW OF LUCKNOW.

IN THE FOREGROUND IS THE MAGNIFICENT TANK, BUILT BY ALI SHAH; THE CENTRE BUILDING IS THE GREAT UNFINISHED MOSQUE; AT THE RIGHT, IS SEEN AN UNFINISHED WATCH TOWER, DESIGNED TO BE SEVEN STORIES HIGH.

out the bills and receipts them; the servant presents them for payment and takes the money.

Engaging a carriage to take us to the station, and giving an extra rupee for the privilege of stopping at the garden on our way, we asked the khansamah, who spoke English, to give the driver, who also belonged to the house, the necessary directions. As we were going out of the gate, he came and spoke to him; then saying to us, "all right," we passed on. Soon after, we saw that we were passing the garden, and made signs to coachee that we wanted to stop, pointing to the tall, white gothic screen in full view. It was of no avail, on he drove to the river. Just before going down the bank we met Capt. C——, a resident of Cawnpore, who has a kind, good humored English face; he immediately undertook to set matters right.

Coachee said in explanation of his conduct, that the waiter told him at the gate, not to stop, for we had not paid for going there. When asked if he did not see the money given, and understand the first directions, he answered "yes; but I must obey the waiter."

Capt. C—— very kindly stepped into the carriage and drove to the place with us. He said they were all liable to have just such servants as that waiter; he urged us to write and inform the proprietor of the hotel of what had been done, or some other strangers might fare much worse, as the waiters had abundant opportunities for doing these things.

The gothic screen stands on a terrace that occupies the site, and encloses the well which was near the old Assembly Room, used by the Europeans of this station, at the time of the mutiny in 1857. Nana Sahib, the rebel leader, captured the little band of English and Indo British, who, under Gen. Wheeler, within their hastily formed intrenchments, had withstood a constant fire for three weeks, and who at last capitulated and marched out unarmed, under assurance of safe conduct down the river to Allahabad. All went down to the ghât, where they were to embark, without suspicion of any treachery. The officers and men had, necessarily, in the order of march, been much separated from the women. A few boats only, lay at the Suttee Chowra ghât; and a few moments necessary delay ensued, before any one entered them; when suddenly, from behind a mask of low brush wood, a whole battery was opened on the crowd of men about to enter the boats. Then Nana's guards rushed in between, and kept the women back, while the horrible slaughter went on among the men, until all were slain, except two.

Lieut. Thomson and private Murphy, being near the boats when the slaughter commenced, cut one loose and jumped into it and reached the strongest part of the current, before any attention was directed to them. They then flung themselves on the bottom of the boat and let it drift down the rapid stream while pursuit lasted, and finally reached Allahabad.

The women and children who escaped death on the river bank, were driven back to the Assembly Room, in the now deserted European part of the town. Hundreds of miles lay between them, and any help, but God. The women crowded together in the great room of the building. There was some effort, it is said, made by their captors, to separate a number of the women from the others; but they clung together as if they dreaded some darker fate than death. Finally as the night was closing in, some food and water was brought to them. Very few, except the children tasted either. When morning came, few or none had known sleep; the grief and woe, the dread that yet hung with such dreadful weight over them, had in one twenty-four hours so changed their looks, that friends could scarcely recognize each other. Towards the close of the third day, Nana Sahib sent his butchers in, with swords and cutlasses, among this unresisting crowd of women and children. The doors were left open; as the first blood was spilled, a few children ran out screaming; but not an English woman moved or offered to leave; they knew escape was impossible. These butchers hacked them in whatever position they sat or stood until obliged to desist, from weariness, and from the heaps and blood of the slain.

THE MEMORIAL IN THE GARDEN AT CAWNPORE.

When they left, a set of the lowest caste and condition of native men were sent in to clear the place. The children who ran out in their fright, were directed around the corner of the building, where another man with a sword killed them with a stroke, as they turned the corner of the house. As no Hindoo would ever drink from a well that the English had used, it was decided to throw their bodies in the one near the building where they were slain.

It is said that the mutinous native troops, when they met Sir Colin Campbell's highlanders in their peculiar costume in battle, were almost panic-stricken, and when they saw how they fought, they declared they were not men, but the spirits of the women who had been murdered, and who could not be conquered.

The garden includes several acres of ground, very beautifully laid out, where bloom flowers sent from Scotch hills and English vales by distant friends, to grow on the graves of loved ones, whose lives flowed out here. The Ganges water ripples musically through the little white, open conduits, among shrubbery here, and flower beds there, and past green turfed, nameless graves, as if it would gladly wash out every mournful memory from this loveliest and saddest of all spots of earth.

These grounds, Capt. C—— assured us, were, eight years before, as dry and barren as the arid plain outside, which is swept over by the hot winds from the south west; but these little streams of water have clothed the efforts of man with success, and crowned it with such loveliness, that it almost seems a spot of enchanted land rising out of a Sahara.

On a raised mound around the well stands the memorial. It consists of a circular platform, built over the well which is in the centre, covering the spot where the Assembly room stood. On the outer rim of the platform rises up a lofty gothic screen, most beautifully wrought in purest marble. A circular pedestal rises over the well, on which stands a draped female statue with drooping wings and saddened features, having palm branches in her hands. A soldier,

William Murphy, one of the survivors of the massacre at the Suttee Chowrie ghât, has charge of the garden.

The site of the intrenchment is nearly a mile and a half from the river; no trace of it now remains except the well which supplied the troops with water. A handsome stone cross marks the burial place of those who fell during the attack.

There is a mystery about Nana Sahib; he conveyed himself away to some remote part of the earth, and his whereabouts has never been correctly ascertained, though the most stringent efforts have been made. Rumors of him have gained footing at different times, but when traced have always proved to have originated by some one personating him.

I have alluded to the Ganges canal. It looked like a new world institution; indeed it appeared like something that I had seen before, with its massive stone locks. I had supposed it was a channel for irrigation only; when lo! it is a highway of inland commerce. Boats laden with clean, golden grain lay at its banks, and I looked around for the great warehouses that Anthony Trolloppe saw, when he told of the "rivers of corn," but they were wanting—although this canal in one sense is a river of corn, for it has changed 5,000,000 acres of dry desert land into possible fields of waving grain.

The grain buyers have been busy to-day; each one spreads a large, strong cloth on the dry earth on which is piled the grain he owns in the midst of the busy mart close beside the track, and he fears no harm. God's cloudless sky roofs his granary; he has a lease of good, dry weather for some time to come, and he can sit there as he does now, calm and serene, until every pound of his wealth is sold. Water is near for ablution, he will spread his praying carpet, and pray. The stars will look down on these piles of grain at night and see a turbaned head by the side of each, whose vigilence will keep it safe.

This canal brings the water from the head of the Ganges

CHOULKULHIRE PALACE, OR HOME OF THE BARBER, LUCKNOW.

where it comes out of the mountain chain. The main line is four hundred and fifty miles in length. My informant states the entire length at 700 miles. It is eighty feet in width. It must wonderfully influence vegetation in an arid region, whose entire fall of rain comes within three and one half months of the year.

Along our way to-day, lay many very pleasant fields of wheat, flax, and patches of peas in bloom. It is the 20th of January, and those vegetables which with us are only seen in the summer months, are now in luxurious growth. With the sun nearly verticle, as it is when at the Tropic of Cancer, it would be—as it is at Singapore—too hot for any temperate zone plant to live a single day; but with the sun near the southern tropic, as it is this month, and with means of irrigation, the condition is favorable for their growth. Frost is quite unknown on the bottom lands, and only found in this latitude, near the foot hills of the Himalayan mountains.

There has been a great change for the better, in the province of Oudh, since its annexation to the English territory. The peasantry are very industrious, and only need to be sure of receiving the small share that is their due, as an encouragement to work.

Formerly, when under the rule of their own kings, if the land which was tilled by the natives of a village had yielded well, and a store of grain had accumulated, the chief or noble to whom the king had given the charge to collect the chouth or revenue, would come down suddenly with a large armed force, lay seige to the village by surrounding it perfectly with armed retainers, and then make his demand of so many human ears, or so much grain, which would in all cases be as much as the chief thought that he could possibly extort, by any cruelty he could inflict. If the grain was paid without much trouble, the chief would repeat his visit, and collect the taxes from the villagers two or three times a year, or whenever his own funds got low. On the other hand if it was not paid over, there would be a battle; if the villagers were conquered, their stores of grain would all be plundered, many of their huts burned, and they themselves tortured and maimed. If the villagers conquered, the chief's party would receive the same treatment at their hands that it would have subjected them to, had the case been reversed. Some of those chiefs in the course of a few years nearly depopulated the district or section over which they collected the chouth. A people coming out from such a rule will prosper under a heavy tax, if there is anything like an adequate support left for themselves which they are secure in.

The stories that are current among the Europeans here, of the barbarities of the satellites of the court during that time, are enough to make one shudder, and look to see if the coast is clear now. The nobles set at naught every principle of justice and humanity. Predatory excursions were often made into the territory of neighboring chiefs, during their temporary absence. Cruelties, and horrible outrages—such as maiming, digging out the eyes with a dagger and filling the sockets with salt and lemon juice; roasting the hands and feet by placing them in the fire—were common occurrences, only innocent and proper pastime for soldiers. The country was infested by robbers; whenever there was a chance of plunder, a band of land pirates would swoop down and seize it, regardless of any territorial lines or prior claims of chiefs. The kings had neither power nor force of character to govern their country, or to remedy these evils. From the first their rule was an usurpation.

This province was a part of the Empire; its first king was a vassal of the royal house of Delhi, named Ghazhee-ood-deen-Hydu who, during the reign of Ahmed Shah and the troubles with the Mahrattas, took the opportunity to revolt. He formed an alliance with the East India Company which enabled him to withstand any effort Delhi could make to subdue him, he binding himself to govern well, and protect the interests of the company; thus virtually leaving in the hands of the East India Company, the right to declare the throne vacant, whenever, in their opinion, he or his heirs did not sufficiently protect their interests.

SOUTH SIDE VIEW OF KAISER BAGH.

We arrived about one o'clock at the station of Lucknow, and took a carriage to the "Imperial Hotel." A Mr. Hill was the proprietor and was not too spiritual to be seen; we found in him a very obliging host. The carriage drove into an enclosed court-yard, a ruin forming one of the sides.

We were led into a room on the ground floor paved with tile; on looking around we saw that this was a central hall reaching from the ground to the roof of the building; the windows of the first and second story opening into it. It was also used as the dining room of the hotel, from which we were ushered up a steep, narrow stair, leading out of it. At the top of the landing we were shown into a room for our use. It struck us as being a curious apartment, and I commenced exploring it. On one side the windows opened into the central hall, on the other into the court below, and a curtained one, very high from the floor, opened into the street. Drawing the curtain, I discovered that there was a good strong iron grating on the outside, to keep out intruders, but it did not hinder a good view of the Kaiser Bâgh and Kaiser Pasund, that is, the king's garden and palace.

On the other side of the room hung a huge, worsted padded curtain, before an alcove; taking hold of it, I found it was weighted, and intended to serve as a door; indeed, this is the Turkish style for inside doors of a suit of apartments; it led to the bathroom, around which stood huge jars of water, holding thirty-five or forty gallons each. About half of the floor was cemented and had a raised wall across it, to prevent the water flowing over on to the part that was matted. Here the bather stood and poured or dashed water over himself.

Fastidious to a fault in personal cleanliness, all Orientals set their faces against bathing tubs, on the principle that they are unclean institutions. I am inclined to favor their views. The village trough is sometimes scorned by a neat horse, and I have tried in vain to place a higher value on a hotel bath that different persons have access to, unless the integrity of the keeper is of the real old Roman stamp. In these oriental baths the water does not come in contact with ones flesh twice. It is the only safe process of bathing in a country, where the people who do the work are not addicted to the sin of over cleaning and scrubbing articles that are used frequently.

On the flat roof of the house, was a small room, similar to a cupola, where a night watchman kept vigils. Looking out from the window into the court, there were visible a number of one story buildings, used as kitchen and servant's rooms.

I have been thus particular in describing this house, because it is a genuine oriental one. It was, until the Sepoy mutiny in 1857, the residence of the brother of the king of Oudh, who vacated it when the king and court left Lucknow.

The apartments on the second floor were immense, and in them doubtless a whole regiment of children, with head-nurses and sub-nurses, according to their dignity, bivouacked at night on cushions, in the Turkish style. Here also the inmates of the zenanah, or harem, could look down on nâch, or dancing girls' performances in the central hall below, which was constructed with that object in view. Native people of rank would hardly think an entertainment acceptable to their guests, unless supplemented by something of this kind.

The rooms are now partitioned off into smaller ones, by stretching cotton cloth tightly over great frames, across the room, and then laying on a thick coat of white-wash which renders it quite opaque. It is a cheap and expeditious method of making two smaller rooms out of one large one.

Towards evening when the sun had lost something of its glare, we walked through the lofty gateway into the Kaiser Bâgh—king's garden. It is a great quadrangular enclosure, surrounded by ranges of palaces and suites of apartments for the members of the household, their attendants, and such officers of government as were in immediate attendance on the king. The Vizier of the ex-king, Nawab Ali Nuki Khan, used to reside in a splendid apartment over the Lukhi gate, called also the Mermaid gate, because two mermaids done in plaster stood on either side of it.

LUKHI GATE, KAISER BAGH.

KAISER PASUND PALACK.

We entered the gateway opposite, and had the white marble Baradarri or palace on our right. It is built in the form of a pavilion with a double row of pillars, which are adorned with black marble in such a manner as to make the white appear whiter. The floor in the palmy days of the king, was overlaid with silver. Strictly speaking, it is only a throne-room, though detached from all that forms the quadrangle. It is now used as a theatre by an amateur club.

Eastern sovereigns, unlike King Henry IV, had no fear "that being daily swallowed by men's eyes they will surfeit." They knew that they must be often seen; and so their throne rooms were detached pavilions, whose pillared arches could be adorned with richest fabrics, and the royal person still be visible. The body guard on gala days, when the king sat in state, or when he went about, required almost as much room as a moderate sized army—to say nothing of the great nobles present, who were allowed attendants near them.

There stands near the throne pavilion, two square towers with a pretty arch springing from one to the other, with steps to ascend and pass over. It had a very pretty appearance at a distance; good taste did not seem so far disregarded by the free use of buff and white bands of color on the stucco, as in some other buildings.

The Kaiser Pasund, a new palace with a gilt semicircle on the top, stands at the right of the Durbar pavilion. It was built by a vizier, and afterwards confiscated by the king and given to a favorite begum, or princess. It is now used as the head-quarters of the police and has an untidy ruinous look, as if the master was absent and decay was being written over it. In the lower story of this palace the Dhowrera party of English captives was confined, and from it taken out to be killed, during the mutiny of 1857. The sun was setting as we looked upon it, and one or two elephants with trappings of scarlet cloth were standing just inside the lofty gateway. My thoughts went travelling back to days when Lucknow was under the luxurious, though profligate rule of her native kings. What gorgeously caparisoned elephants and horses with their bejewelled riders have waited at these gates, or filed through this garden from gate to gate, before the throne, on festival days. No native state in India, has in this century, been as prodigal of wealth and show as was the court of Lucknow, before the deposition of the king of Oudh.

The quadrangle, called the Kaiser Bâgh was finished in 1850. About four million of dollars was expended on it. It was poorly built, and war has left some marks upon it; whenever a few bricks fall very many others show an aptitude to follow them. This suggests a reason why there are so few ruined dwellings about the older cities. Heroic Gen. Neil fell in the attempt to capture the Kaiser Bagh, at the foot of the open space at the west gate. Resistance was madness behind such mere shells of walls as these were.

Apartments which were built for the king's favorites, are now empty and dirty, and fast falling into decay. Our enthusiasm went down and down as we went on. There is seemingly less to merit the care of the present government in the architecture of the Kaiser Bagh, than in that of the other palaces here. I would not advise a stranger on arriving here to pay it the first visit; one is disenchanted too suddenly.

Within a short distance, on the bank of the river, is a group of tall white buildings with graceful cupolas and domes, surmounted by umbrellas—the symbol of royalty. There is an air of dignified beauty about these buildings—known as the Chutter-Munzil—that is very different from the Kaiser Bagh quadrangle. They were designed as a retreat for the ladies of the harem of Nus-seer-oo-deen-Hyder, and were built on ground adjacent to the river. It is a charming place—this river bank—with the group of palaces rising in such majestic outlines, out of the midst of gardens.

The Furhud Bux (Giver of Delight) was the palace mostly occupied, during two or three reigns. The ground about it connects with the Chutter Masjid and the Lal Baradarri—

THE CHUTTER MUNZIL AND FURRUD BUX PALACES.

THE HOSEINABAD IMAMBARRA AND GARDEN, LUCKNOW.

the free-stone Throne-Room, at present occupied as a post-office. This is the room or pavilion where all the kings of Oudh were crowned, and is often spoken of as the Bed Palace, and is also called Kusr-ul-Sultan.

It was the custom for the East India Company's representatives to seat the new king on the throne, in this room, and then to be the first to lay their presents at his feet, as token of alliance. Here, an usurping prince once attempted to compel that Company's representatives to do him that honor, and so confirm him in power.

This part of Lucknow is certainly very charming, indeed it is quite indescribable. To see it perfectly one must be in the vicinity of the old stone bridge across the Goomtree river, where his vision will cover the numerous tall minarets, standing out clearly against a soft cloudless sky; the domes with delicate tracery of arabesque; and the lofty gateways that seem as beautiful as frost work and almost as frail; causing him to secretly wish that some Medusae would change all this stucco to stone, that it might wear through long centuries of coming time.

The Hoseinabad Emambarra was the only architectural work completed by the third king of Oudh, Mahomed Ali Shah. Himself and mother, both lie buried here in a place of fairy like beauty: a tomb palace—I will not call it a mausoleum, for that word always suggests gloom as well as grandeur; while here there is nothing to indicate death or the presence of a grave, until one suddenly comes upon the silver railing surrounding the spot where the king and his mother sleep beneath the pavement.

Entering through a gateway so light, airy and lofty, and of such beautiful design that architecture seemed to have leaved, grown, budded, and at last blossomed into a white kiosk over the large centre arch—the color is pure white, on grey—we came upon a paved walk beside a fine walled tank or fountain, at the lower end of which was a cow and calf sculptured in black marble, which relic of Hindooism seemed out of place in a Moslem Emambarra. Before us was a fine stone chaboutra, or platform on which the building stands—an appropriate pedestal. On each side of the avenue through which we came, stands a model of the Taj at Agra; but its domes and minarets are too crowded to seem as harmonious as the grand original, yet they give an airy, graceful finish to the garden.

While standing there we noticed innumerable little steel sockets set in the white stucco, covering all the face of these buildings from base to dome, minarets, cupolas and niches, as well as the bridge that spanned the miniature lake. These were for illumination. Every available three inches of surface, of even the lofty facade of the Hoseinabad itself, could be grandly illuminated when desired.

The vestibule was hung with many beautiful chandeliers. Passing through a row of pillared arches we stood in the grand central hall. Directly under the dome are the tombs of the third king, Mahomed Ali Shah, and the Sultana his mother. Both tombs are overlaid with chased silver, with a heavy balustrade of solid silver around them. Twelve or fifteen feet above them hung a canopy of cloth-of-gold, the silken threads of which were somewhat discolored but the metal gleamed brightly out; it was fringed with twisted shreds of gold. There was nothing sad or gloomy here, nothing like a grave; all was light, cheerful and beautiful. On the left were four or five steps overlaid with filigree-work of silver, where the Grand Mouloie sat during the funeral obsequies of the king. A copy of the Koran lay on this seat. The floor was laid in black and white marble. The peculiar characteristic of this tomb, is the preparation made for illumination on the king's birth day.

In this hall, about the tomb, rising in conical form from massive stands overlaid with gold resting on the floor, are arranged immense chandeliers. Thousands of pendant brilliants hung from them, and large mirrors against the wall reflected in all directions the rays from white green and crimson lights. Chandeliers on the right of us; chandeliers on the left of us; the ceiling was hung thickly with

GATE OF THE HOSEINABAD EMAMBARRA.

MODEL OF THE TAJ, IN GARDEN OF THE HOSEINABAD.

chandeliers; chandeliers sprang out from the walls in unlooked for places—the spaces between being covered with mirrors, to reflect chandeliers; from the floor rose up monstrous chandeliers with rows on rows of globes and burners piled one above the other, with thousands on thousands of pendants to refract and reflect the light. I had read of a feast of lanterns but I had never expected to come as near seeing one, as all this seemed to be. I asked the attendant keeper how many lights were required. He said six thousand for that hall.

This Emambarra has a princely endowment for its maintenance; and though the Sepoy mutiny left marks everywhere else, this place was unscathed. Here amid the play of thousands of water jets, and flash of innumerable lights from the whole facade of this great building, the two Taj models in the garden, and those mounds of light within, the yearly festival of the Mohurum is duly celebrated with a splendor that befits Ali Shah, although the royal family are in exile. European guests are sometimes invited; and rumor says that a servant is stationed at the door, who throws a gold necklace across the neck of each lady as she departs.

Near the entrance to the Hoseinabad, is seen a grand mosque which was nearly finished when the monarch died; his successor did not choose to finish a work which would not take his name when done; so the scaffolding stands rotting around the lofty minarets to day, though the king has lain in his grave more than a score of years.

A magnificent tank: a miniature lake in the vicinity, of irregular form, with massive stone steps leading down to the water, was also the work of this king.

THE GREAT EMAMBARRA.

This building is well known all over Hindustan. It stands upon a stone chaboutra, or platform that extends along the entire front of 303 feet, and is said to have a very deep foundation; so that no settling has ever disfigured it with rent or crack.

Oriental monarchs, willing to relieve their successors from the task of preparing their tombs, build each a palace while living, and at death, order their graves made in the great halls, which ever after insures them against confiscation, by any Moslem; but we shall soon see that other people are not so scrupulous; for we espy through a lofty gateway, pyramids of cannon balls and gun carriages. This place is now used as an arsenal by the English. The gateway leading to it is called the Rome-i-durwaza, literally the Roman gate. These Moguls once learned that the capital of the Roman Empire was removed to Constantinople; and to this day they are not quite willing to unlearn it, or believe that it is not so now. Hence a city or palace gate standing at a point of compass that would indicate that city and the Bosphorus, is called the gate of Rome. This gateway is richly decorated though not as crowded with ornament as the gate of the Kaiser Bagh, and impresses one with an air of grandeur, by the height of the arch. Shot and shell have left their mark and given it a look of decay; though the work is yet firm and strong.

The garden, since its conversion to the present use, has become simply a great bare yard, flanked on one side by a very large mosque with tall minarets, and three melon ribbed domes; on the other side, against the wall, is a row of two story cloisters, which terminates near the building, in a tower with a lofty arched doorway. The style of these cloisters is in perfect keeping with their surroundings; they were doubtless apartments for attendants and guards of the king. The now dry tank in front, is abundantly supplied with water jets, which once must have made a fine display.

The building presents its great length facing the approach; with nine high Saracenic arched doorways; and four smaller ones with panels between. Two semi-pavilions project from the front of the corridor, and two corresponding towers shoot up from the centre building, whose battlements rise above a lower row, from which spring up slender minarets, crowned with bird cage pavilions.

THE GREAT EMAMBARRA, LUCKNOW.

THE KUSR-UL-SULTAN, LUCKNOW.

Entering the broad, spacious corridor, which is really a splendid ante-room, we find it filled with English cartridges.

The thickness of the partition walls is sixteen feet, the arched ways leading into the grand hall are of sufficient height to prevent an appearance of gloom. We learn from an inscription the place was built in 1783, by Asf-oo-dowlah whose tomb we see in the centre of the great hall, covered with a towering conopy of silver and gold cloth and precious stones.

We were told that this is the largest single vaulted-room in the world, which statement we did not deny. Its dimensions are one hundred and sixty-three feet in length, width fifty-three, and height forty-nine feet. It certainly is a room of great strength.

Here, in former years, was kept a collection of valuable curiosities, made by several of the Kings of Oudh. Standards embroidered with gold and precious stones, and a great throne plated with silver. They have been removed from this place perhaps to the tomb of the first king of Oudh, as we saw several things of that sort there, and an immense amount in value, of jewels and gold wrought into queer nondescript things.

At each end of the central hall, is an octagonal apartment. Our guide, an old soldier here during the seige of 1857, conducted us through narrow passages in the walls, which opened into little balconies high up in the vaulted ceiling of this apartment, where only one person could stand, and intruders could have but small chance. It seemed to me to be formed more for witnessing a nâch entertainment below, than for keeping treasure or valuable trappings of any kind.

From the roof we had a most charming view of this part of the city; beautiful, though so much in ruins. English rule brings peace and plenty to all classes, but builds nothing to compare with these structures, unless it should be a christian India in the ages to come.

THE TOMB OF THE FIRST KING OF OUDH.

This is often called Shah Nujeef. Nujeef being the name

of the hill on which the tomb of Ali, the son-in-law of Mahomed, is built, from which this mausoleum is said to be modelled; it certainly is very unlike the usual form of mogul tombs.

Here rests Ghazee-ood-deen-Hyder, who began his career as Grand Vizier, soon after the accession of the Emperor Ahmed Shah in 1747. His qualifications are told in a few lines: "Restless and ambitious, as reckless of consequences as he was regardless of principle; as skillful in dissembling his passions as he was incapable of controlling them; he looked on perfidy and murder as the natural means of attaining his ends."

The court and people soon wearied of his tyranny, and the Emperor plotted to capture his powerful vassal, who was at all times surrounded by a large body of retainers. A royal hunting party well equipped and attended by a large body of royal guards and nobles of the court supposed to be favorable to the Emperor, and each with his retainers, marched out one day with him and his Vizier. The Emperor intended to capture this haughty noble during the hunt, while separated from his party, but Ghazee-ood-deen under a calm exterior, concealed his knowledge of the Emperor's plans and contrived a counterplot to draw him towards Deig, where the Vizier had stationed a large force, and suddenly turned upon the Emperor, captured him, and ordered his eyes put out, also those of the Queen his mother. He then deposed him, and raised to the throne a young prince, Alumgir II. Aided by the Mahrattas, he took possession of Oudh and made the treaty before mentioned with the English, establishing himself as king.

The tomb stands in a comparatively strong enclosure, which is surrounded by an open garden of shrubbery and fruit trees; an ample endowment being left by the king for its care and maintenance. It is surmounted by a culic or spire and a low dome, near the base of which are windows, a very unusual place for them, truly; a garland in arabesque is festooned above them around the exterior of the dome.

TOMB OF GHAZEE-OO-DEN, FIRST KING OF OUDH.

The gateway is a covered portico, extending from the wall to the mausoleum. The whole is well built; the materials are brick and stucco. During the mutiny in 1857, while marching to the relief of Lucknow, Sir William Peel planted his heavy guns close under its walls, and battered away for two hours on this structure before an entrance was made by breach, and the rebel Sepoys driven out of it.

We were shown a curious collection of ivory pictures—miniature portraits of the Kings of Oudh and their wives, and other noted persons: one where Claude Martin was being presented to the king; and another of Noor Jehan, the Emperor Jehan-Gir's favorite Queen. There seemed to be stored here a great number of gaudily, though richly ornamented towers and canopies, glittering with gems and gold, which, judging from their form, are carried in their religious processions. The Mohamedans of Oudh belong to the Shea wing of that faith. The King lies buried beneath the pavement, under the dome. By his side lies the Queen his mother, and his favorite wife; a conopy of faded silk and gold hanging over them.

After paying a fee to the keepers, who, dwelling among tombs, make a very good income by their salaries and the fees of visitors combined, we entered the carriage and drove to Wingfield Park, which is beautifully laid out with walks and trees, and borders of flowers. It is a refreshingly charming place. Resting ourselves in a small, white marble pavilion, we could not help thinking how much the old King of Oudh at Calcutta, must regret his beautiful city here, by the Goomtee.

There are many things in Lucknow that will not bear too close scrutiny. The mosaic of this little pavilion where we rest, is made of painted bits of gloss instead of real cornelians, agates and emeralds.

THE MARTINERE, OR CONSTANTIA.

Strangely beautiful must this palace have been in its fantastic freshness. It is said that it is a combination of every species of architecture; and one can very well believe the assertion when looking at round towers with loop-holes and battlements as if taken from a castle of the middle ages; at Corinthian columns; and at capitals and kiosks and pinnacles everywhere, made to give standing place to some god or goddess, or some flower girl in quaint French dress, with basket on her arm. Near by, on dizzy pinnacles are *le grand hommes et dames*, in the toilet of "*Le grand Monarque.*" Some of them appear in stately attitude, others with appealing, upturned faces, or with uplifted hands gesticulating as French people do. One, on the loftiest height, seemed to be *La Somnambula* just walking off from her airy pedestal. What love for *La belle France*, the old self-exile must have had, away down deep in his heart, to prompt all this collection of plaster casts, with few European eyes except his own to look upon them. Moss and grey lichens have gnawed into their limbs and robed them with a sombre color.

The highest story, if I may call it so, is a strange union of four round towers connected by open galleries. Two immense arched stairways intersect at the highest point where a flagstaff stands. The building rests on the usual stone chaboutra, or platform, which has to one of these structures the same relation as the pedestal to the statue. Entering, we find the great hall filled with seats and desks for a school. Though designed and built for a palace, the builder Claude Martin died before it was finished. He left an ample endowment for a military school to be maintained in it and ordered his body buried in the vault beneath the chapel within the palace.

A danger existed of such palaces being confiscated. This was done, not because their owners had committed crime, but simply because some who had the power to take, coveted them. This could be effectually prevented in each case, by the owner or some of his family being buried within it: placing a ghost to guard the property, as the old pirates did.

The building was solidly built; the apartments are vaulted and many of the ceilings beautifully frescoed. On the

CONSTANTIA, OR MARTINIERE PALACE, (NOW MILITARY SCHOOL) LUCKNOW.

second floor, in an apartment that a princess might covet, we found the neat beds where the boys of the school slept. The chapel it is said, formerly had a door of carved ivory—a statement which should be received with caution, as there are no remains of it now to be found. Native guides are proverbial for retailing the marvelous to strangers.

Claude Martin, the builder and founder was a private soldier in the French army in India, and deserted. He entered the service of the King of Oudh, who employed him to organize and train his soldiers. Under the native rulers, such men were eagerly caught up by them, and patronized very liberally and very many reached high positions. Claude Martin rose step by step, until he became a brigadier general in the army of Oudh, and amassed a large fortune; but his desertion was a bar against his going to France to enjoy it, or even venturing into French territories in India again; so Lucknow became his home, and there he died; but he remembered France, for he bequeathed a sufficient sum to build and endow a similar school at Lyons and one at Calcutta.

During the mutiny the rebel Sepoys occupied the building, defaced the statues and desecrated the chapel, opened the tomb of the founder and scattered his bones. Some kind hand collected them and secreted them until Lucknow was in the hands of the English again, when they were restored to the vault below.

Driving out to the ruins of the Residency, where Sir Henry Lawrence, the English resident minister at he Court of Oudh lived at the time the mutiny broke out, one wonders how a single soul ever came out of that siege alive. It was a large three-storied house, as little suited to defence as any ordinary brick house of its size would be. It tells its own story. It is now roofless, the walls are all battered with balls and peppered with shot as thickly as if a hailstorm of lead had scarred it. Here and there a cannon ball has bored its course through the two opposite walls. In the northeast corner is the room, marked by a tablet, where Sir Henry

Lawrence was wounded by the bursting of a shell in the apartment, and where he died. Near by is the house of Major Bailey, commander of the Residency Guards. The present surroundings, mournful as they may be, are eloquent with glorious deeds of heroism; and those vine clad ruins awaken admiration even in the hearts of strangers, as they remember the gallant defence of those heroes, and against what odds they fought.

Across the way from the Residency is the house of Dr. Fayrer, where a piazza fell, from the effects of the cannonade, killing and wounding sixteen persons out of the little band of defenders. Round holes cut clearly through the walls mark the passage of huge shot. Their little bulwark, a wall hastily thrown up and in no place exceeding four feet in height, enclosed only a few houses; among them was one with a very deep underground room, called Tykhana, (cool place) such as are frequently seen in that country. The side walls of this room were not less than eighteen feet in height. The room was as well finished as ordinary sitting-rooms are there, showing that it was probably made for a cool resort when the weather was intensely hot. It was lighted from small windows at the top of the ground, only one or two panes of glass in depth.

Here in this cellar, as it might be called, were crowded all the wives and childen of the soldiers of the European regiment, for three of the hottest months of the Indian season; and it was here if anywhere, that the Scotch lass heard, or thought she heard the slogan of the Campbells, three days before their arrival, for no woman could lie down calmly to sleep outside in the large enclosure enfiladed by shot and shell. I must write here, that the old soldier our guide about the Emambarra, who was in the defense and had access to this room, said that he had never heard of the story before, and was very incredulous; which fact I regret very much, as it tends to spoil what I considered a beautiful story, and one that had wiled out of me considerable sentimental feeling, and swindled me out of many hot scalding tears.

ENGLISH CEMETERY AND RUINS OF CHURCH, LUCKNOW.

TOMB OF GENERAL HENRY HAVELOCK.

This quarter of the city was formerly crowded with large buildings adjoining the little entrenchments, which the mutinous Sepoys and their leaders occupied. Among these was a palace of the Begums, a Mosque, and an officers' Mess House: a spacious, roomy place, beyond the English lines, which gave shelter to hordes of mutinees. Scarcely a fragment of a wall above the foundation of any of these is left standing. The foundation of the little English church near the cemetery has only just enough of wall and buttress standing to show on a near view what sort of an edifice it was formerly.

So many large buildings razed to thin foundation stones, show what kind of fight the defenders made during those dreadful months, waiting for reinforcements to come, and mark the quality of English nerve and of English faith in English soldiers. All the world knows how gallantly Havelock came to Lucknow; but nowhere else will the thought give one's pulse such a gladsome thrill and bound, as it does standing beside these ruins.

An elephant creeper had begun to climb over the ruins of the Residency; I picked a few seeds, and in the cemetery my friend gathered a few leaves near the grave of Gen. Neil as mementoes of the heroic dead, and we left Lucknow to take the train for Agra.

CHAPTER XI.

AGRA.

AT the station, after reaching Cawnpore, we were told that the train was two hours late. The up trains are said to be so heavy that they constantly lose time. It was due at midnight and the idea of waiting in the great, dreary, dimly lighted waiting-room, was certainly not a happy one; and that of recrossing the river Ganges on that crazy old bridge of boats again, was still less so; therefore the thought of going back to the hotel was given up.

Just as we were settling down to the fact that we must wait patiently, sitting bolt upright, a kind thought seemed to come to the little Hindoostanee waiting woman, and she went into a sort of closet and brought out a charpoy, as it is called, which is really a low four-post bedstead with a bottom made of strong interwoven tape. We understood that act, even if we did not understand her language, and she understood a piece of silver in my hand, though she knew no word of English. All around the place were large posters: "*Servants discharged for asking gratuities.*" The station-master was remarkably wide-awake and attentive to the very few passengers who took the belated train; but the little woman knew how to manage; while her master was talking to us, she bustled about and helped me to put on my wraps, and when I left her, the silver which was in my hand went into hers without his knowledge.

About dusk the next evening we left the station near Agra,

AGRA, FROM THE OPPOSITE BANKS OF THE JUMNA.

in a carriage drawn by a small pony. We crossed the Jumna on a bridge of boats, modeled after those that Xerxes brought into Greece when he made that famous western excursion. There is one thing quite certain about these little Indian ponies, they can travel fast enough to keep out of the way of a carriage going down hill, so we reached the foot of the first bank with sufficient momentum to run the carriage some distance on the bridge, without much outlay of strength on the part of our pony, and he did not become quite discouraged until he reached the opposite bank, when the same scene was enacted as at Benares: the human spiders crept out of dark corners in the old boats and swarmed over the wheels until they began to roll up hill and pony was forced to get out of their way; and then they vanished in the dark with the same chorus of backsheesh, followed by a small sprinkling of copper coin.

It was quite dark—though not later than seven o'clock in the evening—when we found ourselves passing through a noble gateway in a lofty battlemented city wall. The idea of a city wall creates a feeling as if one had stepped back a score of ages of time, and one looks for hoary antiquity in everything. We drove to the North Western Hotel and the next morning were thrown into doubt as to whether that was not an institution of the middle ages also. The landlord was sick and cross, yet no one who sat at his table could possibly suspect that he had the gout. His temper broke over all bounds when we drove back from sight-seeing in a carriage which we did not hire of him, and therefore he would not allow it to come in on his driveway. Thinking frequent scenes of this kind would not materially add to our comfort at his house—for we designed stopping some time—we changed our quarters to a hotel kept by a gentlemanly old Mussulman, where, if the fare was no better, the attention to our wants by the servants was decidedly improved.

We found Hosein Khan a very intelligent person, better posted in the details of the city's history than the ordinary

English innkeeper could be, because it was the history of his own people; he knew every ruin for miles around the city; he also spoke very good English which was of service to us, considering our imperfect knowledge of the Hindoostanee language.

THE FORT, OR CITADEL AT AGRA.

Every Oriental monarch builds his palace within such fortifications that it can be well defended, even after the city has been taken. The citadel and palace of Akbar stand on the bank of the river Jumna, and are surrounded by a wall of red sandstone sixty feet in height, with a machicolated battlement with towers at intervals, outside of which is a deep paved moat into which the waters of the Jumna could be turned at a moment's notice. The form of the citadel is irregular, and has a circuit of one mile and a half of wall.

We drove to the Delhi, or north gate, so called because it is in the direction of that city, and there our Jehu stopped, and said that strangers' carriages were not allowed to enter without permission. He was a man of medium height and much stronger built body than the Hindoostanee people; indeed—if not so pinched by the Rhamadan fast—a fair-sized man, probably belonging to some hill tribe, with a complexion resembling light colored Russia leather—possibly water would have abated one or two shades more—for he had been driving through clouds of dust. He seemed to think that this was a good opportunity to ask for backsheesh, came to the carriage window, opened his cavernous mouth, and passed his clenched hand under the strong leather belt about his waist—a startling gesture if he had been a Feejee islander. I consoled myself with the thought that I did not look tender, and if his appetite did compel him to eat me, the priests would haul him up for breaking his fast. I bestowed an orange and he turned away, mournfully drawing up two or three notches in his dingy leather belt, and laid the orange away till after sunset. Not a drop of water or morsel of food must pass his lips while the sun gives light. During

NATIVE LIFE IN INDIA.

the night he must take food enough to last him another twenty-four hours. Thus he will go through forty days' fasting with a faithfulness that might shame many christians.

Mr. S—— returned with the permit, and we crossed the draw-bridge over the moat and entered a lofty gateway flanked by two enormous towers, pierced with embrasures and crowned with light, airy pavilions of stone; thence up a narrow, steep passage between walls closely loop-holed for musketry. At the top of the passage we enter between twin towers ornamented with stone fretwork and high balconies, with a loggia over the gates for a few musicians. Passing through, we find ourselves in a covered arcade with buildings on each side, showing a beautiful succession of alternate niches and small arched openings, adorned with carving and mosaic, all looking like a section of the middle ages. These were the offices of the royal guard, and where they were mounted each day.

This palace was built by Akbar, in the early part of his reign, which began in 1596. His father, and grandfather Baber, seem to have made old Delhi, or Firozabad as one of the old cities was called, their residence; but this Emperor built a new capitol in a new place. Each emperor of Hindoostan seemed to have been very desirous of giving his name to a city, and therefore forsook the city of his father, on ascending the throne.

We now entered a very spacious court-yard, about five hundred feet in length, surrounded by arcades. On one side, stands the Dewan-i-Aum, or hall of public audience, where Akbar in person heard the causes of the people, and gave judgment. One knowing only the luxurious ease of modern kings, is surprised at the amount of daily business that the Mogul Emperors encumbered themselves with.

Here in a pavilion one hundred and eighty feet in length, pillared and arched on three sides—though now walled up—daily sat the Sultan, where any subject could come and plead his cause before him. Justice was a very prominent trait in Akbar's character; it is said he had the plaintiff, defendant and witnesses stand nearer the throne than to the Cadi or judge, who sat on a raised slab in front of the throne, in the centre of the floor; thus giving little chance to that officer to pervert evidence. The throne in this Hall, is in a recess in the side wall, so as to front the people. This was entered from a small room behind, where doubtless much favoritism was essayed, in important cases. The throne had a canopy of white marble, supported by pillars inclosed by a low balustrade of the same material; it is furnished now with two chairs, and a sofa of filigree marble work. It was formerly richly inlaid with precious stones, which have in some places been dug out, but enough are left to show the design, even through the coats of whitewash which have been applied to it very freely. This building has for many years been used as an arsenal, and long rows of blue flags are seen on the arched ceilings, on which are inscribed the names of the different battle-fields that the English have won in India.

At one end of the hall a faded curtain was drawn aside and a relic of antiquity displayed itself, which was no less than the veritable old gates of the Hindoo temple of Somnauth, captured in Guzerat in the year of the Hegira 415, or the year A. D., 1024. As no visit would be complete without recounting the old, well known tale, I here give it:

The Afghan Sultan Mohammed of Ghazne, made one of his plundering expeditions across the Indus and the Indian desert into Guzerat, where a rich and famous Hindoo temple stood by the sea. After a short resistance, during which the people did more praying to their great corpulent idol than real fighting, the outer wall was battered down, and the Moslems, on entering were dazzled by an array of golden idols around the walls, and one of colossal size in the center, in the same metal. The priests gathered about the conqueror and made offer of a great ransom, which Sultan Mohammed was inclined to take; but while looking at the great ugly image that they worshipped, his religious fury was kindled, and he dealt the gigantic idol such a blow that its body was broken in, when out poured such a quantity of

THE MOTEE MUSJID, AGRA.

treasure, jewels, pearls and diamonds, that the plunder became general. He returned to Ghazne with these old gates, and with such a vast amount of gold and treasure from that and the adjoining countries of the Scinde, that he kept a festival for one week, which he called "The field of the cloth of gold." At this festival he exhibited all the valuables he had plundered, to arouse and incite his subjects to the conquest of Hindoostan. He also plundered all the temples at the head waters of the Jumna. When his capitol was changed to Cabool, the old gates were carried there, where they remained until the English war, when Lord Ellenborough had them brought and deposited here in Agra, which is now the capitol of the North-west Provinces.

These gates are about twelve feet high and very richly covered and inlaid; they are composed entirely of sandalwood; are very much worm-eaten, and show great age. They stood for centuries in that old Hindoo temple, while its treasures were accumulating, and the fame of its wealth was travelling to distant points.

THE MOTEE MUSJID OR PEARL MOSQUE

stands in this great court, confronting the entrance; its outer brown wall being fringed with small marble kiosks. It stands on the spur of a hill, and a long flight of red sandstone steps on the east side lead up to the gate, which is massive and lofty. When the door is closed, one seems to stand in a temple of alabaster, or some ice palace that would melt away with the rays of the sun; so fine, so pure, so spotless, so well polished is the marble of which this royal praying place is made, that time, war, nor conquest, have left stains on this gem of art. It is to-day, as worthy of its name Motee or Pearl, as it was two hundred years ago, when Shah Jehan built it. Here doubtless, accompanied by that gentle, lovely and devoted princess, his daughter Jehanira, he daily came to pray in his adversity, when he had been deposed and imprisoned by his son in this citadel, where he remained during the last seven years of his life.

The court of the mosque is a quadrangle about one hundred and seventy-five feet square, with scarcely a flaw in the polished white marble pavement. A tank to hold water for ablution is sunk in the centre, and is adorned by rich, heavy mouldings, raising the brim a little above the surrounding surface. The mosque extends across the western end and is a colonnade with matchless Saracenic arches. Three rows of massive polished mouldings and panels constitute the only ornamentation, except that peculiar wavy work on the under side of every arch. Just under the cornice is a long row of Persian characters, recording the mosque to have been built by Shah Jehan, in the year 1656; and that two years later he was confined here by his son, as a state prisoner. Above the cornice, on the margin of the roof, and along the top of the arched and cloistered gallery that surrounds the court on three sides, runs a row of diminutive little kiosks, surmounted by a little white bubble of a dome, making a border exquisitely beautiful. "It is a sanctuary so pure and stainless, revealing so exalted a spirit of worship, that I felt humbled as a Christian to think our noble religion has never inspired our architects to surpass this temple to God and Mohammed." Thus wrote the celebrated American writer, Bayard Taylor, whose sparkling genius has often led my heart captive, and to whom I yet make my profound saläam, at a very reverent distance.

I waited long, and I waited conscientiously and expectant beneath these arches—as pure as any ice cavern near the poles—for that humility to come over me; but it came not. In its stead came faint glintings at first, and then almost a vision of that marvelously beautiful Christian cathedral at Milan, and hid itself in my soul to be there a joy forever. Grand old Strasberg, and Cologne too, put in reminders of themselves and their claims, and I was compelled to admit them. So it came about that I walked out of that quadrangle of polished marble blocks without feeling any particle of shame for the architects of Christian temples.

AKBAR'S THRONE-ROOM AND BATHS AT AGRA.

THRONE-ROOM OF AKBAR, OR DEWAN-I-KHRAS AND BATHS.

Our guide, a gray old fungus, who drew his first breath among these walls and has grown to them as lichens grow to rocks, conducted us into another court which was laid out as a beautiful garden, with marble fountains and tanks, whose sides are wrought into a Saracenic wavy work which some have imagined was fashioned in this way to form a seat for individuals when in the water; but if they had taken the trouble to compare it with the ornamentation on the arches, they could not fail to see in them the same design, which was a favorite one, and used wherever it could be. On the further side of this court overlooking the river Jumna, is raised a long stone chaboutra, or terrace, edged with an exquisite border of marble lace.

Conspicuously among the buildings on this raised foundation, stands a fine brown stone pavilion with projecting roof, and brackets of precisely the same pattern that has recently been so much in vogue in our own country. The roof is crowned with two light and graceful kiosks, and there is the same peculiar sweep in the wavy finished arch, as in the marble mosque, which was doubtless copied from this. The pillars are square and massive with highly polished panels and mouldings severely chaste and simple, made to last just as it has done, through ages. Three windows filled with perforated marble slabs, are in the back wall, which look down seventy feet into the waters of the river. A row of sculptured and polished pillars and arches across the back part nearest the river, which formerly hung with curtains of the costliest fabrics, made a small room or passage behind the throne. By some strange mistake, a faithful cut of this one story pavilion, the apartments of the harem at the right, and the Taj in near distance, is published (page, 395) in Mr. Seward's travels, as the "Tomb of Akbar at Secundra." That Emperor's mausoleum is eight miles from the city of Agra. It is nearly a solid pyramidal structure of five immense terraces, raised one above the other. The lower one is five hundred feet on each side; each terrace decreasing in size to the fifth, which is ninety-six square. The pavilion above described is about sixty feet front, and if it could be lifted up and placed on that fifth terrace at Secundra, it would not crowd it at all.

Nothing about this first great audience hall of the old Emperors of Hindoostan is much injured, or has a neglected look. A few meshes in the marble lace work balustrade in front, may have dropped out like broken stitches; but nothing is really wanting to hinder the Grand Master of ceremonies from giving orders for putting up the hangings; replacing the huge black marble throne; covering the floor with gold cloth and costly cushions, and then promulgating the order for the durbar, or reception, when we might expect to see the Great Emperor, cotemporary with Elizabeth of England, come in preceded by the bearers of the gold rod, walk beneath the great golden umbrella fringed with pearls and broidered gold, seat himself upon the throne under these emblems of royalty, followed and surrounded by the highest nobles in the land, who range themselves according to rank on each side of the throne.

Here Akbar first introduced that magnificence of style that is associated in our minds with the Mogul race of kings. Here Shah Jehan, the building Emperor—as he is sometimes called—inaugurated his reign by showering upon his subjects on coronation day, seven millions dollars worth of jewels and gold.

Let us call out venerable old Ferishta the historian of those times and make our best saläam to his white beard and whiter turban, while he seats himself on this pavement, once so familiar to him, to give us the story of one of those magnificent festival days at the end of the Rhamadan fast, as celebrated by Shah Jehan.

The Emperor's usual place, says the historian, was in a gorgeous pavilion tent of huge proportion, which was placed in the center of a wide space of smooth, hard ground entirely covered by stretching and fastening over it one or two thicknesses of firm, white cloth. Inside the royal tent

THE EMPEROR AKBAR AND RETAINERS.

above the white cloth is spread a carpet or sittringee of the richest silk, in which elaborate figures are woven of fine shreds of beaten gold. The color of the outside of the tent is red; it is lined and hung with the richest of satins and velvets in delicate colors; some of the curtains about the throne of cushions in the centre, are fringed with pearls and embroidered with wrought gold studded with diamonds. The Emperor has what is called "good presence," the fine oval features of the Tartar race, and a tall commanding figure. He sits *a la Turc* on the cushions, with his feet folded under him; his turban is all a glitter with diamonds, and from the aigrette in front rises a heron plume. His robe is well adjusted for effect, and as thickly studded with diamonds as the night sky with stars. The throng of nobles and courtiers are all shimmering in garments of gold cloth and jewels, with the richest of the shawls of Cashmere for sashes and turbans. The Grand Vizier and the Omrahs, for they are the great barons of the realm, have each a tent—a little distance away—almost as gorgeous as the Emperor's, though smaller in size, where they receive visits from each other and sometimes from the Emperor. Each one of these high nobles keeps a small army of retainers in his own pay, and absorbs in this manner the revenue of one or more of the petty Indian kingdoms.

When all is ready on this festival day, great golden scales are brought. The Emperor steps in on one side; the other is filled with a medley of rich stuff. There are robes of the costliest fabrics, as satins and velvets embroidered with pearls; silks embroidered with gold; and gossamer muslins of Decca. Robes fit for a king are jumbled in with a horse's bridle embroidered with wrought gold; and rich crimson velvet tent hangings with gold embroidered saddle-cloths, for some Arabian charger; there are also embroidered crimson velvet cushions and hangings for an elephant's how-dah. Thus the scales are filled up, and when the beam is level the Emperor takes his seat in the center of the tent again, and the contents of the scales are then waved about his head to impart to them a peculiar influence, supposed to be very fortunate to the receiver, and then laid aside. The Emperor again steps into the scale, and into the opposite one drops almonds made of pure gold; jewels for the neck; jewels for the ears; and jeweled bands for the wrists and ankles of the fair ones in the zenanas of the nobles. An aigrette of diamonds, fit to grace the Grand Vizier's turban, lies beside another of emeralds, topaz and crystal, that will grace the forehead of some favorite elephant. Thus the list goes on until the scale beam is even; the Emperor takes his seat, and the contents are waved over his head, when he is weighed again, until his great store of gifts are exhausted.

Then commences the distribution; the smaller articles are thrown out among the crowd of nobles and courtiers to be scrambled for, like nuts among children. Whatever of eagerness, avarice, or curiosity there may be below the surface, the true Oriental courtier would not show it; he wears his face as a mask, and politely professes to prize the gift for his Sovereign's sake; but internally it is rated at its worth; and no Jew dealer in London or Paris could quicker detect its real value, or want of value, than he. The new Emperor is supposed to be in a gracious mood, and pardons are asked and granted, and petitions are presented. Then the grand closing procession gaily marches past the royal tent, in which all the high officers of the court, and the great commanders of the army perform their part, and make their presents to the Sovereign.

Leading the front, come the splendid troops of the household and the palace, followed by one thousand stall elephants with velvet housings embroidered with gold, the leading ones with frontlets of diamonds and gems on their foreheads—these representing the empire. Next in order come the retainers of the nobles, bearing the presents of the Grand Vizier, Asf Khan—the father of the Emperor's wife, the beautiful Moomtaz-ee—the minister who so quietly paved the way for Shah Jehan to ascend the throne. Next, one thousand tall Afghans, all mounted on splendid Persian

PROCESSION OF NATIVE CHIEFS.

horses with silver bridles and embroidered saddles, led on by the Governor of Candahar, and followed by camels laden with his presents.

Then come five thousand war elephants with howdahs filled with archers, escorting the presents from the Nawab of Bengal, and followed by cages of lions and tigers from its jungles; and hunting leopards or Cheetahs, for catching deer. Then come trained hunting hawks and wild foreign beasts, followed by platforms borne on the shoulders of men, carrying dancing girls, and performing jugglers.

A host of cavalry from Oudh and Behar, come next in order, all glittering with cloth of gold. Troops of brave old Rajpoots from the countries of Guzerat, Marwar and the Punjaub, with spears and shields, led by their princes who are Omrahs—great commanders in the army of the empire—born of families who have held their Rajahdoms for fifteen hundred years, and thought it stooping when their daughters married the new Emperors of Delhi. Gookars, and men of the northern hills, and Cashmerees brought tribute of gems, and the gorgeous fabrics of that famous valley. Thus the subjects of all this vast empire, one after another were represented in the pageant passing in sight of the throne.

Thirty years later, comes the contrast of this festival day. The Emperor is an old man now, and his beloved Moomtaj-ee has laid long years in her grave in the Taj; and he is dying, a prisoner within the same palace walls where all this gorgeous pomp was displayed. His sons are all dead, except the one who has closed these gates against him, and rendered him weak and powerless. Only the gentle Jehanira, and the children of her murdered brother Dara are with him. All that throng of great and powerful nobles have long since transferred their allegiance to his foe. After the reign of Shah Jehan, this citadel and palace was not much used as a royal residence.

A grand Durbar or vice-royal audience was held in Agra in 1866, where the Viceroy of India, Sir John Lawrence, as representative of the Queen of Great Britain—now seated on the throne of Akbar as Empress of India—received all the native princes according to their rank. At that time within these old walls, something of the old life returned, and something of that old gorgeous display was re-enacted.

This reception formed one of the most striking spectacles of the age and being considered by those interested, as one of the most important events connected with English rule in India, is entitled to more notice than a mere mention. The 20th of November was the day fixed upon for the grand display, although festivities commenced much earlier. The Viceroy entered Agra on the 11th accompanied by a splendid retinue and staff. The cholera was raging severely yet seemed to be forgotten entirely by the immense throng which crowded into the city. Entertainment followed entertainment, given by one and another of the native princes. A magnificent fete was given at the Taj by the Maharajah Scindia one of the most powerful princes in Hindoostan, at an expense to himself of 20,000 rupees. On the 17th of November the Viceroy presided over a grand assembly of the Order of the Star of India, at which several were invested with the insignia of the Order. The investiture took place in the Shamiana or tent of the Durbars, in the center of the Imperial Camp. The ceremony was simple. The candidate for knighthood stood before the dais of the Viceroy; the Queen's letter was read aloud; the Viceroy embraced him, and fastening the ribbon and collar around his neck, declared him a knight.

On the 20th of November, Agra was a scene of the greatest excitement. The ceremonies of the Durbar had attracted thousands of Europeans and natives to the city, who encamped mostly outside of its limits in tents, in spite of the dreadful epidemic raging. An eye-witness of the scene thus describes the grand reception.

"At noon the esplanade in front of the camp presented a magnificent *coup d'œil*. Each rajah, surrounded by his court and displaying all his riches, took up the position assigned to him, from which he was to proceed to the Durbar.

Hundreds of elephants of gigantic size, rivalling each other in the magnificence of their trappings, some with howdahs of gold and silver, others bearing the standards of royal insignia; thousands of horsemen, Rajpoots, Mahrattas, Sikhs, and Boundelas; soldiers in every imaginable uniform; thousands of eager spectators from every province of India,—such was the crowd which thronged the Maidan of Agra.

At two o'clock the procession commenced. According to etiquette the highest in rank came last. Each Sowari in turn, advanced up the great avenue; the English troops presented arms; the batteries fired a salute; the royal elephant knelt down at the entrance of the Shamiana; and an English official, taking the rajah by the hand, conducted him to his seat. The procession continued without interruption, increasing in magnificence from the Boundela chief of Alipoura to the high and mighty lord of Gwalior. At length all were seated; the Indian princes on the left of the dais, with their nobles and ministers behind them; and to the right the English governors, generals and officers, whose rich uniforms appeared quite simple beside the Oriental magnificence of the rajahs. There was a pause; after which the choubdars clad in red and armed with long golden canes, announced the Viceroy, when the assembly rose, and Sir John Lawrence, in full uniform, with head uncovered, slowly crossed the pavilion and ascended the dais, amidst the firing of cannon and the strains of the National Anthem. At a given signal all sat down, and the Secretary of State declared the opening of the Durbar."

He then describes the ceremony of the nuzzur, which was the presentation of gifts to the Queen by each rajah, through the Viceroy as her representative, and adds:

But during the ceremony, which does not last less than an hour, let us take a glance of the princes present. The first on the right of the throne was Scindia Maharajah of Gwalior. He represented at the Durbar those terrible Mahrattas who, for a whole century, filled India with fire and blood, overthrew the Mogul Empire, and, by their lawless atrocities, paved the way for the British conquest. Scindia was dressed in robes of brocade, with a few diamonds around his throat, and a turban with raised wings. On the immediate left of the Viceroy was Ram Sing, Maharajah of Jeypore, wearing the robes of the Order of the Star of India, and a turban covered with precious stones. He and the Maharajah of Joudpore, who was seated next to Scindia, are the representatives of the Solar race, of the god Rama; and they rank next to the Rana of Oudeypoor. Then came the Begum of Bhopal, the most important Mohammedan sovereign of Rajasthan. She is about fifty years of age, of an energetic and almost masculine type. She was dressed in a manly costume, with tight pantaloons of cloth of gold, and a satin tunic decorated with several orders. Among the nobles of her suite was the dowager-queen Goadsia Begum. Then came the Maha Rao Rajah of Kotah, and the Rajah of Kishengurh, both of them Rajpoots, wearing the ancient kangra or short-plaited muslin petticoat. The Maharajah of Kerowly, the young Jât Rajah of Bhurtpore, and the Maha Rao of Ulwur formed a group resplendent with jewels; Sheodan wearing a long tunic of black velvet, blazing with strings of diamonds."

Hosts of others are enumerated whom we will omit after mentioning one party more, viz:

"Six Mirzas, members of the ex-emperial family of Delhi, descendants of Akbar, richly dressed and wearing the dress of the princes of the blood, saluted the English Viceroy, from whom they receive pensions."

After the ceremony of the nuzzur came that of the khillut: the presentation of gifts to the rajahs. These consisted of elephants, horses, jewels, precious stuff &c, which were displayed in the pavilion and presented to each rajah as he came up. After this distribution, an address was made by the Viceroy, and the Durbar closed. Festivals were however continued till the end of the month. At a grand ball given by the Ram Sing, a Hindoo prince the descendant of Rama, was seen to figure in a quadrille with an English lady upon his arm.

THE SHISH MAHAL, OR PALACE OF GLASS,

standing on the same terrace as the throne room, and at the left of it, and separated from it by only a few feet, was one of the Emperor's suite of rooms. It is certainly the most singular apartment in the palace. It was planned for a cool retreat from the glare of the day, and was the favorite apartment of Jehan-Gir when in Agra, or Akberabad as it was named in honor of that Sultan. There were no windows to light it from without. At one end of the room the water

IMPERIAL DURBAR AT AGRA.

was made to fall in a broad sheet from the mouth of a conduit high up in the wall, over slabs of marble inlaid with zigzag lines, to which it is said the motion of the water gave the appearance of fish swimming. An outlet led into a tank in the terrace.

In the walls and ceiling of this apartment are imbedded thousands and thousands of small mirrors, so very near together, that a delicate vine of white stucco in arabesque, connects them all, making meshes of white frost-work on a ground of silver, which shivers and shatters the light into ten thousand glittering rays, as if the whole were an incrustation of crystals. The builder must have endeavored to realize some dream or story of fairy palaces built of gems, by the old genii. Here, Jehan-Gir, or Selim and his Noor Mahal must have wiled away much of the time of the twenty years that they spent in Agra, and have found it a charming retreat. Beautiful as the conception of it must have been in its freshness,—for it is now dimmed with the smoke of torches—light and water were such essential parts of it, that one gets only a meager idea of its beauty with its channels dry, and by the glimmer of *one* faint light.

Emerging from the "Hall of Mirrors," which is wholly below the pavement of the terrace, we come into a fine, airy saloon used for private reception. Numerous other apartments opened from the Hall; one, a charming combination of bay-window and balcony, hangs from the top of the massive, inaccessible river wall like a bird cage, on the otherwise blank rampart. Here amid gorgeous cushions, sat the Sultan, as the day declined, and perhaps smoked his narghileh; but during the reign of Jehan-Gir, an edict was issued against the use of tobacco, then a new luxury introduced from Europe.

The zenana, or harem, is reached by passing out on the platform in front of the throne room, or through the arched gallery at the back of it. The apartments are not numerous or large, but opening out of them on the rampart, is the same combination of bay-window and balcony, closely curtained in with marble lace. Along the pillars are flowers and vines inlaid in fine mosaic; borders of agates and cornelians, lapis lazuli and blood-stone, and traces of gilded bands, scrolls and flowers, all showing that this suite of rooms was adorned for the great Sultana, the mother of the reigning Emperor, and next to her in rank, the mother of the heir-apparent.

Here sat the royal mother on carpets of gold cloth amidst glittering cushions and rare flowers in vases of crystal and silver, while a young Persian girl sang the songs of her country and thrummed her ziraleet; when her songs ceased, another related stories, the quaint romances of her native country. In this manner, if not in this place, prince Selim first saw his Noor Mahal, while entertaining his mother and sister.

A little court adjoins this suite of rooms, adorned with fountains and water jets, and great vases of flowers and plants. There is a large brown-stone palace at the right, built by prince Selim when he became Emperor; a corner of which is seen in the engraving, and which was also devoted to the harem, but at the present time it is occupied as barracks for European soldiers.

We did not feel inclined to explore the subterranean passages which are said to exist beneath these structures; one is reported as extending as far as the Taj, but no outlet has been found; another, as ending in a deep well, where it is said the faithless members of the harem were launched out of life. Such wells were known to exist in Europe at that time in old baronial castles, where the bodies of persons secretly executed were thrown.

Doubtless, very many of those places were used as treasure vaults, where gold and jewels were stored. Elphinstone says, that this palace contained, at the time of Akbar's death, many millions of pounds sterling in gold and jewels, and that while Shah Jehan was a prisoner here, he would not allow his son Aurungzebe to remove the jewels and treasure that were stored in the palace, which were estimated at

THE JUMMA MUSJID, AGRA.

twenty-four millions of pounds sterling, besides almost countless jewels, which were all removed after the death of Shah Jehan.

The garden probably retains only a faint semblance of its former self, a sort of royal shabbiness appears in the mass of tangled jessamine, moon flower and roses, with here and there an orange tree; probably not a tree or shrub that remains, the Great Emperor or his grandson saw planted; but their representatives are here, growing in the same parterre, by the same paved walks and marble fountains. There is also a small court paved with blocks of black and blocks of white marble, so arranged as to form a pachisi board. Here the Emperor and his courtiers played chess, not with ivory pieces surely, on this gigantic board, but with warriors for knights and bishops, and pages or eunuchs for pawns. Sometimes there was a more domestic assortment of pieces, the eunuchs or girls of the harem trotted from square to square, as the moves were made.

On our way back to the hotel we went into the great Jummah Musjid, which stands in the open space between the citadel and town. It is a massive structure of brown-stone, with inlaid ornamentation of white marble; and were it not for its domes, it would resemble a fortress more than a place of worship. There are three massive gateways, each having a high arched way which rises into dome shape. On either side of the central passage the gate building is divided into two or three stories, each one being arched and having ports or windows looking into the passage. In these gate buildings, a portion of the household guards were stationed on great days, as the feast of the Rhamadan, when the Emperor came to this mosque in state.

The court is a broad, paved enclosure, with the fountain in the centre. There is an arched gallery running all around the three sides of the interior, which would hold several thousand people. Across the western end of the court, rises the mosque. On going into that part, we perceived a congregation listening to a priest expounding the koran. They sat with their legs crossed under them, on a thick cloth spread on the white marble paved floor. The priest sat in the same fashion, a little in front of the people, and talked or read to them in a conversational tone. We had quite forgotten that Friday was the Sabbath of the Mussulmen, and this day particularly holy, being the last one in their long fast of forty days. We looked very inquiringly into the face of the attendant who had met us at the gate, and was conducting us around for the fees, but there was no demurring look; so we waited until the priest and worshipers were gone. The women do not worship with the men, and none were in sight. There was a narrow place on one side, separated from the audience hall by a screen, where they might have been. From there they might hear the voice of the priest, but could not see the kiblah, the point in the wall which indicates the direction of Mecca; but as no good Mussulman could hope that his prayers would be answered unless his face was turned *exactly* towards it, it may be inferred that Moslem ladies do their praying at the public mosque by proxy.

The immense size of the blocks of white marble in the pillars and arches under the domes, impress one with a sense of great strength and grandeur, being eighteen feet from side to side, forming a leading feature of this mosque. The lofty entrance and vestibule is a niche whose top is a semi-dome of marble, opening out, which is carried far above the roof. This architectural peculiarity has probably travelled eastward from Egypt, as it is seen at Cairo, in the mosque of Sultan Hassan, which was built about A. D., 1360.

Leaving six rupees—nearly three dollars—in the hand of the attendant, we took our departure.

GATEWAY TO THE TAJ, AGRA.

CHAPTER XII.

THE TAJ—THE MARVEL OF INDIA.

THE TAJ was built by the Emperor Shah Jehan, as a mausoleum for the remains of his wife, whose title was Moomtaz-ee Mahal, and who died about the year 1629; he having been seated on the throne of his ancestors a little more than a year. It is situated about a mile from the palace, on the bank of the Jumna. We drove along the river margin, over a good English made road, cut through piles of ruins and the débris of generations of old buildings, and halted at a broad stone terrace in front of a lofty and imposing portal,

THE GATEWAY OF THE TAJ.

This is a fitting adjunct of the marvelous structure to which it leads. It opens into an enclosure which is a magnificent garden, and beside it on either side stand broad spreading tamarind trees. A lofty niche with a pointed arch similar to the one just described at the mosque, rises nearly to the roof, which is about seventy feet from the ground. Up the sides and over the top of this great doorway runs a band of white marble, on which is inscribed texts from the Koran, inlaid with black marble. There are four tall, arched recesses in front, in place of windows; the space over the top of each, as well as that over the lofty entrance, is entirely covered with a ground of white marble adorned with flowers and vines, with leaves and scrolls inlaid with cornelians, agates, lapis lazuli and other stones, with green marble leaves. The entrance is flanked by two octagonal towers of brown-stone—each block of which is inlaid with narrow band of white marble—the towers surmounted with beautiful marble-domed pillared cupolas. Supporting each base, we noticed the same pattern of brackets—placed here two centuries ago—which, introduced at home, we flattered our vanity with as a new style that some fertile genius in architecture had invented within the last score of years, when in truth we had only "looted" it from these unchristian Mussulmen. I felt almost courage enough to confess the fraud, but on considering that we had never appropriated the style of ornamenting with rows of small white domes about the size of turbans, like those over the arch, the fraud committed, was left to balance the one omitted.

Passing through the gate-building, we emerged upon a long stone platform, extending through a magnificent garden which is eighteen hundred feet from east to west, and one thousand feet from the gate to the river; it was laid out in walks and planted with flowers and shrubs. The fruit and flowers of the orange and lemon trees shone out among the dark-green foliage of the cypress. It is enclosed by a high red sandstone wall, around the inside of which is a row of cloisters, or arched and pillared galleries. In the middle of the platform is a fountain basin which extends the entire length of it, a distance of nearly six hundred feet, with rows of water jets on each side, and a larger row through the center. There was formerly a large stone basin for fish about half the distance across, which stood a little higher than the other and poured a circular sheet of water into it. This has now been filled with earth, and set with roses and heliotropes; the jets remaining as they were. A charming sight it must have been, when all these jets sent their sparkling waters into the air, while beyond was seen the Taj with its tall dome, cupolas and slender minarets rising above, as pure as alabaster against the blue heavens.

Across the further side of the garden on the bank of the Jumna, is a brown stone chaboutra or platform nine hundred

GARDEN-VIEW OF THE TAJ, AGRA.

and sixty-four feet in length, and three hundred and twenty-three feet in breadth, and four feet high. I like dimensions, stiff as they may seem, they pin a thing fast to the memory. From the four corners of this great terrace rise octagonal towers built of the same stone and crowned with white marble kiosks. Two mosques, one on the west, and the other on the east end, stand between these towers on the same grand pavement. They are built of red sandstone like the gateway; every block in them having its border of white marble, inlaid. Their domes and cupolas are all of the same stone, and their grace and ornamentation would make them models of beauty, were they not so absorbingly eclipsed by the wonder that stands so near them. Only one of these mosques has ever been consecrated, or used for prayer, for it stands with the kiblah wall to the east, while every good Mussulman here, prays with the face to the west, toward Mecca. It was built to preserve the symmetry of the group, and this is the only reason given for the erection of an edifice that would be the pride of any city in the world. The natives call it the jawab or answer, and have no religious reverence for it.

From the middle of this immense sandstone terrace, rises a superb platform of white marble. Its sides are panelled and highly polished; it is three hundred and thirteen feet square and is ascended by a flight of seven steps. Four lofty marble minarets rise from the corners of this second chaboutra, to the height of nearly one hundred and seventy-five feet from the river bank. They are crowned with light, graceful cupolas, each supported by eight pillars. A spiral stairway leads to the top of each, and at equal heights a door opens on a balcony, a resting place in ascending. From the center of this higher terrace rises that gem of wondrous beauty: the Taj; lifting its dome and spire two hundred and sixty feet from the level of the ground. The dome is seventy feet in diámeter, very highly polished, and through the lapse of two centuries, retaining the purity and color of a pearl. The plan of the building is octagonal; the larger sides face the four cardinal points, and are each one hundred and thirty feet long, and in these are lofty entrance recesses which rise about sixty-five feet high, and are forty feet wide. There are two window recesses twenty feet high, one above the other, on each side of the four large entrances. Slabs of perforated marble in the place of glass, soften and subdue the light that comes into the central hall.

We chose to commence our survey on the outworks, so we went up the winding stairs of one of the minars, resting our feet and taking fresh breath on the little balconies, till at last we stood in one of the kiosks on the top.

A wide range of country was presented to our view, and the Jumna was traced for a long distance, glistening out from behind its winding bank, such a slender stream that one can scarcely believe that it fills its banks and becomes so powerful a river in the rainy season. Here our eyes could wander freely from the minar, among the slender spires and minarets that shoot up from every angle, and the glistening white marble domes of the kiosks, that are set like little pearls around the great one in the centre. A broad girdle of mosiac encircles the centre pearl, the dome is a fitting framework to this jewel here uplifted to the heaven. Along the edge of the roof runs a low parapet, a rich border of mosaic. Every slender minaret, from the pavement to the spire, is inlaid in wavy lines of black marble in the white, in such a delicate manner as to impart to it, as a whole, a bluish or pearl white color at a short distance.

Descending from the minar, we approached the lofty portal facing the gate. A beautiful wainscot of the purest marble, with lillies and roses of Sharon in base relief, framed in by a most exquisite border; a jewelled vine which puts forth buds of rubies and cornelian, and leaves of malachite and emeralds, passes around the inside base of all the entrances and window recesses.

It was well that our party had thoroughly surveyed the exterior before entering, for the enchanting scene before us would have unfitted us for it afterwards. Instead of entering

THE TAJ MAHAL, AGRA.

directly the grand rotunda beneath the dome, we chose to first visit the sloping passage that descends to the sewers, or true tombs. This passage is worn smooth and shining by the bare feet of the thousands who have passed over it every year of the two centuries since its erection. It conducts one to a spacious vaulted apartment of marble, containing two tombs. The only light comes from the door and falls directly on the sarcophagus of the queen, whose title "Noor Jehan," is written in Persian characters on it.

This, one of her very many names, is apt, at first thought, to confound her with her famous aunt, the Empress before her, whose title "Light of the world" was fastened upon her, when the original was excluded from power. A train of maidens had filed in before us and strewn the grave with roses and jessamines for the daily tribute—either to the dead, or to the sentences from the Koran that are written among the countless mosaic flowers, which the old Persian artist of Shaiya wrought in the stone above the tomb, or to the prayer also there inscribed: "Allah defend us from the power of the Infidel,"—it was not easy to say which.

There were no fresh flowers on the Emperor's tomb, nor any texts from their holy book. It is said they were withheld by Aurungzebe, for fear some impious foot might tread on the words of God and Mahomet. The sarcophagus of the Emperor bears this inscription written in Persian:

"The magnificent tomb of the king; inhabitant of two heavens, Ridwun and Khool; the most sublime sitters on the throne in illeeynn; (starry heaven;) dweller in firdos; (paradise) Shah Jehan; Padshah, Gazee; peace to his remains; heaven is for him; his death took place the 26th day of Rujub, in the year 1070 of the Hegira. (or 1665 A. D.) From this transitory world, eternity has marched him off to the next."

This is said to be a correct translation of the Persian writing on the sarcophagus. Directly over his face were traces of a large star-shaped figure said to have been composed of diamonds, but they have all been "looted," (plundered) long ago, and not one remains in this figure, while work done with less valuable stones, is as perfect as the day it was finished.

We stood looking at the exquisite workmanship before us. The ceiling, walls and tombs are one mass of mosaic work, representing birds, fruits, flowers and other designs; all the usual expressions seemed too tame and hackneyed to do them justice; one does not in the presence of anything so much beyond previous conceptions, feel like expression. At last, when astonishment had a little worn off, we commenced counting the stones in the flowers; we went up into the grand hall and stood beneath that matchless dome by the screen, and were so demented as to count stones, and estimate, and hold our breath; when we had reached far up among the millions, the actual number on the steps of only *one* of the *four* tombs, we laughed at our folly and stopped, lest our sanity should be doubted.

Then one or two of the party relapsed into the old silence, and stood gazing upwards with enraptured faces, while Mr. C—— sang a few notes which seemed to float up against the lofty dome—that concave a hundred an fifty feet above our heads—reverberated and floated from side to side, in exquisite melody; then slowly died away , as if the beautiful gates above had been left ajar, to let us catch a few notes, and had been reluctantly closed again. We can scarcely imagine the effect of that first Persian funeral refrain that was chanted here, when the Emperor and his sons and daughters, accompanied by his splendid court in all its grandeur, spread their mats on these terraces, while this dome caught up and prolonged the sweetly wild lament of the Persian mourning women. Even the old historian only gives the meager facts.

The form of the screen surrounding the two sarcophagus in the rotunda, is similar to the building: octagonal. The circumference of it is ninety-six feet; its height about six and one fourth feet; and the diameter of the space inclosed by it is thirty-two feet. Each side or face is composed of a slab of delicate marble fillagree work, hung like a curtain of rich lace between pillars, and beneath a cornice, on which

INTERIOR OF THE TAJ MAHAL, AGRA.

SARCOPHAGUS OF SHAH JEHAN.

thousands and thousands of cornelians, agates, rubies, emeralds, bloodstones or carbuncles, garnets, onyx, lapis lazuli, green marble and malachite,—in short the whole list of stones are elaborately wrought into the most exquisite patterns and vines. Each stalk, and leaf, and bud, is represented in its appropriate color and shade, and each leaf, and shade of the leaf, by the different shades of the varieties of stones of that color. A few small flowers, about one inch in diameter were selected at random and the stones counted, the different pieces in each varied from thirty to fifty in the coroll alone.

One person estimated the stones on the two pedestals alone on which the sarcophagus of Noor Jehan rests, to be one hundred thousand in number, and those on the Emperor's at three hundred thousand; but this—as will be readily seen—is *far* to low an estimate. Lines of black marble on the white of the paved floor, form a sort of star pattern that is very pleasing to the eye, and does not at all detract, or in any way mar the delicate color and beauty of the place, that stands unrivalled in all the world. It has had no peer, nor is it at all probable it ever will have.

Yaverner, an early traveller in Hindoostan, says, that twenty thousand workmen were employed on this building twenty-two years. Another account states that it was completed in seventeen years. The list of the kind of stones and where they were obtained, together with their price, the Emperor caused to be engraved in Persian characters on a stone tablet, on the premises; as also the names of the master workmen, and their salaries, as follows:

Head master, or architect, Isa Mohammed; chief, or head illuminator and master of the mosaic work, Amarand Khan, of Shiraz; and the master mason was Mohammed Hunif, of Bagdad. Each one of the head workmen received the same salary, viz: one thousand rupees per month, equal to five hundred dollars of American money. The list of stones given, is as follows:—turquois, from Thibet; lapis lazuli, from Ceylon, which was also abundant in Afghanistan, then under the dominion of the Emperor; coral, from Arabia;

garnets, from Bundelcund; diamonds, from Punah; crystals, from China; rock spar, from Nerbuddah; chelcedony, from Velate; amethyst, from Persia; sapphire, from Lunka; cornelians, from Bagdad; blood-stone, or carbuncle, from Gwalior; onyx, from Persia; white marble, from Rajpootana; yellow marble, from Nerbuddah; black marble, from Charkow; pudding-stone, from Jassilmere; jasper, from the Punjab; emeralds and rubies, and so on to the end of the list.

This plain, clear record, written on a stone tablet at the time of its erection, ought forever to set at rest the idle speculations of some, who at once jump at the conclusion on seeing the Taj, that an Italian architect was employed, because there is a resemblance between the mosaics of that country, and this ought to have saved Mr. Seward his regret on page 401, that the name of the architect was already lost.

On coming out from the Taj we encountered outside of the gate a host of venders of polished stones, for which Agra is famous. It is amusing to see how sharp these fellows are on the track of strangers; they had followed us from the city and waited at the gate during our stay in the garden. They had paper-weights of pure jasper, of onyx, and of gold stone, and a few of marble, inlaid in precisely the same patterns of vines and flowers that we had just seen in the mausoleum; also agate paper-knives, and seals, and buttons; and beads made of cornelian. From this display we concluded that stone-cutting had taken root in the soil, which this beautiful work made long years ago, yet fosters and cherishes.

There were about fifteen of these stone merchants, and each of them in an agony to make a bargain, but their Hindoostanee was as unintelligible to us, as our English was to them. Presently a boy about nine years old, from the public school, came, who spoke very fair English. His samples of stones were quite limited. Seeing that his stock did not suit us, he turned and snatched up the stones belonging to

MODE OF CARRYING IN INDIA.

the others, and began a thriving commission business, insisting on his share before any money went into the girdles of the owners—they wore no pockets.

Suddenly every stone was slipped away or covered up, and they commenced fierce, angry gesticulations toward a native man in the outskirts of the crowd. We turned to see the cause of this disturbance, and beheld a leper. He appeared to have the kind of leprosy described in the Bible. When he saw us motion him away, he did not dare remain. He made a forlorn effort to laugh at his own impudence in thrusting himself into the presence of others, where he knew he would not be allowed, then walked away. Instead of a healthy brown, his skin was a reddish white, and had a rough, swollen, unnatural look, and his hair looked dry and stiff, and instead of being black, was a dull, brick red. My heart ached for such a pitiable object, a sort of animated corpse walking the earth, enduring years of agony, waiting for the grave to kindly open and hide his suffering. We entered the carriage and drove through the city. The bazaars and queer little shops are all on the same scale as at Benares and Calcutta.

On the north-east side of the city is Rambagh, a pleasure ground, laid out in the same style as the Taj garden. It has marble pavilions and stone kiosks, and in former times it was a magnificent garden, on which the Emperors expended vast sums of money. It is still a very charming place. Near this garden is the tomb of Itmud-oo-dowlak; it stands on a white marble platform of the same material as the mausoleum, which is about fifty feet square. Four round marble minarets, forty feet high, rise from the corners, and are surmounted by kiosks.

In the center is a circular apartment crowned with a marble dome, where lie the remains of Kwaji Aeias, whose title was Itmud-oo-dowlah. He was the father of the first Noor Jehan, and grandfather of Moomtaj-ee, the Noor Jehan who lies buried in the Taj; indeed, this name is one of the syllables in her title. This is the Persian who had the fate to emigrate to Hindoostan on one little bullock cart, which carried all his earthly effects, afterwards to become Lord Treasurer, his son Grand Vizier, and his daughter an Empress, who wielded more power in India than any woman since Sultana Rezia; and lastly, to have his grandaughter lie in state as it were, in the Taj, and receive homage through centuries of time, from an admiring world. Very few who have made such unostentatious journeys have succeeded as well.

That evening we made arrangements for a carriage to go to the Secundra Bagh, eight miles out of Agra early on Monday morning. Very weary, we retired at an early hour and slept soundly until about eleven o'clock, when we were awakened by some one tugging at our door, which was clumsily fastened with a chain and our own padlock. I involuntarily gave a little scream, while my husband called out in the sternest voice that he could command on a sudden emergency: "Who's there? What do you want?" No answer came. Of course the first thought on such an occasion is, a midnight intruder and self-protection, and there is no knowing what amount of damage might have been done, if we had had anything to do it with. We both sat bolt upright, straining our eyes to peer into the darkness. Presently the voice of the old khansama (landlord) giving some directions about something—in the ordinary tone of that individual—put to route all thoughts of adroit Indian thieves.

As soon as we were dressed in the morning, a gentleman of our party put his head in at the door, exclaiming: "Hee-yah! there is an American arrival!"

"How do you know, have you seen him?"

"Well no; I cannot say that, but I have seen the back of his coat, and I *know* that it was fitted to that back in America. There are more than one. I am off to reconnoitre." So saying, he sauntered off to the front verandah.

A pleasant surprise awaited us, for the party consisted of four American Methodist Missionaries—three gentlemen and a lady. They were returning from a conference held somewhere in the vicinity of Agra.

That evening we took our tea in *table-d'hôte* fashion, with the Revs. Mr. Brown and Scott; the other missionary with his wife, had gone to preach at some station out of the city, and were to join our party at Secundra Bagh. After rising from the table we bowed the knee and mingled our prayers, at that, our first and last meeting with those gentlemen.

Next morning we breakfasted by candle light, and started in the grey dawn for Secundra Bagh, over a splendid English road, between double rows of trees, a dreary sort of black foliage pine, and miamosa, the last in full bearing, their large pods shelling out their ripe seeds. They resemble our locust, and belong to the same class of plants. Long trains of loaded camels passed us, laden with produce for the Agra market. These camel trains are made up by tying the head of one camel, by the halter, to the tail of another, making a row of ten or twelve. The driver puts a bell on the last one and rides the first; but woe to that one bringing up the rear, if he should abuse his trust and get loose and browse; his bell would betray him.

Our friend said *that* camel would fare like the Chinaman's last duck. Of course we all wanted to know how the last duck fared. He said the poultry-men on the Canton river had boats fitted up for raising ducks in them, and when the tide was out the keepers were in the habit of letting the ducks out to feed, on the ground which had been overflowed. They wish them to come promptly to the call when they throw down food, and the last one, no matter how fast he was travelling, was caught and badly whipped and flung far away to go without his supper, and come back alone. After a little experience, there would be no loiterers, though there would always be a last duck.

Trains of huge, wooden-wheeled wagons loaded with fair, golden wheat passed us, coming from queer little clusters of blue clay houses—villages they call them—near some great tank, where the ryots, the cultivators of the soil live; men, among whose ancestors—if traced back as far as the time when Joshua entered Canaan—not one could be found who ever aspired to be, or had ever been anything more than this one, who sits there driving that antediluvian wagon. He sits on the broad tongue of his rude cart, with his lank, bare limbs folded under him. His only clothing is a narrow cloth about the loins, and a piece of coarse wool blanket which has been folded in the middle and sewed part way across one end to form a hood over the head, a leather string fastening it under the chin. There is no waste of cloth in this primitive cloak; it falls about his body, reaching to the hips; and by sitting on his heels, with a good deal of management, he can bring it so as to cover his limbs; for the morning air is quite chilly—with the mercury at 65°—to those who are used to a temperature three-fourths of the year, varying from 90° to 115° Fah.

His wagon is a compound of a frame house and a child's toy cart made of a cigar box, with spools for wheels. Four strong pieces of square timber seem to be framed into a parallelogram; over that is laid a floor; then four cross sections of the largest trees that can be obtained constitute the wheels, which turn on four iron bolts driven into the wooden frame, to which the broad tongue is also fastened. Put a row of stakes in the frame, pass a few ropes between them and stretch a coarse hemp cloth on them to secure the grain, and you will have one of these wagons, which need fear nothing less than a locomotive. The oxen are sleek, strong creatures, with high hump on the shoulders and a long frill hanging from the neck, who hold up their heads as proudly as if they were drawing the state carriage of the Emperor.

SECUNDRA BAGH.

Our carriage drew up in front of the terrace before this grand entrance to the mausoleum. It is the finest portal in Hindoostan; the only ones that can compare with it in proportion and finish are the other three gates to this garden. Secundra is the way Alexander is pronounced in India. The

GATEWAY TO THE TOMB OF AKBAR, AGRA.

name is often heard; it is applied to great personages, and seems to be a lingering memory of the old conqueror, handed down through all the intervening centuries.

The lofty, pointed, arched entrance-recess is said to be seventy feet high, containing the door and a window-recess above it. There are also two high, arched window-recesses one above the other, on each side of the entrance, which opens into a great rotunda reaching from the ground to the roof. Around this vaulted hall are rows of small openings for musketry. The structure is of brown stone with very strong walls, and every apartment is a vaulted arch, of such strength as to render the roof capable of sustaining the weight of four tall white marble towers. Exterior stones on every side are inlaid with marble, in the mosaic patterns indicated by the illustration; much defaced, however, by the wars which have swept over Agra in the two hundred and sixty-seven years since it was built. The rear and front are precisely alike, two cupalos standing over each. A spiral staircase leads to the top of each of the four white marble towers, but some are in a very unsafe condition. The towers were formerly higher and surmounted by graceful cupalos; but when the Mahrattas captured Agra about a century ago, Holkar their chief, turned his cannon upon them in sheer wantonness, to leave his mark. A native has taken posession of one of the deep window-recesses, and set up his business of making coarse mats, which he stores in another recess around the corner.

The garden is about twenty-five hundred feet on each side, and is enclosed by a wall of brown stone, in which are inserted panels of elaborately wrought, perforated stone of the same color. On the garden side of the wall, an arched gallery passes from gate to gate making the usual row of cloisters, except at the left of the gate, where were fourteen stables for the Emperor's elephants; these stables have been changed by the English into convicts' quarters.

From the four gate-buildings, fine causeways of dressed stone, each one thousand feet long, converge on the central terrace. In the middle of each of these causeways are long fountains with numerous water-jets capable of making a very charming display. The central terrace on which this pyramidal building stands, is five hundred feet square. Standing just in the edge of the masonry are two or three old tamarind trees, said to have been planted by Akbar's hand; and when his widow built this tomb she had them included inside the foundation. They have the appearance of great age. There are still many trees in the garden, though we saw a large portion of it was planted with American cotton.

In the middle of this central terrace, a flight of steep stairs lead to the second. Cupolas adorn this entrance on each side. In the Saracenic arched alcoves which surround the whole structure are buried members of the Emperor's family. On the right is the tomb of his daughter, named, as the inscription which was carved on the foot of the sarcophagus informed us: Aram Barnoo (maker of peace.) On the sarcophagus also was a sculptured arabesque in bass-relief. There was the usual slate framed on the cover, to denote her sex. A grandson of the Emperor was also buried in this apartment, which seemed to be formed on the corner of the terrace. The top of the white marble sarcophagus of the child was scooped out, forming a cavity, which, our missionary acquaintances informed us, the friends of the child filled with water, and daily placed fresh flowers therein. In case of a very young child, such a cavity is usually filled with milk, as a pious offering to the departed spirit of the babe. A sort of winged star was sculptured at the foot instead of the name; which I thought was intended as an emblem of the little soul's flight; but others chose to regard it as a mere ornamental flourish of the sculptors.

In the alcove in the left corner, another daughter of this family lies buried; a maiden princess who devoted her life to good works and prayer, and spent much of her time at her father's tomb. She was a very pure and saintly character. Texts of the Koran, mingled with the arabesque, crowd every part of her large white marble sarcophagus. Even

A NATURAL CRADLE, SOUTHERN INDIA.

the sculptured slate was covered with inscriptions detailing her numerous virtues; and as if that were not enough, a large tablet was inserted in the wall of the alcove, which was also full of inscriptions. Her name "Sukerum" (sweetness) was inscribed on the foot of the tomb. The old fungus, the keeper, started off in an eulogistic strain about her, as though she was a very holy saint. This struck me as very peculiar, coming from a Mahomedan—a sect reputed to believe that women have no souls. Men are often better than their creeds.

The entrance to the vault, where the real tomb is, opens from the ground terrace. The long sloping passage is paved with slabs of stone, now smoothly polished by the friction of bare feet, through more than two and a half centuries. Entering any house with shoes on the feet, here, would be as woful a breach of good manners, in either a Moslem or Hindoo, as it would be in a christian country, for a gentleman to sit in church with his hat on his head. The vault is spacious, and the wall appears to be covered with a coat of cement or stucco, without any ornament whatever. The sarcophagus is a plain solid block of polished marble and stands in the centre, it has that peculiar glossy surface that is produced on old stone by the constant friction of hands, caused here by the feeling out of the outlines in the dim light that comes from the door, visitors by doing this save the price of a torch.

Leaving the large ground terrace we ascended the flight of stairs, before mentioned, to the second, which extends three hundred and sixty feet on each side, and has a balustrade. This great surface is built up solidly from the foundation, except the vault—which is not more than forty feet square, and the alcoves in the corner, where the daughters are buried. Here we find four pavilions over each entrance from the four causeways, coming from each gateway, and two very large octagonal ones on each side of the corners of this terrace, making twenty-four in all on this story; the same Saracenic arched alcoves of no depth surround the solid body of the structure.

Up another flight of steps to the third terrace extending about two hundred feet on each side, having a balustrade of stone on the outer edge and the same row of shallow arched alcoves around the decreasing central structure. The same number of pavilions adorn the porches and corners as on the lower one; the same solidity is seen everywhere; only here and there have the rains and the sunshine which have fallen on it through all these long years, left any marks of decay on the pavement. Time and changes have dealt lightly with it. After the capture of Agra by the English, one thousand of their soldiers were quartered in this mausoleum and garden, for some time.

The fourth terrace, extends only one hundred and fifty feet on each side; here is the same repetition of the alcoves around the body of the structure, which without them would be a blank wall. The space between it and the balustrade is comparatively narrow. The pavilions have diminished in size, as we have come up; there is now only twenty, but those over the porches have their domes covered with brilliant emerald colored tiles that reflect the sunlight from them like monstrous gems, producing a very charming effect, reaching as they do to the base of the lovely white marble screen above.

We now pass up to the fifth terrace and find ourselves translated into a frostwork temple that has hardened into alabasta; only the blue heavens roof it over and blend exquisitely with the curtains of marble lace that enclose a court of ninety-six feet on each side. The sun does not look down upon a fairer spot than this. I could no longer wonder why the maiden daughter loved to come here to pray. It was doubtless her pure mountain top, where the gentle in spirit have always loved to pray; and I can easily believe her fervor and devotion increased, as she conned over the ninety and nine names, or attributes of God, written on her father's sarcophagus. Here she may have had clearer views of a holier heaven than Mahomet portrayed, for the story of the Saviour was known in her father's palace. His favorite

THE TOMB OF AKBAR, SECUNDRA.

SARCOPHAGUS OF AKBAR, SECUNDRA.

wife was a christian Portuguese lady, whose tomb half a mile away to our left, is now occupied by a mission press, that is telling of Jesus to millions in this valley.

All the dust and noise is far below; all the dark gloomy brown stone has disappeared; everything is as cheerful, graceful and beautiful as if the Titans had begun a huge pyramid, and carried it up and up, and then angels had stopped them suddenly, and changed all with a brush of their pure white wings into alabaster.

The pavement of this court is laid in porphyry, white marble and goldstone. In the centre stands the marble sarcophagus of Akbar*—a single block of very fine grained white marble, which is superbly sculptured in scrolls, vines and flowers; among which are traced the words, "God the giver of life. God the merciful. He that setteth up, and He that putteth down. God the giver of our daily bread." Also, standing out in relief, appear the seventy-nine names by which the Almighty is invoked, or addressed by Mussulmen. There is no mention of Mahomet; Akbar put him out of sight as much as possible, and changed the era of the Hegira and the Arabian months for the solar year. Arabian names were disused. He allowed no one to approach him with a beard, although wearing the beard was enjoined in the Koran. No deeds of dark ferocity stained his occupancy of the throne. He made wise and just laws for the people, and in the Hall of Public Audience, often sat below the throne to see that the laws were properly carried out.

He allowed perfect toleration in religious matters. He sent to Suret for the Portuguese missionaries, and supported them at his court for two years. He delighted to call together the notables of different religions and listen to their arguments. His grandsons were instructed in the New Testament. Their lessons, says Elphinstone, did not begin with the usual Mahomedan form "In the name of Allah!" but in the name of

* The body of Akbar, it is reported, does not rest here, but lies in a plain marble sarcophagus, without ornament or covering, in the cypt of the mausoleum, reached by a long, narrow passage, leading from the main entrance.

Jesus Christ. He seems to have thrown off the shackles of the Moslem faith, but did not embrace a new religion in its place; his own ideas of religion seems to be comprised in this: "There is no God but God, and Akbar is his Caliph." M. Thevenot a French traveller, who visited Agra in 1666, says that there were at that city twenty-five thousand christian people. They were mostly Dutch or French, and Portuguese, their half caste descendents employed in the arsenal and army. Very few traces of them are to be found there now.

The Christian Begum's tomb, is less than a mile from Secundra Bagh; it is a large structure and stands in a region of ruined walls and brick foundations of large buildings; indeed very much of the distance from Agra there, is covered with broken brick walls and mounds of rubbish. Here and there are little plots of ground that have been cleared from debris and are yielding good returns to the cultivator. A neat little church with a tall spire and cross, and a grassy lawn around it, —much as if a piece had been cut out of christendom and dropped down on this plain — fronts the tomb where Bégum Marie, though dead more than two centuries and a half, is doing a great amount of teaching.

On reaching the enclosure we were met by the children of the Episcopal or Church of England mission school and their teacher, or rather an assistant, who had charge of the little ones at the time. He probably had unmixed Saxon blood in his veins, but very sluggish, for on being asked if that was the Christian Begum's tomb; he replied; that he had only been at the building *three months*; the gentleman was absent that day; if he was at home he could tell us all about it. "I have heard," continued he, "that one of the Emperor's wives was buried here; I do not know about her being a christian, for I am sure there is no cross on her tomb." It did not seem to occur to him that a christian could be a christian without a sign. However, he conducted us into the interior through a long corridor, to a Portuguese half caste who was working at a printing press, and who readily gave the information that we asked; and then brought the gentleman who had supervision of the mission printing. I regret very much that I cannot recall his name, for he kindly gave us much information, not only about the ruins, but about the work the mission was doing there, and also specimens of their printing. I purposely avoid making any report of what the missionaries are doing in this country, not from a want of sympathy in their good works, but because I think they, having the facts and evidence, can do it better. The orphanage and school here have in their charge more than three hundred children.

After the mutiny of 1857, the mission repaired the mischief the rebel Sepoys had done the tomb, and walled up the arches in the corridor—for it was a very solid and firm building—and set their press at work in it, and it has been used for that purpose till the present time.

Bégum Marie's grave is under a solid mass of masonry more than one hundred feet square which forms the centre, and there is no access to it. As she died before the Emperor, he probably had her tomb constructed in such a way as to effectually prevent any indignities being offered to her remains, on account of her religion, after his death. Thus he entombed this woman, whose only known history may be summed up in a few words. She was an accomplished Portuguese lady, who no doubt, exercised a great influence over the Emperor, and to whom he was tenderly attached. As it was but a fraction of time that the Emperor could spare from the duties of government and his numerous wars—involving long campaigns—and as this fraction must be divided between herself and two other wives of higher rank, whose children and relatives occupied the highest positions in the kingdom, and upon whose society or friendship she could not rely, her life must have been a very dreary and monotonous one. It is said he built a splendid palace for her at Futtehpore Sikri. It is more than probable that she did not become his wife before the court forsook that place, and Agra was built. The building near her tomb now occupied as the orphanage, is said to have been her garden house.

The tomb has nothing light or airy about it, it is a massive, gloomy square pile of arches and corriders without a dome. On the flat roof of the structure, in the centre, with no screen or sculptured ornament of any kind, is a solid block of pure white marble, the size and form of a woman's tomb, without a slate to denote a Moslem, or a cross to denote that a Christian was buried here; its plainness no doubt has saved it from the fanatical moslem rage against unbelievers.

We entered the carriage and drove back to Agra. Among the ruins we passed on our way were several small tombs; the sides were enclosed with perforated marble, which, though small, looked so beautiful that we got out and went to them; there were no inscriptions on them, they evidently belonged to the middle class of people.

But it must not be imagined that all the people of India are buried in such costly graves; far from it! A traveller thus describes a scene he witnessed in Agra in 1868:

"In the course of the morning, while walking among the ruins of palaces which adorn the banks of the Jumna below the Taj, I witnessed a strange and touching scene. I was about to descend one of those ghâts, or great staircases which lead to the river, when a plaintive song, interrupted by sobs, struck my ear. I approached softly, and hiding myself completely behind a tree, saw an old and poorly clad woman sobbing, with her face hidden in her hands, seated on the steps of red sand-stone. At the foot of the staircase, on the brink of the water, stood two young Hindoo girls, one of them naked to the waist, standing upright with her arms raised to heaven, and singing in a strangely plaintive tone, one of those cradle songs with which Indian mothers lull their infants to sleep. As she sung, she took flowers from a basket, and let the bright-colored leaves fall into the water. I could not make out the meaning of this strange ceremony until, leaning forward, I perceived a sort of small wicker raft floating on the water, on which lay the dead body of an infant.

"This explained the spectacle. The poor mother, unable to pay the expenses of a funeral pile to consume the remains of the poor little creature, had resolved to confide them to

THE HINDOO MOTHER.

the sacred waters of the Jumna; and she was there, accompanied by her mother and sister, bidding her infant a last adieu. She was accomplishing no rite; her heart alone had inspired her with the idea of singing the usual song once more to the little one; and, with a not less touching inspiration, she was throwing over the frail body leaves from those flowers which were true emblems of its brief existence; while her sister, leaning over the water, held the little raft, reluctant to abandon the tender prey to the monsters of the stream."

Next a deserted garden attracted our attention. Its high brick walls were perfect, and so were the towers at each corner—crowned with pretty little kiosks. Not a tree or blade of grass was in it. We walked up to the deserted house, it looked far more desolate than the tombs, for there is a feeling that a house ought to have people in it. It was built of dark brown stone; a fountain with water jets was in front of it, in the platform on which it stood. The walls inside and out, were of brown stone and long slabs of the same, formed the ceiling. The windows were of perforated marble; a good stone stairway leads to a second story, and another flight to the roof. On the ground floor, a shepherd, who probably lived in a clay hut himself, had piled up loose brick in the door between the larger rooms, so that he could *pen his sheep in one of them.*

A few facts concerning the history of Agra may not be uninteresting to the reader. It was a place of small note until 1488. In that year the Emperor Secunder established himself there, and from that time it grew in importance. In 1556, as has been mentioned, Akbar made it the capitol of the Mosque Empire, naming it Akbarabad (by which name it is still known among the natives); and built monuments, palaces, mosques, and a vast citadel. Millions were lavished upon it during the reigns of Jehan-Gir and Shah Jehan, until the latter took up his residence at Delhi.

Since then it has met with reverses. In 1761 it was sacked by the Jats, and a few years later by the Mahrattas, and in 1803 was taken possession of by the English. Its population once 700,000 was reduced to less than 20,000, but under British rule has increased to about 200,000, and Agra now bids fair to become a great commercial emporium.

One night, we went up on the roof of the hotel to take our farewell view of Agra. Beyond the old palace we saw the Taj looking indescribably lovely in the light of the setting sun, and the domes of the Motie Musjid shone like huge pearls among cupolas and minarets of the old citadel of Akbar. As we turned to leave the roof we saw a tall figure with long, white patriarchal beard, and white turban, dressed in a long robe of a light soft color; on another part of the roof, it was Hoseim Khan looking out for the first glimpse of the new moon, which inaugurated a moslem festival. As our party descended the stairs, we left him there outlined against the evening sky, and I asked myself if that style of dress had really come down from David and Solomon; it is so very difficult to realize how stable and changeless are the modes of dress of the orientals.

CHAPTER XIII.

FUTTEHPORE—SIKRI—BHURTPORE—DIGH.

IN the vicinity of Agra are several places of note, among these are Futtehpore—Sikri, Bhurtpore and Digh. The former is an old walled city containing many beautiful palaces with gilded domes, gardens and fountains, in a good state of preservation, and although deserted and left in almost utter solitude when Agra was built, they still give an idea of the magnificence of the place, three centuries ago. Futtehpore was Akbar's favorite retreat and on it he lavished untold treasures, and one can but wonder at the caprice which should induce him so suddenly to give it over to such utter desolation. He is declared to have removed his court to Agra, because the business and bustle of it disturbed the meditations and life of a famous old Mussulman saint who resided there. Other accounts attribute his building the city to the fact, that Sheik Selim Shisti—the name of the anchorite—occupied a cavern in the hill on which the city was built, and that Akbar established his court there, in order that he might have daily intercourse with him; and that the death of Selim was the cause of the sudden change of his plans.

It is also related that it was through the sacrifice of the life of his own son, by the Sheik Selim—by some miraculous process—that an heir was born to Akbar; that this heir was named Selim in honor of the saint, and afterwards became the Emperor Jehan-Gire. The building was commenced by Akbar about 1570, and proceeded with great rapidity, until the summit of the hill was covered with glittering domes, and long lines of palaces marked the existence there, of a populous city. Tales of the magnificence of Akbar's court while at this place, reached the ears of Europeans, but were scarcely credited; but the evidences still existing among these ruins, prove that the truth was not half told. But for some cause, within a score of years after the first stone was laid at Futtehpore, Akbar abandoned it, and leaving all its magnificence behind, removed his court to Agra, and Futtehpore became again a solitary desert.

The fame of Selim, however, had gone forth, and pilgrims flocked to his tomb in multitudes, and two small villages sprang up for their accommodation. The tomb of Selim quite eclipses the royal palaces; judging from that, he must have been a very opulent saint during his life. The gateway is reached by a splendid flight of steps, the height of which is one hundred and twenty feet, and the *inside* measure of the arched portal is seventy-two feet. This gigantic gateway opens into a grand quadrangle five hundred feet square, which is surrounded by a majestic colonnade fifty feet high. On the west side of this court is a magnificent mosque surmounted by three domes of pure white marble. Fronting the lofty gateway, stands the tomb of the Saint. It is forty-six feet square, built of white marble and very elaborately carved. The sarcophagus containing the body is surrounded by a perforated and carved marble screen of surpassing beauty; having an arched canopy covered with mother-of-pearl. The floor is paved with jasper, the marble walls are inlaid in a most beautiful mosaic with cornelians, agates, carbuncles and jasper. The doors of this jewel box of a tomb, are of solid ebony.

The mosque is a very beautiful building, with an exquisite marble basin in front used by the faithful in their ablutions. The Imperial palace consists of a great number of buildings, connected by galleries, and covers a great extent of ground. Its exterior is plain, and contrasts in this respect with other palaces we had seen. The zenanah was surrounded by a high

THE HINDOO EGG DANCE.

wall, and each wife had her own palace within it. A richly ornamented verandah is said to be one used by the mother of Jehan-Gir, the favorite wife of Akbar, while a magnificent palace is pointed out as that of the Begum Marie. As before stated, it seems probable that this Christian Begum never resided at Futtehpore; yet there is some ground for supposing she did, for in one of the apartments is a fresco representing the Annunciation of the Virgin Mary. Wonderful it is, that in the sixteenth century, a monarch ruled in India so tolerant, as to allow almost every kind of religion to be represented in his kingdom. He even went so far as to build a little Hindoo temple called the Gooroo-ka-mundil, "Temple of the Medicant," and supported at his court a Gooroo or religious mendicant, as a token of his respect for the religion of a portion of his subjects.

The Pânch Mahal, is a curious structure of sculptured stone, and great doubts exists as to its use. It is built against the wall of the zenana and communicates with it. It consists of four distinct terraces placed one upon the other, supported by pillars and growing smaller in size as they ascend, with a dome upon the upper. The effect is remarkable. Other buildings are worthy of note. The palaces of the nobles of Akbar's court, are specimens of architecture of which any city in the world might well be proud; and the "Palace of the Public Audiences," and of "The Council of State" are models of beauty. The provisions made by Akbar, for the amusement of himself and wives, were very extensive. The "Court of the Pucheesee," arranged for playing the game with sixteen young slaves from the harem acting as pawns, was frequented by the Emperor, who afterwards continued to play the game at Agra, as before mentioned. One building, filled with galleries, corridors and passages, was used by the ladies of the court for the game of hide-and-seek.

The walls of the city are well preserved; they surround an area five miles in circumference. There are five gates for entrance to the town; near one of these stands the "Tower of the Antelope." From this tower it is reported that

Akbar was accustomed to shoot antelopes, driven past. It is curiously ornamented with elephant's tusks, in stone.

Bhurtpore, about twelve miles from Futtehpore, with a population of about 100,000, is in the centre of the Jât kingdom. The Jâts are a brave and warlike race and furnish the best soldiers of the empire. They opposed the Mussulmen with great vigor, and were never controlled until the English obtained possession of India. Their history dates back for centuries, but their origin is a matter of conjecture. The town of Bhurtpore has but few points of interest. It is sadly delapidated. The citadel is famous for the obstinacy with which it was defended by the natives, during two sieges laid by the English: one in 1805, and one in 1825. During the former, the English were repulsed several times and suffered severe loss. After three weeks of blockade, the siege was raised. The citadel and town were taken in 1825, after a most desperate resistance. The walls of the town were destroyed by the English, after they got possession, and are now a mass of ruins.

But little remains in the way of architectural beauty in the town. An ancient palace, said to be the oldest in the place, remains tolerably preserved. The "Lake of the Pearl," a body of water of considerable volume, is situated in an elevated plain, and supplied water for the moat which surrounded the town and protected the ramparts. The visitor will find but little to interest him, and will gladly avail himself of the first opportunity to leave.

Digh, one of the oldest of the old cities of India, dates back centuries before the Christian era. It has many magnificent specimens of architecture, and is strongly fortified. Here it was that Lord Lake was successfully resisted in his march in 1803, and for a time stayed. A beautiful edifice is the Gopal Bhowan, situated on the banks of a lake. It is a part of the magnificent palace, built by Souraj-Mull, in 1730, which consists of several pavilions or Bhowans built between two lakes, and which make a beautiful appearance with

THE INDIAN PRINCESS, SHAH JEHAN.

their balconies, colonnades, and kiosks. This palace is looked upon as one of the most perfect of its kind.

But a most wonderful building is the great Audience Hall: the Dewan Khas—with its columns and carved corridors. It is a specimen of architecture hardly equalled in elegance. It is surrounded by beautiful gardens, amid which are built exquisite pavilions, the abodes of the ladies and nobles of the court. These pavilions are connected by terraces. Immense reservoirs supply innumerable fountains with water. One of these throws water in the shape of bouquets. The simultaneous playing of all these fountains produces a charming effect. Digh is at present the capital of the Jât kingdom.

But farewell to Digh, to Bhurtpore, to Futtehpore and to Agra. We looked forward with the deepest impatience towards another city, whose renown eclipses all these others, and whose history is the history of India. Delhi was before us; Delhi, to whom Hindoo chronology assigns a descent from cities founded thousands of years before the christian era. Delhi, whose ruins cover miles upon miles of the earth's surface. Delhi, around whose name clusters all the romance of eastern history, magnificence and glory. Off for Delhi!

The thought sent a thrill through my frame, and made my heart leap with enthusiasm. A drive to the station at Agra upon a cloudy morning, a ride in the cars through a drizzling rain—the first we had seen during our long journey, and even then unexpected—a short jaunt in a sort of an omnibus, and we alighted safely at the dâk-bungalow—the traveller's dwelling;—one of those institutions kept by order of the government for the accommodation of strangers, in places where, as in Delhi, hotels have as yet not sprung into existence. We found our quarters quite comfortable.

The next morning was clear, the clouds had rolled away and we strolled down Chandni Chowk, the great thoroughfare of Delhi, which runs in a straight line from the Lahore gate to the grand entrance of the citadel.

It is really a fine avenue, and although its former magnificence has passed away, and the gorgeous displays which were wont to appear upon it are no longer seen, yet much interest is awakened, by the appearance of this really business street. Multitudes fill it hourly, women in rich attire—the style designating them as of Hindoo or Mussulmen extraction—stroll as leisurely up and down as they do in Broadway; natives of Delhi mingle with those from every section of India—merchants, bankers, laborers, in fact all classes, are seen here, as in other cities, actively engaged in their legitimate business. The stores are crowded with goods and customers, and everything betokens a thriving place.

CITADEL, PALACE, AND GATE OF THE JUMMAH MUSJID.

CHAPTER XIV.

THE FORTIFIED PALACE OR CITADEL OF DELHI, AS IT IS NOW.

WE crossed the deep and now dry moat by the drawbridge, and entered that famous, grand old Delhi gate of the Palace, between two hexagonal towers crowned with kiosks, or light, graceful pavilions, built of the same red stone as the towers. The walls enclose a circumference of ground of one mile and a half, in which the several buildings stand, which constitute and are known as the royal palace of Delhi.

The wall is forty feet high, flanked with towers at regular intervals, which are pierced with ports for large guns, while the walls themselves have only loop-holes for musketry. High above the gate is the lookout from which the guards could hold parley with any one desiring admittance. The cornice over the gateway is crowned with a row of small, white marble domes, similar to those over the gate of the Jumna Musjid or mosque, which seems to have been a favorite style of embellishment with Shah Jehan; and these are flanked with two very slender minarets, crowned with the most exquisite little bird-cage like pavilions of white marble. Indeed, pavilions seemed to have been perched wherever there was standing room for them; and when towers failed to offer a convenient site, a slender minaret shoots up and offers itself as a graceful pedestal for a kiosk or pavilion. This peculiar feature of Mogul architecture takes away all the gloomy, frowning look, so usual to a fortress.

Having entered the gate, we passed over a road paved with round stones, which led up an inclined plain between two parallel walls, thickly loop-holed for musketry on each side. What a fearful gauntlet of plunging fire might here be rained down on a foe, if the walls were well manned. At a distance of six or seven rods we entered the second gateway, similar to the first, but opening into a high covered gallery of considerable length, built with the same red sand-stone as the outer wall. Around us were numerous rooms opening out on little verandahs, which, in the palmy days of the Moguls, were occupied by important officers of the court.

A little to the left of this was the building once occupied by Col. Ochterlong, the English resident councilor at the court of Delhi, who bravely saved the city in 1804, when that fierce Mahratta chieftain, Holkar, laid siege to it. The lamented Capt. Douglas occupied that position in 1857, and was the first victim of the mutiny. High over this second gate is a red stone balcony, called Naobut Khanah—Music House. Here the palace band discoursed music, and banners floated out, when Shah Jehan the magnificent, or Aurungzebe his successor, was wont to pass with gorgeous processions on his way to battle; or perchance, on a hunting excursion, with a retinue like an army corps; or in celebration of a birthday, with squadrons of gorgeously caparisoned elephants in crimson velvet embroidered with gold. Following the Emperor, were the foreign kings and princes at his court, all glittering with the famous gold cloth of Benares, each with as many retainers, or troops, as his exchequer could possibly allow. Hooded hunting-leopards, trained for catching deer, were led along by their keepers, and perhaps, one or two royal bengal tigers in cages, to be pitted against a wild buffalo in fight, for the later afternoon recreation.

From this gate, Aurungzebe went to the Jumma Musjid—Sacred Mosque—which one may see beyond on the hill, on the first of the Ramadan fast, when the Hindoo people, sitting and standing, blocked his way, clamoring with an importunity peculiarly oriental, for the abatement of the

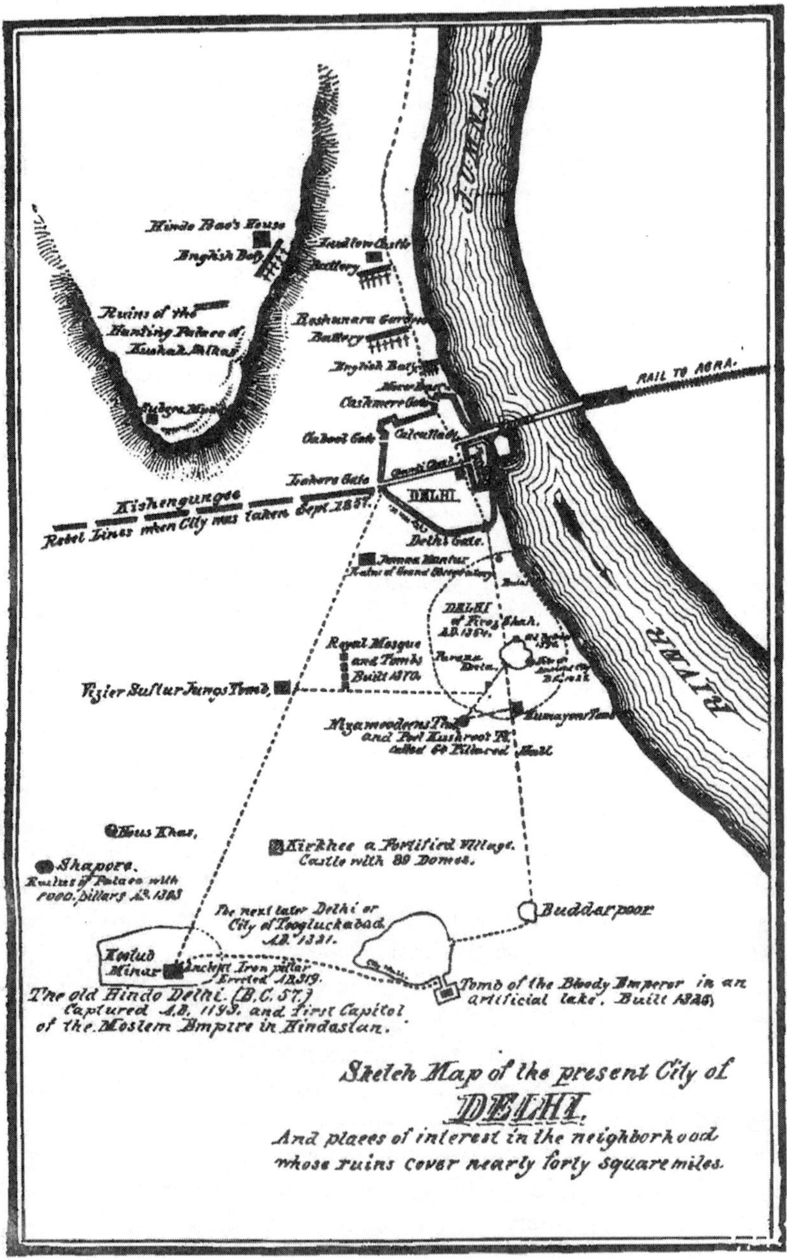

JUMNA
RAIL TO AGRA.
Hindo Rao's House
English Baty
Ludlow Castle
Battery
Ruins of the
Hunting Palace of
Roshunara Gardens
Battery
English Baty
Cashmere Gate
Cabool Gate
Calcutta
Lahore Gate
DELHI
Kishengungee
Rebel Lines when City was taken Sept. 1857.
Delhi Gate.
Jumna Muntur
DELHI
of Firoz Shah.
A.D. 1354.
Royal Mosque
and Tombs
Built 1370.
Vizier Suftur Jungs Tomb
Humayons Tomb
Nyzamoodeens Tomb
Kus Khas.
Kirkhee a Fortified Village.
Castle with 89 Domes.
Shapore.
Ruins of Palace with
1000 Pillars A.D. 1343
The next later Delhi or
City of Toogluckabad
A.D. 1321.
Buddarpoor
Kootub
Minar
Ancient Iron pillar
Erected A.D. 319.
The old Hindo Delhi. (B.C. 57.)
Captured A.D. 1193. and first Capitol
of the Moslem Empire in Hindastan.
Tomb of the Bloody Emperor in an
artificial lake. Built 1325.
Sketch Map of the present City of
DELHI
And places of interest in the neighborhood
whose ruins cover nearly forty square miles.

jezia (capitation tax on Hindoos,) and he ordered his elephant driven over them. What, to the Grand Mogul, were a few men trampled to death! All this magnificence and tyranny has passed away, as also the turbaned guards, their officers, and the thousands of courtiers at this once powerful court. The British flag has long waved where the banner of the Mogul once floated. A few sepoys were now on guard, and from their officers we obtained permits to visit the palace.

Crossing a broad court—which was unpaved—by a dusty, untidy walk, we passed the old canal of Ali Murdan, built in 1650. Here our guide pointed out an ordinary brick building, where the late king's Prime Minister lived, near which were two or three trees about the brow of the hill, where, he said, twenty-five English women were either hung or shot, in the late mutiny. It seemed almost too horrible to believe did we not know, only too well, what crimes were perpetrated at Cawnpore in 1857.

We walked towards the Dewan A'm, or Hall of Public Audience. The lesser zenana or women's apartment is situated in the rear of the Hall, a door opening into it. We entered upon a number of soldiers cleaning their belts and blacking their boots, and perceived that the apartments once allotted to the favorites of royalty, were now occupied as barracks for English soldiers. These apartments were of fair dimensions and tolerably lighted—for women's rooms two centuries ago;—but if ever there were any ornaments attached designed to cater to a woman's taste, they have disappeared long ago. This was probably a sub-zenana for the lesser " Lights of the Harem," for the builder never married but one wife. The walls are of red sand-stone and there is an arched gallery or verandah that opens towards the Dewan Khas and the other zenana by its side. One of these red sand-stone rooms which once had elaborate gilding and flowers painted all over it—though now covered with whitewash—was one of the private apartments of the Emperor. If one, in imagination, will hang the walls, windows, doorways and verandah with rich, crimson silk curtains; and cover the bare floor with a thick stuffed and quilted mat or carpet, here called a sittringee; and then dot over this with dainty rugs of rich, heavy silk brocades glittering with beaten, inwrought gold; and immense cushions of the same material embroidered with seed pearls and gold, and gems fastened by being set in a small socket of gold and then stitched on; this room would be arrayed in eastern style, and be very far from mean looking, though not suited to present wants and tastes.

Through the door opening into the hall of justice, those great old Mogul Emperors were wont every day, when they were in Delhi, to enter upon this throne, to sit and hear the cases of the people tried and decided, according to the principles of justice laid down in the koran. This then was the lobby, in reality, though the term was not then known; it was just the place where the power of the favorites could be exerted over the royal mind, to influence the Emperor to decide a certain case a certain way, before taking his seat to hear the case tried.

We will see from the glimpses we have of them in history, in peace and war, that the lives of the most powerful rulers: Baber, Humayun, Akbar, Jehan-Gir, Shah Jehan and Aurungzebe, were of constant activity. In battle, the sovereign, if he commanded in person, must be found at the front, conspicuously mounted on the tallest war elephant, dealing his best blows if need be, and directing the movements of his army; if he was lost sight of for a moment, as in the case of Dara Sheks—the rightful heir instead of Aurungzebe—the army would lose heart and flee. Emperor Humayun mounted with the scaling party, the walls of one of the strongest fortresses in India by means of steel spikes thrust into the crevices of the stone wall, and overcame the garrison. Each Emperor held his power by his own right arm. A part of every day, in time of peace, he must be seen by his people, hear and judge their causes; or some leader would soon spring up that would relieve him of his power, his throne and his life.

PLAYING CROQUET IN THE TROPICS.

We will now open the door and step upon the throne of Shah Jehan and his son Aurungzebe, the culminating Mogul stars.

We are under a white marble domed canopy supported on four pillars. The floor is also of white marble, and raised about ten feet above the floor of the hall or pavilion; this being in the centre of its back wall, is very well situated for the royal person to see and hear what is going on among his subjects in the crowd below him. On scraping away the white-wash—and it is to be hoped the English Government will finish the good work it has begun and clear it away from all these works of art—we shall find traces of very elaborate inlaid work. The whole of the wall behind the throne, says Beresford in 1856, is covered with mosaics in precious stones, representing the most beautiful flowers, fruits, birds and beasts of Hindoostan, in a very natural manner.

There is a low ceiling of marble along its top and up the pillars which support the canopy over our heads, and along its cornice also, we even now—after all these changes, the conquests and sacks of the city, and the flight of two hundred years—see cornelians, agates, jasper, onyx, green marble, amethyst, jodestone, lapis lazuli, etc., etc., wrought into beautiful flowers and figures, discernable through the vile white-wash.

This Dewan A'am was a Hall of Justice, an open pavilion on three sides. The roof is supported by pillars connected by Saracenic arches standing upon a raised platform approached by steps. Nearly in the centre of the floor, and at a convenient distance in front of the throne, is a raised slab of white marble, once richly inlaid, but of which few traces now remain. That slab marks the place allotted to the learned Cazi, or Mufti (judge) when he sat to expound the laws of the koran.

A novel sight to our western eyes, would an oriental court of two centuries ago present, if we, with a magician's wand, could bring back the turban-headed crowd in their flowing robes, and the dress of each caste and tribe of people. The prevailing color of the mixed assembly would be white, but there would appear dashes of blue, red and yellow, with the green robes of a Suiad or a Pilgrim to give a faint hint of a flower bed, minus the fragrance. The Cazi would sit a' le Turc on his embroidered mat with the koran on a silver book-stand before him. Little could be gathered from his face as to which side he inclined. The pleaders would gesticulate with a rapidity and warmth, that, in any except an oriental man, would foreshadow a coming collision with somebody, or something; but in this case, it would prove only a cloud of dust. The features of the defendant, were he high or low, would not betray any signs, by which his enemies could triumph, before the final sentence was pronounced. If judgment was given against him, he would accept it and say: "God wills it." There would be no appeal, this would be the highest tribunal of his country. The execution would speedily follow.

One old traveller witnessed a ludicrous scene here. A rich widow bowed before the throne, as the Emperor was taking his seat. She was asked what complaint she had to present. She replied "No complaint, your majesty, I only wish the Emperor would explain in court, what kin he was to my late husband, that he should inherit the largest part of his estate; as it will amply compensate me for my small stipend and my sons, who are left but scarcely enough to save them from servitude." The Emperor was amused at her ingenuity in placing his rapacity in the light of a relative, and immediately wrote an order for the full restoration of all the property, of whatever kind, that his officers had taken from the estate.

The court of the Dewan Khas, or throne room, was the centre of attraction here; it was the place where foreign princes and ambassadors, and the highest nobles in the realm were received by the Sultan, in a style befitting the rank of each. These receptions were called durbars, in oriental phrase, the magnificence of which culminated in the reign

4

LIFE IN INDIA.

of Shah Jehan and Aurungzebe, and dazzled the world at the time when Milton wrote:

> "The gorgeous East with richest hand,
> Showers on her kings barbaric pearls and gold."

Those scenes have forever passed away and in future will only live in story, showing, however, the civilization to which the people of this country had attained.

On the further side of this court, at the edge of the bank overhanging the river Jumna, is a long marble chaboutra, or terrace, on which stand three detached marble buildings. The throne room occupies the centre; at the left of it are the royal baths and private apartments of the Emperor. On the right is the zenana buildings, occupied by the royal ladies of the harem.

We commenced our survey, beginning at the baths, which were not accessible to visitors until the last Emperor had been banished with the royal family forever from Delhi.

Passing into the corridor, the baths are on the left. The room is about thirty feet square and seems as perfect to-day as when the Emperor left it. There are no windows in the walls, it is lighted from the roof, by a sky light—ordinary sashes of plain glass, which look too modern to have been placed there by Shah Jehan. The walls are of the purest of white polished marble, each side is adorned with exquisite, intricate designs of flowers and scrolls inlaid with precious stones; each shade of color in the different parts of the flowers, leaves and buds, was represented by a shade of the same color in the stones. The Roman and Florentine mosaics were, generally, made of artificial colored stone. The mosaics of the old Moguls are no shams, the stones are real.

An exquisite border of mosaic runs around each side of the apartment, framing within a panel, almost countless corneliaus, rubies, emeralds, agates, turquoise and crystals, wrought into beautiful representations of the flowers of that country. On one side, under a low arch in the wainscot, was a reservoir, where, it appeared, water was heated from below.

The third side of this apartment, was a long arched alcove; the inlaid floor of which was raised six or eight inches above the level of the room; it was decorated with the same rich mosaics. Here the Sultan could robe, safe from moisture. In the centre of the floor was a raised slab of marble, bordered and exquisitely adorned with mosaic, on which the bather sat *a' le Turc*, while water jets from all sides of the room spouted their spray over him which trickled away over countless jewels wrought into a woof of flowers, in glistening polished stones, like a carpet with its rich border, and fell into a narrow channel running all around the room, then flowed out into a wider one, which conveyed it away.

Passing out of the bath, across the corridor, we entered another apartment about the same size, but evidently intended for a royal sitting-room. No lovelier spot could be imagined could we restore all the gorgeous paraphernalia that once belonged to it, as set forth by the writers of those days. Standing within these apartments of Shah Jehan, it flashed into my mind that the "Arabian Nights" may not be all fiction, for Shemselnihar's palace is outdone here; the mosaics in one of these apartments far outnumber those enumerated there.

Nearly in the centre of the room was a charming little fountain about four feet wide, of a most perfect scollop shell pattern, with a *jet-d'eau* in the middle, all exquisitely inlaid from brim to brim, and as fresh and perfect as ever. When the sun hung in the hot sky over these walls, how cool and soothing the plashing of the water on this shell-fluted basin must have been. Opening out on the rampart above the river, is the same style of balcony and bay-window that we saw at Agra; the same, yet not the same, for it is fresher and richer in decoration. The design and arrangement of the whole citadel and palace seem to be an effort to reproduce the one at Agra in a more highly embellished condition. From the window we looked on the ancient palace of Selim Gurh, which was built by Sher Shah, who drove out the Timorlane kings and ruled the empire sixteen years. It was

NATIVE LIFE IN INDIA.

there that Aurungzebe first placed his brother Morad, after getting him so intoxicated that he had to be placed across his horse like a bag of grain. Morad was his confederate in dethroning their father. That being done, Aurungzebe got rid of his brother by sending him to prison for life, in the fortress of Gwalior, which is now used as a military store-house.

The opposite bank of the Jumna is dressed in the green velvet of young wheat, striped with wide golden patches of blossoming mustard. Cultivated fields on this side come close up to the water. Very anxious, haggard, and watchful eyes have looked out from this beautiful window, when these walls were beleaguered by hostile camps, during the sieges and numerous captures of this city. Nidar Shah, king of Persia, captured and plundered the city in the year 1739. Seven years later, Ahmed Shah Dourani, the Afghan king of Candahar, swept with resistless force over all the provinces, and Delhi fell again. One year later came the plundering Mahrattas. Hitherto, her conquerors had been Mahomedans, but the rage of this Hindoo race was insatiable; they robbed and defaced temples, tombs and shrines, and the silver ceiling of the throne-room was taken down by them and melted into 1,700,000 rupees, the current coin of India. (Mr. Seward, erroneously says—page 411 of his travels—that it was sold in the market at London for 170,000 pounds sterling.) Two years later, Ahmed Shah Dourani again took Delhi, to humble and break the Hindoo Mahratta power, and then returned to his own country.

We bent down over the low screen of perforated marble lace that surrounds the balcony which is still perfect and strong, to see where the water of the river flowed into the moat, to augment the strength of the citadel. This walled rampart, seventy feet from the water on this side, seems not to bear a single scar from all the wars that this city has seen. Here in these rooms, amidst his luxurious cushions and mats glittering with shredded gold, and curtains of the richest fabrics from the famous looms of Shiraz, sat the builder of all this splendor, Shah Jehan the magnificent; in the later years of his life resigning nearly all the cares of his vast empire to his eldest son Dara Sheko whom he designed should succeed him; surrendering himself to the enjoyment of the palace and the society of his tenderly beloved daughter Jehanira. It was during this period of Dara's brief prominence, that the younger sons conspired to depose both father and brother. When their plots ripened into open revolt and marshalled armies, the scene shifted to Agra.

Dara Sheko led on the army against his rebellious brothers and was defeated. The Emperor remained with his daughter in the citadel at Agra, never again returning to Delhi; his son making him a close prisoner at Agra for the balance of his life, during which, he ruled within his own palace walls. He would not allow the daughter of the murdered Dara Sheko to accept the proffered hand of Aurungzebe's son, nor allow that monarch to remove the jewels and treasure in the palace. His favorite daughter Jehanira preferred captivity with her father to the splendor of her brother's court. He was buried in the Taj by the side of his beloved Moomtaj-ee.

The few glimpses that the history of that time gives of Princess Jehanira, show that she, as well as Akbar's daughter, was a most lovely character. She early embraced the christian faith as taught by the Portuguese missionaries, at her grandfather's court. According to Elphinstone, page 368, Jehan-Gir allowed two of his nephews to embrace the christian religion.

When Morad and Aurungzebe, Jehanira's two younger brothers, at the head of their two splendid battalions—after the defeat of the Imperial army commanded by Dara Sheko the elder brother—presented themselves at the gates of Agra, the defeated brother fled north to save his life if possible. The aged father not daring to meet his rebel sons, shut himself in his fortified palace within the city walls, distrusting in that dark moment, every one except his daughter, whom he chose to go without the gates, to arrange a peace between himself and his younger sons.

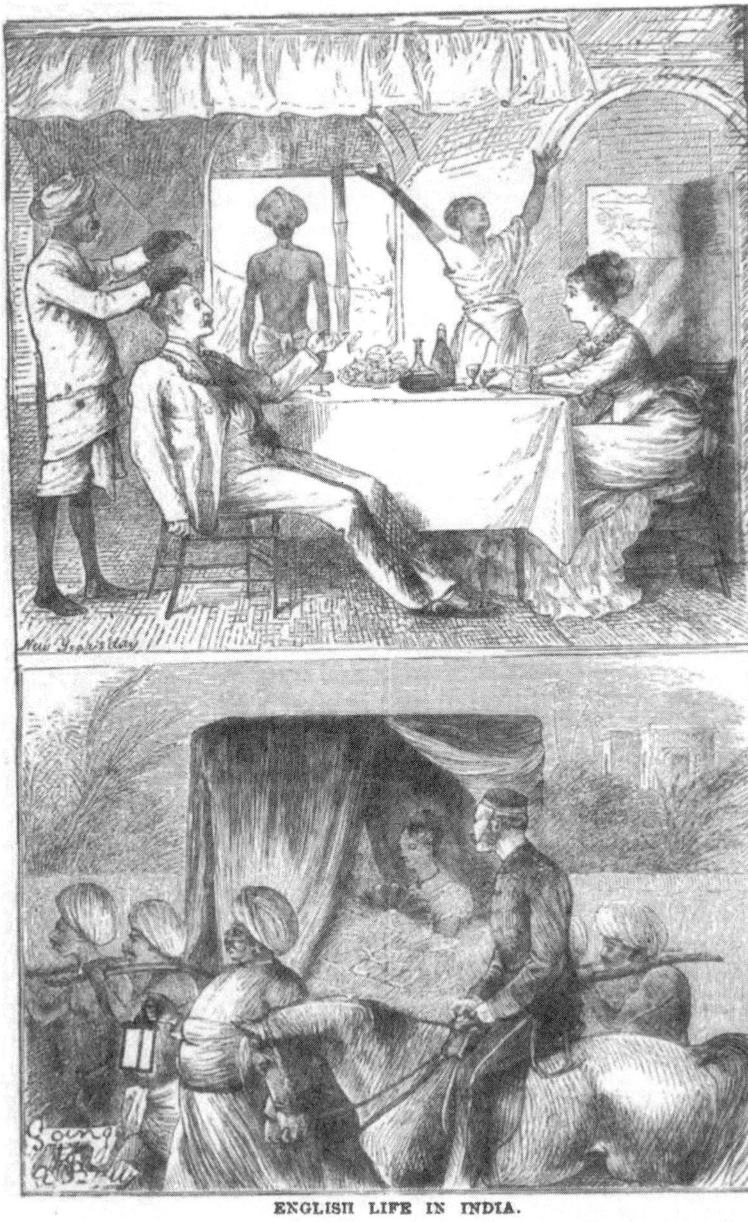

ENGLISH LIFE IN INDIA.

Morad repulsed her coldly, but the dissembling, subtle Aurungzebe, with mock penitence on his lips, besought her to entreat their father to receive his son Mahomed, by whom he would send a message of submission. This grandson of the Emperor, when once admitted with his retinue, disarmed the guards, and made his grandfather prisoner in his own palace.

The magnificence of her brother's court at Delhi has never been surpassed during any succeeding reign, but no inducement could draw Jehanira from the prison of her father. She was his solace, when he mourned so many of his family slain by this son, during the seven years captivity. Twenty years later, a plain grave was made by her request, among the royal tombs at old Delhi, bearing this inscription in her own words: "Let no rich canopy cover my grave. This grass is the best covering for the poor in spirit, the humble, the transitory Jehanira, the disciple of the holy men of Christ, the daughter of the Emperor Shah Jehan." Her mother was the beautiful Moomtaj-ee for whom the Taj was built. Shah Jehan, though he survived his wife thirty-six years, did not marry again, he had but one wife.

Aurungzebe, being a successful commander of the army, mounted the throne—after he had slain, or caused to be slain, all of his brothers and their sons—to be haunted during his reign of fifty years, by the suspicion, that his own sons were conspiring against him, as he had done against his father.

Few, very few Timorlane kings of Delhi lie buried about this city. Baber, the first of that family who resided in the Indian empire, requested his son to carry his body to Cabool, and, bury it in a beautiful spot that he loved in his early eventful life. His son and successor, Humayun died and was buried at old Delhi, and those three white marble domes, three miles to the left of the city, crown his mausoleum. Akbar the son of the latter, is buried at Secundra Bagh near Agra. Jehan-Gir and the famous Noor Jehan, his wife, are buried near Lahore on the bank of the Ravee. Shah Jehan his son, as already mentioned, lies in the Taj at Agra.

Aurungzebe, the son and usurper of his father's threne, died at Ahimedabad, and was buried there in a modern tomb, which Elphinstone says, the Emperor directed should be built with five rupees ($2.50) which Aurungzebe had himself earned copying the Koran. His wars with the Mahratta and other chiefs, kept him twenty-two years away from his capital.

According to Kafi Khan the historian of those times, the display of power in Aurungzebe's armament and marches, and the luxury exhibited in his encampment, in the Deccan, were very imposing indeed. His cavalry consisted mostly of hardy mountain men of his Northwest provinces and the borders of Persia. They came from Cabool, Candahar, Mooltan, Lahore, Goorkah, Cashmere and Rajpootania.

There were huge, powerful bodied Afghans, Beloochees and Cashmerees, who were born to spear and lance, as were also the fierce, haughty Rajpoots, descendants of a long line of warrior ancestors; these were opposed to the slender, frail, though lithe and supple bodies of the Hindoos of the peninsula.

His infantry was very numerous, composed of musketeers, matchlock men and archers; all well equipped. Of these, the Mewatteers from Mewatta, long accustomed to hard usage and robber expeditions, were of especial service in tracking the Mahrattas to their piratical dens or forts in the Ghats. His cannons were manned by Hindoos, but directed and aimed by Europeans. Several of the guns that were called cannons, were small insignificant things no doubt, but there are a few monster guns of that day yet in being, one, a brass gun at Bejipore, fifteen feet long, and four feet eight inches in diameter at the muzzle, the calibre two feet four inches, and weighing forty tons; the big guns in our late war seem not to have been a new thing, by any means. He had light artillery, composed of small guns which were mounted on camels instead of gun carriages, and fired from their backs. War elephants went into battle with miniature castles on their backs filled with armed men.

When the Emperor marched, his wives and young children went with him, for he knew not what enemy might seize them in order to extort some concession from him, by placing them, like young Akbar, in range of their own father's cannon-balls. Following his vast army of castled elephants and camel batteries, came long trains of baggage elephants and burdened camels, carrying the royal ladies and children, and baggage of the royal household, while a thousand and one armed liveried men run before the carriage of an Eastern Grandee, shouting, "Clear the way for his Sublime Highness, the King of the world, who graciously allows the sun to shine on us;" or "Make way for the grand Sultana Begum, Light of the world and Glory of the palace; sister of Rana of Oodipore," and as many more titles as the fertile minds of ingrained flunkeys or courtiers could invent; for their own dignity was elevated just in the proportion that they could raise their master's.

They were singularly safe in that direction, from offending any modest scruples of master or mistress, for that is a plant that never flourished in such soil. If the Grand Vizier was present, and passing along, he was sure to have a large body guard, a retinue of armed men in livery, shouting in a tone they thought most befitting a person next to the Emperor in position and power.

Then would follow a train of rare animals in cages, for a large menagerie constantly attended his marches for the amusement of the court. Here would come a fine lion, a veritable old king of the African desert, brought to this far spot to swell the pomp and show of the great Mogul. Next a huge Bengal tiger that would be pitted in combat against a monster buffalo, with horns four feet long. This would be an important item for the evening sport after getting into camp. Then came hunting hawks, or falcons, for sport in the field at catching birds on the wing. Hooded hunting leopards trained to taking deer. Dogs, hounds, and hunting elephants, with every accessory for a royal hunt.

As the sun that had hung so hot in a cloudless sky all day,

touched the top of the western mountains—those gigantic ghats or steps of the Malabar coast—would come a discharge of fifty cannons, announcing that the Emperor Aurungzebe had arrived at his camp, which, according to Kafi Khan the historian, would occupy a space five miles in diameter. The troops—the sinews of war, were arranged according to the best military skill of the day, and constituted the wall of the canvass city. One could walk through streets of gorgeous tents of noble Hindoos, and princes of Rajpootania, whose families ruled there before even the birth of Mahomet; proud Moslem warriors; Khans of tribes on the river Oxus; princes from Cabool and Candahar; and refugees from Persia.

A broad avenue led to the entrance of the royal enclosure. A continuous canvas wall thirty-six hundred feet in circumference, enclosed what may be called a magnificent cloth palace. The spacious portal was flanked by two elegant pavilions which were fitted up in the same style as the rooms at Delhi. From the pavilion on the right extended a row of twenty-five cannons; also one from the pavilion on the left. At the end of each row of guns stood tents for the band and state drums, and a little further on a royal guard was posted, which was mounted every day by a high nobleman of the realm. Near these was a separate tent for the Emperor's armor and harness. Further on, a tent to keep water cool with nitre; a third tent for sweetmeats; and a fourth tent for betelnut and hookah, and the various apparatus for smoking.

The kitchens were behind all of the others. Conspicuously placed, for effect and show, was the grand Durbar tent pavilion, a hall for giving receptions to foreign princes or high nobles of his own realm. In the centre, magnificently lined with the richest satins, velvets and tapestries, was the throne, which was surrounded by gilded pillars, on which rested a canopy of velvet, embroidered with gold and precious stones, and fringed with pearls. The floor was covered with Persian carpets (sittringers) of cloth of gold, and the richest satins and damasks of Persia and China were laid down for such guests to walk or stand upon, as were

AN IMPERIAL PROCESSION.

considered of rank worthy to be received into this hall.

Gilded cupolas surmounted the tops of all the royal tents of every sort. There were halls for private councils with all the cabinets attached to them; halls for giving audience to the people presenting petitions or grievances; tents to be used as mosques or oratories; tents for baths, and galleries for archery and gymnastic exercises. Separate suites of tent apartments for each of his Queens and their children and attendants, made the zenana as luxurious and private as when at Delhi or Agra. These tents were of a variety of lively colors on the outside, and the insides were lined with most gorgeous silks and velvets, according to the rank of the person that was to occupy the apartment. White muslins of gossamer firmness, were festooned with azure silks with glintings of interwoven gold, making a princess' tent look like the bower of a fairy.

Thus the court travelled, or as it is said there, went into marching cantonments for the whole dry season which lasts eight months of the year; or, if its object was a pleasure trip to the mountains and valleys of Cashmere, or up the Khyber Pass to Cabool, or to Candahar, the same gorgeous tent-city with all its palacial appointments and furniture, took up its line of march. Each tent and each article of furniture in all this magnificent array and profusion, had its exact duplicate, so that while the camp was dwelling in one set of tents at night, the other set was moving forward to be pitched at close of the morrow's march. Such was the magnificence of the four greatest reigns of the Emperors of Delhi, commencing nine years after the close of the reign of Henry VIII of England, and extending over a period of one hundred and fifty-one years.

CHAPTER XV.

DEWAN KHAS OR THRONE-ROOM AT DELHI.

THIS palace was built by the Emperor Shah Jehan, about the year 1638. The Empress had died eight years before, and her mausoleum, the Taj, was in the course of erection, which occupied, as one historian says, seventeen, and another, twenty years. In either case, they were both in process of erection at the same time. The same workmanship is seen, the same skill and perfect finish in all the details of the mosaic, and the same kind of precious stones wrought into the various designs; which fact goes to show, that the same chief illuminator and master of mosaic work, Amarand Khan of Shiraz, who wrought the Taj into such a marvel of beauty, superintended in this work also. No Parian or Carrara marble was ever finer or purer or more susceptible of high finish than this, from the quarries of Rajpootania.

The Dewan A'am as described, was a far less pretentious edifice than this; although it had its throne, it was only the Hall of Justice; the Emperor sat there as a sort of lord chief justice in the court of the king's bench; but when he sat upon the throne in the Dewan Khas, it was in his royal capacity as Sultan: Ruler of the Empire, to hold durbar; that is: to receive ambassadors from foreign courts; royal princes; guests of the empire; and the great nobles of the realm; who were here arranged on either side of the throne, in the strictest adjustment of rank. The stranger, to be introduced, advanced up between these rows of dignitaries, to near the foot of the throne, which is raised to such height as to enable the Emperor to overlook from his seat all that is passing within this enclosure.

The Dewan Khas, or throne room, as before stated, is the middle building on the long marble terrace. It is an open pavilion on three sides, as all oriental throne rooms are. It has two rows of pillars connected by beautiful Saracenic arches, and a low balustrade of the most exquisitely wrought marble filigree, which form a matchless colonnade around the inner room.

The roof is adorned with four small marble kiosks, one on each corner. From side to side, this building is about sixty feet. All the pillars are square and very massive, with pannels on either side, formed by rich mouldings; within these, are birds and flowers done in a most perfectly finished mosaic, composed of agates, cornelians, rubies, emeralds, malachite, goldstone, lapis-lazuli, turquois, on through the whole list of precious stones. Turquois, or cornelian flowers bloom on stems and vines of the purest *verd antique*, bud out with emeralds, leaf out with malachite, and go twining and waving in and out, up and over all the concave, scolloped Saracenic arches far over our heads, making them wonderously beautiful. Bishop Heber, viewing the architecture of the Mogul Emperors said: "They built like Titans and finished like jewelers."

I opened Mr. Seward's book, page 412, and read, "The frescoes of birds and flowers on the polished marble walls are now dim, certainly they must always have been a blemish." Bowing in all due respect and reverence to the lamented statesman, I must say, I applied the microscope to detect the deception; I found no paint, found no sham, all the stones real, and remarkably excellent ones of their kinds.

Turning again to the page, I read, "The solid silver plates of the great audience chamber have been stripped from the ceilings and sold in the market in London for 170,000 pounds sterling." In the year 1803, Lord Lake marched the first hostile English army against the city of Delhi, defeating and utterly routing, in its vicinity, the great Mahratta army and its chief, who had held the Emperor and city in the most oppressive vassalage since its capture by them in 1751. The people formed in procession, marched to the gates to welcome the English as their deliverers from the Mahrattas, and rejoiced as Lord Lake passed through the streets to the palace. Here the aged Emperor unfolded to him a startling tale of all the barbarities that these walls had witnessed. Sixty-four years previous, the Persians under Nadis Shah had plundered Delhi, flooded it with the blood of its people, and carried away the Peacock Throne. Twenty years later, the Mahrattas, under their prince, Sedasheo Bahao, captured and plundered the city and palace, taking down the gold and silver filigree ceiling, and melting it into rupees, the current coin of India; retaining afterwards, possession of the palace, city, and the revenues of the empire; only allowing the Sultan a stipend of $23,000 per annum. Eleven years later, a rebel Khan, the commander of the army, conspired with the Kotwal, or governor of the city, to plunder the palace again. These brigands tortured the Emperor, Shah Alum, tearing out his eyes in the vain endeavor to compel him to bring out treasure that had long since been plundered and carried away. There was not a brilliant prospect for spoils in 1803, even if Lord Lake had been a born vandal. It is true he might have stolen the Emperor, but there was no money for ransom; there were just the city and country left; they were a temptation, an irresistible one; they were just the things the Honorable East India Company coveted; so they took them—the Emperor aiding and abetting the taking, preferring the English to his Mahratta captors. Thus came the Protectorate with the resident British ministers behind the Mogul throne, which began with brave Col. Ochterlong and ended with slaughtered Capt. Douglass, in the mutiny of 1857.

In this Throne-Room stood the famous Peacock Throne. The seat was six feet long and four feet wide, composed of solid gold, and inlaid very elaborately with the most valuable

THE IMPERIAL THRONE-ROOM, DELHI.

THIS ROOM FORMERLY CONTAINED THE FAMOUS PEACOCK THRONE, AND IS IN THE PALACE MENTIONED IN MOORE'S POEM, AS BEARING UPON IT THE INSCRIPTION, TRACED IN LETTERS OF GOLD: "IF THERE BE A PARADISE ON EARTH, IT IS THIS, IT IS THIS, IT IS THIS!"

precious stones that a monarch might covet; as rubies, emeralds and diamonds. Its back was formed of jewelled representations of two life-sized peacocks, with tails spread, and between them stood a life-sized parrot, carved from a single emerald. Over this seat of gold was a dome of burnished gold, having on its lower edge a fringe of pearls. This was supported by twelve pillars of gold. On each side stood the symbols of royalty—not a crown, not a sceptre, not a shadow of an European royal toy—but two huge umbrellas with handles of wrought gold, which, like the canopy over the throne, were fringed with pearls.

A rogue of a jeweler at Bordeaux, France, finding Europe would no longer be safe for him, after he had imposed on one or two princes by selling them counterfeit gems, thought the air of Asia would agree with him, and thereupon took his way to the court of Shah Jehan, and was employed by that Emperor to make this throne, which made for himself a world-wide notoriety. The cost of the throne and adornments was estimated at one hundred and fifty millions of francs.

Over this gorgeous throne of gold glittering with its countless gems, spread out a whole ceiling of fretted gold and silver, made by a native jeweler, whose descendants yet linger about Delhi and far excel all others in filigree jewelry, which they make of good, honest sovereigns, without alloy. This ceiling the maker valued at twenty-seven millions of francs. Just beneath the ceiling and the cornice, at the right and left, the architect wrote in Persian letters of gold:

"If there be a Paradise on earth, it is this; it is this; it is this."

Ah! how this hand would have faltered had some wise seer caused tableaux after tableaux of one-half the cruel history that these walls have since looked upon, to pass before his eyes.

The zenana, or women's apartment is seen in the view of the Throne-Room, on the same marble platform at the right. This building is of white marble, gilded and painted in flowers and other ornamental designs, and from all appearance, never had any very elaborate mosaic work upon its walls, which were undoubtedly covered with hangings of silk. Only one or two of the rooms were of passable size. The small cramped sleeping-rooms, where the royal wives and children slept while in Delhi, would be condemned by our advanced knowledge of the laws of health. Doubtless, there were other houses appropriated to them within this enclosure, that have been allowed to go to decay, because their architectural style and finish did not entitle them to be preserved as works of art, as this has been. Perhaps this was oftener the abode of the King's mother, who, if she possessed a fair share of native good sense, was always a power behind the throne, and was usually made regent when the king went to battle, and was the woman (instead of the wife as in Europe) on whom the highest dignities and titles were conferred.

The zenana has another of those graceful pillared balconies to correspond with that of the baths and private apartment of the Emperor, yet more suggestive of a huge bird-cage than the other, because the spaces between the pillars are enclosed to their tops by a curtain of marble lace. Why was this made so secure and the others left so open? Was it because it was feared that some half-frantic woman, whose brain was maddening with the life she led, might seize an opportunity and fling herself down, to dash out her life on the stones at the bottom of the moat?

The room on the opposite side, opens into a white marble court, requiring only flowers and shrubs in graceful, sculptured vases and pots, to stand around the fountains and mingle their fragrance with its cool spray, to make it like the lewans, or cool saloons in the houses of the old Mameluke princes at Cairo. In the center is a fountain of dark or nearly black marble in the same scollop shell pattern as the one in the king's apartment in the baths, but it is much larger, and, as if making some amends for lack of decorations elsewhere in the zenana, it is more elaborately inlaid all over the polished, fluted ribs and brim of the basin. Fadeless flowers are in leaf, bud and bloom, done in jasper, rubies,

THE MOTEE MUSJID, DELHI.

agates and cornelians. On the side of the court next the throne-room, entered that broad channel communicating with the baths, the bottom of which was inlaid with green and white marble in zigzag lines, which, it is asserted, when full of water, gives the appearance of fish swimming in it. Over this channel stands the most exquisite marble lace-work that is to be found anywhere. Through this screen, the ladies could command a full view of what was passing in the throne-room, or court in front of it, without exposing themselves to view.

I thought of the many toddling little feet that had pattered over this court, and the little hands that had dabbled in this fountain, grasping at the sparkling gems under the water, that in after life held the reins of government with hands stained with the blood of brothers that here played in these waters with them. Beautiful white-robed young daughters, that here sported and played beside this fountain, and here bloomed, under an Indian sky, into maidens as beautiful as the poet has painted Lalla Rookh, at this threshold bade adieu to Sultana mothers, who, proud and stately, sent their daughters away with grand old Fadladeens, or trusty, crusty, pompous officers, with gorgeously mounted guards on Persian horses and elephants marvellously decorated, bearing in their lofty howdahs scores of maids of honor. These Princesses were carried in magnificent state palkees, on couches of gold cloth strewn with roses. Trains of camels burdened with presents, were followed by others carrying troops of players, dancing-girls and buffoons, to amuse the Princesses in their evening camp; then came the baggage-elephants carrying tents and camp equipage; then guards, guns, and music and banners everywhere. Persian and Afghan Khans or chiefs, dashed off or pranced and curveted as outsiders.

If the same Lalla Rookh and the characters represented in that wedding procession, and long march to Cashmere, where she was to be wed by the king of Bokhara, had any shadow of foundation, she must have lived some part of her early life here, by the side of this fountain; and that procession must have started from the foot of this platform. The author of Lallah Rookh was never in India, but the English Government had sent their ambassadors there nearly a century before this; and the East India Company were scarcely ever without some one in their interest in this court. It is probable at least, that an account of the wedding procession of some one of the Emperor's daughters, gave Moore the hints that led to the poem.

The history of India abounds in many very beautiful and romantic incidents, which, if they were separated from the deeds of blood with which they are closely connected, and represented in the quaint manner, and magnificent habiliments in which they were enacted, would be as charming and as readable as the poems of Moore or the fascinating stories related of the Caliph Haroun Al Reschid of Bagdad. Many native women have made their names famous by their heroic acts, when placed in circumstances requiring them.

The story of Chande Beebre is a veritable history of a sort of Joan of Arc, who was cotemporary with Queen Elizabeth and Catherine de Medici, and was regent for the young king Ahmednugger. She was a Hindoo woman, an Asiatic who had never mingled in the society of men—even those of her own family—as their equal, and certainly had no masculine training to fit her to harmonize conflicting interests. But certain it is, her influence had its weight among the princely chiefs of the Deccan. She said to each one, "Let us know no enemy but the Mogul." When this same enemy had battered down the walls of her own city, she rushed into the gap and stood there encouraging and directing all, till the invader was repulsed.

Gholam Khadis—a son of a man whose love of intrigue and blood was fully inherited from his fathers—on coming into posession of his estate, rebelled against the Government, and confederating with the Commander, marched his troops to the walls of Delhi. The whole court was corrupt; the Nigam or Governor of the city traitorously admitted a portion of Gholam's guards within the walls, though not within the citadel. Gholam immediately demanded the viziership from the Emperor, but the Begum Sumroo and a few other adherents, brought their troops to the timely rescue of the Emperor, and drove the rebel to his camp.

The Emperor, Shah Alum, rewarded the Begum Sumroo, with the office of Major General, for the timely and important service, which she had rendered at that critical moment. She was the daughter of a Moslem Chief, a lineal descendant of the Prophet Mahomet. Sceiads is the name usually given such men, a kind of pedigree that is current anywhere in a Moslem country, no matter what the ruling dynasty is. Sirdhana was her father's jahzir, or military station. Having no brothers, she inherited her father's estate and titles. She had force of character and energy enough to maintain her position and dignity, amidst the predatory chieftains ever on the alert for any advantage to be gained over the weak and defenceless. She was early in her married life converted to the catholic religion, and built a church and convent at Maruth, which had schools under its care, for the instruction of her vassals. She showed herself willing to promote the interests of her people in industrial pursuits, and in giving them protection of life and property. A little more than half a century had elapsed since Aurungzebe's hands had dropped the reins of government, and Shah Alum was the ninth Emperor of his family who had attempted to hold them. Stormy and troublous times came on, as one weak, indolent, inefficient Prince after another, ascended the throne of Delhi.

India was full of European adventurers and refugees, who went there to elude justice—deserters from ships, navy and army of different nations—who were attempting to get a foothold in that country. The native rulers in attempting to cope with, first the Portuguese, and then the Dutch, French and English, had learned from very mortifying experiences, that European military tactics and discipline, were in all respects, vastly superior to their own. Hence these refugees were eagerly sought for, to train their contingent of troops, and were allowed a share in the spoils of war.

Such an one named Reinhart, in the Begum's early life, had fought in her father's wars, and had so conquered his way to the old man's heart, that he thought it would be advantageous to marry him to one of his daughters. Their wedded life passed on evenly enough between themselves, she sharing his confidence, trials and plans in a greater degree than she would have done, had she married one of her own faith and nation.

Thus she was unconciously developing, and maturing strength of mind and sagacity, for the stormy years of her widowhood. Often after the return from a campaign where the spoils had been few, and the retreat to Sirdhana more than usually embarrassing and difficult, the usual quiet of her zenana would be broken by messengers to tell her, that their troops of wild irregular cavalry had mutinied, and had bound her husband to one of his own cannon, until he should give them the money they demanded of him. Sometimes they would emphasize their clamor by building a fire at the other end of the gun making the heat approach him slowly, giving him time to choose whether he would wait to be roasted by the heated iron to which he was bound, or yield to their demand.

There was only one son born of this marriage, and he, unlike either parent, had a very weak, infirm mind, and had nothing of the bold dash of the young Moslem men of his mother's race, or the sterner virtues of his Teutonic father. According to the customs of India, the Begum had him married to the daughter of a friend, and there was born from this union a daughter who was married at a very early age, to a Mr. Dyce an European, and this granddaughter's son became heir to the wealth of the Begum.

Reinhart had prudence as well as sagacity. His troops often amounted to five or six battalions; this gave him power and the dignity of a chief. He died in the latter part of the last century, leaving his wife in the full vigor of womanhood, to wrestle single-handed with her fate. Her mind naturally shrewd and penetrating, had become imbued with the rude strength of her husband, by his making her his confident and sharer of his plans. It did not take her very long to see that she must employ and command her husband's battalions, or be murdered and robbed by them. She built a fine large residence at Delhi, where she kept a part of her troops. Her retinue in passing through Chandni Chowk made a very noticeable figure. She built a fort at Sirdhana, and garrisoned it with troops in her pay. As weapons were necessary for her own soldiers, as well as others, she determined to manufacture them on her own estate at Sirdhana; and built a gun foundry and established an arsenal. It was about this time, during one of her temporary sojourns in Delhi, that she was able to bring such force to the Emperor Shah Alum, as before related, as to drive his rebellious vassal out of the city, after he had been treacherously admitted by the Governor, who was in league with him to depose the king, and plunder the city. For this, as before stated, the Emperor formally commissioned her as Major-General, and henceforth she was capable of making her power felt in the politics of the court.

Her troops once became very turbulent and disorderly and plotted to rob her treasury; even the women of her household being enlisted in the plot. Two of her slave-girls set fire to her house, while their lovers led on the soldiers who plundered it. The girls and their lovers eloped; but she caused them to be arrested at a village where they stopped, and brought before her. The trial was brief, for their guilt was very evident. She ordered them to receive a great many lashes; in fact, flogged nearly to death, and then ordered them to be buried, while life was yet warm in them, in her own tent, close beside her and under her own supervision. This prompt action ended the mutiny.

She soon after gave the command of her troops to a French adventurer named Le Vassoult, who not only performed this duty, but managed at the same time to successfully woo the Begum. It is said he professed himself so enamoured of her, that he declared if she should die he would kill himself. His trial came. A dissatisfaction arose among the troops and their sullen mood soon ripened into open mutiny, and such hostile demonstrations were made, that the loving pair sought protection in flight, but their wild, hard-riding troopers were not long in overtaking their fugitive commanders. When it was certain that they would be overtaken; dreading the indignities from this rabble more than death, the Begum drew a dagger and stabbed herself, as she was being carried along alone in her palkee. Vassoult was some distance in advance of her; the maids perceiving their mistress covered with blood, set up the usual wail for the dead, tearing their hair and beating their chests. They ran howling to Le Vassoult and told him the Begum was dead. He immediately drew a pistol and blew out his brains. Their pursuers finding Le Vassoult dead, but the Begum still alive, carried her back to Sirdhana and after some days of sulliness and annoying menace, they again acknowledged her authority. It is said they chained her to a gun-carriage for a week, which is not improbable.

But a storm was gathering; the Mahrattas had brought on a war between themselves and the English. The Begum hired her battalions to the former and fought at the great battle at Assai, where they sustained a crushing defeat. The Begum predicting from their prowess in battle the final triumph of the English, sought alliance with them—this certainly showed a good degree of foresight—while the English in their turn, sure of controlling the guns that were manufactured at her foundry—thus preventing their being used against themselves—encouraged her advances, and were thus enabled to turn her troops to their own account. They reinforced her six battalions with an European battery and a troop of cavalry, which augmented her power in no small degree and enabled her to maintain her rank with princes, as the protection of the English considerably increased her

ENGLISH LIFE IN INDIA.

revenue. The expenses of her establishment were six lakhs of rupees ($300,000) per year.

Besides building a church and convent, and establishing schools at Sirdhana, and building similar institutions at Maruth, she built palaces in other cities in India, and left in her will a million of rupees (half a million of dollars) to various charitable purposes. She died in advanced age, leaving to her great grandson, Dyce Sombre, sixty lakhs of rupees, ($3,000,000) who, after coming into possession of this inheritance, visited England, and though he was a miserable debauchee, he made a brilliant match for himself by marrying a nobleman's daughter, whom he rendered very miserable while he lived. After his death his property was the subject of a long suit in Chancery, and it has been stated that his wife received very little of it. Though he died in England, a large monument was erected to his memory in the church at Sirdhana where he was buried in a chapel at the right of the altar, where were also statues of the Begum and some of her descendants.

The sister of Lord Aukland relates an incident of the Begum when in quite advanced life. The Governor-General, as representative of the Queen of England, was marching in a goodly sort of royal state, such as would not disgrace the Queen herself, having with him all his councilors, and the ladies of his household, and officers of the vice-royal court at Calcutta, and a retinue of 12,000 men at arms and followers, through the upper provinces of India, to exchange civilities with different Princes, whose rank was supposed to be sufficiently exalted to entitle them to such an honor. Of course there were nice points of rank to be settled, for if on one hand they bestowed the honor of a visit upon those not of high rank, those who were, would not value it.

Upon nearing the Begum's territory, the council of the Governor-General and Master of Ceremonies or Aid-de-camp decided promptly against His Excellency's going in person to visit the Begum, as she was not of royal family. It was quite honor enough for the Aid-de-camp to make the visit, carrying His Excellency's compliments. Accordingly the second made the visit. The Begum, concealing all anger, represented how much the cause and prestige of the English would be injured if they passed her by—an old ally—so cavalierly, and followed up her eloquence with a polite offer of backsheesh of very valuable jewels. Of course the visitor refused them; it was against—says the narrator—the express rules of the East India Company to receive them. But somehow there was a radical change in his views when he went back, for he advocated the visit so earnestly as to overcome the other members of the council, and the visit with all due form, was made by the Governor-General in person.

RUINS OF OLD DELHI.

CHAPTER XVI.

RAMBLES ABOUT NEW AND OLD DELHI.

THE new or present city—that is, the citadel and palace, the walls and public buildings, were built by the Emperor Shah Jehan after his accession to the throne in A. D. 1628, on the outskirts of the old city built by Firoz Shah, and named after himself Shahjehanabad. As soon as the Emperor occupied the new palace the inhabitants of the old city came within the walls and made their homes, on account of both business and security.

The Chandni Chowk is a very broad street, a great departure from the rule in oriental cities. Through the centre of it runs an open conduit supplied with water from an old canal, which one Ali Murdan built two centuries ago. A broad walk is on one side of it, paved with stone and bordered with trees, with a wide carriage way beyond. Here in the early part of the day is a great commercial mart, and here, in the afternoons, under the old rulers, was the great show of Delhi. The grandees rode on elephants, with hosts of livered men running before them shouting their titles, while the whole space was filled with a glittering throng. All the marriage processions of any note passed through this great avenue. In the absence of the royal family these processions have lost much of their former brilliancy and show. Then, in case of the marriage of a son of a person of high rank, the ladies of the Emperor's family would come in native carriages with scarlet hangings, attended by a portion of gaily equipped Royal guards, followed by camel batteries, or trained elephants gorgeously caparisoned, and trains of palkees with bearers in bright colored clothes. Then followed the bridegroom, with his friend, each mounted on an elephant—the former carrying on his person the whole family stock of jewels and gold ornaments, so arranged as to give the greatest effect—accompanied by chobads (mace bearers) with gold or silver canes or wands, and servants carrying enormous peacock fans. Every gay or beautiful thing that the bridegroom or his friends could bring, was made to swell such a procession.

This street once witnessed a different sight, when Nadir Shah, the king of Persia, sat on the gateway of a small mosque not far from the Jumma Musjid, while the sack and plunder of the city went on remorselessly through all the hours of that bitter day, and when the old Mogul Emperor came to him, bowed down and besought him to stay the slaughter. Nights of carnage followed, more horrible than the day if possible, in which the inhabitants were tortured, mutilated and butchered in every way, to obtain money. Men killed their own wives and daughters, and then rushed into the streets to die.

We walked to the Jumma Musjid, (sacred mosque) which stands on a spur of a hill, about a quarter of a mile from the citadel gate. From its roof we overlook the wide space between this and the palace, which is planted with trees and neatly graded, and has winding and intersecting walks. There are no buildings in this part, excepting the government dâk bungalow, and a small tomb mosque where a daughter of Aurungzebe is buried, built of red granite and white marble with slender ribbed minarets; a sort of toy model compared with the grand old structures, from which it was evidently patterned.

We passed up a broad flight of thirty-six red sandstone steps and entered a lofty gateway, having very high doors faced with brass, that were only opened on grand occasions, when the Emperor went in person at the close of the

Ramadan fast. There is a wicket, which appeared from the ground to be a little hole, but we found it to be the height of ordinary doors, and entered into what I shall call the gate building. An oriental gate is quite an imposing structure; this, is three stories high, built very solidly with a rotunda in the centre reaching to the roof, with three tiers of windows opening into it from rooms on either side of it. The rooms in each of these three stories are arched, the top of one forming the foundation and floor of the story above it.

We now passed into a large open court, four hundred and fifty feet square, which has three noble gateways opening into it. In the centre is the reservoir for ablution. The koran requires its disciples to wash before prayer. A few of the poor had washed their outer garments and spread them on the pavement to dry, showing an economy of time and a regard for cleanliness next to godliness. A high red sandstone wall encloses this court, it is plain and solid without; within, a cloistered gallery of stone elaborately ornamented, extends along three sides; the ever present accommodation for poor travellers, that every Mosque affords.

On the west side stands the mosque. It is two hundred and one feet in length, and one hundred and twenty feet in breadth, flanked by two tall minars, each, one hundred and thirty feet high, and crowned with marble cupolas. The roof is supported by interior rows of massive pillars of huge dimensions, similar to those at Agra, and is surmounted by three white marble domes, crowned with culices or spires of gilded copper. Just beneath the cornice, are ten tablets of white marble, each ten feet long, and two and one half feet wide, on which are inlaid inscriptions with black marble, in the "Miski characters," giving the name of the founder, Shah Jehan, and date of erection A. D. 1626. It also states its cost to have been ten lakhs of rupees or $500,000 of American dollars, and that it was ten years in course of erection.

There is the same lofty arched portal that seems to pertain to all of Shah Jehan's edifices of this kind. The upper part of it is a semi-dome with all its slender ribs of white marble, bending and meeting in its high pointed arch. It has the same breadth as the centre dome, which is about forty feet in diameter. The kibla and the Inam's station is a niche in the west wall, not far from six feet in height, indicating the direction of Mecca; it is composed of very fine white marble, and profusely ornamented with sculptured fruit and flowers in bass-relief, in exquisite finish and workmanship.

Near it stands, apparently, a single block of marble, four feet wide, and six feet long, cut into steps, on which, on grand occasions, sit the dignitaries. The floors are paved with slabs of white marble, bordered by a band of inlaid black marble forming an oblong figure, which has a Saracenic inscribed arch at one end; the effect is very beautiful. Coming out, a priest volunteered to show us some old relics contained in a sort of shrine in one corner of the cloistered gallery, for additional bucksheesh. Before the mutiny, these things were entirely too sacred for infidel eyes to look upon. Her Majesty's riflemen use very convincing arguments.

These relics are considered very sacred, and are daily strewn with orange or other flowers. First, there was a reddish brown bristle, a veritable hair from Mahomet's beard, inserted in a chased silver holder and kept in orange flowers, in a silver case. Then a very old copy of the koran, written by Mahomet's grandson, about twelve centuries ago. It was a heavy, dark lettered book, held apparently in great veneration we judged, from the amount of care and orange flowers and work lavished on its silver case. Cabool, Samarcand, Bagdad, Damascus and Jerusalem, each have doubtless one just like it; and they probably are all exact copies of the one deposited in Arabia, which no amount of gold that the old Emperors could send, would ever buy. The third was a pall of very rich silk brocade, that one of the Emperors about two centuries ago had brought from Mecca, where it had lain on the tomb of the Prophet. It was an ancient rag, and looked as if the moths had waged a fiercer war with it, than with the old parchment book.

The Governor of Mecca does a very thriving business in

THE JUMMA MUSJID, DELHI.

the way of chudders, or palls that have lain on the Prophet's tomb only a short time; it forms quite an item of his revenue, besides spreading the oder of sanctity. The Commanders of the Faithful, are expected to invest in such marketable piety as this. The last and—next to the atom of beard the holiest —was an old shoe of the Prophet's, as rude in make as any old shoe could well be. It had good, thick, honest soles, which were evidently too much for insects of any kind. It was an unsightly thing, yet there it lay encased in silver and orange flowers, and guarded by priests. We paid our rupees and salaamed; for it was near the hour of prayer; we had read the regulations in the gateway, requesting visitors not to be present in the court, so we took that opportunity to ascend the minars; which are without question among the most graceful in India. They are built of brown stone with vertical stripes of white marble extending to the top. Balconies of white marble divided it into equal sections, and charming cupolas of the same material surmounted the top. A flight of stairs led to the roof, from which there is an entrance into the minars. From the cupolas we looked down into the court, on a row of eighty or ninety men going through their prostrations and prayers. They knelt, bringing the hands to the face, and then bowed the forehead to the pavement, then rose and recited their forms of prayer, during which, the face was bowed three times to the earth. An erroneous statement has come out, that the Mahomedans were not allowed to worship in this mosque since the mutiny.

We looked down on the flat roofed houses of the city, into cosy little places where the native people were at work, some of them were twisting silk with a few bobbins and a hook or two driven in the wall, others were making mats or weaving; warmed by the kindly sunshine. Near by was the old black mosque with fifteen small domes on its roof. It looked firm and strong though blackened with age and dust. It has almost completed its five centuries of existence, having been built by Firoz Shah in A. D. 1380. Eleven miles away the Kutub minar stands among the wide spread ruins of the

Hindoo city of Delhi, which Mahomed of Ghazui, captured in the A. D. 1193.

To the left, were the ruins of another walled city of the Delhi kings, built by the Emperor Tvogluck Shah in A. D. 1321. Nearer still is to be seen the domes of the mausoleum of the Emperor Humayun, standing amid ruins of the two old royal cities, one of which stood on the site of a Hindoo city which has date of a birth recorded by mentioning the position of the seven stars, from which astronomers reckon back to the year 1430 B. C. Therefore 3302 years ago, a certain Hindoo king named Parik-sheta, was born in a city whose site is now occupied by the citadel called Indraput or Purana Killa or Keela. Not a carved stone of that ancient city is supposed to exist there. The Jumna once flowed close under its old walls, but it long deserted them.

On our way back, we stepped into the old, black mosque. The court was paved with round stones—Firoz Shah must have liked round stones—and was occupied with silk spinners; the fine black marble kibla has been very much scribbled over, and on some parts there are caricatures, and in the cloistered, domed gallery, some family had penned its goats. It is said, the Government intends having this mosque cleansed, and if occupied, done so in a proper manner, for the building is strong, though it has seen so much storm, wreck and pillage. The next day we drove out to the old ruined palace of Firoz Shah—the building Sultan who was mentioned in connection with the garden at Allahabad—where is one of those old columns of king Athoka. It was originally set up at Kumaon, and though Buddhist in origin, the Hindoos had claimed it for centuries as the "walking stick of the Shepherd God," and said it could not be removed from there till the day of judgment.

The Emperor Firoz Shah, who reigned from 1351 to 1385, hearing of this tradition, caused it to be removed to Delhi and set up at the entrance of his own palace, in the place where it now stands among the ruined walls. It is forty-two feet and seven inches in height, a solid shaft of pale,

MIRZAS OF THE IMPERIAL FAMILY OF DELHI.

pinkish granite. It has the Buddhist inscription of king Athoka engraved on it, which ends with a short sentence in which the king directs the setting up of the monoliths. It is similar in all respects to those already mentioned, namely: one at Benares, and one at Allahabad. An English traveller who saw it in 1611, says that it had black and white stone work on the top, surmounted by a gilt pinnacle with a globe and crescent.

There were in this vicinity many massive, lofty walls, through which secret passages were still visible, which are said to connect with vaults and treasure wells in the foundation, and also to have outlets on the Jumna. The stone is not dressed, and these old walls only impress one with their rude strength; there could never have been much beauty or finish about these buildings. Near by is a lofty gateway, the arch of which belonged to a later city; it is called the Lal Durwaza, or red gate. This city was built two hundred years later than the former.

The Purana Keela, which is only a short distance from the old stone monolith, was the citadel of old Delhi, with walls sixty feet high, having four gates which were defended by towers and circular bastions at the corners. It was built by Shir Shah, who reigned from 1540 to 1545. He drove the Emperor Humayun, who had made his residence here, from his throne.

It was to the old city near the Lat, or stone pillar, that Timorlane came and flooded its streets with the blood of one hundred thousand of its inhabitants; there, too, came Baber, the sixth in descent from the Tartar conqueror, one hundred and forty years later, after he had captured Agra and subdued nearly all the strip of county south of it from the mouth of the Indus to the Ganges—including Behar—and established the house of the Timorlane emperors, whose line comprises some of the most powerful, enlightened and tolerant rulers that swayed sceptre in that age of the world. Elphinstone says:—" Baber was the most admirable, though not the most powerful prince that ever reigned in Asia. He was an accomplished scholar and no mean poet; his diary abounds in descriptions of the countries he visited; their scenery, climate, productions and works of art." He had a kind and affectionate heart, and once when his son and successor was apparently very near death, the charlatan physicians said he could only be cured by some one volunteering to give up his own life to save him.

The noble father, then fifty years old and in good health, at once said he would give his life freely, if they could transfer it to his son, and submitted to the juggling ceremonies by which they pretended to convey his life to the prince; he then took to his bed and died in the belief that his act saved the life of his son. He was buried in Cabool. Humayun his son led a life of strange vicissitude. Ten years after he came to the throne of the empire, the victorious army of Shir Shah thundered at this old gate for the surrender of the citadel, while its fugitive sovereign—with a broken army—was fleeing across the desert of the Scind, toward Persia. This was the stronghold around which the conquering Pathan built a city wall nine miles in circuit; finished the beautiful mosque; and built a part of the palace.

We entered the old gate and made our way through a very extensive clay village within the walls, to the Keela Kona mosque and the ruins of the old palace, occupied at different times by the contending emperors: Humayun and Shir Shah. This musjid is the finest specimen of Pathan architecture, or of the older buildings of that kind, in the neighborhood of Delhi. Its front has five horse-shoe arches; and is in a good state of preservation, with the exception of the top of the middle arch. It is remarkable for its fine inlaid mosaic of black and white marble, appearing in the exterior cut stone of the lofty center arched niche. The small interior arched entrance is composed of beautiful white marble, which retains its color perfectly, even after a lapse of more than three centuries. The side arches are picked out with pale yellow, glazed tile, and black stone, carved so the color shades from dark to light in the center. The stones in the walls are massive, and with little care it may stand for centuries yet to come, in all its beauty and grandeur.

We made our way to the roof up a narrow stair composed of thick blocks of stone, and enjoyed a fine view of the country down the river, and the old eleven-arched stone bridge, built between four and five centuries ago. The old palaces near this and the Shir Mundel—a handsome stone pavilion, used as a library by the early emperors—are in a ruinous condition. In this library Humayun was sitting, about six months after his restoration, when hearing the call to prayers in the mosque, he rose up suddenly, slipped, fell, and died from the effects. His widow, Hazi Begum—the mother of Akbar—built the large-domed mausoleum, which is seen about half a mile away.

As we made our way back to the gate through winding paths among clay houses, we eagerly looked for some carved stone, either great or small, that might be a relic of that old city, where king Paricksheta was born thirty centuries ago; but we saw nothing except the clay, and we forbore to take that, lest some avenging spirit might haunt us, and claim it as a part of his earthly tabernacle, a thousand years ago. We passed outside to our carriage, and drove along a road cut through old foundations and stone walls of buildings, where there appears to be material enough to build a dozen ruined cities.

As our driver drew up at the gate, we saw another opposite to it opening into a high walled enclosure, with towers and cupolas covered with a very brilliant blue encaustic tile. There was a mosque in the back part of the enclosure, which was ornamented extensively, with the same colored tile. The effect of such brilliant colors combined with the brown stone and that style of architecture, is very different from what it would be with ours. This musjid was built in A. D. 1540.

THE TOMB OF THE EMPEROR HUMAYUN.

A paved walk leads to the centre of a large garden of about four hundred square yards, which was originally laid out in a beautiful manner with shrubbery, and walks, and fountains and marble fish ponds; and surrounded by high cloistered walls. The garden is entered by three noble gateways. The mausoleum is raised on two fine terraces, the lower one is only three feet high, and extends out twenty-five feet all around the second, it is the foundation on which the labyrinth of arches rest that compose the second chaboutra. This is twenty feet high and forms a superb plinth on which the mausoleum rests. There are four great flights of steps, three of them are opposite gates and lead up to the second platform, which is two hundred feet on each side.

This spacious mausoleum is octagonal, and nearly one hundred and fifty feet from one opposite side to the other. Three sides have each a lofty niche, within which are the windows and entrances. Each of the shorter sides form one face of the four beautiful octagonal towers, that we see for the first time joined to the buildings of this kind. The narrow neck to the white marble dome, is here first introduced in Mogul architecture. The grand central hall up to the bending dome, is lined and paved with white marble; in the centre stands the sarcophagus beautifully cut and polished. A corridor leads to the four octagonal apartments in the towers, where the two widows of the Emperor were buried, and some other members of his family. His marriage and his affection for his wife—the mother of Akbar his successor, —was almost as romantic as that of Jehan-Gire, his grandson. Fleeing from one petty state of the Scind to another, while at the stronghold of a chief who had opened his gates to give him and his small band of followers shelter, he chanced to meet his future Sultana. Though his fortunes were at a low ebb —he had neither throne or army to defend himself—yet he was immediately married. Darker clouds still gathered about him during the year that followed, his enemy was on his track, and the chiefs of the Scind dared no longer to give him shelter.

Humayun and his family with a few followers took their way across the desert that stretches along the East side of

TOMB OF THE EMPEROR HUMAYUN, OLD DELHI

the Indus, men and animals suffered fearfully on the march, half famished with thirst they reached a little oasis and village, where his son and successor was born.

It was customary to distribute valuable gifts on the birth of an heir, but Humayun had no treasure to distribute; so he took a pod of musk in the presence of his friends, and broke it, saying, he hoped the future renown of his son would travel as far as that perfume would. While the child was yet an infant, both he and his nurse were secretly abducted by the Emperor's younger brother Kamran, the Governor of Candahar, who was in rebellion against him, and his bitter personal enemy. After years of exile and wandering, the Emperor obtained some assistance from the king of Persia, and then treacherously got possession of a frontier city, and with its army and treasure he was enabled to lay siege to the city of Candahar and capture it. Kamran was cruel enough to expose young Akbar—whom he had stolen so long before—on the walls in range of his father's cannon. When Kamran was brought in as prisoner and the chiefs were in favor of putting his eyes out, the Emperor did not interfere to prevent it.

Humayun's widow, Haji Begum, the pilgrim queen, survived him many years, during which she built this mausoleum; she is buried in one of the octagonal apartments in the towers. There are several tombs in the arches on the lower terrace. It was here—one hundred years later—that the body of Dara Sheko, the rightful heir, was buried after he was beheaded by his brother Aurungzebe.

It was near this place that Captain Hodon of the Guards so summarily disposed of the sons of the Emperor of Delhi, when an attempt was being made to rescue them, after the capture of the city in 1857. It is better told by the gallant Captain himself:

"I laid my plans to prevent access to the tomb or escape from it. I then sent in one of the inferior scions of the royal family, whose life had been promised him, to say that I had come to seize the Shah-jadahs (princes) for punishment, and I intended to have them, dead or alive. After two hours of wordy strife they made their appearance and asked if their lives had been promised them by the Government? I answered them, most certainly not. I then sent them towards the city under a guard. I took the rest of my men and went to the tomb * * * * It was crowded, garden and terrace, with, I should think six or seven thousand people, the scum of the palace and city. I then demanded, in a voice of authority, the surrender of their arms. They obeyed with an alacity that I had scarcely dared hope for. They brought out about five hundred swords, and more than that number of firearms; besides horses and bullocks, and covered carts. I arranged these, with the arms and animals in the centre and placed a guard around them. I then rode off to look after my prisoners. I was just in time, as a large mob had collected and were turning on the guard. * * * I rode in among them at a gallop, and addressed a few words to the crowd. * * * * * * *

"Seizing a carbine from one of my men I *deliberately shot them* (the princes) one after another. Their bodies were then taken to Delhi in a bullock cart and exposed in a public place. These men inaugurated the massacre at Delhi, and would have been court-martialed and executed for their crimes had they reached the city alive."

While giving the chuprasse at the gate his *douceur*, some men having scented in some way a backsheesh—though half a mile away—came to conduct us to

THE TOMB OF NIZAM-OO-DEEN.

We did not understand their Hindoostanee, nor did they our English; but one of them, the speaker of the crowd—the rabble here cannot be called the "great unwashed"—said: "You come see; backsheesh give." As that comprised his entire stock of English, the sound of it pleased him, and he said it over several times. We followed him into a labyrinth of old ruined streets, not very well knowing what we were going to see, but resolved to see the sights. The guide opened a gate leading into a large square enclosure, crowded with native people all in holiday dress, representing all the colors of the rainbow in a confused jumble. With happy, good-natured faces, they made way very respectfully, right and left, for us to pass to the tomb of Nizam-oo-deen.

NIZAM-OO-DEEN'S TOMB, OLD DELHI.

AT LEFT HAND IS SEEN THE TOMB OF MOHAMED SHAH.

This structure was built A. D., 1350. It has a white marble dome, and its verandah with Saracenic arches gives it a very graceful appearance. The roof and dome are supported by pillars, and the spaces between are filled with perforated marble, forming a screen about the sarcophagus which is covered with a pall that had once been embroidered with gold, but is now so loaded with the dust and dampness of ages, that only here and there a glittering thread could be seen. A low guard-rail of carved wood surrounds the grave, and from each corner rises a stone pillar, which supports a canopy above the sarcophagus. The interior and ceiling are finely painted in arabesque. It is in a good state of preservation and shows less soil and stain, and fewer marks of time and the elements, than one would suppose the 522 years would have left on it.

Nizam-oo-deen has been held in great veneration, though for what, seems a little mystified. We chanced there on his festival day, when pilgrims were present from all parts to do him honor. His title or name is that of a high officer or governor, and does not imply great Moslem sanctity. General Sleeman who caught more Thugs, and studied their ways more than any other person, gives it as his opinion, that this Nizam-oo-deen was the head of the Mahomedan Thugs of India; the founder of that society of assassins for causing death by strangulation. The object was plunder, for it would be very singular that a Mahomedan could be brought to believe in Bhowanee, and reject all the other gods of the Hindoo mythology. He amassed great wealth by some means—not very clear now—which enabled him to set his king, by whom he had been mortally offended, at defiance. It is supposed that he had a hand in the plot and in the contrivance of that pavilion, by which the son of Toogluck Shah freed his own father from mortal coil and took the throne.

As the two gentlemen of the party stood looking in at the door of the screen, a tall native was standing at our backs, with nods and winks to the crowd, making passes across his throat and neck with his hand, a sort of Thugee pantomime, which turning around suddenly, I caught him in the midst of. It did not alarm me, for I knew the English rule was too strong here for him to put his joke into practice; but I gave him a scowling look, and he lost no time in slipping back out of sight in the crowd.

THE POET KOSHROO'S TOMB

is a less pretentious one, and near that of Nizam-oo-deen. He was a Persian by birth, but resided in Delhi, and lived to see five or six emperors ascend the throne. Elphinstone says:

"The poet Koshroo was a friend and companion of the eldest son of that gorgeous old Emperor Bulbun, who supported at his court with liberal pensions, fifteen kings that had been driven from their thrones by Chengis Khan, and in their train came poets and men of letters from Bagdad, Persia, and Ghazni, to that old Delhi by the iron pillar."

He is mentioned again in Ala-oo-deen's reign, as having wrought into beautiful Persian verse, the romance of Caula and Dewal Devī, the wife and daughter of a Hindoo king; the former of whom Ala-oo-deen had taken captive in one of his expeditions, and whose beauty so won his heart, that he made her his favorite wife. She was so contented with her lot, that she besought the Emperor to send Alp Khan his nephew to the army in the Deccan, expressly commissioned to capture her daughter if possible, to save her from being married to a Mahratta prince.

When the Hindoo father heard that another Mogul was approaching, he sent the princess, his daughter, to her betrothed in charge of a trusty officer. When Alp Khan came into the vicinity of the caves of Ellora, he met the retinue of a person of rank coming out of the Buddhist temple. The usual quarrel about precedence ensued, and the opposing party was defeated and driven away; and the Khan found his prisoner to be the very princess that he had been sent after, to bring to Delhi. Her beauty made such an impression on the heir-apparent that he soon married her, and the poet celebrated their love in the poem that has been mentioned. Says Sleeman:

"His songs are yet the most popular. He is one of the favored few who live in the thoughts and feelings of millions of people, while the crowned heads who patronized him in their days of pomp and power, are forgotten."

Our chuprassee was eager to win his backsheesh, and with his hurried "come see" led the way to the

TOMB OF PRINCE MIRZA JEHAN-GIRE.

This is a most exquisite piece of workmanship. The tomb is raised a few feet from the ground and entered by steps. The sarcophagus is of white marble, and is covered with sculptured flowers in bass-relief. It is surrounded by a charming screen of most delicate marble filigree. The prince was the son of Akbar II and was banished from Delhi on account of his frequent attempts to procure the assassination of his brother the heir apparent. He was sent to Allahabad, where he soon killed himself drinking cherry brandy. This is quite a recent structure.

Very near this is the tomb of Jehanira Begum, the christian daughter of Shah Jehan, whose name was mentioned in the slight sketch of the father's imprisonment in the palace at Agra. It is said that her conversion to the christian faith, through the efforts of the Portuguese missionaries, very much exasperated the Sultana, her mother, who, as may be seen from the prayer inscribed on her tomb in the Taj, was much more bigoted in her faith than the Shah. He only seemed to see in Jehanira the loving, dutiful daughter, whom he could trust and rely upon in any emergency, long after all other friends had forsaken him, during the weary years of his imprisonment in the citadel. Her tomb is enclosed by a handsome screen of marble filigree, in which is inserted a slab of marble having on it the inscription that has been given in another place (page 381). She says, she is a disciple of the holy men of Christ, but there is no cross on her tomb anywhere, doubtless it was omitted to save it from insult by the rabble who in all countries are the most intolerant.

It must have been a great departure from his rule, for the bigoted Aurungzebe, the zealous stickler for the Moslem faith to bury his own sister with such an inscription on her tomb. The sarcophagus is without a cover, the hollow open part is filled with water, and flowers are kept in it.

Near by enclosed by a white marble screen, is the tomb of Mahomed Shah, that unfortunate Emperor of Delhi, who was the last occupant of the gorgeous Peacock Throne. The Shah's army was no match for the hardy veterans of a hundred battles, led by the first commander in Asia, and were easily routed and Mahomed Shah had no resource, but flight or submission, and he chose the latter. He sent his vizier to the Persian camp, and then repaired there himself. The Persians had agreed to spare the city on the receipt of a certain sum of money. The two monarchs entered the city together and sat down in the royal palace, to take a friendly cup of coffee. The master of ceremonies was perplexed between duty and etiquette and prudence. If he served his own master first, he would offend the Persian, and he might lose his head; and if he should serve the guest first he would incur his master's displeasure. So he solved the difficulty by presenting the tray first to his master, with a low salaam and a neat little speech saying, I know your Majesty will not allow your illustrious guest to be served by any except royal hands. The Shah replied; "if all of your subjects had performed their duty as well as this one, I should not be here."

In the evening of the third day, the inhabitants were so insane as to attack the Persian troops which were quartered in the city. At daylight, Nadir Shah mounted his horse and rode through the city, endeavoring to suppress the tumult; but seeing many of the Persians murdered, and being attacked himself, he dispatched his troops over the city with orders for a general massacre. The Persians were used to that work; and Nadir Shah sat upon the mosque in the Chandni Chowk watching the work in gloomy silence. The city was set on fire in several places, presenting a scene

TOMB OF MIRZA JEHANJIRE, SON OF THE EMPEROR OF DELHI, DELHI.

of horrible, bloody carnage, which was attended with all the horrors of lust, avarice and vengeance.

When this first day of slaughter was far advanced, Mahomed Shah, accompanied by one or two high officers of his court, came into the presence of Nadir Shah, and on his knees humbly besought him to stop further carnage. The Shah gave his orders, and his soldiers obeyed,—like fate. Before nightfall, quiet was restored, and the slaughter in the streets was stayed; but from street to street, and from house to house, went the Persians, in search of treasure to pay the city's ransom, and the inhabitants writhed in untold torture. Sleep forsook all eyes during those fifty-seven days and nights. The gates were closely guarded; none could escape; and no provision could come in; famine and pestilence adding their horrors to the ill-fated city.

When there were no more jewels to be obtained, the Persian king reinstated Mahomed Shah in his government, and arranged a marriage between his son and Mahomed's daughter. Nadir Shah returned to Persia carrying with him, up through the grand old mountain passes, that unparalleled PEACOCK THRONE, which a French jeweller estimated at six million pounds sterling. The lowest estimate, says a reliable historian, placed upon the amount of treasure carried away by this invasion, is three hundred and twenty millions of rupees, equivalent to one hundred and sixty millions of dollars.

The chuprassee began to repeat his stock of English words: "Come see; come see; backsheesh give," and led off through a narrow opening between ruined walls, and past an ancient mosque, which I stopped to look into, and caught sight of a Hindoo woman at her household duties. She was cooking chupatties over a little fire-place, built by placing about six bricks in a semi-circle. She hurriedly covered them, and her face also, for my shadow, the shadow of an unbeliever, falling on her food would render it unfit for her to eat; her religion would compel her to throw it away, and she probably valued them higher than any acquaintance with me; and I hurried on, fearing I should stray from my party. We soon entered a covered gallery partly surrounding a deep tank or reservoir, just in time to see a half-clad boy drop down through the air and disappear below the surface of the water. We watched for him till the water grew smooth, and my heart almost stood still for fear he would never come up, when a small head showed itself on the surface, forty feet below where we were standing; he took breath a moment and then struck out for the stone ghâts on the other side of the baolee or well. In a moment more he stood before us in his dripping garment, holding out his hand, crying backsheesh, between his chattering teeth. A generous one was cheerfully given, which warmed him into a laugh.

Seeing the success of the little fellow, a full-grown man jumped from a wall the height of the houses. One of the party held up a rupee, signifying to him to jump from the top of the mosque near by, but evidently he did not feel equal to that, so he plunged off from the wall and received the same reward as the boy. But the first diver had seen the coin come up out of the pocket, and by a sort of pantomime—putting his fingers on the money and then on himself, and pointing to the dome of the mosque—he made quite an intelligible proposal to accept of the offer. In a few minutes he appeared on the top of the mosque and took the leap in good spirits. These divers wore the usual loins cloth, and plunged head downward at the start, but when about half the distance down, they reversed, turning the feet downward, so that when they reached the surface of the water, the feet were firmly together, and the hands and arms were straight and close by the sides. This pool or well is oblong, about eighty by fifty feet, and at this dry season the water is about sixty feet below the ground level. It is said the old saint Nizam-oo-deen, either began or excavated this well in A. D., 1330. The natives believe its water has miraculous power to heal diseases.

CHAPTER XVII.

THE OLD OBSERVATORY ON THE ROAD TO OLD DELHI OF 1193.

WE drove out at the Lahore gate, with the intention, and confident expectation of being able to do (as the phrase goes), any reasonable, or unreasonable amount of ruins. We had heard that they covered forty square miles in this direction; but what of that; what of all those miles, when one feels so fresh, that climbing the tower of Babel itself, would not seem too much for one's strength!

There they lay, grim, old, nameless walls and foundations, through which our road had been cut, but we passed on. Two miles out from the gate, looms up the lofty gnomon of an observatory, surrounded by a number of buildings which, at first sight, seem to be in a very sound condition; at least, no wall is much broken. The largest of these, is an immense equatorial dial, named by the builder—Rajah Jei Singh of Jeypore—the Semsat Yunter,—Prince of Dials. The gnomon towers up fifty-six feet, with a base of one hundred and four feet; and the length of the hypothenuse, is one hundred and eighteen feet five inches.

These buildings were never intended to be roofed over, and had they been placed on a solid stone platform and adapted to the true system, not a more fitting or lasting monument need any man desire than this one, left by this Hindoo Rajah. This observatory was built some forty years later than the one at Benares, and is planned on a grander scale. It is constructed of brick and stucco, which would have stood the elements in this climate well enough, but could not stand invading armies as well as stone, especially if it had a few texts of the Koran written on it.

While the gentlemen went to the top of the great gnomon to take a survey, I crossed over to a combination of sun dials inclined at an angle of forty-five degrees to the horizon, which are yet in a fair state of preservation. The design was to correct the markings on the great dial. Stairs lead to the top. On one side a seed had lodged in a crevice; the sun and moisture had nourished it, until now it was a large tree toppling down the parapet, and so shading the dials that the sun did not reach them at that time of day. The parapet wall of the staircase forms gnomons to the concentric, semicircular dials, which are inclined, as mentioned before, to the horizon. The outer walls form gnomons to graduated quadrants, one on the east and the other on the west. A dividing wall reached by the stairs unites with the gnomons at right angles. On its northern face is described a graduated arc for taking the altitude of celestial bodies.

Recrossing the road to the side of the gnomon, we looked into two circular buildings exactly alike in all respects, thirty or thirty-five feet in diameter, open at the top. Each of them had a round pillar in the center; and from this center, thirty horizontal stone *radii*, including equal spaces between them, spread out and join the circular walls. In the walls between each radius are two open spaces, like windows, to enable a person to climb up and read the number of degrees of altitude on the perpendicular wall, and to pass through and read them when the shadow is thrown on the *radii*. These buildings were erected in the early part of the reign of Mahomed Shah, when the Mogul Government was just plunging into the abyssmal gulf from which it never arose.

Entering the ghari, we drove about three miles further south, where there is a group of four large domed tombs; a musjid and a bridge of seven arches are on the left hand side of the road. They have quite a fine appearance, and must be the resting places of persons of distinction, whose great, solid, spacious mausoleums have confronted the eyes of people for four or five centuries; while the memory of the persons buried there have died out of the minds of those living in the shadow of their walls, until they have entirely forgotten who lay there.

The antiquarian, Gen. A. Cunningham, had the mosque cleansed so he could read the inscriptions. He fixes the date of the two square tombs at 1370. The largest octagonal one is assigned to Secundra Lodi, who ascended the throne of Delhi in A. D., 1488. His father belonged to a family that had been leaders and high officers in the Empire, when Timorlane captured the old Firozabad Delhi, and drove the Emperor into exile. Then succeeded half a century of anarchy and struggle among the great nobles to get and retain possession of the throne; when Behlol Lodi, the father of the one resting here, concerted with the last Emperor's Grand Vizier to divide the power between them, and obtained possession of the army and throne.

One of his first public acts was to put his colleague to death. He held the reins of government firmly for thirty-eight years and then died, and his son succeeded him. Secundra Lodi was a bigot, and persecuted the Hindoos to the full extent of his power, destroying their idols and temples. A Brahmin being reproved for worshipping idols replied: "All religions are equally acceptable with God if practiced with equal sincerity." He was then ordered to accept the Mohammedan faith, or suffer death. He thought it was safest to die a Brahmin, and he suffered death.

THE MAUSOLEUM OF VIZIER SUFTAN JUNG.

This mausoleum stands in an enclosure which is nearly three hundred yards square, having the usual cloisters for visitors on three sides. The only gateway is planned somewhat after those that have been described in other places. It is built on a stone terrace and has a fountain in front of it. It is said to have been modeled after the Taj; but one would hardly suspect it, so little does it resemble that beautiful edifice. It is surmounted by a narrow-necked dome, beneath which, in the grand hall, is an elegantly carved sarcophagus; and directly beneath this is a vault containing a plain grave of earth, where the remains were interred. The four towers join the building, as in Humayun's tomb; and there are the same lofty entrance niche and window recesses that we have seen elsewhere. It was built in the year 1746, and though only a little more than a century old it has a battered look, for it has often sheltered the people during the numerous invasions and sieges. It is the property of the royal family of Oudh.

Standing before a tomb of such pretension, the question that presses itself upon one is: who, or what was this person? Surveying the structure does not satisfy one, till he has probed his way down to the vault, or stood by the empty sarcophagus. When he can go no further, he wishes to know the history of the person who lies buried there.

Suftan Jung belonged to a noble, powerful family, and was made Vizier by Ahmed Shah, who ascended the throne of Delhi, in the A. D., 1747. Prestige had forsaken the Mogul banners, and the hill tribes on the north invaded the valley of the Ganges; the Vizier led an army against them and was defeated, and when he returned, he found a new favorite in his place, whom he assassinated. This exasperated the Emperor; and Ghazee-oo-deen, grandson of Asf Jah—whom the Vizier had temporarily promoted to his position during his absence—was now used by the Emperor against his former Vizier, and civil war was carried on in the streets of Delhi for six months; when the Mahrattas, a foreign force, were called in to settle the strife between these two powerful barons of the realm. In the settlement, Suftan Jung retained the possession of Oudh as a Viceroyalty, until the time the East India Company entered into an alliance with a member of the family, and recognized him as the first king of Oudh,—but after some years, set the family claims aside, on account of its breaking treaty. The king, that has been heretofore mentioned as living near Calcutta, on a pension from the English Government, is a descendant of this family.

Taking the ghari once more, we drove through a level country dotted with huge piles of broken, half prostrate old walls, and foundations of dwellings. We saw an old black structure on the left of the road, towering as high, and appearing as strong as an old Scotch castle, only it had a number of small black domes on the top, resembling a village of beehives; there were also a number of tombs and smaller buildings about it. This group with the massive object in the centre, had a very picturesque appearance from the road. A halt was called and we discussed the pros and cons, and concluded we had been entombed long enough for live people, and if this was not a castle exactly, it must certainly be a very ancient mosque. Mr. S—— said that he had had enough of ruins to nearly kill him, and he would prefer to stay in the carriage, and hear our report when we came back. So we started off, and walked over a rough, native cart track eight or nine hundred yards through the fields. On our way, we saw only one man, who seemed to be busy with an ox cart, and we came to the conclusion that this building was quite deserted, but when we entered the enclosure people swarmed out of the old black structure like ants; they came out of queer little dens that did not appear to be much more than crevices in the old wall.

A muddy, filthy pool of water occupied the centre of the enclosure, the children of the hive were innocently engaged in working buffalo chips with their hands and sticking them on the wall to dry. On duly considering the aspect of things, we thought there was more dirt and filth than would suit us to encounter, even in search of quaint, oriental decorations, and contented ourselves with what we could see from the road. We afterwards learned that these buildings, consisting of a mosque and caravanserais or resting place for travellers, was erected by the Emperor Firoz Shah, and were somewhat over five hundred years old. I almost regretted that I did not explore every nook of the old ant hill.

The old historian says, that the beautiful decorations this Emperor put upon the mosque which he built, so charmed the eyes of Timorlane that he dragged off all the artizans of Delhi to Samarcand, to build mosques there. As we proceeded, ruined buildings increased on every side until we reached the ancient city.

We drove through streets of the dead but not buried place, and alighted near the finest old gateway that the sun ever shone upon. I know he looks down on Thebes and Karnak, and yet I will not take back a word; *they* are grand, but the Alla-oo-deen is charmingly beautiful as well as grand. As we had digested considerable antiquity on our way out, and did not feel remarkably refreshed by it, we proposed having our lunch in this unique porch. As there was nothing suggestive of a gate, or of being closed up, porch or vestibule is a more fitting name for it. I was conscious of being satisfied with food, but looking at the delicate tracery and beauty of this building as a whole, my eyes could not take in enough and were not satisfied.

The title of the Emperor Alla-oo-deen, is several times repeated in the inscriptions over the entrances, with the date of erection, year 710 of the Hegira, which corresponds to A. D. 1310. The building is made of brown stone and white marble, and is fifty-six and a half feet each way on the outside. The walls are nearly eleven feet thick, leaving thirty-four and a half feet interior dimensions.

On each side is a lofty doorway, its form is a pointed horse shoe arch, the stone on the outer face of which, is carved in a delicate arabesque, while the under surface is fretted and panneled. The corners of this square building are cut off by bold niches; in the lower part of which are windows, one third the height of the doors, which are closed by beautiful slabs of marble lace; the head of the niche above them is fitted with series of five pointed arches, the middle one is the largest.

The interior is covered with an unrivalled carved ornamentation and frost work, away up to the centre of the lofty

TOMB OF SUFTUN JUNG, VIZIER OF MAHOMED SHAH, DELHI.

dome. The exterior walls are panneled and inlaid with bands of white marble in the brown stone, of which the edifice is made. The roof is edged around with a fringe of battlements, and the white marble dome glistens fair and pure above it, covered with carved work, as beautiful and white as though traced in new fallen snow.

General Cunningham the English government antiquarian says, he considers this the most beautiful specimen of the Pathan architecture that he has ever seen.

If no other monument of that Emperor remains, this one will, while it stands, always suggest by its beauty, some pleasant thoughts of him, whatever he may have been five hundred and sixty-five years ago, when he built this entrance to the grandest temple dedicated to God and the Prophet, in Eastern Asia.

RAMBLES ABOUT OLD HINDOO DELHI OF 1193.

We passed through a strong, high stone colonnade into a court, the pillars of which could never have been placed here, by those masterly architects of the great mosque and minar, for their beauty. Their presence here was probably to commemorate some very important event.

They look very much as if some giant had taken an afternoon freak to play builder in a chaos of old ruined square pillars, and had set up rows of such columns as would stand one upon the other; without a qualm of hesitation, if the lower one happened to be the least in size; then roofed it over and settled it down into the enduring thing that it has been for six centuries; all before nightfall.

Within this outer court was another, smaller one, immediately in front of the lofty ruined arches of what was once a magnificent mosque. This had a weird look as though goblins had commenced work, when the giant left off, with their best endeavors to outdo him in grotesque buildings, and had succeeded admirably—as might be expected from them—in bringing together the most hideous forms carved in pillars, and had set them up here to warn or admonish the

Faithful as they went to prayers in the mosque. The execution is good, and the fruits and flowers beautiful; but the grotesque human forms are as ugly as the gargoyles on the churches that were built in the middle ages. It was formerly supposed that these were the remains of a temple of Vishnu, built by the old Hindoo kings; or at least, a court of pillars, where he had wrought in these combinations all the gods in his mythology, to have them near his palace.

There is no doubt now, says the antiquarian before mentioned, "that these pillars were placed in their present position by the Mohammedans; they belong to the ninth and tenth centuries, and are among the very few examples that seem overladen with ornament." We noticed Ganesh and several other Hindoo gods without faces, having been unmasked by Moslem chisels which had left a part of the elephant god's proboscis; many others were readily recognized, although the faces were mutilated.

These pillars are now supposed to be the remains of twenty-seven idol temples in this old city, that were torn down by the invaders, and were gathered into this place to commemorate the triumph of religion over idolatry. To make them consistent with the rules of the Koran, the faces were mutilated, they certainly are not in harmony with the mosque or minar.

In this court stands an ancient *wrought iron pillar;* it is sixteen inches in diameter, and rises twenty-two feet above the surface of the ground. A recent excavation was carried down *twenty-six* feet without reaching the foundation on which the pillar rests.

This pillar, as the inscription informs us, was erected in this place in the A. D. 319, by a Hindoo, Rajah Dhara, who resided here only at intervals, and at other times at Kanouj. The legend concerning it is this; the Rajah fearing his kingdom might be wrested from him by some foreign power consulted with the Brahmins. They told him if he could make an iron pillar and sink it in the earth until it pierced the snake god's head, his kingdom would remain forever. The

GREAT ARCH AND IRON PILLAR, OLD DELHI.

pillar was made and sunk until the priests said that they had pinned the snake god so fast there was no trouble to be apprehended from him, and things moved on in the old way for more than eight hundred years.

During the eleventh century, Rajah Pitthora was on the Hindoo throne. He began to entertain doubts whether this iron pin did actually prick the great snake god's head; so to satisfy his mind on the subject, he ordered the pillar to be taken up and examined; blood was found on the end of it. He was satisfied, and caused it to be reset, but in this they were not so fortunate the second time; the spell was broken, and the Mohammedans came, in less than half a century and took the kingdom.

THE GREAT ARCH.

This was the central one, in the row of seven pointed arches which pierced the front of the first musjid built in these parts. It is twenty-two feet wide and fifty-three feet to the apex of the grand entrance. The side arches have fallen, or been thrown down. The foundation indicates great strength, the walls are about eight feet in thickness. The great arch is surrounded, on the front face by a band of inscriptions, outside of which the brown stone is finely carved in a delicate tracery with a finish that is quite surprising for nearly seven hundred years ago. It was built by the conqueror Shahab-oo-deen, the king of Ghazui, at the suggestion of Kootub-oo-deen his successful general. The English government considering both this and the minar, works of art that are worth preserving, have expended considerable sums in repairing them.

We pass a little beyond the mosque and court, to the right, and find the tomb of the Emperor Altomsh the slave, and the son-in-law of the first Emperor. This is called the oldest authentic Mohammedan structure in India. There is an inscription on it, saying it was erected to his memory by his children, Sultan Ruqu-oo-deen, and Sultana Rezia. Altomsh died in the year 1236. The interior of his tomb measures twenty-nine and one half feet each way. The walls enclosing the square are more than seven feet thick, and do not appear to have ever had a roof. They are built of brown stone and white marble, and covered with the same delicate carving in arabesque as the mosque; which some suppose that he either finished or greatly embellished. He had two or three sons, and a daughter who was a very remarkable young lady for a Mohammedan spinster of that era. She understood the laws of the koran so perfectly that her father made her regent when he went to carry on wars in the neighboring kingdoms. She evinced great knowledge of business, and talent for governing. Whenever the Emperor was asked why she was made regent instead of one of his sons, he answered honestly, because she was more competent and trustworthy than any one of them. When acting in this capacity, she put on the imperial robe and sat upon her father's throne in the public hall or court of justice, judging the people's causes, as the Emperor was wont to do, and giving judgment in accordance with the laws of the Prophet.

Says Shams-i-Siraj, the old chronicler, "this princess was adorned with every qualification required in the ablest king; the strictest scrutinizer could find no fault in her, except that she was a woman." Not a bad thing truly, to say of a female lawyer and judge, who practiced the profession six hundred and thirty-six years ago, among a people that were not in the habit of paying much respect, or many compliments to women.

After the death of the Emperor her father, his eldest son Ruqu-oo-deen succeeded to the throne, but being very dissolute in his habits, the people became discontented, and he was deposed in seven months. The reputation she had gained during her father's reign now placed the Sultana Rezia upon the throne. By her justice and power of persuasion she soon reconciled and overcame the prejudices of the majority against the fact of a woman wielding the empire in her own name. One of the party who had united to depose her brother, was equally opposed to her elevation to the throne.

He succeeded in collecting a large army, and began his march to the capital. An army was sent against him, but it was defeated. The Sultana proved herself equal to the emergency, she resolved to sow dissension among her enemies, and by her address and persuasion, the confederacy against her soon melted away and peace and good will were restored.

On being again invested with the supreme power, she wore the imperial robes in public, and daily appeared on the throne and transacted all the public business in the usual manner of the Emperors—particularly of her father, who was considered by historians, a brave, learned and pious king, though originally a Tartar slave who rose to his position by his merits.

When she had been upon the throne about three years, the old commander in chief of her armies died, which occasioned several changes among the great officers of state. One of the generals was originally an Abyssinian slave, and his promotion to master of equerry gave great offence to the nobles, who formed a combination to assassinate him and depose the Sultana, as soon as an opportunity presented itself. The Sultana became aware of their plans and opposed them with great energy.

The governor of Lahore was one of the party; she led an army against him, and came upon him suddenly; his confederates could not render him aid, and he was obliged to throw himself upon her clemency. She pardoned him, and led her army away to reduce to submission another refractory baron; a mutiny occurred among her own forces in which the Abyssinian was slain. Not knowing what the extent of the conspiracy might be, she determined to throw herself upon the honor of Alturia and went to his stronghold. He was one of the great nobles who first rebelled against her.

On becoming more acquainted with her he was so captivated by her great beauty and accomplishments as well as her intellectual attainments, that he offered to marry her; and pledged himself to support her right to the throne against all of his former confederates and friends. Their marriage was duly celebrated, and by their united influence a large army was collected and marched to Delhi. In the meantime the nobles in her capital had elevated her younger brother, Meiz-oo-deen Behram to the throne. A battle was fought in which the Sultana's force was defeated, and herself and husband taken prisoners and put to death.

Thus died a princess, who, considering the age and the people among whom she lived, and the false, degraded position, they usually assigned to women, was certainly one of the most remarkable characters in Mohammedan history. Her reign continued three and one half years.

While standing by these tombs, among ruins evincing such high architectural taste and refinement, it is very natural to wish to know how these people lived who piled up that lofty tower that stands there so fair and perfect after a lapse of more than six hundred years, and who embodied their ideas of beauty in such enduring and unrivalled forms.

Seven years after the death of the Sultana, a saintly man, the youngest and the last of the Begum brothers, was on the throne; and when his turbulent nobles let him have quiet from war, he spent his leisure time in making copies of the koran, and used the proceeds of this pious labor to supply his own simple wants, considering himself the servant of the state,—yet was at the same time, surrounded by one of the most gorgeous courts in the world. His Vizier and successor was a Turkish slave, who rose from one position to another, till now he virtually ruled the empire. The following extract is taken from Elphinstone's History, and shows how ambassadors were received in this old city six centuries ago. A minister came from Tartary, bearing the courteous wishes of Haluka, or, as he is sometimes called Koubli Khan, grandson of the renowned Ghengis. His herald had made known his approach:

"The Grand Vizier went out to meet the ambassador with 50,000 cavalry, composed of Arabs, Agims, Turks, Khiljees and Afghans, all splendidly mounted; 200,000 infantry fully armed; 2000 of the choicest war elephants, and 3000 carriages of fire-works. He drew up in order of battle, twenty deep, with cavalry and infantry properly disposed.. After having gone through a sham battle, and displayed his power and pomp—doubtless as a wholesome lesson to all the Tartar Khans—he escorted the ambassador to the royal palace. There the court was splendid, everything being set out in the most gorgeous and magnificent manner."

All the omrahs, commanders and officers of state, judges, priests and great men of the city were present; besides five princes with their retinues, who had been driven from their thrones by Ghengis Khan; many Rajahs of Hindoostan, subject to the Emperor, stood next to the throne.

When the saintly Emperor died without children, the Vizier Bulbun ascended the throne without opposition. His court was probably the most magnificent of any in the world at that time. The sovereign princes that had been driven from the thrones by Ghengis Khan, were still in exile; the hospitality they received attracted others, so that at one time there were twenty fugitives,—one of whom was a grandson of the "Commander of the Faithful," the Caliph of Bagdad. Bulbun gave them palaces to live in and pensions from his treasury for their support; and in compliment to them, gave their names to streets, or quarters of the city. On all public occasions they stood on the right and left of the throne, according to their rank. With them came men distinguished for their learning in the arts and sciences. Cordova in Spain, Bagdad, Samarcand and Ghazne had one after the other been the great centres of learning, where science and philosophy were developed. These latter cities having been overrun by the destroying Tartar, Delhi became their ark of refuge. Poets were especially favored. Another extract from the pen of the author before quoted, will show how the nobles spent their time at court, in this old city seventy-two years after its capture, or A. D., 1265:

"In the retinue of these princes, were the most famous men for learning, war, arts and sciences, that Asia at that time produced. All the philosophers, poets and divines, formed a society, meeting every night at the palace of Khan Shedid, the heir-apparent of the Empire. Another society composed entirely of musicians, dancers, mimics, players, buffoons and story-tellers, met constantly at the house of the Emperor's second son, Kera Khan, who was much given to pleasure and levity. The Omrahs or Commanders followed the examples of their superiors; so that clubs and societies were formed in every quarter of the city."

The Sultan, or Emperor, had a great passion for splendor and magnificence in his palaces, equipages and liveries, and he was imitated by the whole court. Such was the pomp and grandeur of the royal presence, that none could approach without terror. The ceremonies of introduction were conducted with so much reverence and solemnity, and everything was so disposed, as to inspire the beholder with awe and astonishment. Nor was Bulbun less magnificent in his cavalcades; his stall elephants were caparisoned in purple and gold; his horse-guards—consisting of one thousand Turkish noblemen in splendid armor—were mounted on the finest Persian steeds, with bridles of silver, and saddles adorned with rich embroidery. Whenever he went out of his palace, five hundred chosen men in rich livery, with their drawn swords upon their shoulders, ran before him proclaiming his approach and clearing the way before him. All the omrahs followed him and were arranged according to their rank, with their various equipages and attendants. This monarch seldom went abroad out of the city with less than 100,000 armed men; this, he used to say, was not to gratify any vanity in himself, but to exalt him in the eyes of the people. What a very martyr he must have been to his kingly circumstances! One is reminded of the Caliph and his Vizier passing through the street to visit Shemselnihar.

Once when Bulbun was suppressing an insurrection in Bengal, he massacred his prisoners so cruelly, that he gave great offence to his court, whereupon, all the learned men, cazees and mufti, poets and philosophers, uniting in one petition to the king on the subject, caused him to show more mercy; which certainly proves there was considerable independent thought even under the rule of a Sultan, whose will was his law.

The celebrated Kootub Minar, is now conceded to have

KOOTUB MINAR, AND DOME OF ALBA-OO-DEEN GATEWAY.

been built by Shahab-oo-deen, at the suggestion of his general and viceroy, Kootub-oo-deen, the first Moslem Emperor that resided in Delhi. It was used by the muezzins to call the people to prayers in the mosque across the other side of the pillared court; the great arched entrance of which, we have seen in the illustration. This tower, or minar, stands entirely separate from any wall or building; and is at present two hundred and thirty-eight feet high; but is supposed to have been higher, as there is now no cupola on the top.

The diameter of the base is forty-seven feet and two inches, while at the top it is only nine feet. Four balconies supported by brackets seem to divide it into stories. A spiral, stone stairway leads to the top, with doors opening out on the balconies, and narrow windows on the stairs. From the base to the first balcony the exterior is fluted into twenty-seven divisions, alternately semi-circular and angular. In the second story the flutings are all semi-circular; in the third, they are all angular; and from the third story to the top, it is all of white marble and smooth. Around the first division, there are six horizontal bands of engravings, in one of these are the ninety-nine names of God, and sentences from the koran in broad relief. On the second, there are only four belts of engravings, and on the third, there are only three. On the second division, the inscription over the door records the fact that the Emperor Altomsh had ordered the completion of the minar, and his name and praises are repeated over the third story where it is supposed he commenced building. The walls are massive and firm, the central column, around which the stairs wind, is larger at the base, which gives greater firmness to the structure. Three hundred and seventy-nine steps lead to the summit. From the top we obtained a fine view of a vast extent of country. The old walls of the Hindoo fortress could be traced for a long distance to the right and left, and the ditch is a deep tangled glen in some places. In the northwest corner in this moat near the citadel gate, is a small, white-washed, stone tomb; there is nothing remarkable about it excepting its great age. It is the tomb of the general who led on the assault on the wall in front of it, six hundred and seventy-nine years ago, at the time of the invasion. His name was Hazi Rose Begh, and his position in the army shows that he belonged to the old warrior family of Samarcand of mighty valor.

Looking over the landscape, we saw what appeared to be domed pavilions, moss grown in some instances, like gentlemen's garden houses. I asked: "What are those high, octagonal domed structures; they look as though they were pleasant residences?" They were standing in a small grass grown field, cleared of ruins. "Indeed they are very pleasant residences: and are fitted up to let to those people who wish to come out here to rusticate among these picturesque old ruins, but they are all tombs nevertheless." Truly these people had a cheerful way of burying their friends. In the group on the right, the larger one is called the Metcalf House, because it was a favorite resort of Sir Theophilus Metcalf, when he was the English Resident Minister at the court of Delhi. Here you can have a living exegesis of the scriptures, of the man who lived among tombs and cut himself with stones; and G. added—for two rupees per day.

We turned, and took one more sweep of the eye around the horizon before leaving our lofty perch. There was the present city of Delhi with its red sandstone walls, and lofty white towers, domes and minars, and the river Jumna glancing like burnished steel, eleven or twelve miles away. Near it was the old red fort, and the ruins of the old cities, that have acted their part and have given place and life to newer ones, growing up around them. Three miles to the left of the minar where we are standing, is another ruined royal city. Its massive walls loom up dark and strong; making the fourth old capital mourning in her gray desolation. This last one was built and resided in by the father of the Sultan Kooni, the bloody Sultan, referred to in the siege of the old city of Pundoah; if he had lived in our time, we should probably consider his sanguinary proclivities insanity;

but this Emperor had the misfortune to be born four or five hundred years before it was the fashion to put as many breadths in charity's mantle as we have now.

He was in the habit of going out as if for hunting accompanied by a great many retainers, and men at arms; and sometimes he would enclose a large extent of country, and drive every thing toward the centre, then give the order to slay every human being in it. That a man could repeat such a horrible pastime, during a course of twenty-five years, and then die otherwise than by an assassin's knife, shows what great wrongs the low caste Hindoos, the tillers of the soil—would submit to. The best act of his reign was to die. He was buried in the large domed tomb beside his father and mother, in the midst of an artificial lake, which is connected with his old citadel by a causeway six hundred feet in length, carried over arches. It has been related before, how his cousin and successor, a wise and excellent ruler, after he came upon the throne, searched out the families of the sufferers and provided for them by pensions, on condition of their granting full pardon and forgiveness to the late Emperor Kooni, in the presence of the holy and learned men, whose names and seals were affixed to the documents as witnesses. "The whole of these documents, as far as lay in my power," says Firoz Shah, "have been procured and put in a box, and placed in the tomb where Mahomed Togluck is buried." They are, doubtless, there at this moment, ready for the dead man to clutch, and show the angel Gabriel that his bloody score was wiped out by his cousin. I wish some sacrilegious Anglo Saxon would get the box and place it in the British Museum in London, it would be so interesting to read the account through.

As we came down from the minar Mr. G—— proposed calling at the "Metcalf House," it was readily agreed to, and we started out through the great arch, and through the ruins of the old palace, in the terrace of which, was an enormous open well of great depth; one of our party, called Padre Sahib, who was the least given to probe old ruins, suddenly took it into his head to peer down to the bottom, leaning over the smooth cemented edge, when G—— seized him like a frog, by the foot, telling him to "Hold on! there is no use looking for immortality where everybody is dead, and nothing recollected but the old walls; and there is not the slightest chance of our being remembered." After laughing in its hollow depths and sounding it with his voice to hear it reverberate back from the water far below, with a ring like a great metal tube, it was so smooth, he gathered himself up, and we continued on our way to the domed palace.

There was not a living thing to be seen about it or anything to indicate there had been, except some dried grass stored in a little kiosk near by. It was built of brown stone, and about forty feet through, from side to side, and possibly fifty feet to the top of the dome. We did not meet the dead man; but we did meet his sarcophagus or cenotaph, a solid, oblong block of marble, standing on the porch,—the remains are always placed out of reach far below the pavement, under the centre of the dome.

We peered through the modern sash door and had a good view of the lofty hall reaching to the top of the dome where the cenotaph *had stood.* It was covered with neat matting, and furnished with table and chairs in a very cheerful way. Just then the stillness was broken by a crashing sound, as if thousands of bricks had been poured down upon the roof. We started out of the vestibule with, I should say, rather an accelerated movement, and looked at the dome against the clear, soft blue, afternoon sky, and saw that was all right; whereupon one of the party in a deep stagely tone began "Hark from the tombs a doleful sound," looking at the ornamental coffin on the verandah. Padre who had started off a few moments before, now returned with the report that a whole herd of goats had charged up a back flight of stairs to a covered wooden porch, a cheap wooden thing to make it more passable as a traveller's bungalow. The goats had heard our voices and supposed the keeper was there, so the whole herd charged pell mell up the stairs.

This is the tomb of Akbar's foster father; that Emperor had four foster mothers, and probably as many foster fathers. He must have had great, tender and delicate regard for his nurses to manifest it so indirectly as by burying all their husbands handsomely; this is the second foster father's tomb that we have noticed, but have nowhere seen a grave of one of the foster mothers; probably like the wandering Jew, they are still travelling over the face of the earth. His name was Mahomed Khan, and this pavilion may have been erected during his lifetime, and used by him as a garden house. It was fitted up for a country-house by Sir T. Metcalf, Resident Minister at the court of Delhi.

We now drove through the little village of Mehrowlie; which is near to the Kootub, and saw two very ancient, large, square and deep baolies, tanks or wells. One of them was built by the Mahommedans about the year 1263; and the other was excavated much earlier, by the Hindoo king, who was driven out by the invaders. Wells, fountains and tombs seem, in this old country, to have inherent germs of endurance, and live on in blessed immunity from harm. Before we were hardly aware of it, a diver, running across the roof of a high building sprang out, and came dropping down through the air, but with his limbs much more extended during the first part of the descent, than those we had seen at the other diving well, because the distance is greater; they were very straight, and firmly closed together when he entered the water. This well is very deep, the water became perfectly smooth before his head appeared above it.

These leaps seemed so very perilous to me, that I could not enjoy them. The thought of any human being going out of the warm air into the cold deep water to amuse us, was abhorrent to my feelings, so I led the way to the carriage.

Seeing near at hand a tall, domed pavilion in an inclosure, with cool shady trees around it, we went to it. An oblong block of very highly polished marble representing a sarcophagus, was on the porch; we looked in through a window and saw a great round hall under the dome, furnished in about the same style for a bungalow, as the other; but more shade around it. Among the trees I noticed a rare kind of miamosa.

This was the tomb of Adam Khan, a haughty nobleman of the early reign of Akbar. He was a high commander in the army and was sent to subdue the Rajah of Malwa. When he had done this he refused to give up the spoils. His young Emperor marched suddenly against him, and quickly reduced him to his normal position; forgave him; and carried him away from Malwa to Futtehpore Sikri where the court was then residing. Only a few days elapsed before this haughty man had a quarrel with the grand Vizier—who lies buried in a beautiful marble tomb nearer the city—and when the latter spread his mat for evening prayers, the omrah stole up behind and stabbed him. The Emperor was in an adjoining apartment of the palace and hearing the outcry rushed in upon them. The punishment was speedy—for there were fewer loop holes in their law, than in that of some others,—the evidence was clear, and the execution came almost as soon as the sentence: "Let him be hurled from the battlements of the fortress." This took place in the year 1572, but this tomb was built some thirteen years later.

Our next ramble took us through the Victoria gardens, which are within the walls. There is a small collection of wild animals in cages, disposed among the shrubbery, and the English church, where the Beresfords, and a great multitude of people who were cruelly slain during the mutiny of 1857, lie buried.

We drove out of The Cashmere Gate, where the adjacent wall shows abundant marks of the English batteries. I can not forbear telling the story of the gallant "six" who blew open the gates to the city. The history of the mutinous native troops of the Bengal army, the way they swarmed into the city on May 11th 1857, and the wholesale massacre of the English officers and residents till not an Anglo Saxon was left in the vicinity, that followed, are facts too recent and too well known to the world to be repeated here.

CASHMERE GATE, DELHI, SHOWING EFFECTS OF BOMBARDMENT IN 1857.

The following September, a small army of English and loyal native troops, numbering seven thousand, laid siege to a strong walled city, containing sixty thousand rebel soldiery. Under the trees that lined the side of the road, stood six soldiers—the advance guard of civilization, breathlessly awaiting the signal to rush up to the gate of the city, bristling alive with Sepoy muskets, and place bags of powder to blow it open, and admit an assaulting column that was to follow. The signal came, and Lieutenant Home with four bags of powder, ran swiftly to the outer gate, passed the drawbridge and laid the bags at the inner gate, and then jumped into the moat unharmed. The rebel Sepoys by this time began to comprehend what was doing. Lieutenant Salkeld followed swiftly after, with four more bags of powder, and a lighted port fire. He had just placed the bags, when he was shot through the arm and fell back on the bridge; he gave the port fire to Sergeant Burgess bidding him light the fuse, but the latter was instantly shot dead. Sergeant Carmicheal took up the fire, and succeeded in lighting the fuse, but fell mortally wounded. Sergeant Smith, seeing him fall, advanced on a run, but finding the fuse lighted, jumped into the ditch, where the bugler Hanthorn, who was to sound the call, had already conveyed poor Salkeld. The next moment came the explosion, the shattered gate, the buglers' call, and the assaulting party rushing across the drawbridge above their heads, through the gate, and into the city. That is the way the English went into Delhi on the 14th of Sep. 1857.

The northern suburb is the European quarter, and is by far the pleasantest and most tasteful spot about Delhi. Shah Jehan in his palmy days expended a million pounds sterling on a magnificent garden in this quarter, adorning it with fountains, marble pavilions and kiosks, and planting it with cedars. This garden, as well as those at Lahore and Cashmere, he named Shalimar—The house of joy. The European cantonment is said to be on the same site , and scarcely a trace of the garden has been left by the invading armies.

Two centuries ago the suburbs were filled with tombs and palaces and gardens of the Mogul nobility.

But our visit at Delhi must come to a close, and we prepared with great regret to leave it. Months might be spent among its ruins, and yet, at leaving, the same unsatisfied craving for a longer stay would exist. The legends and tales of past splendor and magnificence, which one hears hourly here, are so entertaining; and captivating recitals of deepest romance and most devoted love, mingled with stories of bloodshed and horror, so abound, that one feels as if in an enchanted dream, and holds back from the awakening.

Wishing to proceed to Beas River—the rail road was not then in operation—we were very glad of the opportunity of trying the Indian Dâk, on that superb highway—the English Grand Trunk Road—which has been mentioned as the graded and macadamized road, extending from Calcutta, northwest to Peshawar, the very gate of the Khyber Pass in the mountains of Afghanistan, a distance of 1,600 miles.

The Dâk is a strong, square built Indian carriage, a flat roofed house on wheels, with four good sized windows with venetian blinds. It is provided with means to bridge the well or place where the feet rest, so as to make it level, that a mattress may be spread for a bed at night; many persons, if the journey is long, prefer to lie upon it in the daytime also. The horse is changed every five miles. These carriages are chartered, and one keeps the same one the whole distance whatever it may be, with the privilege of stopping over and resting, whenever it is desired. One coachman and a syce or assistant, accompany the carriage. We found it on the whole a very comfortable way of travelling.

We passed out of Delhi by the Lahore gate. On each side of the road were ruined, roofless, brick walls, and tall arches, and a wilderness of piles of broken bricks, until we had passed the coss (or one mile and a half) monument—that being the name applied to their linear measure—and then we came out upon the fine, fertile plains of this region. Long trains of camels ladened with cotton were coming into market, and huge wooden-wheeled antediluvian carts, drawn by fine, large zebus or Indian oxen covered with blankets, they being more warmly clothed than their drivers.

We had some of the most abused, as well as some of the most abusive horses—I cannot say that was ever any one else's lot to have—for I knew by their bleeding necks, and sides, that a good many had had them before us. Here is a wide field for Mr. Burgh and Rarey. Rarey should go first, and teach the horses to be docile; and then the other, to see that they are not abused. Poor, lean, melancholy beasts, with shoulders and sides raw, were put into the shafts, and they utterly refused to move a step. I do not think their drivers resorted to hard beating as much as the English or Americans do on such occasions, but on the other hand they did not know how to break and teach their horses submission, nor how to care for them. The usual methods are, first, to put a rope around one of the forelegs at the knee and pull directly forward, the knee bends and the horse must step, a timely application of the lash usually sets all the feet to moving. If that fails, however, they call help enough to put a man on every spoke of the wheels, tugging and pushing to roll them forward, until the animal finds it much easier to go than to hold back, so he starts off on a run, and the coachman takes good care not to let him stop very soon.

Toward evening we pass Paniput a small city enclosed by a brick wall, forty miles west of Delhi; this vicinity has been for centuries a famous battle ground where the fate of the Empire and Delhi has often been decided. Here Ahmed Shah Dourani in 1761 nearly annihilated the power of the Mahratta nation. "These plains," says the historian, "drank the blood of 200,000 men that day; never was carnage so dreadful."

While we were exchanging horses a young man came about the carriage with what we were inclined to think was a dwarfish straw cutter, and endeavored to sell it, he asking five rupees ($2.50) for it, but was told to go away, that we did not want it, and had no use for it; but he continued his importunities, until Padre Sahib said he would disgust him by offering him half a rupee, and then he would go away. Holding up the coin in his fingers, the fellow quickly said, "I take," and handing out the machine he ran off nimbly, leaving Padre Sahib astonished, and us to think that perhaps his necessities had driven him to sell at a ruinous price. On showing it to a missionary he said, "your conscience need not trouble you any more on that point, for the youth got his usual price for the article," which was a betel-nut cutter.

About eight o'clock in the evening we arrived at Kernaul. There did not seem to be inducement enough about the city to keep us, and the traveller's bungalow presenting very few attractions we came to the conclusion to push on and travel all night.

Wheeling over this grand trunk road is, if anything, a little easier than riding in a baby cart over a carpet, because there are no seams in it to jolt over, for above all the rolling and smoothing there was laid on a coat of hard-finish, which was polished to give it a shine. Conversation had long before ceased, and certain drowsy sounds came from the Padre's corner; then there was a jolt and he sprang with a "Halloo! we are off the track! Halloo! Coachee wake up!" and with considerable ado he aroused him. Horse and carriage were half way down the embankment at the side of the road, the horse had stopped the headway by turning as nearly at right angles as the carriage would allow. The poor, lean, sorry creature had not life enough to gallop down hill, out of the way of the carriage, so he turned out for it to go past him, but as it did not go, he stood still and waited to see what would come of this new turn of affairs. His inherent lowness of spirits and chronic melancholy were our safe-guard, for the driver and every soul on board were asleep.

After much ado, we got safely back upon the track, and Padre thought that coachee would bear looking after, and therefore nerved himself to keep awake, and succeeded in doing so, until we arrived at the place for changing the horses. Having seen the horse put into the shafts and actually moving over the finished road, the Padre subsided into his corner, and I knew he was bound for a short trip in dreamland, but I felt safe as long as he was on guard, even if he did drowse on duty a little. I had just arrived at that point where care and don't care meet and blend in a happy oblivion, when Padre jumped up again, saying, "We have stopped! We have surely stopped! Can you hear the horses feet?" Out he sprang, and found both horse and coachee asleep; probably the horse, from polite instincts, waited until the driver went to sleep, and then followed his own inclination. Padre turned to get into the carriage, when he espied an additional native's head peering out from among the trunks and valises. He made him get down, and the fellow had the audacity to pretend he was the company's chuprase, but Padre Sahib found that the driver had slyly passed his own belt, in the darkness, to the fellow to keep up the cheat; when a match was lighted the fraud was detected. The fellow was left standing in the road. Though it was far from morning, there was no more dozing; as Padre had to refrain from sleep to keep the driver awake, we thought it only fair to keep him company.

Gray dawn at last came and whitened into light, and we found ourselves passing through a rich and fertile plain that surged up into low hills in the distance, where the toiling cultivators lived in clay villages. A mile away was a brick serai. The coachman had stopped in the road mending his harness, and we saw a turbaned horseman, armed with shield and spear come out of the serai and sweep down over the ground at almost flying speed; his was no jaded steed, I assure you it never drew a dâk. He looked very quaint and picturesque in the distance; and for a moment I enjoyed the sight immensely; but when he wheeled and came down upon us at such speed, I began to fear his errand was not quite friendly; some vague remembrance of wild robber horsemen of former years flitted through my mind; but when he came up and rode around the carriage, and addressed a few words to the driver and then galloped away, I began to feel more comfortable; and as I really saw him leaving, my admiration returned.

Coachman got upon his box at last, drove about a mile and passed into a small grove of trees, on the further side of which we saw eight horsemen equipped with spears and shields, sitting upon their horses in line across the road. Our driver slackened speed, and finally stopped; one after another, we put our heads out of the door and took a survey of the situation; I distinctly remember there was nothing said about the picturesque or beautiful, but I instinctively thought of Colt revolvers, and that it would be a profound consolation to know that our gentlemen had two or three apiece in readiness; but the next thought was, what could the gentlemen do against eight armed men? Just then one of them rode up to the driver, and a few low words in Punjabee passed between them, I hardly heard them, my heart made such a pounding in my throat, probably from a sudden touch of heart disease. The horseman then rode up to the door on my side of the carriage, looked in, then rode around to the door on the other side. I concluded he was going to pay his attentions there first. Each one during that brief moment kept his thoughts, there was less desire for conversation in that carriage then, than there would be in a respectable Quaker meeting. After taking a good survey of the party, the horseman rode back and our pony started on. When we came up to the horsemen they opened right and left for us to pass through. When we were about eight or ten rods from them, their backs certainly did look well. I admired them decidedly, they even looked like fine fellows, splendidly mounted. My heart disease got better rapidly.

A little further on was a station for the Queen's mounted police, and the thought slowly dawned on us as we saw the same sort of troopers going to relieve the others from duty, that those wild, Punjabee horsemen with spears and shields, whose horse's hoofs we had heard thundering past us in the darkness, at intervals, and whose appearance drawn up across the road in the morning twilight, was rather striking to strangers like ourselves, had been the guardians of the road during the night.

About nine o'clock we came upon an officer in the civil service and his family in marching outfit; they had encamped under some trees and had just finished breakfast. A tent was near by from which the servants were bringing different articles of furniture, and loading camels, while a grand, old elephant was waiting to be ladened with the tent. The lady and her children entered a covered carriage, while the husband mounted his horse and rode by the side of it.

An hour later we reached the Umballa hotel. It is situated in the cantonment, on a street with pleasant European residences near. One readily detects where occidental civilization crops out, and we were glad to look upon it again. These houses were built after the same pattern of every house that we had seen in cantonments or European quarters; they began to seem like old acquaintances, and we came to have, in time, a great affection for a huge, haystack roof, it was an object that our eyes lingered very kindly upon, to say nothing of the pleasant inmates.

The Rev. Dr. Morrison, an American Missionary, resided at Umballa. He came out in 1838, and was first stationed at Loodiana. The missionary field, with which he is connected, skirts along the foot of the Himalaya mountains nearly five hundred miles in length, and fifty miles in breadth, reaching from the fords of the Indus at Attock, down to the Ganges; making an area of 25,000 square miles, occupied by ten missionary stations, and three white ministers, (I do not know the number of native helpers) which gives each one ample elbow room truly. How rapidly would gospel truths spread in New England with only one well organized, working christian church in the centre of Massachusetts, Connecticut and Rhode Island? How many years it might be asked with only three churches in all New England before the people of those states, were they heathen, would know there was either a God or Saviour in the universe.

As I passed out to step into the dâk, I heard a gentleman,

who had just come over the road, telling another how very bad they were, and emphasizing his assertions with very hard words. We drove hour after hour with a dismal dread of something that did not make its appearance, but certainly would very soon. In such a state of mind, one might go through paradise and see nothing to excite his admiration. We had been gradually nearing the foot hills of the Himalayan range, which are so closely backed by the kingly, old snow-capped peaks, that we were nearly on the line where the warm, humid air of the plains, meets the colder air of the mountains, and the resulting mixture was a Scotch mist, which moistened the upper layer of fine dust just enough to make it stick to the wheels, and load our feet with an untold weight of clay, if we stepped out of the carriage.

Towards night we came upon a party of men, engaged on a dent in the track, repairing it, or as Mark Twain would say, sand-papering it down to propriety. They had fenced us off the track, and we were obliged to turn off on the bare earth-road for five or six rods. It was easy to turn off but not so easy to accomplish the five or six rods. However by the aid of the workmen and a yoke of oxen standing near by, we were finally reported safe again on the track, much to our great joy and relief.

We were glad to find the old khansamah had no other lodgers, so whatever the scanty larder of a house far from any town contained, we could have the benefit of it. In reply to our enquiries, he said beefsteak and mutton, no got; potatoes, no got; bread and tea, no got. Still we were not discouraged, for we saw by the cut of his chupkin that he was a Mohammedan, and would have a moorghee (chicken) or two, somewhere on his premises, ready to die for a traveller. Moorghee got; rice got; broccoli got; coffee got; chupatties got. This last is the most unleavened of all unleavened bread; being simply wheat flour wet with cold water, and baked in a pan over the fire, in pancake fashion. G—— said he was hungry enough to eat through the whole bill of fare, and ordered the old khansamah to bring it all on.

In the dining-room we discovered a wee bit of a fire-place and chimney, like a triangular closet built across a corner of the room; it was a novelty, we had not seen one before in all the Orient; we voted with great unanimity to celebrate the event by having a good fire, though not a bonfire. In due time we rejoiced in its cheering warmth, and the dancing light and shadows, glimmering and quivering over the wall, gave to this room something of the charm of a far off home scene, amidst which, dinner was brought in, and in eating, we almost forgot the vexations of the day. The moorghee had been broiled, and a splendid head of broccoli did duty in the place of other vegetables; the chupatties I did not consider a successful substitute for bread. The rice and curry made amends for the other short-comings, and G—— remarked, as he passed over for the second plate, I am going to enjoy this curry while I can, for we shall soon be out of the region where they know how to make it.

As we had a little store of tea among our baggage, we enjoyed what consolation a cup of it afforded our weariness. This dinner has been described at length because it was the shortest bill of fare that we found on our way through Hindoostan.

After giving orders for an early breakfast, each one retired to rest. Perhaps the lonely situation of the house made us a little sensitive to noise; in the early part of the night we had heard the watchman going his rounds bravely, and the servants crooning their stories over, so we slept well until about two o'clock, when a slight movement outside the venetian blinds—for there were no glass windows—awoke me. I listened breathlessly; a long, dead stillness was followed by the same light, rustling sound, closer under the window; each particular hair manifested such a remarkable proclivity to stand up and listen, that my head would not lie on the pillow, without great effort of the will. Listening, we could hear some one breathe, and we lost no time in going to the window, and looking out, we saw a man crouching down with the cold, vainly endeavoring to protect his bare shoulders with a sort of curtain, made of reeds, which he tightly drew about him, so folded as to get an additional thickness to keep out the mountain air. He was one of the million poor, low caste, out of door servants, one of the people who labor all day with only a cloth about the loins, and at night sleep on open porches or verandahs, with about as poor covering as this man had. I confess that I felt that the world, and myself in particular, had been very unjust to him. I found no difficulty after that, in keeping my head on the pillow till five o'clock, when the old khansamah notified us to be ready for breakfast. We had nearly completed our toilets, when G—— came to the door and called through the keyhole, "Come out, the snowy peaks are in sight!" We rushed out in the dim twilight to see innumerable domes, pinnacles, points and peaks all glowing and radiant with a rosy light, like a beautiful city in the clouds. No direct ray of sunlight reached any part of the valley where we stood, yet it touched those lofty peaks of snow, so gloriously, that they seemed to us in the dim light where we were, like the vision of St. John, of the "Holy Jerusalem descending out of heaven from God." Below them lay the foot hills like walls and towers of purple amethyst, whose peaks and depressions, and opening passes shone like beautiful gates of pearl. We watched this glorious sight, that seemed more vision than reality, till the flashing gem of rose colored light, caused by the refraction of the sun's rays when below our horizon, faded into shades of pearl color, which the peaks retain through the day. It is worth a journey around the world, to have the pulses thrill once, with such a vision as this.

Our thoughts were at last called down from the clouds, by the coldness of our feet; when we noticed for the first time that the ground was covered with a crisp, white frost, the first we had seen; I thought of that poor creature on the verandah, trying to keep warm by wrapping a fence made of sticks around him. Babies, and children under five or six years old, are not supposed here to be old enough to know when they are cold. I saw one the day before, in full dress;

AGED HINDOO VOTARY AT HURDWAR.

he had half a dozen bracelets on each arm, and a small *brass* spoon about as large as the palm of one's hand.

We were not particularly talkative at breakfast that morning, the sublimity of that scene did not leave us at once. I felt as if the grandeur of the last two chapters of Revelations had been portrayed upon the clouds. Were I to see them again, I should wish to see them at the same hour of the day.

We packed ourselves in the dâk once more, knowing we should still have the mountain in sight. The air was cool and crisp, and I wrapped myself in all the blanket shawls at hand. Padre Sahib drew on the third coat, he had only worn two up to this point of the journey, and he had warmed himself heretofore with promises of another if pressing, or rather, if shivering need of it came, he sat down complacently informing us that he had one more in reserve.

An old elephant came down the road at a swinging pace, as though he was walking to keep warm; it really does not seem possible that such bulky creatures can walk as fast as they do.

We had already entered on the great water-shed between the waters that flow into the Ganges and Jumna on the right, and the tributaries of the Indus on the left. Hurdwar, a city on the banks of the upper Ganges, is the very cradle of the River-God, it is at the foot of the mountains. It is a very holy, and must also be a very sinful place, if the 3,000,000 of pilgrims who visit there in April, really do wash their sins away, and leave them there. Dr. Morrison and the other missionaries from Lahore, Loodiana and Umballa, improve the opportunity to preach the truths to the crowds that come from all parts of Hindoostan; they erect their preaching places, and spread their mats where the people pass, and very many will drop in to hear what they have to say. No opposition is made to their teaching the truths of the Bible at their sacred mela or fairs.

Trafficers in all sorts of rare and curious things, come here to trade or to buy. They bring rare gems from distant countries, shawls from Cashmere, silks and velvets from

Europe, and curious things from Thibet and China. White oxen from Burmah are wonderfully jumbled in with splendid Persian and Arabian horses, and the lank, lean ones of this country. There are princes, nobles, beggars and saints; bathing, praying, bargaining, screaming, and altogether making a perfect pandemonium. An English poet writes:

> "But night drops down—and what a change!
> An Eastern dream of beauty strange!
> Forest and islet, street and shore,
> With magic lights are blazoned o'er;
> Midst the green foliage, soft lights glow;
> Down Ganges, lights of worship flow;
> Each palace-house is opened wide,
> Midst light that gushes like a tide,
> And dancing forms and music sweet,
> Fill house and garden, tent and street."

A few of the very fanatical ones, climb the lower range, and wearily pick their way along precipices, and frightful chasms, and across mountain torrents; brave every privation and hardship in a colder temperature than they have ever before known, in order to plunge into this sacred river where it rises from under the glazier, from perpetual snows. The opening is called the cow's mouth; and is the birth place of the River-God. There are here, one or two temples, and a few priests and their attendants; the place is called Gangotri. Our party displayed a vast amount of perversity and original sin by declaring they did not care for the cow's mouth, or any of the hill places, and would not go to them.

Landour is one of the many delightful health retreats that the mountains of India afford her foreign inhabitants. Darjeeling is in the eastern, and Munsooree and Simla in the western part of the range. The last mentioned place is made particularly gay and brilliant during the part of the year that the Viceroy and his court, from Calcutta, spend there, it is then as gay as any watering place on the continent of Europe.

To these places the soldiers and officers are sent when health has failed. Here also, are boarding schools for the children of those, who either have no friends to leave them in charge of in Europe, or are too poor to send them there; here they have as cold and bracing air as they would have in England. Landour is delightfully situated on the summit of the spur of the lower range, and is but a few miles from Munsooree, which is lower and more sheltered. The former place is about 6000 feet above the sea.

This lower range is covered with trees. Gullies are said to be cut deep and sharp into the heart of the mountain by the great rain-fall of all the centuries since the creation, and deep chasms rent in the rocks by the convulsions in past ages, making bold, rugged and beautiful scenery, especially when looking towards the narrow secluded valley of the Dhoon, on the north of Landour, which dips down hundreds of feet, while beyond it rises range after range, each higher than the preceeding one, and above and over them all, appears the grand and sublime snowy range, so far above, that one is apt to mistake it for clouds. The highest part visible from Landour, is 23,000 feet. The vicinity of this mountain is the mother of two of the grandest river systems in the world, whose banks for more than three thousand years, have had a teeming population, and whose authentic history reaches so far back, as to place it second only to that of the Nile and Euphrates. The sublimity and vastness of these mountains, and the magnitude of the streams, that have gathered their forces here, long ago so awed the heart of man, that he made them the dwelling place of the Gods, and their traditions have long outlived those of the Gods of Greece and Rome.

It is remarkable that the sources of all these rivers are so near together, that if the spaces between them were level, one could visit them all in a very short space of time. The Indus, and its tributary the Sutledge, rise on the northern side of the Himalayas in the valley of Cashmere, and force for themselves grand and beautiful passes through the mountains to the plain below. The Jumna and Ganges —twin River-Gods—have their birth place amidst the awful grandeur of the eternal glaciers on the southern side of the same mountain peak. An English traveller writes thus: "By dint of untiring perseverance, we at last reached the confines of eternal snow. We found the river gliding under arches of ice. The most holy spot is upon the left bank, where, from beneath a mass of quartz and silicious schist rock issues forth five hot springs into the bed of the river, which boils and bubbles at a furious rate. The height of the snow bed here at Jumnotree is about twenty thousand feet."

We arrived at Loodiana about two o'clock in the afternoon, in time for tiffin—the mid-day meal. We had scarcely risen from the table, when a half dozen traders in Cashmere shawls and Tussore silks, presented themselves, each avowing their wares were made in Cashmere, though it is a well known fact, that none made there ever come into the hands of these traders; theirs are wholly made at this place and Rampore, up in the mountains. They are made from the same material however, that is, from the inner, finer fur of the Thibetian goat; and Cashmere workmen make them. After having refused all their offers of splendid bargains—they asserting I would be very sorry for I would never meet with them again, I astonished them by saying, I did not like Cashmere shawls, I liked the Rampore better. They looked at each other half a second, not a whit moved, then each one extending the same that he had offered me before, exclaimed eagerly, "Got! Got! Rampore got! All same, Rampore!" This turn was executed admirably, not one of them lost balance, it was edifying to know these heathen Punjabees were equal to the Jews in enlightened Chatham St. New York.

There were no antiquities in Loodiana; it is the centre of a rich tract of country which was formerly a part of the Soodi Afghan principality of Jalunder. When the English made the treaty with Rungeet Singh, king of Lahore, it was stipulated, that if the prince died without heirs, this territory should escheat to the Honorable East India company, instead of the king of Lahore. This was a small town of only 16,000 inhabitants, but as soon as it was known to be under English raj, or rule, native traders and capitalists flocked in from all

VIEW OF LANDOUR SANITARIUM, AMONG THE HIMALAYAS.

parts of the adjoining country, for they understood very well, there is more equity and safety to life and property, with the Honorable Company, than with their own rulers; so the population was quadrupled immediately. There are bankers here who have correspondence with all parts of the country, from Calcutta to Cabool. One of the largest printing establishments connected with the American Mission is at Loodiana.

We went out to see the place, which is finely situated on a high bluff. We stopped at an old fort just outside of the town; and it so happened, the commanding officer rode up to the gate at the same moment. Perceiving we were strangers, he very kindly showed us about, and then took us upon the wall, where we had an exeeedingly fine view of the country, which is like a level prairie, and I should think, about as fertile, judging from the luxuriance of the crops. We could see glintings of the rivers here and there in the distance. The few remaining arches of the railroad bridge across the Sutledge—which had been destroyed in the recent flood — were in sight. It was a grand structure, but its foundation at the bottom of the river was ploughed out of the sandy bed, and it fell. The great difficulty is to tell just what these streams will do, when their vim is up. Sometimes—when they cannot do anything else, when they cannot overcome and destroy—they will leave their old banks, ghâts, bathing worshippers, and all, and go madly across the country and make a new channel; then the old one is called a nullah; which was just what we were looking into then. This river is the Hydespes of Alexander's time, and the farthest limit of his eastern march.

The town, and this little fort, stand on the old banks of the Sutledge; but it did not go far enough away to bring the city to naught, as in one or two other cases. The commanding officer pointed out two cities standing where the green fields meet the horizon,—one on the right, and the other on the left; they were, he informed us, thirty-two miles apart, yet the objects in them are quite distinct. Then he told us to turn and look in a northerly direction; there, in the cloud region, was anchored a continent of pearl, just beginning to take on the delicate tints that a clear, beautiful sunset, gives to vast regions of ice and snow. The sun was not low enough in the horizon for it to take the charming colors of early morning; but the light was clear and strong enough for the officer to point out, and for us to distinguish, the depressions that mark those beautiful, but dangerous passes, that lead into the valley of Cashmere. A broken line of a deeper shade of color, marks the course of this mad river Sutledge, which rises on the northern side, and, though snows and mountains were piled to the clouds, could not be shut in.

The city of Rampore nestles among the higher valleys, and the route—sometimes following the river, but leading as it does through this place, and called the Rampore pass—is the one generally used, when passing from that portion of the country into Cashmere.

In the days of the magnificent old Moguls, the court of Delhi, regularly, every hot season, took up its long line of march towards that spot, and defiled up through the passes, amid scenes of wonderful sublimity and grandeur, to spend the months in the charming valley of Cashmere. The Emperor Jehan-Gir died on one of these return trips from this valley. The advent of this gorgeous court, with all its gay revelry; the splendid tent palaces, and gardens, that rose like exhalations, in such a quiet, secluded mountain valley, must have seemed like enchantment, to the simple gaze of the mountaineers; like the doings of the old genii, bringing about marvels of luxury and beauty.

On our way back to the dâk bungalow, we noticed some very broad spreading peepul trees, in a low walled enclosure; the entrance stood invitingly open, so we walked in. There were one or two small, low, domed temples, the inside of which were blackened with smoke. Two or three men were going through certain ceremonies, and then pouring water upon the roots of the trees, which act is said to be particularly acceptable to their gods; for this tree is the legendary residence of some of the deities. Such is the reverence for these trees, that, at Benares, we saw one that had been allowed to grow in a crevice, between the great blocks of stone composing the foundation and the steps of a palace, in the river front, displacing them, so as to weaken the structure very much; but no axe will ever fall on that sacred tree.

I returned to the bungalow while the rest of the party went into the city to take a survey of native life. A crowd of natives noticing the tall hat and black clothes of one of the party, mistook him, as usual, for a missionary, and followed in the wake, several times calling him Padre Sahib, and seemed to suppose he was looking for some particular person, when he was only looking at the gaudy decorations of the houses and gentry. He finally asked some question in Hindoostanee, which was not perfectly comprehended by these Punjabees, when a young native man came forward, and asked in perfectly smooth English:

"What would the gentleman like to know?

"First of all," said Mr. ——— smiling, and very pleasantly surprised, "where you learned to speak that language so perfectly?"

"At Lahore, in the school of the American missionaries! Are you English?"

"No!"

"Then you must be an American; if you wish, I will guide you to the residence of the missionaries here."

This offer was declined, on account of the lateness of the hour. The gentry here put their gilding on the outside of their houses, that it may be admired by the greatest number.

It was here in this English city that the fugitive kings of Cabool took up their residence, after Shah Shuja had applied for assistance to the old King of Lahore, Rungeet Singh; and lavished on him nearly all of his immense treasure of jewels, among which, was the famous Koh-i-noor diamond; besides offering to confirm his possessions of the country of the five rivers to him, as king.

Finally, a treaty was made between the English and the

king of Lahore, by which they were each to send an army to re-instate the fugitive upon the throne of Afghanistan. After doing this, the troops remained a year to consolidate his power; but he became unpopular and was slain by the people. On the 6th of January, 1842, 16,500 souls marched out of the cantonments at Cabool, on their return march to India. Of this multitude, only one person, Dr. Brydon, survived the retreat through the mountains and lived to reach Jellallabad, one hundred miles away, or nearly half the distance between the starting point and the Indus river. They were constantly harassed by the enemy, and amid storms of snow, were betrayed by false guides into blind paths, where they were remorselessly massacred by the pursuing Afghans. This disaster has scarcely a parallel in history.

Leaving the bungalow, after going a few miles, we came to the end of the pucka road, where the horse was taken off and oxen put on instead; we then went down the bank, on to the black, overflowed bottom lands of the river Sutledge. Crops of oil seeds were waving where the mad waters surge so violently in the Spring. The bridge across the river is constructed in the usual manner, viz: boats chained together side by side; we counted ninety-six of them, while crossing the stream, and judged it would take nearly three times that number in the rainy season.

Upon the opposite bank a horse took the place of the oxen. As we progressed, we passed men and women working in delightful equality on the railroad embankment; the men receiving eight or nine cents per day, and the women a cent and a half less. The earth was all carried in baskets, which held about *six quarts*. The men were employed to shovel, and fill the baskets; and the women and boys to carry them to the place required. They reminded me of an army of ants, each carrying a grain of sand to build some great ant castle. The various grains and oil seed crops, promised an abundant harvest. The land between these rivers appears as fertile as that of Egypt; and it was rich and flourishing when Alexander invaded the country, more than three centuries before Christ.

After crossing the Sutledge, we passed more mango orchards than on any day before; they very clearly resembled our apple orchards at home. Topes, or planted groves were also more frequent than before. It is believed here, that planting a tree merits an entrance into Paradise: and this people were trying to get their reward.

Jellunder is only thirty three miles from Loodiana, and was the residence of the Loodi Afghan princes, who ruled this part of the Punjab during the latter part of the last century, and the beginning of this. There are a number of fine mosques, and a large number of costly tomb buildings, and gardens, which evince the wealth and taste of the former rulers, who were Mohammedans; but the great majority of the inhabitants belong to a sect of fanatical Hindoos, called Sikhs, who were so terribly shocked, and indignant, when markets were first opened here for the sale of meat, that they made much trouble. Similar disturbances occurred at Lahore and Umritzer, in the early part of the English rule.

After our midday meal, we hurried on, in order to reach the end of our journey by dâk, before night closed in. We arrived on the east bank of the Beas river, a few minutes past six in the evening, where the horse was taken off and bullocks put on. They drew us across the river, and to the dâk bungalow, arriving about eight o'clock in the evening. It had rather a fine look on the outside, in the dim starlight; but the interior was in a very neglected condition; panes of glass were wanting in the sash windows, and the carpet had been taken up. Mr. S—— declared he would not stay there, and G. concurred with him; when my opinion was asked, I said we certainly could, as I could not travel any further by bullock stage that night; and I proposed calling for a carpet, a fire, and a dinner. They did not quite settle down on that, and proposed calling on an English officer, who was occupying another part of the same building, with his wife, to see if he would interpret our wants a little clearer, to the old khansamah; the point he was particularly stupid about, was, whether there was a better room to be obtained, or not. So Mr. S—— tapped at the Englishman's door, and aroused a bear, who came to the door with a growl, and in a rough, excited voice, asked:

"How can you have the presumption to knock at a gentleman's door, when a lady is present; past eight o'clock in the evening?"

Mr. S—— replied with some touch of spirit: "I have knocked at your door, as one gentleman may knock at another's, all the christian world over; and I am waiting outside as a gentleman should, to know if you would kindly interpret a lady's wants, who is too weary to travel further to-night, to this khansamah? If you will not, all you have to do, is to reply in the negative, and I will not trouble you further!"

The grizzly dropped his bearishness, and said, "Certainly I will; I only thought you might have sent the word by a servant."

Mr. S—— replied: "If the servants could have understood enough for that, you may rest assured, I should not have knocked at the door of a lodger in the house!"

Then it was fully ascertained, that there was no better room in the house, and things were in that state, because they had already commenced repairs. We could have a carpet spread down, a fire made, and dinner prepared. So when Mr. S—— thanked him for the favor rendered, he was mollified; and did not appear to think that his service had been so very arduous, but that he could do some other favor, if any were wanting. I gladly record here, that this was the only departure from the real English gentleman—in a person of his position—that we saw in all our wanderings. We had a plain, comfortable dinner, of fricassee chickens, vegetables, rice and curry, and tea and coffee; the bill of fare for breakfast was varied, for there was rice, curry, potatoes, bread and moorghee, (chicken).

What an unfathomable, immeasurable blessing, to all who are so very unfortunate as not to reckon their ancestry back to some Hindoo god, that these same worthy deities, never

SIKHS IN BATTLE.

took it into their heads to make a sacred bird of poor moorghee, so that it comes to pass, that it is the main occupant of the flesh pots, everywhere in the country of these fanatical Sikhs. My eyes were running over with thankfulness, aided by the smoke from the fire-place. I have a lurking suspicion that the natives had put a cover on that chimney, to keep it from getting wet when it rained.

This place is simply a station, from which the Punjab railway is in running order to the Indus river; consequently, we here finished our travel by dâk. It was much less fatiguing than we had expected, and less monotonous than railroad travel. We had learned to fathom the depths of its pockets, and calculate the force it took to crack our almonds on the cushions; in fact, to know and like it well, and we bade adieu to it with regret.

CHAPTER XVIII.

THROUGH THE PUNJAB COUNTRY.

WE took the cars here for Umritzer, the sacred city of the Sikhs. It is doubtless the wealthiest city in this province, for its sanctity draws crowds of pilgrims, and none know better than the priests, how to exact valuable presents for their particular shrine. These Sikhs are really a reformed Hindoo sect which rejects caste. The founder, a religious ascetic, enjoined or commanded his followers to dress in dark blue, and to wear iron in some form about their person, which was generally understood to mean arms; this was well suited to the tastes and habits of the proud warlike tribes and their chiefs, that inhabited the country northwest of Hindoostan. Their spiritual leader is called a Gooroo, and like other Hindoos, they worship by bathing. Their fourth leader in A. D. 1581, selected a place here, fed by springs, and excavated a large square reservoir, which he named the "Pool of Immortality," in the centre of which is an island, and upon it is built a temple to Vishnu. Rane Dasso the fourth Gooroo is said to have spent his life in a sitting posture, in a diminutive structure, a sort of cage near it. The island is connected by a causeway with the mainland. The temple is richly adorned with carvings and gold and silver embellishments. The Sovereign Gooroo now sits in it to receive homage and presents, substantial tokens of the piety of his followers. Both he and the temple were formerly considered too holy to be defiled by the visits of Europeans, but his sovereign sanctity came down a little, he would graciously permit them to come in, if they brought plenty of backsheesh, and put on slippers of the priest's providing; which is really a tacit acknowledgement of his holiness and their uncleanness. During one of the Afghan invasions, their king Ahmed Shah, blew up the temple, filled up the reservoir and slaughtered beeves upon it. The Sikhs afterwards rebuilt the temple on the same site. About six hundred priests are attached to this temple.

The society of Sikhs had grown up slowly during the reign of powerful rulers, of whose armies they entertained a wholesome respect, but as soon as weakness began to manifest itself in the capital of the empire, these fanatics began a most horrible work of blood. History says, that the Sikhs, under a new chief named Bandu who had been bred a religious ascetic and who combined a most sanguinary disposition with bold daring councils, came out from their retreats and over-ran nearly all the Punjab, committing unheard of cruelties; whole towns were massacred in the most wanton barbarity; neither age or sex were spared; even tombs were opened and the bodies thrown out. Everywhere mosques were destroyed or desecrated, and the moolahs butchered, the Sikhs even approached Delhi on one side and Lahore on the other. Bandu had several times defeated the imperial troops, but when a very able commander was sent against him, Bandu and his followers were at last captured. A large portion of them were executed on the spot, but the leader with seven hundred and fifty followers were taken to Delhi, dressed in sheep skins with the wool on the outside, and were there paraded through the streets on camels. The whole number were beheaded in seven successive days; each one of them refusing to save his life by renouncing his religion. Their chief was torn to pieces with hot pincers, glorying with unshaken consistency that he had been raised up by God, to be a scourge to the iniquities and oppressions of the age. These heathen Hindoo can boast of many martyrs.

They had, at the beginning of this century, abated much of the barbarous fanaticism that they manifested while this province was ruled by a confederacy of their chieftains, but they found in Rungeet Singh a firm ruler and king, and an able leader.

A very striking object about the city, is the fortress of Gooindghur which he built in the year 1809, ostensibly to protect the pilgrims to this shrine, but in reality so arranged that he could turn his guns upon those dangerous and turbulent assemblies, if they became unmanageable. His treasure was kept in this fort.

Since Rungeet Singh died, English batteries have carried on a very subduing influence among the Sikhs, until they have become about as civilized in their way of warfare as other Indian people; and the majority of their chiefs continued loyal during the late mutiny. The name Umritzer, is derived from Amritsa Saras—the Pool of Immortality—the high sounding name that the founder, Rane Dass gave to the tank, whose waters he taught his followers, were sufficient to wash away the blackest sin, and give the bather right and title to a seat in the Hindoo heaven. His influence previous to the year 1770 was confined to the country lying between the rivers Sutledge and Jumna. Both the people and the chieftains were hardy and warlike, and more easily raised to bitter, fighting zeal, than their countrymen further south, whose towering pride of caste, they seemed to hate almost as much as the Mohammedans. The grandfather of Rungeet Singh was one of these chieftains, they were Jâts before they became Sikhs, a lower caste than the Rajpoots. This prince was about twelve years old when his father died. The petty neighboring chiefs thought it a good time to absorb his little territory, and divide it among themselves *a' la Poland.* The mother, who had assumed the management of affairs during her son's minority, availed herself of a Hindoo custom of sending her bracelet to the most powerful chief in her vicinity, who thereby became her bracelet brother. No knight was ever bound more closely by his vows of knighthood, to do to the letter the bidding of his fair lady, than the recipient of a Hindoo lady's bracelet,

LAKE OF IMMORTALITY, LAHORE.

though they were perfect strangers before. The consequence of this little movement was such, that the lady and her son were so gallantly defended as to retain their possessions intact. She afterwards evinced such love of power, as to become unpopular and was assassinated when her son was about seventeen years of age; it was hinted that it was with his connivance, as he immediately assumed the government of his territory.

For nearly half a century the Punjab, the provinces of the Five Rivers, had been a conquered dependency of the king of Afghanistan. In the latter part of the last century, the weak rule of the two fugitive kings, who were mentioned in the sketch of Loodiana, gave Rungeet Singh who was at a great distance from the court and its plots and conspiracies, the opportunity to perform some service for the Afghan, Shah Zeman, his king; who in return granted him the governorship of Lahore in the year 1799. He took possession, after expelling three Sikh sirdars, or generals; this put him on the high road to the throne of the Punjab. He not only maintained his position, but extended his sway over the whole of the province, and then marched across the Indus and scoured Peshaware, a portion of Afghanistan itself. During this time his king had been deposed and blinded, and a brother, Shah Shuja, was placed on the throne at Cabool; but few years elapsed before the second was driven from the throne, and both expelled from that country; they came to Lahore to plead of their former governor, assistance to regain their lost throne.

An English army accompanied Shah Shuja into the southern part of his country, and crowned him at the ancient capital Ghizur, while the army of Rungeet Singh went into Peshaware, and the two united around Cabool, from which the rival king fled, and there Shah Shuja ascended the throne. The fate of the Shah, and the result of this most disastrous expedition has already been related.

In the year 1831 a little town called Boopore, on the Sutledge was honored with a glittering array of the nobility of the country. A grand durbar in something of the old style was held there. Lord Aukland the Governor General and his council, with a great number of officers and ladies, marched from Calcutta with 12,000 men, to exchange compliments with Rungeet Singh and as many other Rajpoot princes, as would care to march out of their strongholds, followed by their retinues, to overlook this movement; for a treaty of alliance was to be signed, which would make the English a power behind the throne of the country of the Five Rivers.

An hour and a half of railway travel from Umritzer through an interesting and populous country brings one to

LAHORE.

This is one of the most ancient cities of India. It was populous and flourishing at the time of Alexander's invasion, who penetrated only as far as the Sutledge, where the murmurs of his army compelled his return.

It was a rainy evening when we arrived at the station at Lahore, and it was a long, dark drive to the dâk bungalow at Anarkulli, the European suburb of the town, which is as nice as any hotel that we have found since we left Calcutta. On looking out the next morning, we found that it was still raining, and that we were almost under the eaves of a fine, large substantial church, which we were told belonged to the American Mission. The Medical College and Dispensary were also near by.

It was the Sabbath, and though it was pouring rain—the first really copious one that we had experienced since leaving the Straits of Malacca—we attended church, but were not much edified, as the services were in the Punjabee.

THE FORT OR CITADEL OF LAHORE.

This occupies the northwest angle of the city, and contains detachments of European troops, and extensive magazines. Near by is the tomb of the Maharajah Rungeet Singh, generally known in history, as the King of Lahore. He died in 1841. This is the first Hindoo mausoleum of any pretension

TOMB OF RUNGEET SINGH.

whatever, that we have seen. We entered a noble hall, through doors of carved sandal wood; around on the walls of the apartment were arranged statues of Vishnu and Sira and Kahlee; the latter standing on the sacred ox; she had a good assortment of wicked faces for one head, and many brawny arms; one hand had seized a struggling urchin by the hair, which is said to be the way she takes hold of sin; consequently all Hindoo men shave the head, so as not to give her a very good chance for a hold of them, if she should catch them in any peccadillo.

In the centre of the hall stands a lofty marble pavilion, double-arched, so that one pavilion seems to stand within another, over the marble urn, containing the ashes of the king, which is covered with a cloth of gold, now loaded with dust. The dome of this exceedingly beautiful monument, is made of fretted silver; the ceiling between the outer and inner pavilion, is composed of mirrors and an arabesque of frosted silver. The outer pillars are inlaid in mosaic; and the whole monument is much more loaded with ornaments, than the Mohammedan tombs. Its surroundings are at fault; it should stand beneath such a dome as the Taj; or within that incomparable court on the top of Akbar's mausoleum. There is not a little of the Hindoo temple gloom about the great hall in which it stands. Passing through to the other entrance, we were shown the funeral urns of his two sons, and grandson. A musician always sits near, playing an instrument, and doing very fair execution. These urns have no pavilion, only quite a plain cloth, partly upheld by a low balustrade that surrounds them.

Not one of the three died a natural death. The first son and successor reigned only one year, and died from the effects of poison; his young son was proclaimed under the regency of his mother; and was killed before the funeral of his father was ended, by the falling of a beam in the structure where the funeral ceremonies were taking place,—"a catastrophe not accidental, though intended to have that appearance." Then a reputed son of Shere Singh contended with the widowed regent, and finally succeed to the throne, only to be assassinated during his first year's reign. Then succeeded bloody anarchy, which raged with desolating fury all over the province and finally spread across the Sutledge, into the country covered by the English treaty; a war ensued, by which the warrior Company absorbed the province of the Five Rivers.

Adjoining the tomb, is the Huzari Bagh, and a fine gateway, leading from the fort into this garden, which was the work of the Emperor Akbar. A beautiful white marble baradarri, or throne-room stands in the garden. Something about it, some incongruities, and the general hap-hazard, neglected condition of it, made me think that the whole had been filched from the Shalimar gardens—three miles distant—by the late Maharajah. This is put down as mere conjecture, though it is well known, that he removed some of the choicest structures from those renowned gardens; taking them down, and putting them up in other places; conveying some of the most ornamental to adorn Umritzer when he made that city his capital instead of this the ancient metropolis, the one captured by the Moguls in 1009, when its proud old Hindoo king, Jei Pal, having been twice beaten in battle, felt himself so humbled by his want of success, that he abdicated in favor of his son, then ascended a splendid funeral pyre, amid a vast concourse of his subjects; a voluntary sacrifice to his gods, to wipe out his disgrace.

We passed from the garden into the spacious court of the Padshah mosque, built by the Emperor Aurungzebe. Its court looked desolate; one of its huge minars has a vertical fracture, extending from the top nearly half way down; yet, the great central column, around which the stairs wind, seems quite firm. There is a mournful grandeur about this relic of the old iconoclastic Emperor. The Sikhs have visited it with insults heaped upon it with frantic zeal; and the late Maharajah converted it into barracks for his soldiers, and slaughtered swine in the sacred place of prayer. The noble arches are closed with brick walls; the marble work, and the magnificent blocks of mottled porphyry, ninety feet in length, that formed the steps at the entrance, are very badly defaced. Indeed, this mosque has received from Hindoo hands, the same treatment that Aurungzebe was in the habit of bestowing on their temples, in the territories that he conquered.

From the top of the minar, we had a fine view of the city and its surroundings. It is a crowded mass of brick buildings, out of which, rise the domes and the tall, slender minarets, of the mosques. Among them, we discern Hindoo temples; the Sonera; and the Vizier Khan's mosque,—the latter being conspicuous for its encaustic tile, of blue and gold color. Beyond, are ruined tombs, with broken walls and tottering domes, on which a few patches of these gaily colored tiles remain; and in all directions, are huge mounds of broken brick, from twenty-five to fifty feet high, that have been gathered from former ruins. This vast amount of *débris* has probably been collecting for two thousand years, and if it was in available shape, there would be enough to build another city.

SELIM AND NOOR MAHAL.

Just across the river Ravee, on its western bank, stands the beautiful mausoleum of Jehan-Gir and his Noor Mahal. It is built of brown stone, and ornamented with white marble laid in mosaic patterns of fruit, flowers, and sculpture, in bass-relief; and, like the sarcophagus where his father sleeps near Agra, his cenotaph has the ninety-nine attributes of God, engraved upon it. This edifice is about seventy feet high, and is covered with domes. A minar rises from each corner of the platform, and these are adorned with beautiful white marble cupolas.

Rungeet Singh, while king of the Punjab, wishing to show disrespect to Mohammedan tombs, as well as mosques, gave this structure to a French officer in his service, named M. Aunise, for a residence. He caused it to be cleansed from its Hindoo and Sikh pollution, and repaired; but he died before he had carried his plans into full effect. His death was considered, by all good Mohammedans, as the curse of Allah; because he, an unbeliever, violated the sanctity of a tomb of the faithful, by living in it. The river is rapidly undermining this structure; a crevice has been made by the settling of the foundation, and a part of the wall has been carried away.

The widowed Queen, Noor Mahal, lived twenty years after the death of her husband, busying herself in preparing his tomb, with a view of resting, after death, near her Selim; her wish was gratified. With the death of the Emperor and her son-in-law, Sherar, and the elevation of Shah Jehan to the throne, all her power passed away. She forsook the court and all of its intrigues, and dressed continually in mourning; so conducting herself, as to even win the respect of her enemies; but never again took part in political affairs. She also, by many years, outlived her niece, Moom-taj-ee, the wife of Shah Jehan.

Elphinstone, locates the place where Jehan-Gir was captured, by Mohawbut Khan, and the scene of Noor Jehan's leading the army to the rescue of her husband, not far from the old fort, Rhotas, on the west bank of the Jhelum, in the vicinity of the place where the road crosses that river. It is northwest of Lahore, and about half way between that city, and Attock on the Indus River.

Wishing to go to the mosque of Vizier Khan, we took the old khansamah's carriage, or rather the one he called for our use, and passed through one or two streets in close proximity to the houses on both sides, but did not quite touch them, and so we jogged on a little further, when scrape, scrape, crash! and some boards came tumbling down. As the rest of the party had left the carriage, I expected I should be annihilated by the rage of the shop-keeper, who came rushing out and looked into the carriage. Seeing an European as he supposed there, he turned to see the extent of the damage, but he found only a few nails broken, the boards not at all split. I looked at them very sorrowfully and waited for him to say something; he did not do so, and coachee thoughtfully jogged on at a snail's pace, closely scanning the inches and half inches between his wheels and some rickety verandah that projected into the street.

Reaching the mosque without further collision, we found it was the hour for mid day prayers; the few faithful were arranged in a long line across the court, going through their prostrations, touching their faces to the earth while reciting the prescribed formula. We hesitated at the gate for a moment, thinking it not in good taste to enter while so many people were worshipping; when a man who had charge of the place espied us, and knowing buckshеesh would be given, came forward and asked us if we wanted to see the mosque. I replied affirmatively, but that we could wait until prayer was over. "Ah!" said he, "it does not matter, if you do not pass before the kibla" which was certainly a token of relaxed zeal. He then conducted us up the minar and pointed out the objects that were visible from it. These minars are not as high as those of the Padshah's mosque, neither was the view as fine. The peculiar feature of this place is this, the whole surface of the towers and buildings is covered with hexagonal glazed tiles of deep brilliant blue and gold colors. I was forcibly reminded of two tall towers swathed each in a patchwork bedquilt. Very many of the tiles have sentences of the koran inscribed on them in Persian, which those of the Faithful that can read may study, while those who cannot read them, make so many offerings and prostrations before the texts, that it seems almost like worship.

Giving the young man his bucksheesh, we got into the carriage, and gave coachee directions to take us to a certain bank where we wished to transact some business. Somewhere during the morning ramble, Mr. S—— had chanced upon the young native man he met in Loodiana, who was very anxious to show us the mission college; we agreed to go after having been to the bank, which we feared would close. After squeezing through a few narrow streets, coachee stopped before a large brick building, dismounted and opened the door for us to alight. Mr. S—— jumped out and ran in, and was much surprised to find himself in the midst of an assembly of between three and four hundred native people, who were listening to a lecture from a native man. He was beckoned into an adjoining apartment, where sat the Rev. J. Newton, and Rev. W. J. P. Morrison American missionaries. He then discovered that he was in the Mission College instead of the bank. We met with a very cordial reception from them. Mr. Morrison and his sister—who is teaching in the Mission College for girls—had only been out two years, while Mr. Newton, who went out first in 1835, is one of the pioneers in these parts.

The lecture that Mr. S—— so inadvertently stumbled in upon, was what they called the middle lesson. Their session lasts three hours; this time is devoted to Bible instructions, and the lecturer was one of their native theological students. They were all listening with as respectful attention as an audience of pupils would in our own country.

The Rev. Mr. Morrison went with us to the girl's school, and introduced us to his sister, a very interesting young lady, and also to an English lady, who was also engaged in the school. The pupils were seated as they are in our own country. I mention the manner of seating, because in the Normal school, held in a part of the old Sikh palace near the citadel—where they have one hundred pupils, many of them teachers in the public schools at Lahore—the young men were seated *a' le Turc* on cloth or matting on the floor, demonstrating propositions in Geometry on a horizontal board covered with dry sand. The salaries that these students receive for teaching in the city schools after this course of preparation, ranges from five to fifteen rupees per month, that is from $2.50 to $7.50. Not far from the price for teaching in the rural districts, in our own country half a century ago.

Mr. Newton informed me that the brick for his house, the girl's school house, and for the church at Anarkulla, were all quarried, dug up from the grounds on which they stand, and

A TABLE SERVANT.

A HINDOO PERFORMER.

THE YOUNG RAJAH.

from the mounds of *débris* everywhere about the city. They were probably made centuries ago, and composed buildings which may have been erected at wide periods of time, for well burned brick are much more durable than one is at first apt to suppose. The brick in the walls of the old palace at Rome from whence Queen Tanaquil looked out of a window and harangued the people; putting forth that little fiction, that king Tarquin was not killed, when he lay stark and stiff beside her, are good and firm now, though twenty-five centuries have passed since they were laid in the wall. Mr. Newton further informed us that the English Government, to encourage the establishing of schools for native youth, contributed to their building fund 80,000 rupees, or $20,000, and pays into their treasury such a fair monthly stipend as to nearly, if not quite, support the teachers laboring in these schools.

Since the mutiny of 1857, the Government has awakened to the importance of educating the middle and lower classes of native people, in order to balance the Brahmins and higher castes, who heretofore monopolized the learning; and also to furnish intelligent employees for the numerous positions that can be filled to good advantage by them. A law was passed empowering any man, of good moral character, who would teach a school that would bear a certain standard of examination, to draw upon the Government for a fixed amount of money. Doubtless the intention of this broad provision was to include these mission schools; knowing that the missionaries have always been the most indefatigable educators in that country.

THE SHALIMAR GARDENS.

After tiffin, we all drove out three miles to these famous old gardens, built by Shah Jehan, in the palmy days of Mogul power, more than two centuries ago; and celebrated in Moore's poem of Lallah Rookh. Not a more charming spot could possibly have been selected for a princess and her retinue of gorgeously dressed attendants to pitch their tents; where their gay camp equipage, gleaming out from among the dark shade of orange and jessamine bowers, amid the plash and murmur of hundreds of fountains, would make it seem so like fairy land.

There were formerly two gardens, each containing about a square mile, and enclosed by a high strong wall; but one, having been despoiled of all its ornaments by the king of Lahore, has fallen into disuse. We entered through a lofty gateway into a covered arcade having apartments on either side. In the middle of the garden, and in full view from the entrance, an immense fountain basin has been excavated, containing four hundred and fifty water jets; its banks are adorned with beautiful, marble pavilions, one of which is inlaid very artistically with a rich, purplish black marble, on the floor and pillars. It has a broad inclined plane of white marble, beautifully inlaid with black, reaching from the front threshold to the fountain basin. There are jets in the margin of the floor, and when in play the water is caught on the marble pavement and falls over the inclined plane into the reservoir.

Beautiful terraces rise one above the other, and walks lead off from the margin of the fountain into shady isles, planted with acacias, palms, orange trees, limes, and fragrant plants and shrubs. The baths are on the further side, next to the wall, and have their entrance from the other garden; they are crowned with brown stone pavilions, and are now in rather a dilapidated condition, not having been used for years.

There are ruins and razed foundations in other parts of this once magnificent garden, that show, though very dimly, something of its former completeness. Into one of these ruins, whose marble embellishments had been removed and the upper part a mass of broken walls, we made our way. A stair case led down into a very deep, well finished apartment, one of the cool retreats; the floor was probably twenty feet from the ceiling. The walls were handsomely finished, and required only the oriental decorations to make the room delightful, in oppressive mid-summer heat, or when the hot winds blow from the desert of Scind. In addition to the coolness derived from the depth in the ground, a doorway was cut into a large, deep well adjoining, to admit the damp cool air from that. A similar apartment at Lucknow, called "Tykahanah,"—a cool retreat—was described in connection with the ruins of the Residency. Light is admitted at the top of the room. The ordinary method of obtaining a cool moist apartment in India is as follows: the windows and doors are hung with mats, made of a kind of sweet scented grass, on which water is constantly thrown; immense pankhas or fans, suspended from the ceiling and moved by ropes day and night by relays of servants outside, keep the room tolerably cool. So much light is excluded by this process, that reading is out of the question; one can only spend his time in dozing. and praying for night and cool weather.

This garden of Shalimar whose royal mantle of beauty has not all fallen away—like that one so named and so adorned near Delhi—is still the much frequented resort of the European community of Lahore and its surburbs, Anarkullee and Mean Meer, for fetes and picnics of various kinds. As a modern attraction, archery grounds and seats along the promenades have been added; which, with the former beautifully adorned alcoves and kiosks, and pavilions of brown stone and marble and the play of the fountains, make it still an irresistible attraction.

The Government keeps this garden in excellent order, and has furnished in a neat, plain style, one or two of the houses for the accommodation of travellers, or any who wish to avail themselves of such a pleasant retreat for a short time, by the payment of a moderate daily fee.

On our way back to town, we had leisure to notice the gigantic mounds of old bricks, the *débris* of ages past, and the old ruined tombs, whose domes are almost toppling down; out of whose dust and rubbish gleam patches of gaudy, glazed tile; old deserted gateways that now lead to nothing; crumbling old mosques long since deserted by worshippers; and ruined serais that shelter no travellers. This is the sight that everywhere meets the eye within a radius of three or four miles without the present city walls, which have only a circuit of three miles, and encloses a population estimated at about 100,000.

St. James Church at Anarkullee is one of those fine, large, ornamental mussulman tombs, that are often seen in this part of the country, which, in this case, the English have converted into a place of christian worship with but little alteration. The tradition is that a youth named Anarkullee, was enamored of a lady who belonged to the imperial zenanah, and was engaged in a mild flirtation with the court beauty; the king saw smiles pass between the couple and he ordered the youth to be enclosed alive in a brick cell which was built around him, and then—as if to make some amends for his barbarity, or a conspicuous point to hang the moral on, which he would have drawn by all handsome young men, namely, that it was not safe for them to flirt with the ladies of his harem—he built over the spot this splendid mausoleum.

In its palmy days Lahore was known to have been divided into thirty-six guzars, or divisions, only nine of them are included within the walls built by Rungeet Singh. In the sixteenth or seventeenth century its glory culminated; but the decline of the Mogul power has left its mark here, even more than on Delhi. The tide of war often rolled down through the grand old mountain passes; and as Lahore was in its way, it never spared her a visit; and within a century and a half it has had many masters, and but few rebuilders. It dates far back in Hindoo history in its long line of rulers, and appears to have been on the route of Alexander, on his way to the Sutledge.

It fell into the hands of that proselyting old robber, Mahmood of Ghizne, in the year 1009. One century and a half later, the Afghan capital was removed from Ghizne to Lahore; thirty-four years after, it was captured by a rival dynasty; and then it enjoyed a quiet of more than two centuries.

RAILROAD TRAVELING IN INDIA.

Akbar, Jehan-Gir, Shah Jehan and Aurungzebe were her benefactors. In their days, old writers describe it, as "the resort of all nations," and it came to be a proverb, "If Shiraz and Ispahan—two Persian cities—were united, they would not make one Lahore." Akbar built the citadel, and a wall around the city, and tolerated all kinds of religion. It was here that he revived the ancient Persian festival in honor of the sun, and appointed his friend, Abul Fayle superintendent of the fire temple. This tolerant Emperor gave Hindoo Ghebers (Fire-worshipers) Buddhists, Jews and Christians, the same free exercise of their faith as the Mohammedans. He so far conciliated the Hindoos, as to build for their pilgrims a separate rest house, outside of the city, and called it Dharmpura; then he built another where Ghebers, Mohammedans, Jews and Christians could remain, which he named Khairpura. In this wise manner did he conciliate the different sects; and the Hindoos and Moslems began to coalesce in his reign.

The oldest specimen of Mogul architecture in the vicinity of the city, is a marble pavilion on the opposite side of the Ravee; it was probably built to decorate some royal garden retreat; but it is now used as a toll house. It was built by prince Kamran, the son of Baber, the first Timorlane Emperor that reigned in Delhi.

We left Lahore by the Scind and Punjab R. R. Our party was snugly stowed in a compartment of a car, and we hoped to have it all to ourselves. However in this we were doomed to disappointment. Soon after taking our seats a pale, thin, sickly English gentleman came to the door attended by two servants, with blankets and pillows enough to furnish a small hotel. Scarcely was he seated on top of all his bedding, than more blankets and pillows, bundles and boxes appeared at the other door. We felt a little nervous, but the gentleman in bed No. 1 looked aghast, as he saw the pile nearing the ceiling of the compartment, and a feminine face peering from one side to the other to discover where one more blanket, or pillow, or tiffin box could be stowed; and heard children's voices in near vicinity. Very soon their came from the top of the No. 1. pile of blankets and pillows, the sharp, crisp words: "Heavens! I shall be suffocated here; I would much sooner travel in a baggage car!" Bed No. 2. looked batteries at No. 1. but as it was disappearing out of the other door, disdained to open fire on a retreating foe.

The engine bell rang greatly to our relief, for it shut off the possibility of any more blankets coming in. We rattled over a road laid through the most dreary, unproductive region that can be imagined, except Sahara. No smiling, cultivated fields greeted the eye; but pools of dark water, said to be very alkaline, were very frequent, all along the entire route; the land appeared to be covered with a low evergreen shrub, called jouh; it resembles cedar more than anything else, yet it is not quite like that. There were a few camels and goats about the dreary villages around the R. R. stations. If this be the character of the land lying midway between the Raree and Sutledge, I cannot form any idea of the great desert of Scind that lies south of the river, and stretches almost to the ocean; it has large fertile tracts in it, petty states, in which have transpired important events in history. Few invaders have coveted these retreats among deserts sands, enough to ravage them. But to the fugitive prince or nobleman, they have been cities of refuge. To these sands came the Emperor of Delhi when Timorlane took the city; and here came Humayun, the second king of that house, and found a shelter till an invasion of his retreat was threatened; and here also, came Dara Sheko, when fleeing from his brother Aurungzebe.

We arrived at Mooltan about ten o'clock in the evening, having been twelve hours in travelling two hundred and eight miles. There was no regular hotel in the city, we had been told, but there was a good dâk bungalow in the European suburb, three mile distant, and to this we went. Late as it was, the khansamah prepared for us a warm supper of broiled chicken, and a dish of rice and curry; so we retired to rest somewhat refreshed, as our tiffin basket had been our only solace, for the wretched looking stations on this day's travel, were as little attractive as could be imagined. The next day was the Sabbath.

The khansamah made his appearance, and waited for the order, "kazrut loss" (bring in the breakfast). When we had finished, a dhoby made his salaam and asked if we had any washing; there was a short struggle between conscience and civilization. Conscience said keep the Sabbath day, and gospel and civilization both demanded personal cleanliness; being two to one, they out talked the still small voice; and this follower of the koran, who neither knows or is compelled to keep any Sabbath but friday, walked off with a bundle of soiled clothing, promising to have it ready before the steamer which was ready to take us down the river should sail.

The dwellings of the Europeans near by, have a home-like look, except the palms about them, which are the most prominent trees in this vicinity. The gentlemen attended church in the cantonments. There was a large audience, mostly military. The deepest impression left on their minds might be summed up something like this: glittering straps, dangling swords and red coats make a great show in church.

Evidently grass is considered a rare plant in this vicinity; very few can afford the luxury of a plot of grass in their yards; they would probably have to persuade it to grow by treating it to a daily bath of ice water, with a pankha to fan it, and one or two servants to hold umbrellas over it. A solitary starveling clump of bulrushes, excited my liveliest sympathy by its loneliness in this almost rainless region, while the "bilkie" a kind of reed grass, defies months, yea, almost the whole year's drouth, if it grows where the annual inundation has covered the ground. M. S—— plucked a stalk of this grass on the bottom land that measured fourteen feet.

MOOLTAN.

On Monday, the khansamah, butter house keeper, head cook and waiter—for all these offices are performed by him; his dignity is summed up in the title, khansamah; and in some cases it is a matter of astonishment how one small head can bear it all in addition to its enormous turban—announced the carriage had come. G—— rushed to the door to take a view of it, and found a two wheeled chaise of the pattern that Benjamin Franklin used, when he was the first Post Master in the United States. As there were only seats for two, G—— was obliged to walk or take a seat on the shafts of this concern, which we convinced him was better than a three mile walk under a tropical sky. We passed some fields of young wheat, through which trickled the small irrigating rills, down to a lower garden or field of mustard, which looked fresh and crisp, though no rain had probably ever fallen on a leaf of it. Groups of date, palm trees, and shrubs of a fragrant flowering miamosa, called golden rain, bordered the road and the gardens of bananas.

Major B—— told us that when he was sent to Mooltan, soon after its capture in 1849, there was then scarcely any verdure apparent, and showers of rain were almost unknown. During the Afghan and Sikh rule, irrigation had not been attended to, and the surrounding gardens and country lapsed into a desert until the English took it and dug channels for watering purposes, and repaired those that had been made under the Mogul sovereigns, so that now they have pleasant gardens, which modify the heat; and sometimes a stray shower visits the place. It has become a proverb among the natives, "Where Inglies go, rain comes."

Mooltan is in Lat. 30° and is situated three miles from the river Chenab; it is built on a mound said to be formed from the ancient *débris* of cities that have occupied the same site, and is enclosed with a wall; on the highest ground is the citadel or fort, whose brick wall was surmounted by thirty towers, and had a moat, faced with heavy masonry. It was considered under the old mode of warfare, a place of great strength. It was situated on an alluvial sand, but no enemy probably had ever thought of turning the river upon it, to wipe it off the earth. In the month of August, very soon after its last capture, through some neglect, the river then in a great flood, made its way into the ditch about the fortress; its massive outer walls forty or fifty feet high, and towers that had resisted the British batteries so long, were in a few hours hurled down into the ditch with all the guns that were mounted on them; on the day following, the inner wall and domes gave way; and of this fortress, celebrated for ages, there was left only a mound of rubbish, and broken, dismantled walls. Though a wall was again built up about it, which on the outside was probably as high as the old one, on the inside it was only four or five feet in height, and was not pierced for guns, nor otherwise made more defensible than an ordinary inclosure upon the same height. A small fort was built instead nearer the cantonments or English suburb, for its defense.

THE OLD SHRINE AND ITS LEGEND.

Within this enclosure is a very ancient tomb of a Gheber, or fire-worshipping saint, a curious compromise of architecture of two religions, equal to the tolerating principles of their wisest monarch. The dome was surmounted by the crescent, the peculiar emblem of the Moslem faith; while the interior was fitted with gigantic sarcophagi, and the peculiar tripods and lamps of the fire-worshippers. The structure was composed of brick, but near the top, on the outside, were blocks of carved sandal wood, very old, and much worm eaten. The porches were ornamented with tiles, some with Persian inscriptions.

The Ghebers were driven from their ancient home in Persia, by the Arab followers of Mahomet, fled east through the mountain passes to India, and found a resting place among the Hindoos. The Parsees of Bombay are their descendants.

The old keeper said this tomb had been built six hundred years. Sham Tebrez was a gheber saint, who suffered martyrdom for his faith, at the hands of the first Mohammedan invaders. According to tradition, he was flayed alive; and while in his agony he prayed, the sun descended from the heavens, and gave Mooltan such a blast of his fierceness, as to scorch everything about it, and from that time to this, the wrath of the old saint's, sun-god, has scarcely abated. This city has always been noted for its great heat and drouth; and if the old saint's prayers did not bring about the heat, then the heat must have been the cause of the legend. A few free thinking persons, have dared to doubt this notable miracle; but it has been equally apparent that in every case, these persons have been heretics, and not good fire-worshippers.

Within this inclosure is a monument to the two English gentlemen, Messrs. Agnew and Anderson, who were sent by the British Agent at Lahore, to install the new Governor Sirder Khan Singh, at the close of the Sikh war. They were basely assassinated, and a plot was discovered by which all the English were to have been massacred; then followed the second Sikh war, and the capture of Mooltan in 1849.

We entered the city, and drove through the principal bazaars; it was refreshing to see people sitting on mats in the streets, even in thoroughfares, driving bargains as though there was not the slightest probability of any vehicle coming along to disturb them.. Wherever we went, there was a rush of petty traders, with all sorts of curious native trinkets, beseiging the carriage, beseeching us very good humoredly to buy their articles. Knowing that turquois and lapis lazuli were brought from the Afghan country, we told them to bring some one with these stones; they were not long in bringing some spurious European imitations; saying "Good! Good! Inglese! Inglese!" we have always found that laughing at these native cheats was the shortest way of getting rid of them; and in this case it did not require much effort, as the thing was so absurb.

In the principal bazaars are merchants who deal in those beautiful Persian brocade silks, where all colors and patterns are woven in, thickly together, like a French brocha shawl. Tussore silks, cotton goods, and Cashmere shawls are found in great abundance. Everywhere are those little, dingy, native provision shops, whose only counter is a board eight or ten inches wide and four or five feet long, on which the entire stock in trade is usually placed in several small piles of the different kinds of grain and seeds that are eaten by the common people for food. A single dollar would be ample capital to start one here in business and leave some on hand for making "change" as it is called.

Remembering our experience in Lahore, we refrained from going into any of the narrow streets, and finally drove out of the gate without having met a wheeled carriage, or cart of any kind, or having seen an European within the walls; yet this is an ancient and populous city. The crowd and hurrying bustle of Broadway or a London thoroughfare, would frighten these people more than a bombardment, for that is a thing they can understand—they are accustomed to it.

The vicinity of the city, outside the walls, is covered with an amazing number of ruined mosques, shrines and tombs, relics of all religions, except the Buddhist and Christian. Walled gardens, garden houses and kiosks appear everywhere—the wreck of its former greatness and splendor which continued up to the end of the reign of Aurungzebe in the year 1705. This place remained in the hands of its viceroys a few years, and in 1739, when he overran the Punjab, the great Persian free booter, Nadir Shah, captured it, and sifted out its gold and carried it away to Persia. Seven years later, Ahmed Shah, king of the Afghans, took it, and it was ruled by a succession of weak inefficient princes of that nation until the year 1818, when Rungeet Singh, with an army of 25,000 fanatical Sikhs, captured its little garrison of 3,000 men, after having had 19,000 of his army slain by the obstinate defenders, of whom only a few lives were spared. Thirty-one years after, it was taken by the English, as before mentioned in 1849. European ideas have scarcely had time, as yet, to stamp their impress upon the valley of the Indus, as they have done on the more accessible valley of the Ganges, which has been so long in frequent contact with them.

Mooltan, or Multan is supposed to be derived from Malithan, which name Sir. A. Burns asserts is still applied, or at least yet known among the more intelligent natives of this land. Hence this city is supposed to be on the site of that capital of the Mali whose territory must have extended to the Sutledge, which Alexander took, more than three centuries before Christ; and near which he built his fleet of 2,000 boats, to descend the Indus. When, by sailing down it to the sea he found out his mistake in geography, *i. e.* that the Indus was a part of the Nile, as he had formerly supposed, he marched his army across what is now Beloochistan, along the coast to the Persian Gulf, while he sent Nearchus, his Admiral, with his fleet of river boats, to coast along the shore to the same place. If they chose their time in the N. E. Monsoon, the Arabian sea would be perfectly smooth for three or four months, therefore, it is not at all surprising, that when comparing their notes, it was found that the sailing party had not endured as much hardship, as those on land.

Selencus Micator, one of Alexander's four generals who shared his vast empire, formed a Greco-Bactrian kingdom, whose rulers dwelt, it is thought, somewhere on the tributaries of this river; for ancient Hindoo books—the Purans—state that eight Yuwun kings ruled in India. "Yuwun, is supposed to be a corruption of Ionian, the name applied by the Hindoos to the Greeks," (*Allen's History of India.*)

The next time Mooltan comes into historical light, is when Mahomed Cassim came from Bassora, on the Persian Gulf, to convert the idolaters on the Indus. Approaching the city, he summoned them to embrace the true faith or pay tribute, —and generously added—or be exterminated, which was so persuasive, that the city surrendered about the year 714. The next capture was by Mahomed of Ghazne when advancing on Lahore, in the year 1009; he did not care to leave so strong a fortress between him and his own country. The city was also taken by Timorlane, in the year 1400, when he advanced to the conquest of Hindoostan, and was chiefly ruled by his descendants while the Mogul supremacy lasted.

CHAPTER XIX.

DOWN THE INDUS.

WE again took our seats in the cars for Shere Shah, the port of embarking on the Indus steamers. It is situated eleven or twelve miles below Mooltan, to and from which trains run twice each day. As it is low water at this season of the year, the train only makes a little stop at this town, and then runs on three miles, across land that is overflowed every year, and consequently drops one's trunks and baggage out in the wide waste bordering upon the river. As there were three steamers moored at the bank, about a quarter of a mile away, Mr. S—— and G—— walked over to them—for there were no carriages at this place—and I remained seated on the baggage—as there was not even a shed to set down in—expecting they would return before the train left. They found the accommodations on the first steamer so poor, that they could not think of taking passage in it; the second would not sail for three days to come; they then went to the third, and found the accommodations very passable; but the agent was not on board, and the captain could not receive the fare and give out the cabin, but compromised the matter by telling them to come on board that night, and if the cabins had all been taken we could return to town by the train.

While all this had been passing, the time came for the train to depart, and the officials were loth to leave a stranger alone on a wild waste, so they rung the bell two or three times, and still no move; then they very kindly sent a messenger to inquire if our party expected to return to town that night. Here was a dilemma. To return to town and have my friends miss me on their return, not knowing where I had gone, I could not think of; to stay where I was, I dreaded, but concluded to venture it, and so presented my thanks and was left alone. Just as night was closing around us we embarked on board the steamer Indus for a voyage down the river to Kotre, seven hundred miles distant.

These steamers are owned by companies in London, and are constructed in such a manner as to be navigated in very shoal water, and tow a number of barges or river boats, which are freighted with merchandise. In this case, there were two, one on each side; on them were Persian and Afghan merchants with goods and chattels, which they never lost sight of. Each one of the better class seemed to have a servant, who prepared his food, and attended to his wants. The passengers on the steamer were Major B—— of the English army, his wife and three children; an army surgeon Dr. D——, and our own party. We were not crowded, each one had a cabin below, and we all made the deck—which was covered with canvas—our drawing room.

The upper part of the river Indus and the Ckenaub its tributary are, at this season of the year, a succession of deep, broad pools separated by sand bars; very fortunately they have not rocky bottoms.

Half an hour after sailing in the morning, we found the boat turning around and around, as if it had suddenly commenced a waltz; at the third turn the mystery was solved, the bow came into the right position to shoot across a sand bar into another deep place. These pilots must know the river inch by inch. The country bordering the river is low and the towns on its banks, if not built on a bluff, are three or four miles from the channel in low water, while the angry stream that surges past these places in the rainy season, varies from three to ten miles in breadth, according to the height of the adjacent country. These banks where they are not cultivated,

SCENE ON THE INDUS, SUNSET.

and growing crops of grain, are overgrown with a low evergreen shrub called jouh: the home of the jackals and hyenas which occasionally show themselves scampering across some cleared space. Water fowls of all kinds abound; the most numerous are the large, brown and white, bromely duck, and a tall, graceful heron. Smaller fishing birds flit around distant margins of shallow pools. Crocodiles come out of the water and sun themselves on the dry edges of gravelly sand that rises above water level, but do not wait for near admiration before they glide into the stream.

When we had made about fifteen miles we came up with two steamers of the same line, one with one thousand soldiers that were going down the river; the other with about the same number of muleteers having the same destination. We came alongside of them, and after the captains had conferred together, ours remembered, suddenly, that he had left one of the cooks on shore when he sailed, and he must wait for him to come; and the other captains said the water was too low, they could not possibly go on before morning. G—— remarked that a heavy dew was expected that night, and they were going to wait for it to fall!

The cables were carried out, and the boat made fast to the bank. The centre of attraction seemed to be on the boat where the troops were; between nine and ten o'clock, our captain came on board with rather beclouded vision, fell down in a helpless lump at the bottom of the stairs, called for his servant and disappeared inside of his room, where he continued in a state of eclipse all the next day. The steamer got under way very early the next morning, and made fewer turns to shoot over sand-bars than yesterday. Going on deck early, we became deeply interested in an Afghan with an embroidered pelisse, on the barge along-side. He divided his time between fishing and praying, with wonderful exactness. He baited his hook and set his line just as the sun was rising, and then commenced his prayers and prostrations, close by his line; while bringing his face down to touch the deck, the line moved a little; he thought he had a nibble; he instantly arose, drew in his line, and discovered his mistake; after examining the hook, he replaced the line and went on with his prayers until he had nearly finished and was saying Allah Ukber but would not wait to finish, for there was a decided nibble and his breakfast depended on that, so he stopped again, and this time with better results. Setting the line again he went on praying and watching, without the idea of any incongruity in so doing. Another, an elderly Mussulman with the placid manners of a Turk, was waited upon very attentively by a dandy sort of a servant, who wore a little Hindoo skull cap all bespattered with spangles, and a gaudy colored vest over his long white cotton coat. His master prayed some time as if absorbed in what he was saying, until the servant chanced to move some of his valuables, when he gathered himself up and reproved him in a very undevout tone, and then went on praying.

As we were about to sit down to breakfast, we were amused to hear the khansamah ask Mr. S——, calling him Padre Sahib, if he would take the head of the table and carve, saying "Captain, he no can come." At which both he and G—— broke into a hearty laugh. Major B—— and his wife looked rather puzzled; when Mr. S——remarked, he could not see how it came that the Padre Sahib had broken out on him again. "Ah" said the Major, "are you not a Padre?" "No!" replied Mr. S——, "unless I have been made one by a sort of universal acclamation since I came to Hindoostan! I do not see how so much goodness comes to be set down by strangers, to my account."

"Ah; ah! my friend, do not plume yourself too much on that," said Major B——, "for I was told at Shere Shah, that the late absconding chaplain, who suddenly disappeared from his regiment up north with a very small stock of that article, was to be my fellow-passenger down the river by this boat."

Just then there was a dull, heavy thud, and a jar that set the crockery dancing. G—— rushed out on deck, the hurrying footsteps above told us that we were on another sand-bar, but no one apprehended any more danger from that, than a party on a sleighing excursion would, if it came upon a strip of bare ground. G—— returned with elongated visage, and said it was thought they would not be able get off the sand-bar that day. "Oh that is nothing," said Mrs. B——, "I was once on the Ganges in a steamer, and we ran upon a sand-bar, and had to remain there two weeks, and but for the fortunate circumstance, that the Governor General was coming down the river and caused a canal to be cut through the bar, we might have remained there until the rainy season came." When we went on deck we saw all hands hard at work, at what they call kedging it. A small anchor is carried in a little boat until good firm bottom is found for it to fasten to, and then by means of cables and the capstan, the boat is drawn through the yielding sand, and after tugging four hours the steamer advanced about forty feet, and soon after came into deep water.

We passed a number of native boats coming up, constructed with such very high pointed bows and sterns, that it was evident that they were modeled after the half moon, as Sir Hendrick Hudson's were; the current was strong against them and they were tracking, that is, a rope was fastened to the bows and natives tramped along the river bank hauling them up.

The Indus valley is situated in some respects, like the Nile; namely, it has a wide, almost rainless region on each side of it, and it is subject to great inundations. Whether, within the last thirty centuries that it has been known to have been inhabited, it ever had as large a population as the Nile valley, cannot be stated; but one thing is certain, no such enduring marks of high civilization exist here as are found in the other.

The steamer's passengers all took a walk on shore one afternoon between five and six o'clock. The natives, both Mussulmen and Hindoos, were scattered in groups far apart, cooking their evening meal and their food for the next day. As we were making our way along the bank, we came upon a group of Hindoos; they threw up their hands and began to gesticulate in an angry manner seizing their food and cooking utensils, and hiding them under their coats, or whatever came to hand.

"What is the matter? what do they mean?" I asked looking all around, expecting to see a hyena or a jackal about to spring upon us.

"The rascals," said the Major, "are Hindoos, and they are telling us that our shadows will spoil their food, and they will break their caste if they eat it."

To have such creatures, who cook their food in a skillet and all sit on the ground around one dish and take out of it with their fingers, make such a pow-wow about our passing along, and say our shadows, even, would make their food unclean, was rather humbling, yet so it was; if it were a prince, or the Queen herself passing, it would have been all the same. That is caste! I had heard the force of caste was abating.

Near by was a long train of camels, tied one after another, laden with wood; each one was made to kneel down while his burden was taken off, to which he protested with many sullen groans. The wood must have grown away among the northern mountains, for there has not been any forests here for 2000 years. It was brought down the river when the water was high, and stored far inland. A native woman, dressed in blue print trowsers very plain and tight about the ankles and very full of gathers at the waist, was sitting astride of a little pony waiting for her animals to be unloaded; she was the camel driver. Could she belong to the same race as Rajah Dahir's wife, who defended so heroically her capital, when her husband had been slain, and her son had fled? This struck me as rather an unpoetical vocation and I can safely say, I felt generous enough to let her continue her calling if she liked it, without coveting it.

Farther on was a water wheel for irrigating the land, it was constructed on the endless chain principle; small red earthen pots were fastened on a rope that passed over a wheel, and between were arranged evergreen boughs, in such a manner as to relieve the pressure when the pots passed over the wheel which was worked by oxen. Near it was growing a small patch of grain: a kind of dwaft pea which is of a dark color and very sweet and rich in nutriment. In a dry state it forms a staple article of food for man and animals.

The soft mild evening air and moonlight drew most of the passengers into the grand drawing-room—the upper deck—where the evening wore away with songs, fun and stories; while those of us who retired to our cabins had wide gaps in our dreams, filled with the echoes of "John Brown" floating over the tangled jungles of the Indus valley, till it mingled with the dim distant bark of jackals. Then came the song of the Calcutta "Baboo;" sleep could oppose no power to its invincible fun; dreams could throw no disguise over that mirth-provoking jumble of broken English. Then the mirth ceased, and as the "wee sma" hours came, the bark of the jackals came nearer and nearer, then stealthy feet were heard on deck, and the rush up the stairs of the two canine watchers; and then we heard the scurrying feet retreating swiftly over the bank. While all this was passing on our part of the boat, a poor Mussulman among the native passengers, unknown to all, was passing through his last struggle, with the bark of the jackals, the prowlers among graves, sharp in his ears. In the morning his body was carried to a grave in the sand, and laid with his head towards Mecca, by the sons of the Prophet. It is said that though a body may be buried very deep in the sand, these jackals will dig it up in a few hours. His family lived at Kotre, and he had been struggling to reach his home before death came, but he died alone and unwept.

We passed through a very level stretch of country the next day, the banks are so low that Shikarpoor, a city on the west bank twenty miles away, is reached by the inundating waters. A branch of the Scind canal affords it communication with the river. From this abundance of water have grown orchards of mangoes; and groves of dates, oranges and mulberry, gladden and beautify its surroundings, and make it differ widely from the cities on higher ground. It stands on the old route from the Scind up through the Bolan Pass to Khorasan and central and southern Afghanistan. Sir A. Barnes gives the population of the city at thirty thousand.

Khyrpoor is also a city on the east bank, fifteen miles from the river, on the border of the desert of the Scind; it is surrounded by a territory of the same name, about one hundred and twenty-two miles square. It is reached by canals for irrigation and transportation, and though selected as the residence of the Ameers of northern Scind; it is said not to contain anything of interest to the tourist. The city is meanly built and has a population of only about fifteen thousand.

It became known during the late war in Scind, that there was considerable treasure among the Ameers who resided at Khyrpoor, which would, and eventually did, become prize-money among the leaders of the conquering expedition. Sir Charles Napier, the commander, obtained for his portion of the booty $350,000, and his salary as Governor of the conquered territory was raised from $50,000 to $75,000 yearly, when the Scind became permanently attached to the English possessions.

The scathed and bare mountain ridges that had lain all day far away on the horizon rim, seemed to be making toward the river, as if they intended to cross the path of the waters soon. While we were sitting at the evening meal, the first officer came down to ask us if we would like to see a very beautiful view. We rushed upon deck to behold at the end of a long reach of river which the desert ridges were almost overtopping, the tall minars and domes of a city, and a picturesque old fortress at the entrance.

SUCKKUR.

This is an old dilapidated—I had almost written the word dead—city, so very quiet and still did it seem to our western senses, with the clear, bright, cloudless sky, bending so tenderly over it. No carts rumble in its streets; its dray is the camel's back. The Scindians do not gesticulate and work themselves up to a fever heat, haggling about an orange or a piece of sugar cane, as one often sees done in the Ganges valley; but they go about the dusty, unpaved streets, as silently as if afraid to disturb the long repose of ages that hangs over them. This city is on the west bank of the river, and behind it rises the reddish, rocky ridge, over which caravans wend their way hither from Candahar, Bokhara, Herat and Persia, bringing the beautiful fabrics of those countries, and horses from the choice herds of Persia and Arabia.

Clinging to a bold precipice, on the east bank of the river Indus, is the town of Roaree, while below it are gardens of date palms, oranges and other fruits, and long stretches of dark-green, velvety grain, appear in sharp outline against the barren hills. Along the river bank are massive limestone ghâts leading down to the water, bordered by wide-spreading, glossy-leaved peepul trees, and shut off from the quays and streets by screens of handsome walls. Between the two towers, on an island in the river, is the old fortress of Bukkur, perfectly commanding the stream. Here is one of the fords by which the caravans from Persia come into India; it has been an important strategic point, from the days of Semiamis, and as such, it has figured conspicuously in most of the invasions. It is said to be the only reliable crossing-place on the lower part of the Indus. In the slave dynasty, one contest ended here, that settled the power on the second slave, or mameluke emperor.

Sumsh-oo-din Altamsh, and Kubachi Khan, were both natives of Turkistan, and were in early youth captured in war and sold as slaves to different families. Being bright and quick, they were educated with the sons of the families, and trained in the use of arms. When their training was considered sufficiently advanced, their masters brought them to Delhi. Kutub-oo-din, the first Mohammedan emperor that reigned in India, and who had risen from the same condition, purchased them both; he was attracted by the rare comliness of Altamsh, and paid 10,000 gold dinares for him. The Emperor's body-guard were all mamelukes, and these two rose rapidly from one position to another, until they became the greatest commanders in the Emperor's army, and his most trusted supporters. To Kubachi Khan, the Emperor gave his eldest daughter in marriage; and to the handsome Altamsh, he married his youngest daughter, who was a marvelous beauty, and the favored child.

There is a tradition that she importuned her father to build the Kutub Minar, because she longed for a high tower to say her prayers in; it was such a necessity; such an urgent necessity; and her rare beauty pleading more than her words, Kutub-oo-din could not deny her, especially, as building it would have the odor of sanctity; would be very instructive to the faithful; and would give just the opportunity for him to perpetuate the praise of his old master, who bought him, trained him, and finally made him Emperor.

When he had completed one story of that old minar at Delhi, he began engraving on it the ninety-nine attributes of God, and verses from the koran, and sandwiched in between them, for safe keeping, was the name and praise of his dear old master, Abul Muzafur Mahomed Ben Sam, Sultan of Ghazni,—I fear I have omitted a few of his names; they may have escaped my memory—and his son, Moez-oo-din. Kutub-oo-din died before the tower reached the third story.

His son and successor, Aram, was a dissolute creature, and disgusted the nobles by his drunkenness, and they assisted him out of the world in a few months. Then began, between the mameluke sons-in-law, a struggle for power; Altamsh was proclaimed Emperor, at Delhi. Kubachi, who had long been Viceroy of Lahore and Mooltan, and had the army of the western frontier under his command, revolted, and resolved to contest the claim. Altamsh marched out his army of veterans, commanded by his "forty slaves," and Lahore surrendered; Mooltan was captured; place, after place was lost; until Kubachi Khan was driven into the old fortress of Bukkur. He was soon hemmed in by the victorious army, and attempted to make peace, by sending his son, Behram, with all the gold, jewels, money and silk brocades that he had in store, and asked to be allowed to pass out of the country. The tribute of the presents was received and the son detained. When Kubachi saw no signs of the siege being raised, he resolved never to fall alive into the hands of his foe, and mounted the ramparts in full armor, and flung himself into the river.

Altamsh was a wise, intelligent ruler, and a successful warrior; but at his death, left a fearful legacy of the "forty slaves"—mameluke officers—who met a tragical fate, thirty years later, from Emperor Bulbun, one of their own number. Altamsh finished the Kutub Minar which his father-in-law began. His name, and date of reign are recorded over the doorway of the third and fourth stories of it. This old tower at old Delhi has been described, as well as Altamsh's beautiful tomb, only a short distance from it.

The picturesque old towers and minars of Suckkur seemed to beckon us when we first caught sight of them in the evening twilight, and the next morning, our party threaded the dusty way towards a high domed building, through the merchandise on the quay, near the steamer on the river bank. The people glided about in the hot sunshine, in a sort of wilted, listless way, as if just aroused and were glad to hear any noise; even the steam whistle seemed to be refreshing to them, and they were doing their best to be appreciative and lively, but were scarcely equal to the effort.

In this country, one can hardly tell a palace from a tomb, for the reason, that a prince builds a palace just to his idea; he lives in it, and likes it so well, that he dislikes to leave it when he dies, and orders his body buried in the rotunda, under the principal dome. These tombs are always tablets of oriental history, because they contain the remains of noted ruling characters. This building was the last resting place of some Ameer of the Scind, but as we had no interpreter with us, we could not make out his name, to connect him with any history of the country. The body of the edifice was made of brick of a pale color; the dome and the interior being composed entirely of white marble. The rotunda under the dome was surrounded by several galleries, with chambers opening on them, indicating it was once the dwelling of the living; and down in that round hall, where the sarcophagus is now, the prince used to feast and carouse with his friends, while dancers and jugglers performed for their amusement, and the ladies of his family looked on from the galleries. Near by was a massively built tower with a winding stairway leading to the pavilion on the top; bare feet, through all the long years, had polished and worn very smooth the one hundred and eight steps leading to the summit, which commanded a good view of the city and the river for some distance.

The city was built of brick, and the streets were narrow and unpaved. On the rocky ridge beyond the town, was an old caravansary, looking very picturesque indeed. Near the base of the tower, were several *sarcophagi*, profusely ornamented with lacquered tiles of brilliant hues. One of them was of a very fine, grained, pale-yellow marble, like that found in the Nerbudda, and exquisitely carved in leaves and flowers, in bass-relief.

About sunset, all the passengers strolled along the ghâts, for it was the hour of Hindoo worship; we did not see as many in the water saying their prayers as we had in the Ganges and the Jumna. I ventured behind the screen, where a few women, at the brink of the water, were dipping it up in their lotes, or praying pots, and mumbling their jargon while pouring it out. One of these apparently coveted some very especial grace; she placed a very small burning taper, not larger than a match, in a cup formed of cork or some very light material, and then carefully placed it on a miniature raft formed of leaves, already at hand, and gently giving it a very light push, went on praying and watching to see if the light on her frail barque was quenched. The evening was so calm the taper could not do otherwise than burn steadily; the little barque quivered and trembled a little as if afraid of the far off, great current of water, whose little eddies, like tiny fingers, turned it around and around or

HINDOO GIRL.

tilted it up coyly, till one, more kind than the other, gave it a friendly push toward the shore. Joy flashed up in the eyes of the watcher as she eagerly caught it and bore it triumphantly to the roots of the pupul tree, as if her anticipations, whatever they may have been, were already realities; then pouring the water from her praying cup upon it as an offering to her sacred tree, its light went out. When she turned around, the joy faded out of her face at seeing me standing in the open door of the screen, as if the whole thing was spoiled by the fatal shadow of an unbeliever.

She commenced gesticulating in an angry manner. I paid no attention to her wrathful Scindee harangue. A Mussulman youth, twelve or thirteen years old, came up, whose clear countenance, regular features, and polite manners showed the Persian blood, while the long embroidered chupkin or coat, and spangled brimless cap told quite plainly, in this country, where each caste has a peculiar unchanging costume, that he belonged to the better class of Mussulmen. Hearing her vociferations, he flourished his little rattan cane in such a menacing way, that she thought it prudent to go to her praying cup. Then he walked along near us, pointing out with his cane objects that he thought would be new and interesting to us as strangers, which we acknowledged by appreciative looks when we found he did not understand the Hindoostanee and we could not make anything of the Scindee or the Persian. This greatly pleased him, and he set up a kind of protectorate over us. Whenever little Hindoos came within too near staring distant, his cane warned them off, and they obeyed him. His gentlemanly bearing towards strangers would do credit to a youth of his years in any country.

We passed under trees loaded with magnificent clusters of white flowers of most exquisite perfume. I was enraptured with their peerless bunches of bloom that made them seem, in this shady, rainless region, as though some happy, loving spirit that walks among the trees of life by the beautiful river, had planted them here and nourished them into such marvels of beauty, to keep some germ of purity alive in the human hearts pulsating in their shadows. I was flying into raptures over the beauties of these trees, when Mrs B—— clipped my wings by saying:

"These trees are nothing to some we have in the hills; these are horse-radish trees."

"Horse-radish did you say?"

"Yes; we grate the young roots for the table, and eat them as they do in England."

I felt as meek as "Mary's little lamb," and did not mention the trees again in her presence, though I did privately try to bribe one of the waiters, to obtain some of the seeds for me to plant at home. I have mentioned, before, the proverb existing among this people, that "Whoever plants a tree and nourishes it to maturity, merits an entrance into Paradise." I will not say that I think that would be called good sound orthodox belief in the New World, where trees are plenty; but here, this short, easy road is scarcely questioned, if the tree acquire a goodly growth. G—— says, "One would think that the whole region would be planted with trees." "Oh no!" said Major B—— "the people do not like to leave the sands of India, even by such an easy way, they are never quite free from fear of being born again in some animal form."

Our kind little Mussulman friend walked with us to the steamer and made his salaam: bringing the hand to the forehead and then respectfully bending the body.

On the east bank of the river some distance inland, on the old camel route which crossed the Indus at Lucknow, stood that ancient capital of Scind, now supposed to be Alore. Its prince, Rajah Dahir, marched out at the head of 50,000 men, mounted on his tallest war elephant—as king Porus did ten centuries before, when Alexander came—and drew up near his own majestic river, to repel the invasion of Mahomed Cassim; nearly twelve hundred years ago or A. D. 714. The Prophet had lain in his tomb only eighty-two years, when this apostle of the new religion came with the sword, to turn a people from rites and ceremonies which they had practiced since the days of Moses. He had been commissioned by the Caliph Waled, and fitted out by the Arab Governor of Bassora, to convert the pagans in India, and to plunder and exterminate all who refused to receive the true faith. None knew better than he, the work of plunder and blood. The Rajah opposed to him his archers and spearmen, and phalanx after phalanx of fierce well trained war elephants accustomed to trampling over columns of puny Hindoos.

Cassim had an army but half the size yet composed of hardy veterans in mail armor, chosen from the conquerors that had fought in Palestine, and had overrun Persia. To Rajah's elephants he opposed huge machines for throwing the Greek fire, which had first been used against themselves at Constantinople, so successfully, that their bravest warriors fled panic stricken before it.

A burning ball was hurled at the royal elephant which adhered to his proboscis; the tortured animal became unmanageable, and ran and plunged into the river; but the Rajah leaped to the ground unhurt. The more distant part of the army, perceiving the royal elephant rushing madly about with the blazing fire adhering to him, supposing their king had been killed and the battle lost, fled panic stricken from the field. The Rajah hastily gathered his guard about him, and rallied such bands of his spearmen and archers as he could, and fought bravely until he fell among the slain. The panic stricken army carried the sad news to the capital. The widowed Queen's first care was to secure the safety of her son, the heir apparent. She bade him fly and save himself while escape was possible, that the dynasty might not be destroyed; while she would defend the city, or die in it, before the invaders entered it.

Mahomed Cassim soon deployed his proselyting columns around the walls amidst a din of trumpets and horns, and when this threatening display was completed, he sent his heralds to proclaim in the hearing of those image worshippers: "There is no God but God, and Mahomet is his

Prophet;" and finished by demanding the surrender of the city and the idols, and the acceptance of the new faith, or be put to the sword. This short and tough discourse was considered quite sufficient, in that age of the world, to convert all the pagans and infidels that were worth saving.

The widowed Queen, the sole brave spirit left, put the city in a complete state of defense; the moat was filled with water by conduits from the great river; and the walls and towers bristled with archers and spearmen. Animated by her courageous presence and the stern, unalterable purpose that burned in her soul—which she had the power of infusing into her demoralized soldiery, as she personally cheered them and shared their dangers—the garrison could do no less than fight bravely, till famine stalked through the streets, and she saw with bitter pain, that if neither help nor death came to their release, the Moslem invaders would soon capture them.

In this extremity her indomitable spirit did not quail. She said she would never change her religion, nor fall into the invader's hands; she had resolved to die at the last moment,—when defence was no longer possible—in flames of her own kindling, a voluntary sacrifice to her gods. In this stern resolution she was joined by all the noble ladies of her court, then in the city. With solemn ceremonies to their deities, the Queen and her noble ladies and the young children, took a sad leave of their weeping friends, beseeching them to brave, as *they* did, the fierce pangs of death in one short encounter with the last enemy of all men, rather than become the degraded slaves of their hated foes. They then calmly ascended the huge funeral-pyre that she had had prepared in the open space near her palace, in full view of the remnant of her army; the Queen with her own hand applied the torch, and they all died among the consuming flames, fitting deaths, as they thought, for high caste Hindoos, who could look calmly on death but never on dishonor.

A large part of the garrison, inspired by the heroism of their beloved Queen, determined to die fighting; they seized their swords, opened the gates, lowered the draw-bridge, and rushed upon the Moslem besiegers, fighting till all had perished. Maddened by the long defense, Cassim slaughtered every man left in the city, who had borne arms against him, and sold his family into slavery.

Elphinstone relates in his history of this affair, that two princesses of great beauty, daughters of the king, were somewhere found by Cassim (possibly their young hearts had failed them in the last act of the Queen's great tragedy) and he thought their matchless beauty would render them acceptable slaves to the Caliph, who was then at Damascus. Sending them by a fitting escort to the Commander of the Faithful—his master, he continued the conquest of the Indus valley, and was maturing his plan to push his conquests further into India, when he was suddenly degraded from his command, and by order of the Caliph, sewed up alive in the bleeding rawhide of an ox, and thus sent to the palace at Damascus.

The two princesses arrived safely, and were duly lodged in the harem. When the elder and most beautiful of the two sisters was brought into the presence of the Caliph, she burst into a passionate flood of tears. On being asked the cause, she said she was not worthy to be the Caliph's slave, for Cassim had dishonored her before she left her own country.

Maddened with rage, and eager to be revenged for the supposed insult offered him by his general, the Caliph issued the order that resulted in the degradation and death of Cassim. When the Indian princess was shown the black and suffocated body of Mahomed Cassim, and was really satisfied it was that of the conqueror of her country, she told the Caliph that he was innocent of the crime that she had charged him with; but she had taken that course to be revenged upon the destroyer of her family, her city, and her country, and was now ready to die. That dangerous beauty that brought her to Damascus did not save her life this time, she perished, chained to the heels of a wild horse. Her country, by this piece of strategy, had rest from proselyting Moslem invasion for 295 years.

On our way the next morning we passed very near a number of boys who were fishing in a very novel, and I may add rather hazardous way, when it is remembered that the Indus river is as much infested with crocodiles as the Nile. These boys swam out into mid stream, lying across a large, red earthen jar with bulging sides, propelling themselves with their hands and feet, as swimmers usually do. When they reached a shoal of fish, they very dexteriously and quietly dipped them up with a short scoop-net and put them in the jar under them, which also served as a buoy to sustain their own weight. These fisher-boys were very numerous on the lower portion of this river, where it had good fair breadth and depth.

About nine o'clock the next morning, we noticed very heavy, dark clouds in the western sky, rolling up fold on fold, black and gloomy towards the zenith. I felt somewhat nervous, for I could not divest myself of the apprehension of a tornado, as the air momently grew darker. We were not in suspense long, for the storm soon burst upon us and brought nothing but white dust and fine sand. The air was so completely filled with these, that it had the appearance of a fog. The pilot could not distinguish where the channel lay, and the cables were carried out and the steamer made fast to the shore. We braved the siftings of this storm hour after hour on the deck which was protected by an awning, noting the strange disguises of each other that grew with the passing moments. The gentlemen could pass muster after two hours for mill attendants; and the ladies and children, ah! it would not be in good taste to describe their powdered locks, and sorry looks. I retreated to the cabin, but the air was hot and stifling, filled with the penetrating fine dust, making it quite impossible to remain there long. Returning to the deck again, I took my seat with my back to the wind and dropped my head as low as possible and avoided fully inflating my lungs. At last the storm rolled away from us, but hung like a thick curtain on the horizon. "Ah!" said the Major, breaking the long silence, "we shall find the air much cooler and purer than it was before." "These dust-storms," said the Doctor, "are our most coveted blessings, some sickly seasons though, we are rather apt to quarrel with the disguise they come in."

The steamer went on her way nobly endeavoring to make up the lost time. The banks were higher, and palm and mango groves were numerous; it was truly surprising how green and glossy the leaves kept without rain. Irrigating wheels were creaking along the banks under bovine locomotion, making glad the thirsty fields. Spoon-bills, wild duck and tall white herons, were looking for their bill of fare in the margin of the water, rather dubiously, as if it was not a good fishing day. Padre Sahib pushed away his impromptu chess board which was marked on a large sheet of paper and tacked on a table, and said:

"Our friend, the tall Persian in the barge, has lost his labor, he has said his prayer wrong and you will see that he will go through it again."

"Why!" asked one, "did he miss any one of the twelve essential requisites of prayer?"

"Did he omit the 'Bismellah,' before he began his ablutions," chimed in another, "or did he slip past one of the bodily positions?"

"No! he was all right there, but these dust clouds obscured the setting sun so perfectly and the boat has turned around so many times, that he has lost his bearings, and prayed toward the east; he will not believe that prayers can reach the right place if started in the wrong direction."

Presently the clouds lifted, and disclosed the setting sun. The Persian looked surprised, he evidently thought the sun had set some time before; he betook himself to praying his prayer over again, this time with his face toward Mecca.

KOTRE AND HYDERABAD.

The latter city is the capital of southern Scind. It is situated on a spur of a low range of rocky hills which are opposite Kotre. It is enclosed between the point and an old channel of the river, which was partially deserted centuries ago. It stands about eighty feet above the low country about it. The plateau of the hill is about a mile and a half long, and seven hundred yards broad, the southern part of which is occupied by the fortress and the suburbs called Pittah. This fortress, contains the residence of the Ameers or Princes, and has a strong tower to contain their treasures. The walls are very thick and solid at the base and are flanked by round towers or lofty bastions, at short intervals, which, added to the height of the hill, give it a very fine appearance. Near it are some fine tombs of the old Kalora dynasty which was overthrown by the present Talpoor Ameers. One is a beautiful mausoleum in a lofty central hall reaching from pavement to the dome, where rest the remains of Gholam Shah Kalora; it is of beautiful polished marble, decorated with elaborate inlaid figures and flowers, handsome mosaics of stones flanked and bordered with sentences of the koran, which have preserved it from Moslem spoilation through the changes of dynasty.

There is a very extensive bazaar, forming one street the entire length of the town, with queer little five by nine shops, abounding in curious, polished, lacquered, wooden boxes and balls, one fitting inside of the other, with great exactness and ingenuity. Tussore silks and embroideries are curiously elbowed in these places, by swords, spears, and shields; these are manufactured in this city, and said to be scarcely inferior to the best European manufacture. Sir Charles Napier captured this city and fortress on the 28th of Feb. 1843—having already conquered the northern Ameers, —and the next day marched to hunt out and defeat, the last chief of the confederacy at Meerpore.

The condition of the country has greatly improved since it has been under English rule. A line of railway has been projected along the east bank of the river Indus, to connect with one coming up the coast from Bombay, passing through all those old, drowsy, oriental cities, whose people have vegetated on the same sites, and trod the same sandy paths ever since the days of Alexander; only awakened at long intervals by invasion, sack, plunder and conflagration. At such times they would scurry away over the sands to some safe retreat until the invaders were gone; then return, level down the old ruins, and build anew on the same site, and live on under the same Princes, whose family ancestors were contemporary with the Heptarchy, and whose descendants have continued to rule their principalities. They still exercise a modified authority, if loyal to the English. There are Rajpoot families, it is asserted, who can show an unbroken family record for fifteen hundred years.

Kotre, where we terminated our river voyage, has no antiquity; it has grown, in less than thirty years, from a mean native village opposite Hyderabad, to a very pleasant place of considerable importance in a commercial point of view. It has about fifteen thousand inhabitants, the streets are laid out on a scale of width that shows European ideas to have been the guage. The numerous English built houses which are surrounded by gardens and shrubbery have a very comfortable home like appearance. Doubtless this place being the *termini*, both of steamboat navigation, and the rail road from Kurrachee, a large portion of its inhabitants will always be Europeans. Towards evening, when the sun had lost its fierce glare, we walked along the bunds or quays, which extend a long distance on the river front. They are built very substantially of finely dressed brown stone, with ghâts leading down into the water and numerous rows of trees skirting them, forming a most delightful evening or morning promenade. The traffic and merchandise is mainly confined to the immediate vicinity of the steamer's landing and the railway station.

We here bade adieu to the steamer, and took our last look at the ancient river that has been the pathway of nations for four thousand years, ever since the days of Semiramis, whose army was defeated on its banks; and seated ourselves in the cars bound for Kurrachee. Think of following the track of Alexander through Gedorosa, whirling along after a locomotive; if he had thought his marching would ever be so far outdone over the same soil, there would have been more tears shed than there was at leaving one obscure corner of the world unconquered.

One passing over this region at the present time, is surprised into wonder at its strange, weird appearance. We passed blackened, scattered ridges of rocks that had the regularity of artificial walls, and loomed dark and frowning from the barren level plain, like the ramparts of some old fortress. It is said by antiquarians, that there are remains of Roman camps and towns further north, relics of the Empire when it spread its legions over Persia and its dependencies, to the borders of India.

The soil of this region, where excavations have been made along the railway, shows a yellowish loam, very like that of western New York; very different from the gravel and coarse sand of the Egyptian deserts. The only needed condition for abundant vegetation is the requisite amount of moisture. There was not a blade of grass or leaf along our route; the only vegetable was a leafless plant whose form and habits resemble the African stapelia, which here grows two or three feet high. We passed a fine old tomb whose domes and a few trees just peered above the small garden wall, enough to show that trees could grow if cultivated. Mr. S—— fell into conversation with a passenger, an English gentleman, who said he had opened a cotton plantation near one of the small streams in the vicinity of Kurrachee, and by irrigating, realized good returns from it; he makes his water wheels do duty for the clouds of heaven, and lives independent of the special providence—ready made rain.

KURRACHEE.

We arrived in the evening at the station, and I took my seat in a carriage, while Mr. S—— and G. were looking for porters to transfer our baggage. The coachman carelessly left his box a moment, when the horses became frightened and plunged furiously in among a crowd of hacks and other

FORT AND HARBOR OF KURRACHEE.

FORT OF HYDERABAD.

vehicles, that usually surround a railway station on the arrival of a train. The night had set in dark; only a few feeble lanterns glimmered about the place, and there were many chances for broken bones; but a gentleman caught the horses by the bits, with a firm, strong hand, and held them fast. Though I could not see him, I knew that was an Anglo Saxon grasp; no native ever had courage enough to approach a frightened horse and stop him, in that manner; there was something refreshing in such a grasp. A gentleman looking for some one, rushed up and asked:

"Is that lady a widow?"

"A widow!" said Mr. S——, "I think not; but *I* came very near being a widower!"

The hotel was rather full, as the mail steamer for Bombay, would sail in three days. After our late dinner we retired to our apartments, and discovered—by sundry phials with druggists' labels, in a small recess—that our room had been tenanted by some invalid. The khansamah was called and questioned as to the person's malady; but he strenuously denied that any person had been sick in the house. This was not a state of things to early tempt coy sleep to one's pillow, but it came at last in snatches and such disjointed fragments, that we scarcely felt refreshed by it.

This is a perfect Sahara; rain is almost an unknown blessing, and the fresh water that is obtainable is so brackish and bad, as to be quite beyond the power of any one, not a native, to drink it. Steamboat officers send presents of pails and bottles of condensed water, as the most acceptable gift, to their European lady friends and it is carefully treasured under the hand of the mistress of the house, to allay her own, or children's thirst. Everything was loaded with a fine, white dust, like pulverized clay or ashes; shrubs, trees, garden walls, houses, all appeared to be mourning in the true Bible fashion,—in dust and ashes.

The old fortified walls that we passed, were made of unburnt or Egyptian brick, or clay that has been mingled with straw, which, in this rainless region, is quite serviceable. The old city contains about 16,000 inhabitants, while the European quarter or suburb—which has entirely grown up since the English have had possession of the country—contains about 10,000 inhabitants; and very many edifices solidly and elegantly built. There are two newspapers printed in English, at this place; there is also a Chamber of Commerce; and numerous wealthy banking firms; and a large number of European merchants, who communicate directly with London, by the Indo-European telegraph, which has its head-quarters at this place. There are also many officers, connected with the army, stationed at or near Kurrachee; so that, notwithstanding nature has framed it in such forbidding, arid surroundings, it has some good society. It has also been dowered with richer advantages than any city on the coast, north of Bombay. It is now, and must continue to be, the port of embarkation for all the immense valley of the Indus, as there is no other harbor along the coast. The mouths of this great river are so obstructed by the sand and silt that is brought down the stream, that large vessels cannot enter with any degree of safety, during the S. W. monsoon. Thus has nature written its destiny in very enduring characters. Beloochistan and Afghanistan must send their trading caravans across the parched, arid plains, and through the mountains to this place, for there is no other seaport until the Persian Gulf is reached.

The Brahsoie mountains hem in the city, on a narrow plain, between them and the sea. A rocky head-land, called Munorah Point, juts out from the shore; it is about five miles in length, and encloses a breadth of water nearly that distance across; it finally terminates in a rocky promontory, one hundred and fifty feet high, near which the mail steamer was anchored.

Mr. S—— had made arrangements with the captain, for us to go on board the evening before she started, in confident hope of avoiding sea-sickness, by being on board and at rest, a few hours before starting. We were rather late in leaving the hotel, as we had not calculated for darkness to set in so quickly after the sun had gone down. When we reached the quay, three miles from the town, and embarked in a boat to be rowed out to the steamer, twilight was just fading into darkness. It had been expressly stipulated that no sail should be used; but we had proceeded only a short distance, when the boatmen attempted to run up a sail, though by this time it had become so very dark, that one could scarcely see an object twice the length of the boat away; so the idea of sailing was not a cheerful one, as there were more chances of going to the bottom of the bay, or of being stranded on a rocky islet, than of reaching the steamer.

Objection being made to the use of the sail, they essayed a flank movement, proposing to run the boat over to the north side of the bay, where a number of native boats were anchored, to get some help; there were three lazy fellows at the oars already, and what could be wanted of more—unless it was for mischief—we were at a loss to tell. The thought of the police being four miles away, and of having a swarm of Arabs, Beloochees and Scindees alight in that little boat, in such a pitchy state of darkness, was not at all attractive to Mr. S——, and he made "muchee loud talkee," in English, Hindoostanee, and Malay—anything except Scindee—and flourished his cane in vigorous wrath—which is a world-wide language, if the others are not—and the fellows began to fear he would do something rash. G—— and Mr. S—— watched the boatmen and I watched the top of the rocky headland, which, fortunately, I could just discern outlined against a starless sky. Between nine and ten o'clock we reached the steamer, which lay almost under the walls of the fort, which was perched like an eagle's nest, on the top of the rocky crag, so far above it.

The next morning we awoke with the dawn, for boats were crowding around and passengers and baggage coming on board. The monotonous song of the native sailors at the capstan raising the anchor, made a limping, halting kind of music, half comical, half doleful, but suggestive of the fact, that if I wished to see Kurrachee again I must hurry on deck.

In the dining-saloon, we encountered our old friends of the steamer Indus, Major and Mrs. B. They had put off coming on board with their little ones till morning, and were hurrying to their particular cabins, intent upon settling themselves there before the boat began to move, and had only time for a passing salutation; but it was quite easy to see, that the bitter separation of this family which would take place at Bombay, had already began to cast its shadow before it, upon the face of each parent. Heaven only knows what death in life, what dearth comes and mingles itself with the wine of joy, in these hard sunderings of families. Years roll on relentlessly; the winsome child goes from the father's arms and only returns after long years, a young lady, or young gentleman, as the case may bé. The father, returns to the lonely home, that is no longer home without wife and children; how the dark shadows will weave themselves in and out, over the walls of the most cheerful Indian house, and blue devils lurk in every corner, ready to charge on the lone one with bayonets forged of melancholy.

The steamer began to move, and I passed out upon the deck to take a last look at that old land, and the town which was clearly outlined against the bare mountains that had no tint of verdure on them. The atmosphere was of that peculiar mingled blue and gold seen in such arid places, and seemed to hang a soft, pale, purplish veil over all the distant objects, making them positively beautiful, because harmonious. Munorah Point, my friendly landmark of last night, was clear and sharp in all its outlines of crags, walls and towers, frowning down on us so closely, and so much above us, that a pebble might be dropped from the wall upon the deck. It was the last object visible, and when the boat turned her prow to the southeast, it vanished, and my trip "Up the Ganges, and down the Indus," properly ends here.

I turned around and met, face to face, our mild sensation of the voyage,—a Beloochee Ameer of the Scind, and his train of servants. In personal appearance, he was slender and below the medium height, with oval face, and finely cut, delicate features, and pale-olive complexion. He wore a long, loose, sacque coat, made of deep-blue velvet, which was elaborately trimmed in all possible places with wrought gold, and magnificent diamond fastenings in front; a very elegant garment indeed, and worthy to grace the court of a prince. His head-gear—which he wore continually—was a most surprising article, and bore a distant resemblance to an ordinary hat, in a triumphant state of rebellion. The brim had refused to be the foundation and bear the burden of the structure, and had transferred itself to the top, to reign and rule on the same level as the crown, leaving the broad, circular tube of the hat to shut down sharply about the head. It was composed either of leather or pasteboard, and finished with *polish* and *black lacquer*. The nether garment was made of ordinary white cotton, and so was the white frock worn under the velvet coat, which reached down to the knees. His feet afforded a strong contrast to his magnificent coat; they were encased in father Adam's own boots, except when he walked on deck,—then he wore slippers.

He had chosen, instead of a cabin, the broad cushioned place immediately over the screw, at the stern of the boat and end of the saloon, as best adapted to his wants; he could sit there in a sort of princely state and overlook the saloon; if one has not been tried, proved and labelled a No. 1. sailor, that enticing spot, with its seesaw movement, more than any other, is likely to vanquish him most ingloriously. At the nine o'clock breakfast he remained sitting there *a' le Turc*, and apologized to those present—through our fellow passenger on the Indus, the Doctor, who was in the capacity of keeper to the lion—saying he was sorry that he could not join them at table, he could not eat English food. His attendants served him where he sat with pilau, that is in plain Anglo Saxon, a dish composed of rice and raisins stewed up in tumeric dye, which he ate with his fingers. It is needless to say that he was willingly excused from eating at table.

Our steamer, though a smaller craft than any we had yet

tried, was for "a' that," a very pleasant one that voyage. The smooth sea, the tender sky, and the February atmosphere so soft and genial, kept us on deck in a half-waking trance with their charms, which on the second day was agreeably broken by the unexpected appearance of a shoal of whales. First we noticed a tall column of water spouting up from a huge, black head, lifted out of the sea. It was a grand blow and was scarcely finished, when another enormous head threw up another water spout near by, then another and another, in quick succession farther away. It was evident the great leviathans of the deep were holding high festival and we were crossing their play ground and were witnesses of their gigantic sports and gambols. It was a new thing to me, to locate whales in the tropical seas; but the captain, an old navigator of eastern waters, said that he had often seen them spouting in the Arabian Sea, and Gulf of Bengal. Probably, he said, some esculapian whale had sent these up from the South Pole, for the benefit of warm baths.

We were now nearing the Malabar coast, and when it was announced that land was in sight, even sea sickness could not keep the Ameer below; a Persian rug or mat was spread on deck, and he folded his limbs very naturally under him, and made himself comfortable upon it, according to his own fashion.

The great serrated masses on the horizon, that at first seemed more clouds than mountains, came at last into the clear distinct outline of the ghâts, and then the great city reposing at their feet came into view. It was about five o'clock in the afternoon when the steamer dropped anchor in the harbor of Bombay, and we first set our feet on this island, the choicest gem that came to England in the dowery of Katharine of Portugal, Queen of Charles II., and entered the great metropolis of the western coast of India.

PARSEE LADY AND DAUGHTER.

CHAPTER XX.

BOMBAY; HOMEWARD BOUND.

THE Island of Bombay is one of a group, which, lying in close proximity to each other, shut in an arm of the ocean; thus forming a large and beautiful bay, Bombay commanding the entrance. It came into possession of the English, A. D., 1661, and outstripping all competitors, has become the great commercial emporium of India. Its population—about a million—is probably more mixed than that of any other city of the world. Hindoos, Parsees, Mussulmen, Persians, Europeans, Chinese, Afghanistans, Javanese, Siamese, Turks; in fact, representatives of almost every race are here found mingling in the vast trade of the city, each enjoying his own peculiar method of living and worshiping, unmolested.

The Parsees are a race we had not met in other parts of India, and we—naturally turning to that which was new—sought an early opportunity to glean information of them. They are descendants of the Ghebers, or fire-worshipers, and still adhere to the religious beliefs of their ancestors. In their temples fires are burning, which they claim have never been extinguished. As the sun sinks in the west, the Parsees face it with extended arms and assume an attitude of deep devotion. They can be seen on the shores of the bay in long rows, thus engaged in worship. They also worship fire, and the stars. They are an intelligent people and have many virtues. They wield a vast influence in Bombay, and are firm friends of the English government. Honorable and able as merchants and business men, they are as a race wealthy and refined, and boast that neither a pauper nor a prostitute of their caste can be found in the city. They speak the English language fluently and use it almost entirely. They do not eat the flesh of the ox. Their wives and children are interesting and pretty and are reared in a sumptuous manner, surrounded by all that wealth can furnish them. Their dead are conveyed to the "Tower of Silence," which stands upon a high hill surrounded by immense trees. The corpse is received at the door by the priests and carried by them into the tower and placed behind an iron grate in such a position that vultures can tear off and devour the flesh, leaving nothing but the skeleton. It is wonderful how a race so far advanced in civilization can adhere to and practice so barbarous a custom.

But a short distance from the "Tower of Silence" is the spot where the Brahmins burn their dead. The grounds are surrounded by a wall. The corpses are brought on litters and are so plentiful that fires are kept continually burning. A dealer supplies wood on the spot. The pile is prepared, the body is placed upon it, and the nearest relative ignites it. When the body is reduced to ashes, the place is watered and some of the ashes thrown into the sea.

A very curious place is the hospital for dumb animals. Here, under the protection of a sect called Jâins, sick animals are cared for and cured or sustained. Oxen, cows, horses, dogs, cats, vultures, crows, buzzards, rats; in fact, animals of any kind, sick or deformed, are admitted here and nursed with the greatest care and attention.

There are several Hindoo temples in the city; to most of them entrance is denied. Some of the suburbs of the city are infested with the deadly *cobra de capello*, and many deaths occur yearly from their bite. The city itself is free from them. One of the festival days kept by the Hindoos in Bombay, is that of the "*Festival of the Serpents.*" It occurs usually in August. Snake charmers bring to the place the deadly snakes, which are fed with milk, in order to propitiate them. Thousands gather to see this, and the charmers handle the snakes with perfect impunity, although their bite is more poisonous at that time of the year than at any other.

NATIVE WOMEN, BOMBAY.

A short distance from the city are the famous caves of Elephanta, situated on an island of the same name in the harbor. They are excavations, forming a temple, consisting of an immense hall nearly one hundred and fifty feet in length, with high ceilings supported by immense columns. Three smaller halls adjoin the main one. The walls of all three are covered with sculptured statues, representing all the passions supposed to be possessed by the Gods. In a recess in the main hall is a colossal three-headed statue, representing Brahma the creator, Vishnu the preserver, and Siva the destroyer. The statues have all been much mutilated and are in a very imperfect state. These excavations are not the only ones of the kind in the neighborhood. Those of Kerli, near by, are of great renown and present points of much interest to the visitor.

There are many customs in Bombay which strike the stranger as singular. Among them is the one with which we had been accustomed at our home in Singapore, viz: the taking, by one, to a dinner or other party, of his own servants to serve him. This is expected always; even at hotels, each guest employs his own servant, and none are furnished by the host. The system of castes is in full force and is absolute in its control. No one can marry into an alien caste, and no one can choose another career than that he is born into, without loss of caste and property, wife and children; only to be regained by the most humiliating ceremonies and concessions. A faithful member of a caste is welcomed among his fellows, wherever he may be, and members of no secret society so faithfully serve each other as do these caste-men. Each race and caste also has its particular dress; and when as sometimes happens, the caste is sub-divided, the dress of each division varies in some points from the others. The Brahmins are dressed in white linen and turbans; the Persians wear colored turbans of immense size or high Astrakhan caps; the Parsees, their ugly head-gear, which baffles description; the Burniahs appear in calico tunics, red bands, conch-shell turbans, etc., etc.

A few words as to the idolatry of the Hindoos may not be

out of place. To most people the devotions of this race seem so absolutely ridiculous and senseless, that one fails to comprehend how a person with the smallest portion of intellect can practice them. But an intelligent Hindoo will tell you that in the wooden idol he sees but the symbol of the God he worships; that as the church edifice in the christian land becomes sacred in the eyes of the christian, by reason of the service to which it is dedicated, so their idols the work of their own hands become sacred to them, as the medium through which they worship their Gods. In their creed, there is but one Supreme God—one head above all others, and him they worship as the embodiment of all power. To other Gods are delegated powers by the great Master, and the propitiation of these Gods is the great service of their religion. In representation of these Gods, they construct idols, but never do they symbolize the one great and Supreme God. And thus with the Parsees; they claim to worship God through the sun his representative. Much as we may wonder at the delusion and infatuation of these people, their credulity is more than equaled by that of the ignorant papists, even of our own day and country, who blindly believe in manifestations and miracles so utterly silly and preposterous, as to leave Hindoo idolatry far behind.

And now farewell to India. The grand ocean stretched out before us, and as we gazed upon its waves a great longing sprung up in our hearts for that dear land which lay beyond them; and with deep joy we embarked once more with our faces turned homeward. Yet, as we cast our eyes shoreward to the land receding from our view we felt a pang of regret, and a sigh rose involuntarily as we remembered that we were, probably forever, bidding adieu to a land where for years we had lived, and with which thousands of happy recollections were linked. We watched until the last speck of land disappeared, then sought our cabin, realizing that hereafter memory alone would connect us with idolatrous, debased, yet proud and magnificent India.

THE END.

THE PRINCE OF WALES

HIS ROYAL HIGHNESS

THE PRINCE OF WALES

IN

INDIA.

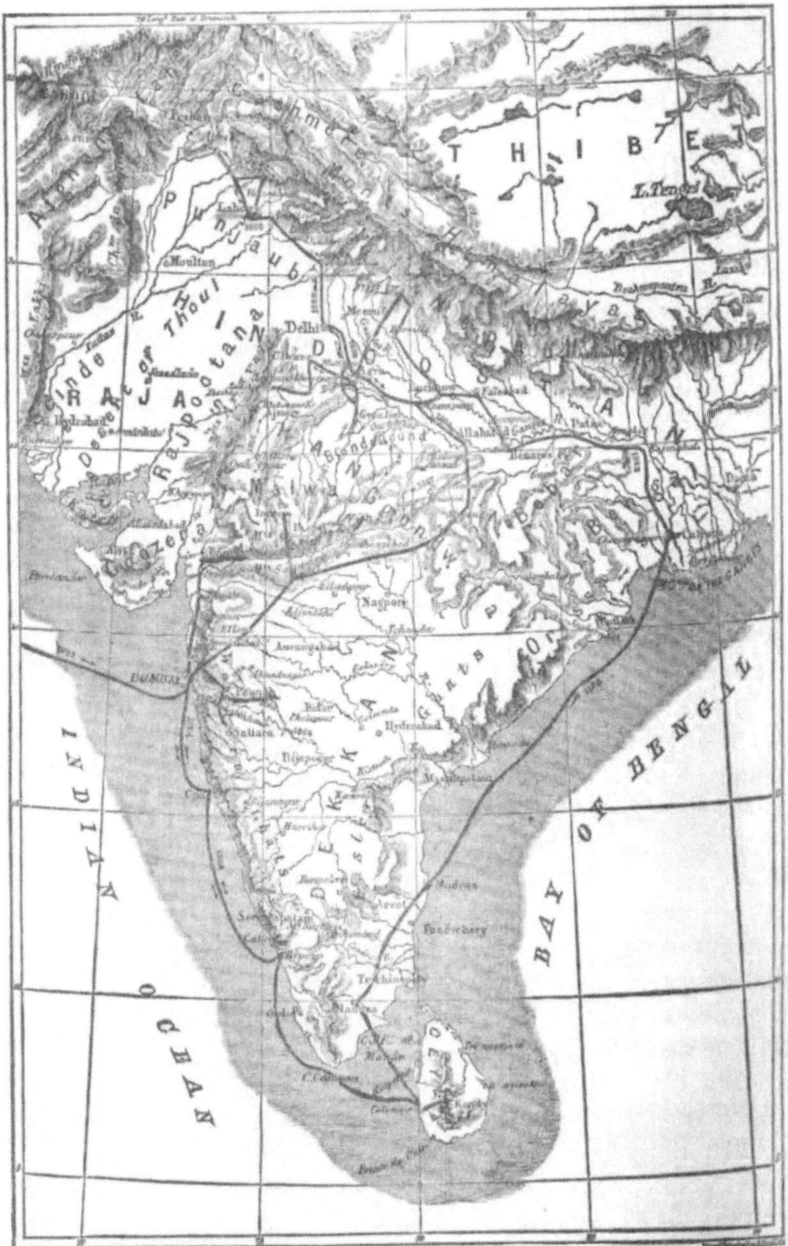

GENERAL MAP OF INDIA, SHOWING ROUTE OF THE PRINCE OF WALES.

CHAPTER I.

FROM ENGLAND TO BOMBAY.

SINCE writing the foregoing, His Royal Highness the Prince of Wales has visited India, where her Majesty's flag floats over more than two hundred millions of subjects, more or less loyal to the Queen of England, the "Empress of India." This has been an event of so much interest to those millions of alien subjects, and may yet prove to be of such great importance, not only to the future ruler, but even in an international point of view, that it is deemed not out of place, and likely to add to the interest of this volume to give a brief sketch of his Oriental tour.

This is the more called for as the Prince is not only Heir Apparent to the crown of Great Britain but seems also destined to reign over the Indias. From this it will be seen that this visit was doubly important, as it afforded, on the one hand, a pleasurable excursion to His Highness; on the other it would produce a favorable impression on the Princes and people of that far off country. It will be seen that the latter is very desirable when it is realized that all this vast expanse of territory with its myriads of people, has been subjugated only by force.

How long this allegiance will continue, is but another form of the question: how much time will be required to civilize and thoroughly educate the natives? It is difficult to believe that an alien sovereign can rule over so many millions of intelligent subjects at so great a distance from the foot of the throne as Calcutta is from London. Even now, when there is a military breeze in Russia it is sure to cause a sensation in the military air of Hindoostan. Perplexing as it is, if there be any nation which can succeed in holding dominion over so many subjects at such great distances it is the English nation, the most successful colonizer in the world.

On Monday evening October 11th the Prince and Princess of Wales left Charing Cross for Dover. A large assemblage of people had gathered to bid him good bye, loud cheers and shouts of "God bless you" were raised on all sides. In two hours they arrived at Dover where a farewell address was presented by the Mayor and Corporation, when they immediately embarked on board the steamer Castalia amid the cheers of the thousands of spectators who lined the pier as the vessel moved off. The Princess of Wales took leave of her husband at Calais and returned next morning to London. On arriving at Paris the Prince was received by Lord Lyons, the British Ambassador, and Marshal MacMahan. During his hasty trip through France, Italy, Greece and Egypt, ovations crowded one after the other.

At Suez, the Royal party embarked on board H. M. S. Serapis, a screw-propeller of 6200 tons burden, which had been fitted up in the most sumptuous manner for the voyage. The Prince's apartments on the upper deck consisted of a reception-room, a drawing-room and a dining-room—divided only by curtains so that they could be thrown into one spacious saloon on state occasions—besides two distinct sets of private rooms for sleeping and dressing, one set on each side of the ship, each being complete in itself, and consisting of sleeping-room, bathing-room and dressing-room. This double arrangement was to secure coolness by allowing the Prince to use at all times the windward side of the vessel. The reception and dining-rooms were richly decorated, the walls were white, blue and gold, with mirrors framed in oak and gold, with fittings of polished mahogany; the curtains bronze yellow; the window blinds green; and the furniture of solid

WAITING FOR THE PRINCE BOMBAY

oak. A double set of punkahs worked by six chinamen kept the saloon airy. A stud of horses for the Prince's use was also on board, and his private yacht, the Osborne, escorted the Serapis. The Prince was accompanied by the Duke of Sutherland, Lord Suffield, the Earl of Aylesford, Sir Bartle Frere an ex-Governor of Bombay, Dr. Fayrer, the Rev. Canon Duckworth and nearly a score of other notable persons. They steamed down the Red Sea, calling at Aden; thence across the Indian Ocean to the beautiful island city of Bombay, arriving there November 8th.

Here they wêre welcomed by Lord Northbrooke, the Viceroy, and, at once, the imposing ceremonies of the long to be remembered visit began. For weeks, the authorities and the whole city had given itself up to the preparation for the grand reception of the Prince, and one can more easily fancy than describe the brilliant scenes and dazzling exhibitions of wealth, and how greatly the effect of the grand receptions was increased in a city like Bombay, especially "fitted for such a display, by its long picturesque streets, composed of quaint oriental houses with overhanging gables; mosques, with gaudily painted fronts; Hindoo temples, ornamented with all kinds of images and shrines; churches, and noble public buildings. The native of Bombay fills his large rooms with huge chandeliers, and suspends others in the verandas and opposite each window, so that on festival days his residence may be a blaze of light." At all times the many brilliant colors of the various costumes of the different castes of the several creeds of this city, dazzle and surprise all who gaze spell-bound upon the scene.

At this time Bombay had become the grand *entrepot* for the native princes, who had come from their principalities with their huge retinues resplendent with variegated costumes; all combining to emphasize every word, act and scene in these royal receptions. Although in a so-called heathen country, everything pertaining to the formal reception of the native princes, even in the smallest details, had been arranged and was carried out according to the nicest rules of Oriental etiquette, as will be seen by the report given by an eye witness of the reception of his Highness Sewajee Chutraputtee Maharajah of Kholapore:

"A little before 10 A. M. the guns began to fire a salute, and, before we could count the nineteen *coups* to which his highness is entitled, the raja drove up, with a great flourish, in a grand carriage, drawn by four horses, with servants in liveries of blue and silver, and a magnificent fan-bearer behind wielding a blazing machine, to keep the sun away. He was received as per programme, led up the steps into the hall, up the grand staircase, then into the corridors, and so conducted to the entrance of the throne room. The prince, who had risen, advanced down the carpet to meet him. At the edge he stretched forth his hand, and took that of the raja, whom he drew toward him kindly. After him trooped the sirdas, each holding his sword by the sheath, which had neither straps, buckle, nor sling. A few phrases of courtesy were exchanged between the shahzadah and the raja, who is an adopted son of the last prince, who died six years ago. He is a boy of twelve, and was attired in purple velvet and white muslin, and was encrusted with gems. His turban was a wealth of pearls and rubies; his neck like an array of show-cases of a great jeweler. He looked as though he would be the better for a course of cricketing. The state which is ruled in his name contains upward of three thousand square miles, and more than eight hundred thousand people, and has a revenue of 3,047,243 rupees.* The face of the raja wore an expression of pleased surprise as his royal highness, coming to the regulation spot on the carpet, took his little hand and led him opposite to the silver chair, where he left him with a bow, and sat down. Soon the sirdars, in turn, advanced to the foot of the throne, salaaming low, and presented to the prince a handkerchief containing gold mohurs. The prince touched this with his right hand and remitted, and the sirdar walked backward to his seat. Then the prince, taking a gold and jewel scent-bottle, shook a few drops of perfume (*uttur*) on the raja's pocket-handkerchief, and from another rich casket took betelnut (*pân*) wrapped in fresh, green leaf covered with gold foil, which he placed in the raja's hand, Major Henderson, as per programme, doing the same for the sirdars. The interview was at an end, and the prince

---

* A rupee is equivalent to about fifty cents; one hundred thousand rupees is a lac.

SOME OF THE ILLUMINATIONS—BOMBAY.

led his highness to the sacred verge of the carpet, and thence he was conducted to the entrance, where he vanished, with his face still turned to the throne."

Of another lad he writes:

"All eyes were dazzled when the little boy, whom the Government of India had installed as the Guicowar of Baroda, stood at the threshold of the door—a crystallized rainbow. He is a small, delicately-framed lad for his twelve years or more, with a bright pleasant face. He was weighted, head, neck, chest, arms, fingers, ankles, with such a sight and wonder of vast diamonds, emeralds, rubies, and pearls, as would be worth the loot of many a rich town. It is useless to give the estimate I heard of their value, and the little gentleman had more at home. He was met at the edge of the carpet, and strode with much solemnity to his seat, side by side with the prince. Sir Madhava Rao, Sir R. Meade, and a notable train of chiefs, came with him. The visit of the Guicowar lasted a minute or two longer than usual, for the prince asked several questions, and conversed with Sir Madhava Rao and Sir R. Meade. The former, the present regent, is one of the men who rise to the surface in Hindoostan by sheer strength of talent, industry, and intelligence. He is a Mahratta Brahmin, forty-seven years of age, and was educated in the High School of the Madras University, where he was at one time acting Professor of Mathematics and Natural Philosophy. He subsequently filled several posts in the civil service, and was then appointed tutor and companion to the Prince of Travancore, and was made prime-minister of that state in 1858. In this capacity he acted for fourteen years, with such benefit to British native rule that he was made Knight of the Star of India, and was offered a seat in the Legislative Council, which he declined. When the viceroy deposed Mulhar Rao, and it became essential to place Baroda in the hands of a native statesman, the British authorities applied to Sir Madhava Rao, who accepted the grave responsibility."

He also says of a lad of thirteen, the young Maharajah of Myrore and says:

"The jewels which literally hung upon him must be of enormous value. One stone of the many of his necklace is said to be worth nine lacks of rupees (900,000 rupees)—$450,000. His neck, wrists, arms and ankles were encircled with strings of pearls, diamonds, and rubies. His turban was graced with an aigret of brillaints of large size, and a large tuft of strings of big pearls and emeralds hung down on his shoulders from the top."

Tuesday, November 9th 1875 was the birthday of the Prince of Wales. In the morning there was a grand reception at Government House, where congratulations and rich presents were exchanged, after which the Prince went on board the Admiral's flag-ship and visited the Serapis, to see the sailors enjoy a banquet given in honor of the day; while with them there he cut his birthday cake. In the evening, the vessels in the harbor, and the streets of the city were illuminated on the most magnificent scale, being literally "one blaze of light," from Malabar Hill to Celaba Lighthouse, an area of seven miles.

Whatever may be the real feelings and future plans of these native princes and their chief men, on all these occasions they seemed to greatly enjoy themselves, and manifested the greatest respect and decorum. In turn the Prince of Wales enjoyed the general enthusiasm by which he was surrounded, appearing not to tire or flag in his interest.

On the following day was held a grand popular *fete*, at which gathered some twelve thousand school children, representing four classes and creeds, viz: Christians, Parsees, Mohammedans and Brahmins, in their costumes exhibiting all the colors of the rainbow. They greeted the Prince on his arrival with loud huzzas, the children sang "God Bless the Prince of Wales," and the others in their languages sang laudatory odes.

During the evening the Europeans gave a grand ball in honor of the Prince at the Byculla Club where he fairly charmed the ladies by his zeal in dancing, and completely amazed Sir Philip Wodehouse by the energy with which he galloped. At the close, the fair sex were quite ready to pronounce this, one of the most successful *fetes* of his visit, being certainly one of the most pleasurable.

The sailors, in turn, to the number of two thousand including some soldier friends, enjoyed a festive day; evidently

THE CAVES OF ELEPHANTA, NEAR BOMBAY.

their picnic was of a different kind from that of the school children, as they were supplied with 500 cold ducks, 1000 chickens, 1000 lbs of beef and the same of mutton, besides cold ham, small pigs, plum duff buttressed by oranges and plantains, clay pipes, cavendish, beer, stout, soda water and lemonade. The Prince was welcomed with tremendous cheers, and with a glass of lemonade toasted the Flying and Indian squadrons, saying in a speech of three lines: "Sailors, I hope you have enjoyed a good dinner and a pleasant day. I drink to the health of the India and Detached squadrons."

From the jolly sailor's banquet the Prince hastened to the site selected for the Elphinstone Dock, and laid the first stone with full Masonic ceremonies. There was an immense procession of the Masonic brethren in full costume; this last produced a very interesting spectacle over the robes of the Parsees, Brahmins and Mussulmen. The banners of the various lodges added much to the real beauty of the scene, as many were embroidered in pearls and brilliants on silk, all indicative of and pleasing to Oriental taste, and by no means repugnant to occidental esthetics. When this grand procession had arrived at the spot, the Prince from his throne struck the stone three times with a mallet and poured over it corn, wine and oil; having performed the ceremony with all the peculiar rites, the chaplain, the Rev. C. Gilder, said:—

"May corn and wine and oil, and all the blessings of life abound among us and all men, and may the great Architect of the Universe bless this undertaking and promote the prosperity of this great work, so mote it be!"

The following day a visit was made to the wonderful Cave Temple of Elephanta on the island of Gharapuri, about four miles from the main land. This temple derived its European name from the figure of an elephant which once stood near the entrance. The main cave measures about 130 feet square, from fifteen to eighteen feet high, and is excavated from the solid rock, a work which is indicative of the patience and perseverance of the worshipers at the shrine of Siva. These excavators designed beforehand, and left, as they cut away the rock, in its proper place, every separate pillar, statue and compartment. At the farther extremity is the bust of a three headed figure, eighteen feet high, representing Brahma the Creator, Vishnu the Preserver, and Siva the Destroyer.

There are side caves in which are representations of Siva's marriage, also the same diety in his double character of male and female and other characters not altogether pleasing, of Hindoo mythology. Especial efforts had been made to illuminate the caves with lamps and chandeliers, yet a serious gloom pervaded the whole place. Still the Prince and suite persisted in dining there, as, in the eyes of an Englishman, no scene, however grand, brilliant, or grim, is complete without a dinner.

Thereafter the Prince made a short visit to Poonah where he was greeted with a warm and popular reception. While here, he visited the Temple of Parbuttee dedicated to Siva, situated on a high elevation, from which a half century since, "the last Peishwa, Bajee Roa, anxiously watched the battle of Khirkee, in which his forces received that decisive defeat which ultimately cost him his throne," but which his son, Nana Sahib, during the Sepoy rebellion, terribly avenged at Cawnpore.

The temple having been visited, the Prince held a grand review on the race course a few miles from the battle-field of Khirkee, and in a few words congratulated the officers on the appearance of the troops, composed of both natives and Europeans. The day closed with a brilliant display of fireworks, when the Prince returned to Bombay, where he spent two days in receiving and paying visits, and viewing the city.

"Among the curious objects seen by the Prince at Bombay was the place on Malabar Hill where the Parsees expose their dead to the fowls of the air, instead of the ordinary mode of sepulture. The Tower of Silence is a lofty square inclosure, without roof or covering of any kind. The top of the high wall is always thronged with huge vultures and kites, which live and thrive on the bodies of the dead. The dead are carried into the centre of the inclosure and there left to be devoured by the birds of prey. His Royal Highness

STATE ELEPHANTS OF BARODA DRAWN UP TO RECEIVE THE PRINCE

also visited the Hindoo burning-ground, the flame of which, night and day, is kept alive, near the shore of Back Bay. At Bombay, and in other towns of India, one constantly meets in the streets a funeral procession, in which the corpse is carried aloft on a stretcher on the shoulders of the bearers. The face is exposed and painted in gay colors. Men playing on screeching native pipes, and a tom-tom, or native drum, frequently head the procession on its way to consign the corpse to the flames." (See page 550.)

Then he declared his purpose of visiting Baroda. This announcement caused apprehension, as the English but a few months before had dispossessed the reigning sovereign, and placed a nominee of their own on the throne. But this feeling was unjustified, as the Prince was received in person by the Guicowar and his Prime Minister and guardian, Sir Madhavar Rao, at the station, where a gorgeous procession of elephants and native troops were drawn up in line, in honor of his reception. The boy Prince, a lad of twelve, entertained his Royal visitor in true Oriental magnificence, exhibiting scenes of real Indian life, consisting of battles between elephants, rhinoceroses, rams, buffaloes and native wrestlers. All these engagements took place within the enclosure of the spacious arena, on the walls of which platforms had been erected, which were densely packed by native spectators. As the young host and the Prince appeared "their arrival was greeted by the trumpeting of four-and-twenty state elephants, which had been drawn up in line under one of the walls. These huge animals had been rendered gorgeous by fantastic paintings on their fronts and trunks, by gold embossings on their tusks, and by the rich trappings with which their sides and backs were swathed; their ankles were decorated with gold bracelets; plates of gold, elaborately wrought, covered the howdahs. As no two were painted alike or bore similar housings, the effect of this long line of splendid animals—for many were of the largest size—was striking indeed."

As the Prince had expressed a desire to see only the *manner* of fighting and not a real fight, there was not much zeal displayed by the animals. Two buffaloes, however, became a little more fierce and one lost a horn; then they were separated. Another pair of buffaloes were brought in, these without losing an instant rushed at each other. "Horn clashed against horn, head dashed against head, with the most passionate fury until one was flung on its side. The victor, at once tried to gore him, but his horns having been carefully blunted, he was unable to effect any injury."

After this a review of the Guicowar's menagerie took place; among the animals which passed before the Prince was the latest caught tiger. This animal, as savage and fierce as could well be imagined, growling all the time, was led in by ten men, five on either side, holding ropes fastened to a leather band which surrounded the tiger's body. It was thus rendered incapable of mischief, though at one time he struck out viciously with his fore legs, and nearly laid hold of one of the attendants. In case of accident, however, numerous spearsmen hovered round, ready to strike the moment his attempts to escape should prove successful.

"On the following day the Prince and his suite proceeded by rail to the Guicowar's hunting lodge at Muckinpoora. Here a great hunt of the black buck with cheetahs had been organized. Gathered round the palace were several bullock carts containing the cheetahs, or Indian leopards, whose disposition is peculiarly intelligent and tractable, somewhat resembling the dog. Also, there was a great assemblage for the hunt, of soldiers and officers, elephants, shikarees (huntsmen), camels, falconers with splendid peregrines and long winged falcons on their wrists, and ugly, fierce-looking dogs, half deerhounds, half greyhounds of the Persian type. After a couple of miles of traveling in bullock carts, a herd of black buck was perceived. The cheetahs had been carefully hoodwinked to prevent their dashing precipitate after the game.

The cart containing one was stopped. His keeper holding the collar of the animal, whipped off the hood, and the cheetah leaped off the cart, and crouched along the ground until within some forty yards of the herd, then singling out one of the deer for his quarry he dashed after him. But the deer was too quick for his pursuer and after a run of some five hundred

THE HUNTING LEOPARD

yards, the cheetah gave up the chase, and allowed himself to be again secured and hooded by his keeper. A short distance further, however, another herd of buck was sighted, and another cheetah slipped, and this time with more success. In a few bounds the leopard sprang upon the haunches of the deer, thence to his throat, thus pinning him to the ground and holding it till the arrival of the hunters. The deer kicked violently, but the cheetah lay across its throat, out of the reach of its legs. The Prince, the Duke of Sutherland, and the shikarees at once ran to the spot, and a shikaree cutting the deer's throat, drew a ladleful of blood and presented it to the cheetah, who quitted his hold of the deer, and lapped up the luxury as his reward. The Prince now dismounted and accompanied by the Duke of Sutherland and a few others, attempted to stalk the deer. On his way back to the palace an amusing incident occurred. The Prince came to a pool where two native girls were keeping a herd of buffaloes. On going forward to get a shot at a paddy bird the Prince alarmed the two girls, for whom the sight of a white man proved too formidable and they fled with piteous cries despite the shouts of an attendant, who was dispatched with a message of re-assurance."

This last scene was no doubt as novel to the Prince as it was terrifying to the girls, as the Prince had hitherto been pre-eminently successful in attracting, not repelling, the fair sex.

On another occasion the Prince drove to Mohtee Bagh, the old palace of the Guicowar, and was received in great state. After an inspection of the Guicowar's jewels the Prince and suite partook of a grand dinner in the pavilion in the garden, the Guicowar appearing only at dessert, where the health of the Queen was drank—it having been proposed by Sir Madhava Rao in the name of his young ward—and then that of the Prince, who returned thanks in a cordial speech, and closed by proposing the health of the Guicowar and Maharanee. In reply Sir Madhava Rao expressed on their part gratitude that "the Prince had come from his distant northern home traversing seas and oceans as the gracious messenger of a gracious Queen." The entertainment closed with fire-works, and music, when the Prince paid a visit to the Maharanee in her private apartments.

His Royal Highness on Sunday evening drove again to the palace of the Guicowar. A most curious spectacle was presented along the entire route. It is thus described:

"Chinese lanterns and oil-lamps were suspended in double lines from frameworks of bamboo and lattice. Every house was illuminated with blue lights and fire-pots. At intervals troops of horse and foot were drawn up. On the bridges stood figures draped in the most fantastic costumes. Their faces were painted chalky white; they wore wigs of scarlet ribbed with gold, and robes of tissue, tinselled; their hair was powdered, and dressed fantastically, or drooping over wan faces with piercing black eyes. Similar figures were grouped on stands on the road; they were brilliantly lighted up, and the lights on masses of white-clothed figures produced an extraordinary effect, along the line of three miles to the old palace. Amid this strange array an escort of the 3rd Hussars pulled up between the Guicowar cavalry."

The next day the Prince was some fifty miles from Baroda, quail shooting; bringing down on that day some one hundred and twenty head of game. He subsequently was initiated into the eminently Indian sport of "pig-sticking." On this occasion the result was not remarkable, as one thousand beaters succeeded in bringing but one pig within the sure range of the Prince's rifle. After that he turned his attention to the smaller game of snipe, and finally left for Baroda and Bombay, being escorted to the railway station with great display by the Guicowar and Sir Madhava, having enjoyed the hunting hugely.

On arriving at Bombay the Prince at once made his arrangements to leave the city. Royal salutes were fired from the fleet and shore batteries, as the Serapis steamed off for the old Portuguese town of Goa, where he was received with great enthusiasm by the Governor, members of the municipality, deputation from the priesthood, and other civil and military officers. While, in some respects, Goa—which calls to mind the name of Vasco de Gama—is quite interesting and pretty, it is at present destitute of enterprise, and all appearance of anything like energy seems long since to have taken its departure. The Prince, following suite, took

PIG-STICKING.

his departure for Ceylon, and was received at Colombo by the Governor, Sir W. H. Gregory, and a guard of honor of the 57th Regiment, in great state.

"The Cingalese had spared no pains to make the decorations of the town as picturesque as possible, wisely eschewing all attempts to imitate European ornamentation, they confined themselves to their own simple materials, namely: bamboo, fruits, and flowers, and built innumerable arcades after their own fashion and their own taste. To begin with, there was the arcade and pavilion at the landing-place, where the Prince received the municipal address, and then the arches along the route; these were first constructed of a frame-work of bamboo, and were then hung with streamers of young and green cocoa-nut wood, the uprights being decorated with thicker strips tied in bows, rosettes and devises of the same material being bountifully scattered over the panels. In the interstices of the lattice-work formed by the bamboo, were placed the varied and many-hued fruits for which Ceylon is so renowned. For instance: areca-nuts, green oranges, mangoes, plantains, red and yellow young cocoa-nuts, the brilliantly colored orange king cocoa-nut, green, red and yellow bananas, and the deadly wild pine, with the juice of which the Malays poison their weapons.

In addition to the fruits, of which, in some places there were pyramids eight feet high, there were strings and trophies of palm leaves, and beautiful flowers; the whole system of decoration showing a brilliant triumph of simple nature over the gaudy, artificial erections the Prince was so accustomed to see. Pavilions and arches of fruit and flowers had been raised upon the boats in the harbor, until they resembled Venetian gondolas. * * * The scene was exceedingly striking and picturesque, the natives wearing their national Cingalese costume—a short jacket, an ample and *bona fide* petticoat, low shoes, and long hair done up in a *chignon*, and fastened with a long, semi-circular comb. This eminently feminine costume gives a curiously womanly look to their already gentle and soft features. The people here were far more demonstrative in their cheering than at Bombay, and the utmost enthusiasm was shown by the Cingalese throughout the route to the Governor's house."

It was natural that the Prince should enjoy highly these novel Oriental decorations of the natives.

From Colombo he went by rail through a country rich with

rice and coffee plantations, to Kandy, where he was received as became his station, with processions, military and civil. In addition, there was the religious festival of the Perehara, described as "a mixture of a Lord Mayor's show with a Spanish religious procession." It has many mystic ceremonies, which occupy its first days. Afterwards, a grand procession is formed, a private rehearsal of which was given before the Prince in the garden of the Governor's house. A correspondent present, gives the following description of the scene:

"The gardens were purposely kept in darkness, except the space immediately in front of the house, so that the component part of the procession—although from the long pauses and breaks it could scarcely be called a procession—emerged in a dim, shadowy way out of the darkness, and faded away in the same ghostly sort of manner—an effect greatly added to by the noiseless tread of the elephants and of their naked-footed attendants. The line of road in front of the house was lighted by torch bearers; and at the head of the procession came some more torch-bearers, who ranged themselves in a large circle, into which entered four priests fantastically dressed in garments glittering with gold, silver and gems. These, to the sound of tom-toms, pipes, and of instruments resembling hurdy-gurdies, began to dance, or, rather, to posture in strange, wild figures, which would have been laughable had it not been for the gloomy air with which the priests went through what to them was a religious ceremony, and thus, with the innumerable torch-bearers, and surrounding circle of absolute darkness, gave a weird and unnatural air to the whole affair. Then came whip-bearers, and fan-bearers, and other officials, and then out of the darkness a mass, at first without shape, but which turned out to be three elephants close together. The central and much the largest animal carried on his back a sort of shrine, of pagoda form, in which were the bow and arrows of the God. Upon each side, upon the smaller elephants, rode priests. The animals were richly caparisoned, and wore coloured hoods or masks with round holes trimmed with gold braid, and looking like big eyes, changing entirely the expression of the face. Upon arriving opposite the Prince the great beasts wheeled slowly round in line, and knelt down in salutation before the Prince. Upon their rising he went forward, patted them, and gave

THE PRIVATE PEREHARA BEFORE THE PRINCE, KANDY.

them pieces of sugar-cane. They went on, and were succeeded by more dancing, more elephants in parties of three, more followers with emblems, until, weird and fantastic as the whole thing was, it became monotonous."

While at Kandy, the chief Buddhist, after exhibiting some curious jewelry—among which was the largest known emerald in the world—he slowly and solemnly opened a silver-gilt, bell-shaped shrine, and took out a golden and jeweled casket; from thence, he took out another and then another—like a conjurer performing the interminable box trick—until at last, the ninth, a beautiful little casket covered with sapphires, was reached, which, on being opened, displayed the tooth of Gautama Buddha,—most holy relic of the Buddhists—reposing on the sacred emblem, a golden lotus-leaf, and surrounded with rubies. All these nine pagoda-shaped caskets are of solid gold and most of them incrusted with gems; the largest and outside one is about three feet high, and about two feet in diameter. They are kept in a room in a cage of iron about nine feet square. There are three different keys to the place, held by three different persons, so that it cannot be opened unless all are present. The tooth is about one and a half to two inches long, and is believed by the incredulous, to be either a piece of discolored ivory, or the tooth of a boar, or a crocodile. So strong is the faith of the Buddhist, however, in this tooth, that at one time the King of Pegu offered $5,000,000, as a reward for its restoration, after it had been captured by the Portuguese.

During the stay of the Prince at Kandy, there was an exhibition of the Veddahs' skill in archery. They also performed some wild dances. They are believed to be the aborigines of Ceylon, and are but a little above the wild beasts.

On the 4th, which was a Saturday, his Royal Highness, with a portion of his suite, left Kandy en route for an elephant shooting expedition in the dense jungles about Ruanwella, a secluded district about half-way between Kandy and Colombo. A correspondent relates the experiences of the Royal sportsman and his companions as follows:

"There were waiting for the Prince two renowned elephant shikarees, Messrs. Varian and Fisher—men well acquainted with the habits of the animal and with the best modes of stalking and shooting them. The jungle in which the big game shikar was to take place is called the Dehi Owitte Jungle. It does not seem to be an eligible spot for an easy walk. It is "batta" or bamboo jungle, where the underwood, tangled with creeping thorns, is so compact that the sportsman finds it almost, if not quite, impossible to force his way through it; while the pliant young bamboos offer no material resistance to the huge body of the elephant. For days hundreds of beaters, under the herd men, had been watching and trying to hem in the wild elephants, of which it was said there were two herds, numbering in all some sixteen or twenty, with several tuskers. A kraal had been built, a square inclosure of strong and heavy palisading, with two diverging arms stretching from the upper corners of the square, and opening out in bell-mouthed fashion as they extended for several hundred yards up the slope of the hill. From the *points d'appui* formed by each extremity of the funnel-shaped mouth of the kraal the beaters stretched in a great ill-defined semi-circle. The scheme of the shikar was to drive the elephants into the kraal, while from a platform close to the outside of its mouth the Prince should have the opportunity of shooting at the animals as they passed. His Royal Highness took post on the platform that had been constructed for him, while the beaters advanced, gradually contracting their cordon. Among the animals so approached was one old tusker with much blood upon his head; he was said to have slain five or six men, and many bullocks. This fellow had his ladies about him, and for them he fought chivalrously, charging against the beaters over and over again. Ultimately he abandoned his females, crashed through the beaters, driving them helter-skelter up into the trees for safety, and made his escape clear. There still remained, however, the prospect of being more successful with a herd of seven elephants still within the beaters' cordon, only they could not be persuaded to leave the cover. His Royal Highness, from his elevation, could now and then hear the huge animals trumpeting and crashing through the dense jungle, within, as it seemed, a short fifty yards of him; but so thick was the foliage that a sight never offered. At length, about half-past four, the gentlemen in the tents heard a couple of shots from the Prince's perch, and rushing out

AN ELEPHANT KRAAL, WITH THE "GRAND STAND FOR ENGLISH VISITORS"

on the sound, were in time to see an elephant stagger on to his knees while the blood poured from his head. From his knees he sank on his side, and the first elephant shot by the Prince lay dead before him. There were others yet to come. The beaters had received orders to force the elephants forward by lighting fires of bamboo behind them, and Fisher and Varian had gone down among the beaters to stimulate yet further the advance of the animals by peppering them from behind. After the first elephant had fallen, Varian came to the Prince and told him how he had several elephants together going along the bed of a small stream, had fired and wounded one of them; and how he thought his Royal Highness would be likely to see sport were he to come down, and by penetrating through the jungle get a second shot at the wounded elephant. The Prince, accepting this advice, went on with Varian and Fisher and Lord Suffield, but got into quick sudden danger that had not been anticipated by his adviser. As he advanced there was a crash in the bamboo jungle close by, and with a thrill of horror there came swiftly to Fisher the conviction that an elephant—or there might be more than one—was charging straight on the little party, almost helpless as they were, owing to the imprevious character of the jungle. He drew the Prince aside, just as the huge beast crashed by quite near, yet invisible; and then, with his heart in his mouth, for he and his mate Varian could realize the imminence of the danger just passed, he put Lord Suffield behind his Royal Highness as coverer, while he and Varian, acting as flankers, advanced in line with the Prince, cautiously and with great difficulty, through the entangled and thorny jungle. In an opener patch close to the stream they came suddenly upon the elephant which Fisher had wounded. Furious with pain, the brute charged at the party with fierce directness; but the Prince, standing forward with steady aim, gave him a ball just in the fatal spot. The great beast staggered sideways a little way, and then, with a last scream, rolled over into the stream stone dead. The noise of the rest of the retreating herd was heard beyond, and Fisher and Varian crept in through the jungle on a scouting expedition. Returning with good news, they brought the Prince up, and he got a shot at another elephant at a distance of fifty yards. He and Varian fired simultaneously, and the elephant first sank on his knees, and then, getting a second shot from his Royal Highness, rolled over dead. Mr. Fisher states that more than once the Prince was in a position of real danger, and that his coolness and nerve were admirable. When he emerged from the jungle his clothes were torn to ribbons, and there were spots of blood on his scratched face. He had lost his hat in the first few steps, and altogether, as my informant stated, the aspect of general dilapidation which he presented was a caution."

Returning to Colombo, the Prince attended a state ball and dinner. After having with due ceremonies laid the corner-stone of a new breakwater, he moved on toward Madras, calling on the way at Tuticorin, Madura, and Trichinopoly.

At the former place he was received with a royal salute, and escorted to a hall where an address was read. At Madura he visited the palace and temple, where he was shown the "golden lotus tank," and the pictures of temples and Gods which are painted on the walls of the inclosure. He was presented with an elegant Benares shawl, on which the figures of the presiding God and Goddess were embroidered in gold. The temple jewels were shown him, and the door of the "holy of holiest" was kept ajar some time, that the Prince might get a good view of the shrine, and the golden idol enthroned within. As the Prince proceeded, the pavement on each side was lined with dancing-girls, who showered flowers at his feet.

At Trichinopoly (place of the three-headed) he was presented some splendid silver gifts for the Princess of Wales, by the ladies of the city, and also by the Princess of Tanjore. He visited Srivungum, about four miles distant, to see the temple there. The ornaments of the temple, consisting of gold vases and other vessels and ornaments of precious stones, all of immense value, were shown him. While he was examining these, twelve of the nautch girls of the temple sang a chorus. These girls were tinged in the face with yellow dye, and their hair bound up with pearls, their arms and ankles being covered with ornaments. As the Prince moved on, they accompanied him, singing and beating bits of wood together. He was also shown two stone horses dragging a car, which are said to have fallen from heaven,

SILVER THRONE MADE FOR THE USE OF THE PRINCE OF WALES IN INDIA.

turning to stone upon touching the earth. The Prince entered the "Hall of the Thousand Pillars," and then drove back to town. In the evening grand illuminations were given, which were most magnificent. It is impossible to give a full description of them, but the following paragraph from the pen of an eye-witness, will give an idea of their extent:

"Facing the tank are some large houses, one of which was occupied by Clive. Behind these again rises the rock of Trichinopoly, a precipitous rock about 500 ft. in height. This is crowned by a great temple, and above it, upon a high knob of the rock, is another temple, or rather the most sacred place of the temple, into which unbelievers are forbidden to enter. Upon the highest point floats the British flag. Along the top of the temple are huge figures of animals, which, as seen from the surrounding country, give it the appearance of a battlemented fort. Not only were the architectural lines of the temple lighted up, but all the salient points of the rock's face were marked out by lines of light, while from the top of the upper temple and from salient corners of the main temple coloured fires were burned. As soon as the darkness was complete the display of fire-works began. These were of native manufacture, and very effective. From a pagoda at the top of the rock Roman candles threw up a stream of coloured balls, while from several large round wicker-work basket-boats, floating in the tank, men kept letting off water-fire-works, which made the lake alive with frisky fire-demons. These were of various sorts. Some disappeared for some time and then came up with a fizz and a spurt of fire; others leaped from the water like fish; some of the great jets revolved in the water like huge fire-fountains, while others threw up great volumes of beautiful sparks for a few seconds and then retired to repeat the performance in another portion of the tank. These water-fire-works, with a new feature added by fiery cascades poured from the top of the walls of the rock temple, had an effect which was extremely fine."

At a visit paid the Prince by the Princess of Tanjore, she was placed behind a screen, where were also seated several English ladies—the Prince and suite standing upon the other side of the screen. The Princess put her hand through a hole in the screen, and the Prince took it and shook it cordially.

On his arrival at Madras he was received with all the respect due to his high position, including the inevitable address. In the Banqueting Hall he held a grand *levée*; the room being beautifully decorated.

At daybreak the next day the Prince turned out with his suite to have a run with the hounds. The sport was good, and his Highness enjoyed it exceedingly. A native entertainment was also given the Prince in the huge railway shed, which was transformed into a hall of wondrous beauty and glitter. An address was presented, to which the Prince briefly replied. A troupe of dancing-girls gathered about the Prince. They are thus described:

"Their dress was exceedingly picturesque. Ropes and wreaths of jewels—chiefly pearls—encircled their heads; their long hair, encased in a thick covering of yellow silk crusted with jewels, hung down in one coil to their waists. Heavy nose-rings of pearls, scarcely,—to unaccustomed English eyes—contributed to the enhancement of their jewellery. They wore short light jackets of embroidered silk in various colours. Their waists were girdled by a belt of elastic gold, supporting loose floating drapery of white muslin, with heavy borderings of gold, studded with jewels and bouquets of flowers. Around their necks hung great strings of pearls down on their bare bosoms; wrists and ankles glittered with jewelled bangles. Moving forward at the signal, they took their places for the dance, standing in a circle, and holding the silken ropes that hung from a common centre in the roof."

While here, the Prince enjoyed one of the grandest sights of his whole tour. This consisted in the illumination of the surf in Madras Roads. There is a frightful surf constantly breaking on the shore, which renders all landing dangerous, except by two kinds of native boats, one called the mossoolah and the other the catamaran. An eye-witness writes:

"Both of these boats were used in the illumination of the breakers, their occupants being furnished with blue lights. On the shore the illuminated buildings formed a brilliant background; seaward the Serapis, Osborne and Raleigh were lighted up, while at a given signal innumerable fires appeared amid the waves drifting landward, which multiplied,

THE MAHARAJAH SCINDIA, OF GWALIOR.

THE MAHARAJAH OF CASHMERE.

dipping and rising now and then through the waves; suddenly from the beach dashed the black forms of mossoolah boats and catamarans, which, amid the wildest yells, charged into the serried ranks of the foam-crested breakers, and dark objects seaward were revealed as the boats tossed violently on the outer ridge of the breakers. There never was such a regatta. Amid a sea now black as ink, now like fire glistening jet in a creamy sea, the catamaran men were swept off and regained their craft, and disappeared beneath the billows. * * * One might fancy the spectacle a contest of water gods."

The day following, the Prince sailed for Calcutta, and on his arrival at the mouth of the Hooghly, Sir Richard Temple, accompanied by deputations from those in authority, gave him a fitting reception at Diamond Harbor and escorted him up the river, and on arriving at Prinsep's Ghaut, the Viceroy received him; and as many native princes had come to witness his arrival, they were presented by Lord Northbrook. The Prince then drove off to the Government House.

"The scene on Prinsep's Ghaut, crowded with all the leading native chiefs of Bengal was singularly striking, each chief being covered with innumerable jewels, many of them of inestimable value. Among the great princes present, the chief figures were the Maharajah Scindia of Gwalior, G. C. S. I., and the Maharajah of Puttialla, G. C. S. I. This latter potentate, is a fine looking man of twenty-two, with rather a heavy face of a Sikh character in its outline. He speaks English, and placed $500,000 at the disposal of the Government during the famine, and gave $35,000 to the Lahore University. He rules over nearly two millions of people, his dominions extend over some 55,000 square miles, and his annual revenue exceeds $2,000,000. His father rendered the British considerable service during the mutiny. The Maharajah of Puttialla is one of the richest and one of the handsomest of the native princes: the jewels he wore on this occasion, including the diamonds he lately bought from the ex-Empress Eugenia, are said to be worth $1,500,000. The Maharajah Scindia is the great chief of Gwalior, and is reckoned as notable a warrior as Puttialla is a millionaire. The Maharajah of Indore, in face and figure is not unlike Henry VIII. This gentleman's wealth is said to be enormous; $25,000,000 of treasure being stored up in his palace. He was anxious to have given the Prince a present, worth some $250,000, but was cut down to the value of $25,000. The Maharajah of Cashmere had also wished to display his loyalty to a similar amount. As he was not permitted thus to do, he decided to make a new road thirty miles long for the use of the Prince when he should make him a visit."

From this it will be seen that love of magnificent display is a large element in the character of the native princes of India, as well as that of the princes of Europe; a single jewel in the necklace of one of them may exceed in value the wealth of any President, or ex-President of the United States.

The next day the native princes were formally received by the Prince, and among them came the Begum of Bhapol Sultana Jehan, and her daughter. The most profuse display of wealth and dress marked the reception throughout. The illuminations in the city were on an extended scale, and many new features were introduced. The next day, Christmas, was in part spent by the Prince on board the Serapis, which was decorated appropriately.

Seventeen miles up the Hooghly is the little French settlement of Chandernagore, the only relic of French ascendency in Bengal. The Prince paid it a flying visit and was warmly received by the people.

In the park of Belvedere, a suburb of Calcutta, the Prince saw a company of wild Nagas — brought down from the mountains for his edification. They went through a series of performances, dances, sham-battles, etc., highly interesting to the Prince.

At a native entertainment, an exhibition of rare skill on various musical instruments was given. Among others, the feat of playing two flutes or trumpets with the neck. The instruments are so finely constructed that the small quantity of air propelled by the pressure of the neck on the mouth of the tube, produces the sound.

Of all the imposing ceremonials pertaining to the Prince's eastern tour, perhaps none was of greater splendor, in accordance with Oriental taste or pleasing to the native princes to

NATIVE MUSICIANS.

such a degree as the holding of the Grand Chapter of the Star of India, on New Year's day, at which the Prince invested several new Knights with the order. On this occasion the costumes of the Oriental chiefs were extremely magnificent; their wearers appeared like "animated nuggets ambulatory mines of jewels." The Chapter was held on the Meridan in a grand Durbar Tent. There were tents there also for each of the Knights Commanders, over which waved the banners of the various chiefs, surrounded by retainers adorned with great magnificence.

"In front of the spectators were the seats for the members of the order. At one end of the enclosure were chairs of state for the Prince of Wales and the Grand Master Lord Northbrook, surmounted by a dais. These chairs were of silver, and differed only in their ornamentation; the back of the Prince's throne bearing the ostrich feathers, and that of the Viceroy a crown. The ceiling of the tent was a canopy of blue silk edged with silver—the color of the order—colors which predominated everywhere, from the banners pending from the roof to the mantles worn by the Knights.

"In the grand procession of the Knights into the Durbar Tent, the Prince of Wales entered last but one, being under the shadow of the regal umbrella of gold, his train being held by midshipmen in the costume of the time of Charles I: cavalier hats and cloaks, tunics, trunk hose, and rosetted shoes, all in blue satin, and wearing cavalier wigs. Lord Northbrook, as Grand Master, came in last of all, and then the Chapter was opened, the Secretary reading the roll of the order, and each Knight seating himself as he answered. The Secretary, Mr. Aitchinson then read out the business to be done, and the Queen's warrant directing the Prince of Wales to hold the Investiture. After handing the Warrant to the Prince, Mr. Aitchinson went in search of the Maharajah Jodhpore—the first knight to be invested.

"The Maharajah entered into the tent in a small procession, the insignia being borne before him on a cushion, and was led up to the royal dais, before which he bowed profoundly. Two Knight Commanders then robed him in the blue mantle of the order; this done, Mr. Aitchinson led him to the Prince, who placed the collar of the order round his neck, saying: 'In the name of the Queen and by Her Majesty's command I herewith invest you with the honorable insignia of the Star of India, of which most exalted order Her Majesty has been graciously pleased to appoint you to be a Knight Grand Commander.' A salute of seventeen guns was then fired, the Maharajah made a deep reverence and retiring was then conducted to his seat, where his banner was unfurled and his full title proclaimed amid a flourish of trumpets. The Maharajah had voluminous pink petticoats which stuck out at right angles to his body, and after he had been invested with the large robe of the order, he had the utmost difficulty in walking, which of course he had to do backwards all down the tent, almost tripping in the attempt. The poor fellow looked in an awful fright, and would have turned his back on the Prince, and fairly made a run for it, if his arms had not been firmly clutched by Mr. Aitchinson and his other companion."

There were several other investitures, similar in their details.

After the state ball, where the Prince enjoyed the presence of the "beauty and the chivalry" of the city of palaces, he left Calcutta for Bankipore where he held a grand Durbar, at which the *native* "beauty and chivalry" congregated in vast numbers. The Prince then went on to Benares,—the holiest of all the holy cities of the Hindoos, who call it the "Lotus of the world." It is here that every Hindoo, or at least every Brahmin, would wish to die, believing he would go straight to heaven if he could but touch the sacred water of the holy Ganges, which has power to wash away the darkest sins of the wickedest Thug. Here the Prince visited the Golden Temple, which is "a marvel of intricately sculptured walls, and where is situated a holy well, formed by the perspiration which once dropped off Siva," as the natives claim. He also visited the Monkey Temple, where hundreds of monkeys play, and sometimes fight, and also make ludicrous grimaces and much mischief for all that part of the city; yet, these apes must be endured, as they are held sacred by the Hindoos. He also visited the burning ghâts, where the bodies of the faithful Brahmins are cremated. He enjoyed the interesting sight of standing on the ghâts and witnessing the scores of thousands of men, women and children

THE MAHARAJAH OF JODHPORE RETIRING FROM THE PRINCE'S PRESENCE

bathe, it being with them a sacred act, cleansing the soul as well as body, such is their belief,—

> "For the Ganges' wave, that is strong to save,
> Hath washed their sins away."

From Benares, the Prince passed on to Lucknow, where he was received in state, and where he had the rare opportunity to witness a scene that deeply touched his sympathy as well as admiration, being a review of the veterans of the mutiny at Lucknow.

"Here the Prince laid the foundation-stone of a monument dedicated by Lord Northbrook to the memory of the native officers and men who fell in the memorable defense of this town, during the mutiny. Well might Sir George Cowper, the Chief Commissioner of Oudh, say in his address to the Prince, that he believed the behavior of the Sepoys at Lucknow, simply to be without parallel in the annals of the world, when they stood firm in their adherence to the British, although fifty yards off their own relations, fellow castemen and former comrades adjured them to forsake the infidel and save their race. The survivors of this heroic band were ranged behind Sir George Cowper, and after the ceremony, were presented one by one to the Prince, the officers holding out the handles of their swords for the Prince to touch as they passed; some had received promotion and rewards, while others were less fortunate, and had prepared petitions for redress of grievances. Many wore the old uniform in which they had fought in 1857, while others appeared in civilian attire. The older men seemed especially affected at the sight of the Prince, and one man fairly burst into tears. Many had lost a limb, one poor fellow had been wounded by the splinters of a shell, while another could not walk at all, save with the help of his hands. Truly a touching 'roll call' of men who, for the simple motto of 'fidelity to salt,' had rendered the English one of the greatest services on record."

After this sad, yet interesting scene, the Prince left for Cawnpore, where he remained a short time, visiting the Memorial Church and Garden, and then proceeded to Delhi, where he was received by the authorities with a grand military display, and with great enthusiasm by the people.

Up to this time, in nearly all the grand receptions attending the arrival of the Prince in the various cities, the civil element had mainly taken the lead; here the order was changed; instead of the inevitable address and civic entertainments being the chief attractions, there were splendid reviews, a grand military ball, and sham fights for two days. On these occasions the populace seemed to turn out *en masse* as spectators, some "on foot, on camels, on horseback, on elephants, in four-in-hand drays, and vehicles of all kinds; all forming a picturesque background to the masses of European and native troops, who were drawn up in line before the Royal standard." While here the Prince had the pleasure of reviewing the brave native troops, called the Goorkas, "gallant little fellows, very small and slight, but with the courage of lions, the activity of cats, and the fidelity of dogs."

A grand ball was given in the palace; in the centre of the suite of rooms used was the throne-room, in which once stood the famous Peacock throne. There were twelve hundred males present at this ball and but three hundred ladies. The Prince visited all the places of note in the city, and also the ruins of old Delhi, and left by rail for Lahore, at which place a grand reception was given by native chiefs. The Prince visited the goal, a model establishment filled with ruffians of the roughest texture. Among these were two Thugs, one of them seventy years old, who had murdered with his own hands more than two hundred and fifty people. The other, who was younger, could boast of only thirty-five. They showed how the cord was used, the old man giving one of the party's wrist a twist with it, which was clearly felt for days afterwards.

A native entertainment was given here also, at which were members of the Royal family of Delhi, and of Afghanistan—one of whom had actually sat on the throne. There were also descendants of Nanuk the founder of the Sikh race, also Rajpoots, Pathans, Belooches, and others, representing almost every tribe and race of northern India. Although

THE PRINCE'S TRIP ON THE GANGES, BENARES.

these chiefs and sirdars had been expressly told how to act on their presentation, and that nuzzars were not to be offered, they forgot the instructions, and frequently salaamed, often to the ground; sometimes kissing the golden carpet or estrade where the Prince sat, and waited in attitudes of reverence, as if to say something or to listen to a word from the son of their Empress.

Jummoo, a frontier town of Cashmere, was the next town visited by the Prince; thither he went to call upon the Maharajah of Cashmere. The town is picturesquely situated on the little river Tani, and on a low spur of the Punjab Himalayas, whose rugged, snowy peaks, form a magnificent background.

Although the Maharajah was a wealthy prince, his troops "presented a quaint spectacle, from the variety of their uniforms and accoutrements; some companies were clothed in steel skull-caps with chain-mail armor neck-pieces, and brass back and breast-plates, and armed with javelins; others with brass helmets and breast-plates; some were in bright-red uniform, white cross-belts and tall shakos; others again were clothed in turbans and a more Oriental garb, and armed with blunderbusses." These lined the road over which the Prince passed upon his arrival, mounted upon an elephant with the Maharajah,—a distance of two miles to the camp.

Hunting parties were arranged, but they proved failures, and fishing parties met with no better success. At a dinner party given by the Maharajah, a performance was given by the Lamas or Buddhist monks. When the floor was cleared, some of these monks came in and squatted down on the floor with drums, trumpets, cymbals and other instruments. When these began to make an uproar, the dancers came in, one with an incense vessel. They wore broad-brimmed hats, with ornaments like vanes and weather-cocks, from which floated strips of fancy colored silks. Their dress resembled the Chinese, but was covered with rags and tags, which flew about as the dance proceeded. After dancing awhile they retired and came back with heads of animals apparently in place of their own. The effect was overwhelming; elephants, bears, and almost every native animal were represented. Again the dance proceeded. These Lamas were from different parts, probably from Leh, Pekin and Thibet. At the party, the Maharajah presented the Prince a sword all studded with jewels, worth at least $50,000.

The Maharajah had been to the expense of building a new road to enable the Prince to make this visit,—and making roads over the spur of the Himalayas, is not a light undertaking; he also had erected a new palace to be occupied by the Prince. He seemed to have treated all his guests with prodigal hospitality, "every convenience being provided for them, even down to combs and tooth-brushes." After the Durbar and fire-works, the Prince and Maharajah enjoyed a grand banquet.

On his return from Jummoo to Agra, the Prince halted to open the "Alexandra" bridge, across the Chenab river, one of the longest bridges in the world, the distance across it being one and three-fourths miles.

On his arrival at Agra, his reception "was as gorgeous and imposing as all the trappings of Oriental pageantry could make it. The Prince rode an elephant, "which was wrapped in a long robe of cloth of gold, the howdah being of silver, relieved by female figures representing Peace and Plenty; the ostrich plumes and royal arms being worked on the sides. A group of mace-bearers escorted the animal." Another elephant had been "completely covered by a chain armor formed of rupee (fifty cent) pieces." The Prince was delighted with the view of the Taj Mahal, that magnificent mausoleum erected by Shah Jehan, which was fully illuminated in his honor.

A most gorgeous procession was formed and passed before the Prince, excelling all modern displays and rivalling those of the old Mogul Emperors. No list could give an idea of its extent and magnificence. Few of the chiefs had less than fifty elephants and perhaps as many camels, with scores of led horses, besides a retinue of hundreds of cavalry and

THE GUICOWAR OF BARODA, VISITED BY THE PRINCE OF WALES.

infantry. It was a gorgeous affair. The Prince visited the tomb of Akbar at Secundra, and also the ruins of Futteh-pore-Sikri, and left Agra for Gwalior.

At Gwalior, in the Mahratta country, is one of the strongest fortresses in Asia; it is said that five thousand men could hold it against the whole armies of the world. This noted fortress belongs to Maharajah Scindia, who was loyal to the British during the mutiny; hence the Prince was extremely anxious to make him a visit, to show the Maharajah his personal regard, and also to see the famous fortress. On his arrival he was received in grand state. While there the Prince held a review of the troops, after which, there was a sham fight, in which the Maharajah came off victor.

At Dholephore the Prince visited the young Maharajah, a lad of thirteen, now under the tutelage of a British officer. He also visited Bhurtpore and enjoyed a very fine reception given by the Maharajah and his retainers.

Early in February the Prince left Agra for Jeypore, that he might enjoy a long anticipated treat, namely: a tiger hunt in the jungle. The Maharajah, Ram Singh had been notified of the intended visit and was awaiting His Royal Highness, being prepared to give him a grand Oriental welcome. His plans were fully carried out.

Upon his arrival he was met by the Maharajah, and mounting an elephant they passed into the town. The procession, with its elephants, camels, bullocks, horses, warriors, and pomp, equalled anything the Prince had seen before. It had one new feature. A large number of Nagas preceded the procession, brandishing long swords, cutting and slashing to the right and left, to the music of tom-toms and serpent-shaped horns. They are a wild race and give the Government much trouble.

"Soon after his arrival, news came that a large tiger had been seen in a neighboring ravine, and the Prince, the Maharajah, Lord Alfred Paget, and Lord Aylesford started thither, and on arriving took places on a low building. The beaters, after much trouble, drove the tiger within range of the Prince's rifle. He fired and wounded it twice, but the animal escaped. Elephants were then brought, and mounting them, the party followed the animal down the ravine, and overtaking it at the entrance of a den, fired two more shots and killed it. On examination, the tiger proved to be a full-grown female, some eight feet four inches long. It was placed on an elephant and bourne in triumph to the Residency and on his return the Prince had a photograph taken of himself and party, with the tiger lying at their feet."

Leaving Jeypore, the Prince entered upon a two week's tiger hunting expedition in the Terai, a small portion of the time being spent with Sir H. Ramsay in the Kumoon, and the remainder with Sir Jung Bahadoor in Nepaul.

"At Moradabad the railway ended, and the Prince bidding adieu to all the conveniences of civilization, entered into the routine of camp life. The hunting-camp had been formed upon the most magnificent scale, there being two hundred elephants, five hundred and fifty camels, one hundred horses, sixty ox carts, one thousand native camp-followers, seventy-five Goorkas, and other troops and police. On Tuesday accordingly, he proceeded to Nynee Tal, arriving in time to see the snowy ranges lighted up with the sunset glow.

"The Terai is the belt of prairie which skirts the great forest at the foot of the Himalayas, and the word is, as a rule, applied to the forest itself. Game of all kinds, from rhinoceroses, elephants, tigers, to the humble pig, or a covey of jungle fowl, inhabit the thick jungle and dense swamps, and are in a great measure protected by the evil reputation this region bears for malaria. The natives in particular have great dread of it, but it has been fairly established that during the winter months the Terai is exceedingly healthy. * * To come to the tiger shooting: the *modus operandi* is to go out every morning after breakfast with about one hundred and fifty elephants in one, two, or three parties, the elephants being employed to beat in a straight line or in a semi-circle toward the Prince, who, on the first day of the hunt, got a long shot at a tiger; but the grass being high, the animal escaped. Indeed one of the chief features of the country is the extreme height and thickness of the grass, which hides the tallest elephants up to their breasts and completely conceals the smaller animals, who can only be distinguished by the track they leave as they crush through the reeds. The difficulty of getting a good aim at any kind of

THE TIGER AT HOME.

game may thus be easily imagined, the course of the animal pursued being only indicated by the waving reeds and the agitation of the elephants."

Everything was done according to the usual custom of hunters here, and the Prince took his chance with the rest for shots. A deer or hog would be started and guns would blaze at him from along the whole line of howdahs; possibly he would fall at the first shot, but the chances were he would run a distance, if he did not escape entirely. The long jungle-grass added much to the likelihood of the last.

"Later on in the day the Prince shot his first leopard. The animal was a large female, and the first game of any importance the Prince shot in the Terai. She was started in the long grass, was fired at, and made for the forest, but, on crossing a patch of shorter grass, was finally brought down."

At the end of four days the Prince took his departure for Nepaul, where he was met by Sir Jung Bahadoor and the British Resident at Nepaul. After an official visit and a Durbar, Sir Jung Bahadoor presented the Prince with two tigers and a collection of Nepaulese birds, and the next day the Prince re-commenced tiger-hunting. This time considerable success was achieved, as Sir Jung Bahadoor had spared no pains to secure grand sport.

Seven hundred elephants were employed in beating the jungle, and the Prince one day shot no fewer than six tigers, the greatest number any man in that country has been known to kill in a single day. One of the six shot, was a man-eater and within the week had devoured a human being. She was lean and lank—none but old and sickly tigers take to man-eating. Another of the tigers had killed nine bullocks and buffaloes belonging to one village. The Prince acquitted himself nobly, and won the encomiums of the natives.

One of the grandest spectacles seen, was that of the seven hundred elephants crossing the river—an arm of the Sarda:

"They crossed the stream in single file, each carrying at least two persons, and some three or four. The Prince sat for three-quarters of an hour watching the display which is said to be such a spectacle as has never been beheld by living man, and indeed it may be doubted if the like was ever seen in past ages." After the elephants had crossed the stream and began to march over the prairie, they reminded one of vast "armies moving in columns."

In one of the hunts the Prince's elephant was attacked by a tiger—a full-grown male—measuring nine feet six inches in length. The scene is thus described by a gentleman of the party:

"The game lay in a patch of forest, which was hemmed in by the pad-elephants. The howdah-elephants joined the circle at intervals, under the direction of Mr. Girdlestone. They all advanced into the wood. The ground was at first rising or hilly, but they soon came to a gully covered with high grass. Into this the elephants went, crashing down all before them. A cry of 'Bagh!' or 'Tiger!' was heard to the left hand and the reports of two guns. The circle of advancing elephants drew in, rapidly narrowing, and surrounded a clump of grass, which seemed alive with tigers. The Prince had the Maharajah on his left hand, and further to the left was General Sir D. Probyn, pistol in hand. The tigers, finding themselves hemmed in, rushed furiously round the circle, roaring loudly. The elephants were trumpeting, men shouting, and it was a scene of great confusion. Above all was heard the shrill voice of Sir Jung Bahadoor, hurling imprecations on the head of any one who should allow the line to be broken. The grass on the side where the Prince was, gradually became trampled down; yet a patch was still left, giving covert to the tigers. Out of this patch of grass they kept charging into the open. In one of their charges, the elephant ridden by his Royal Highness was attacked. Though a staunch animal, this elephant did not keep his front towards the tiger, but turned so as to receive the tiger upon his vast haunch. This movement sent the mahout and the other persons upon the elephant reeling backwards; but the Prince instantly recovered himself, coolly turned round, and fired. The tiger was killed, his head being at that time very near the legs of Mr. Peter Robertson, the Prince's attendant, then seated behind him. Four tigers were killed at this one spot; but the biggest of them, the paterfamilias, is supposed to have escaped."

The Prince went out with a pack of tame elephants to fight and capture wild ones. There is nothing that pleases

THE PRINCE OF WALES IN THE NEPAUL TERAI CHASED BY A WILD ELEPHANT.

a trained elephant better than to beat and batter a wild one so unmercifully as to allow of his being bound. There are elephants of great sagacity, strength and courage that are kept for this purpose in Nepaul. Howdahs cannot be used in these hunts and pads are substituted. The Prince rode on one of these, holding on by a strap. The scene is thus described:

"These trained racers will do seven miles an hour, the usual pace of the animals being only two miles and a half. The fighting fellows were on ahead engaged with some of the wild ones, who, headed by an old tusker, were showing a bold front and giving battle resolutely. 'Forward!' was the word. The Prince had at least a novel sensation now, for the elephant, 'kukereed' before and malleted behind, dashed on at a speed which would have been exhilarating enough. But he went crashing through trees, down ravines, up nullahs, through jungle in the most reckless manner; and he had a store of water in his proboscis which he replenished at every pool and sluiced himself with to cool his sides as he ran, drenching the Prince unmercifully. As they were dismounted, taking some refreshment, runners came up to announce that some of the wild herd had broken back. 'Mount at once,' exclaimed Sir Jung; 'you are not safe. Get on your elephants.' Another scout came in to report that the tusker had struck to the left, and that the fighters were engaged with him. Off went Prince and party full speed again; but they did not see the battle. They only beheld the result; for, about ten miles back, they came on the captive—his legs tied, an elephant on each side and one before and one behind him, his proboscis dejected, his tail bleeding, his ribs punched, his head battered, his bearing exceedingly sorrowful. In the course of the night and early morning the herd, fourteen in all, were brought in captive, and are now fastened up to undergo training and taming, one little creature being reduced to milk diet by hand. Mr. Rose, one of the Prince's suite was actually chased by a wild elephant. This elephant chanced to be one which had broken its left tusk, a stump only remaining; but Mr. Rose had a narrow escape, being for a moment almost within reach of the elephant's trunk."

"On another day the Prince was treed by a herd of elephants, as he was about to lunch. News came that a herd of wild elephants was advancing upon him and his suite. Sir Jung

Bahadoor at once besought every one to seek for safety in trees. Accordingly the Nepaulese constructed a perch in a fine banyan tree, by binding the cross branches together with ropes of creepers, and to this stage, followed by his suite, some of whom displayed astonishing climbing and clinging powers, the Prince clambered. However, the spectators waited in vain, for the elephants did not come, but if they had come, and found a single human being on the ground, the natives said that he would inevitably have been killed." This day ended the Prince's tiger shooting.

On March 9th the Prince arrived at Allahabad, where he held Chapter of the Star of India, and after looking at all points of interest in the city, left for Indore, where he arrived the same day. This place was swept clean and whitewashed, but no special display was made in the reception. The Prince visited the camps of several Central India Chiefs who had gathered to see him. He also held a Durbar, at which these chiefs and others were formerly introduced. On the 10th of March he left for Bombay by railroad, reaching that city the next day, and going at once on board the Serapis. The farewell ceremonies took place on the 13th, on board the ship, which sailed in the afternoon. The shipping in the harbor was dressed and the yards manned. Royal salutes were fired, and the Prince of Wales had commenced his homeward voyage. The Prince carried with him a menagerie consisting of about eighty animals, which to passengers and crew furnished most interesting amusement and employment throughout the entire passage.

The Serapis stopped at Aden, Suez, Cairo, Gibralter, Cadiz, Seville, Madrid, and Lisbon; the Prince spending a week at each of the two latter places, a guest of the Kings of Spain and Portugal. From Lisbon he sailed direct to Portsmouth arriving on the 11th day of May, and proceeded at once to London, having been absent just seven months.

HUNTING A WILD ELEPHANT WITH TAME ONES IN NEPAUL.

The following calendar of the places visited and principal events happening during the journey of the Prince of Wales, will be found of great service to those who may wish to refer to the account of any of them. It can be relied upon as correct.

CALENDAR OF THE PRINCE'S JOURNEY THROUGH INDIA.

1875.

Oct. 11, Left London.
" 12, Arrived in Paris.
" 13, Left Paris.
" 14, Arrived at Turin.
" 15, Left Turin, dined at Bologna.
" 16, Arrived at Brindisi and embarked for Athens.
" 18, Arrived at Athens.
" 19, Spent the day at the Royal Country Seat of Tatoi-Chareau.
" 20, Entertained King and Queen of Greece at lunch and left for Egypt.
" 23, Arrived at Port Said and left for Cairo, reaching there the same evening.
" 24, Attended Service at the Palace.
" 25, Invested Prince Tewfik with the Order of the Star of India, dined at the Pyramids.
" 26, Took leave of the Khedive, went to Suez, and started thence for Aden.
Nov. 1, Arrived at Aden, held a Levee, and left for Bombay.
" 8, Arrived at Bombay. Grand Procession to Government House, Parell; Reception and State Dinner.
" 9, Went on Board the *Serapis* to cut Birthday Cake; Grand Reception of Princes; Illuminations.
" 10, Held Levee, was present at the Children's Fete, dined at Government House, and present at Ball.
" 11, Visited Bombay University; opened Sailors' Home, and laid Foundation Stone of Elphinstone Dock.
" 12, Banquet in Caves of Elephanta.
" 13, Went to Poonah, drove to Government House, Gunesh Khind; State Reception, Banquet, and Ball.
" 14, Visited Poonah Church.
" 15, Visited Temple of Parbuttee, held a Review at Poonah, and started for Bombay.
" 16, Arrived at Bombay; Review of Troops, presented New Colours to 21st Bat., and went to State Ball at Parell.
" 17, Visited the Parsee Tower of Silence, the Hindoo Holy Tank and Shrine of Walkeshwur, the Hindoo Burning Place, Sonapore.
" 18, Started in evening for Baroda.
" 19, Arrived at Baroda; Procession to the Residency; went to the Arena, witnessed Wild Beast Fight.
" 20, Hunted with Cheetah at Mucklnpoora, and returned to Baroda.
" 21, Attended Service at Residency; drove to Mohtee Bagh; visited the Maharanee.
" 22, Went Quail Shooting, held Reception and started for Dutka.
" 23, Arrived at Dutka; Pig-sticking; returned to Baroda and left in evening for Bombay.
" 24, Arrived at Bombay and embarked on board the *Serapis*.

1875.

Nov. 25, Left Bombay.
" 26, Arrived at Goa.
" 27, Received visits from the Governor and Landed at New Goa; Parade of Troops, held Levee, and went to Old Goa.
" 28, Left Goa.
" 29, Touched at Beypore and proceeded to Colombo.
Dec. 1, Arrived at Colombo; landed, and drove to Government House.
" 2, Left Colombo and arrived at Kandy; Grand Reception and Procession of Elephants.
" 3, Reception of Chiefs; invested Governor with the Insignia of Knight Commander of the Order of St. Michael and St. George; Exhibition of Buddha's Tooth; Torchlight Procession.
" 4, Left Kandy for Elephant Shooting at Camp Ruanwella.
" 5, Received Visits from Native Chiefs.
" 6, Went Elephant Hunting.
" 7, Returned to Colombo; State Dinner.
" 8, Visited Cocoa-Nut Oil Factory and Coffee Mills; laid Foundation Stone of Breakwater.
" 9, Left Colombo and arrived at Tuticorin.
" 10, Landed and stayed half-an-hour at Tuticorin, and left for Madura.
" 11, Visited Old Palace, then took Train to Trichinopoly, visited Pagoda and Hall of Thousand Pillars.
" 12, Attended Divine Service and left for Madras.
" 13, Arrived at Madras; Grand Reception, Durbar, and Banquet.
" 14, Remained at Guindy Park.
" 15, Attended Races and laid Foundation Stone of New Breakwater.
" 16, State Banquet.
" 17, Grand Fete to School-children and Illumination of Surf; Grand "Nautch."
" 18, Left for Calcutta.
" 23, Arrived at Calcutta; Procession, &c.
" 24, Grand Reception of Native Princes State Dinner.
" 25, Attended Divine Service at Cathedral and visited the *Serapis*, driving to Barrackpore in the evening; State Dinner; Exhibition of Hill Tribes.
" 26, Attended Divine Service; visited Chandernagore.
" 27, Returned to Calcutta; opened New Zoological Gardens; Dinner and State Ball.
" 28, Returned Visits; Levee and Native Entertainment.
" 29, Returned Visits; went to the Races.
" 30, Lunched on board the *Serapis*.
" 31, Visited the Hospitals and attended Grand Ball.

1876.

Jan. 1, Held Chapter of Star of India and Unveiled Statue of Lord Mayo.
" 2, Went to Church at Fort William.
" 3, Witnessed Snake Poisoning Experiments and went to Convocation of University.
" 4, Left for Bankipore; held Grand Durbar, journey to Benares.
" 5, Held Reception, laid Foundation Stone of New Hospital, opened New Town Hall, visited the Monkey and Golden Temples and the Maharajah of Benares.
" 6, Started for Lucknow, arriving same evening.
" 7, Laid Foundation Stone of Memorial to Sepoys who fell in the Mutiny, and held Levee of Survivors.
" 8, Pig-sticking Expediton at Onao.
" 9, Went to Church at Banks' Bungalow.
" 10, Left for Cawnpore and thence journeyed to Delhi.
" 11, Arrived at Delhi; Grand Military Reception.
" 12, Review; presented Colours to 11th Regiment; dined with Lord Napier and attended Ball.
" 13, Visited the Kootab Minar.
" 14, Sham Fight.
" 15, Ditto.
" 17, Started for Lahore.
" 18, Arrived at Lahore; Grand State Reception by Native Chiefs; Levee; visited the Gaol.
" 19, Returned Visits; opened Sailors' Industrial Exhibition at Meanmeer; attended Native Fete.
" 29, Started for Jummoo; Arrival; Grand Reception and Nautch Dance.
" 21, Hawking, Cheetah Hunting, &c.
" 22, Left Jummoo, opened Bridge over the Chenab near Sealcote, and returned to Lahore; attended Native Fetes in evening.
" 23, Attended Divine Service at Government House.
" 24, Started for Amritsir, visited the Maharajah of Puttiala, and went on to Agra.

1876.

Jan. 25, Arrived at Agra; Grand Elephant Procession.
" 26, Reception of Native Chiefs; visited the Taj Mahal.
" 27, Returned Visits and Illumination of Taj Mahal.
" 28, Hunted with Rajah of Bhurtpore.
" 29, Visited Ruined City of Futtehpore Sikri.
" 30, Divine Service.
" 31, Left for Gwalior; Grand Reception; lunching on way with Maharajah of Dholepore.

Feb. 1 Review and Sham Fight; Banquet and Sham Fight.
" 2, Returned to Agra.
" 3, Lunched with the 10th Hussars.
" 4, Went to Jeypore, visiting Bhurtpore on the way.
" 5, Tiger Hunting.
" 6, Divine Service; visited Ambair; old Capital of Jeypore.
" 7 Returned to Agra on his way to the Kumaon Terai.
" 8, to " 18, Tiger Hunting with General Ramsay in Kumaon Terai.
" 19, Arrived at Bunbussa and met Sir Jung Bahadoor.
" 20, Divine Service; crossed into Nepaul Territory and held Durbar.
" 21 to March 4, Hunted Tigers in Nepaul Terai with Sir Jung Bahadoor.
" 5, Returned to British Territory.
" 6, Left for Bareilly, lunched there with the 18th Irish;
" 7, Arrived at Allahabad; held Chapter of Star of India.
" 8, Lunched at Jubbulpore.
" 9, Arrived at Indore; Reception by Maharajah; visited Rajahs, Banquet and Ball.
" 10, Left for Ellora.
" 11, Arrived at Bombay, received Farewell Address from the Municipality.
" 13, Left Bombay for England.

THE END.